SOCIETY, LANDSCAPE AND ENVIRONMENT IN UPLAND BRITAIN

edited by Ian D. Whyte and
Angus J. L. Winchester

Series editor: Della Hooke

Society for Landscape Studies
supplementary series 2

Published by
The Society for Landscape Studies

© The Society for Landscape Studies and the individual authors, 2004
Registered Charity No 278393

Apart from any fair dealing for the purposes of research or private study or criticism or review, as permitted under the Copyright, Designs and Patents Act 1988, this publication may not be reproduced, stored or transmitted, in any form or by any means or process, without the prior permission in writing of the copyright holders or their agents. Except for reproduction in accordance with the terms of licences issued by the Copyright Licensing Agency, photocopying of whole or part of this publication without the prior written permission of the copyright holders or their agents in single or multiple copies whether for gain or not is illegal and expressly forbidden. Please direct all enquiries concerning copyright to the publishers.

British Library Cataloguing in Publication Data
A catalogue record for this book is available from the British Library

ISBN 0 9539711-1-2 Paperback

Front cover: View of Head of Ullswater, Cumbria
© I. Whyte

Order form for this book is available on line:
www.landscapestudies.com

Printed in Great Britain by Silk & Terry Ltd, Birmingham

Contents

LANDSCAPE HISTORY

Contributors

PAUL A. ARDRON: Countryside Research Centre, Sheffield Hallam University, City Campus, Howard Street, Sheffield S1 1WB

MARGARET ATHERDEN: Director of PLACE Research Centre, York St John College, Lord Mayor's Walk, York YO31 7EX

MARK BRAYSHAY: Department of Geography, University of Plymouth, Drake Circus, Plymouth PL4 8AA

JOHN CHAPMAN: Department of Geography, University of Portsmouth, Buckingham Building, Lion Terrace, Portsmouth PO1 3HE

ROBERT A. DODGSHON: Professor of Geography, Institute of Geography and Earth Sciences, University of Wales, Aberystwyth, Ceredigion SY23 3DB

DAVID EGAN: School of Sport and Leisure Management, Sheffield Hallam University, City Campus, Howard Street, Sheffield S1 1WB

PETER HERRING: Senior Archaeologist, Cornwall Archaeological Unit, Kennal Building, Old County Hall, Station Road, Truro, Cornwall TR1 3AY

GUY M. ROBINSON: Professor of Geography, School of Earth Sciences and Geography, Kingston University, Penrhyn Road, Kingston upon Thames, Surrey KT1 2EE

IAN D. ROTHERHAM: Centre for Conservation and Outdoor Leisure, Sheffield Hallam University, City Campus, Howard Street, Sheffield S1 1WB

R. J. SILVESTER: Deputy Director, Clywd-Powys Archaeological Trust, 7a Church Street, Welshpool, Powys SY21 7DL

ELEANOR A. STRAUGHTON: Department of History, Lancaster University, Bailrigg LA1 4YG

MELANIE TEBBUTT: Director, Manchester Centre for Regional History, Manchester Metropolitan University, Geoffrey Manton Building, Rosamond Street West, Manchester M15 6LL

RICHARD TIPPING: Senior Lecturer, Department of Environmental Science, University of Stirling, Stirling FK9 4LA

IAN D. WHYTE: Professor of Historical Geography, Lancaster University, Bailrigg, Lancaster LA1 4YB

ANDREW WILLIAMS: Department of Geography, University of Plymouth, Drake Circus, Plymouth PL4 8AA

ANGUS J. L. WINCHESTER: Senior Lecturer, Department of History, Lancaster University, Bailrigg, Lancaster LA1 4YG

LANDSCAPE HISTORY

Preface

Ian D. Whyte and Angus J. L. Winchester

The aim of this book is to chart aspects of the history of human activity in the uplands of Britain during the historic period, in order to help illuminate and understand the face of the uplands at the present day. Upland areas, if defined as all land above the 300-metre contour line, account for a third of the total area of Britain, and so are an extensive component of the British landscape. Moreover, they include much-loved landscapes, visited each year by millions, which are deeply etched on the national consciousness. The uplands of England and Wales contain most of our national parks (apart from the Broads, Pembrokeshire coast) — while the first national park in Scotland, Loch Lomond and the Trossachs, designated in 2002, also covers an upland area.

The British uplands have been the focus for a range of important debates in recent years, among them the future of hill farming (particularly following the foot-and-mouth crisis of 2001); rights of access, focusing on the 'right to roam' bill; and pressures on upland environments caused by a range of social and economic pressures, notably tourism. However, much of the debate in relation to upland management is conducted in a vacuum, apparently oblivious to an understanding of management strategies in the past and how these have affected the landscape. There has been a relative lack of research focusing on the societies and economies of upland areas and the landscapes they created, with the result that these well-loved landscapes are not necessarily well understood.

This is unfortunate because, in terms of landscape history, relics of past human activity tend to be preserved far better in upland areas than in the lowlands. Even a modest gain in altitude can result in a substantial improvement in the survival of many kinds of site, such as deserted medieval settlements in the Sidlaw Hills east of Perth (RCAHMS 1994). High tides of cultivation and settlement, from medieval and later times, have often been well preserved in upland areas due to a lack of later disturbance. Pastoral land use is generally kind to evidence of former human activity, though some modern upland uses such as afforestation, quarrying and reservoir construction are notably destructive.

Upland areas and their landscapes have often been neglected and misunderstood by contemporaries in the past and historians in recent times. Viewed from the perspective of lowland-centred, arable-oriented societies, they have been seen as backward and primitive (Pollard 1997). Smout (2000) has shown how disparaging comments about the upland resource base by seventeenth- and eighteenth-century lowlanders contrasted with accounts of abundance and fertility from upland-based writers who understood livestock farming and knew the areas they were describing intimately. Modern landscape historians have only recently begun to focus on upland landscapes. Despite a flowering of work on the Scottish landscape (an environment in which upland areas cannot be ignored) since the 1970s, the lowland focus of the English pioneers of landscape history, W. G. Hoskins (1955) and Oliver Rackham (1986), has resulted in themes applicable to lowland, arable landscapes being seen as the norm. Upland areas have sometimes been seen as deviating from those norms, rather than possessing a rich landscape history of their own.

There is no standard, accepted definition of what constitutes the 'uplands' today. No single variable provides a perfect definition and a combination of factors including altitude, climate, topography and land use is required. Even then, there are problems. The twelve essays collected here combine discussions of aspects of the uplands in general with a number of studies of the landscape history of particular regions. Geographically, the scope of the book extends to all the major upland areas of Great Britain, from the Scottish Highlands, through the northern English uplands, to Snowdonia and Mid Wales and the moors of south-west England.

At the heart of common perceptions of these 'upland landscapes' lies the rough pasture and moorland ecosystems of the hills. But the extent of such quintessentially upland ecosystems has changed significantly since the middle ages. The distinctive ecological character of some former upland areas has effectively disappeared with reclamation and enclosure as Herring shows for Cornwall, and Chapman more generally. A consistent trend from the sixteenth century onwards has been the impact of population increases and economic pressures with the intake of land for improvement and a reduction in the extent of rough pasture and moorland. The result of these and other forces (notably the impact of extractive industry) has been to create a variety of distinctive regional landscapes in the uplands. Far from being the uniform 'Highland Zone' of so many maps of the landscape character of Britain (*e.g.* Rackham 1986, p. 3), the uplands embrace a rich diversity of landscapes reflecting regional differences in human agency as much as physical geography.

If one theme runs through the following essays it is that of change over time. Understanding the processes and chronology of change is central to any understanding of the British uplands, and the essays in this book explore the interface between ecological change, changing patterns of landownership and resource utilisation and wider changes in the perceptions of upland areas. The distinctive characters of the many different upland landscapes in Britain are the product of unique combinations in the trajectories of change across the centuries. Some aspects of change were common to many or most of the areas involved, though with different intensities and chronologies. Long-term ecological change, notably the reduction of woodland cover (explored in the essays by Margaret Atherden and Richard Tipping), was inextricably linked to the principal land use of the uplands, that of rearing and grazing livestock. Themes such as the abandonment of systems of transhumance, the spread of settlement, and the growth of commercial livestock farming recur (as in the chapters by Robert Silvester, Robert Dodgshon, and Mark Brayshay & Andrew Williams, for example). Behind the changing patterns of livestock management lay changing patterns of landownership. The transitions from medieval hunting forest to manorial waste and common grazings and from common land to individually-owned enclosure allotments are discussed by Angus Winchester and John Chapman, while the legal distinctions which underlie the management of surviving upland commons are highlighted by Eleanor Straughton.

But the upland landscape is the product of much more than livestock management. Traditional upland communities won a wide range of resources from the hills, the digging of peat and turf in particular having a significant impact on the landscape, as Ian Rotherham and his co-authors demonstrate. In certain areas, industrialisation in the eighteenth and nineteenth centuries and the collapse of industry in the twentieth have had a dramatic impact on the landscape, as demonstrated by Ian Whyte's overview and Peter Herring's study of upland Cornwall and Mark Brayshay and Andrew Williams' essay on Snowdonia. The pace of change in the uplands varied over time, with long periods of continuity punctuated by moments of rapid change (Withers 1996). The contributors to this volume show that the rich diversity of human landscapes in the British uplands reflects differences in the balance between continuity and change and in the chronology of change from one upland area to another.

Perceptions of the uplands have also changed. The seventeenth- and early eighteenth-century tendency to view uplands with distaste and horror as unproductive and ugly areas (Defoe 1971) gave way from the mid-eighteenth century to the formulaic approaches to landscape appreciation of the Picturesque, epitomised by William Gilpin's guidebooks, and then to the more personal interpretations of the Romantic movement. From the early nineteenth century, upland landscapes have become valued in cultural terms for their therapeutic benefits. As Tebbutt shows, the landscapes of areas like the Peak District became powerful icons emphasising a sense of national identity, particularly in times of crisis such as the First World War. More generally, the twentieth century saw a growing perception of the uplands as a reservoir of semi-natural environments that should be conserved in the face of growing pressure from alternative — and destructive — land uses (such as afforestation) and the explosion in the number of tourists visiting upland Britain. In the final chapter of this book, Guy Robinson explores the 'national planning' and statutory regulation which increasingly determine the direction of change in the uplands. At a time when the future of the uplands is being debated, this collection of essays is a reminder of the importance of an historical understanding of landscape change in the past in informing discussion of priorities and policies for the future.

Ecological changes on the North York Moors during the last millennium and their impact on the landscape

Margaret Atherden

ABSTRACT

The chapter examines a range of sources of evidence for ecological change over the last thousand years on this distinctive and well-researched upland area. Particular emphasis is given to the evidence of pollen analysis, the documentary and environmental evidence for climatic change and the evidence of past ecological changes that can be derived from studies of modern vegetation communities.

KEYWORDS

North York Moors, pollen analysis, climatic change, rural settlement

INTRODUCTION

The landscape at the beginning of the last millennium differed in many ways from that of upland Britain today. There were still substantial areas of native woodland, especially in upland valleys, where survivors of the fauna of the wildwood, such as wolf and wild boar, still roamed. In most of Britain, the woodland was deciduous, dominated by oak or alder, but in the Scottish Highlands there were large areas of pine forest, especially to the east of the Great Glen. On the highest mountains, the moorland graded into montane communities, where arctic-alpine species flourished. Blanket bog and wet moorland covered most of the rest of Scotland north of the Great Glen. Moorland communities also covered acid soils in upland England and Wales, but their plant communities were more diverse than today, with heath and acid grassland species intermixed. The farmed landscape of upland valleys was much more limited in extent and there was a close association between the cultivated land and the meadows and pastures.

This landscape and its ecological communities were far from natural. The main outlines had been established in the prehistoric period and human impact had been increasing in intensity for the past 9,000 years (Atherden 1992). The woodland cover had been reduced significantly, giving way to areas of moorland and grassland not much less extensive than those of today. The most fertile land had already been claimed for agriculture and many of the best sites for settlement were already occupied. However, upland Britain in A.D. 1000 still lacked many of the familiar features of the modern landscape. No coniferous plantations blanketed the Scottish Borders. No patchwork quilts of burnt and unburnt heather mantled the North York Moors or Dartmoor. The Lake District fells carried scrub woodland as well as grassland and no tourists trampled paths to the summits. No ski-lifts intruded on the solitude of the Cairngorms; no road or railway traversed the mires of the Flow Country. It was a relatively quiet landscape, even near the settlements, and at night no light pollution obscured the stars.

The processes by which this upland landscape was transformed into the present one may be studied by a wide range of scientific and historical techniques. The former vegetation cover has been reconstructed through pollen analysis at hundreds of sites in the uplands, where peat bogs or lake sediments preserve a sample of pollen grains and spores from the past. A range of other scientific techniques supplements pollen analysis, including the study of plant macrofossils, insect remains, charcoal fragments and shards of volcanic ash (tephra). These techniques reveal the nature of former plant and animal communities, and also provide clues to changes in climate, the development of soils and land-use patterns. They are complemented by archaeological finds and documentary sources from many upland areas. Another important line of evidence is the study of modern vegetation types, many of which preserve evidence of their history in their species composition or community structure. By combining these techniques, it is possible to build up a detailed picture of the changing landscape during the past thousand years. A case study from one upland area will serve as an example; a comparable but different story could be told for any region of upland Britain.

A CASE STUDY FROM THE NORTH YORK MOORS: THE EVIDENCE OF POLLEN ANALYSIS

Intensive research since the 1960s has resulted in the publication of over thirty pollen diagrams from the North York Moors. Not all of them cover the last 1,000 years and dating control varies from site to site, but there are enough diagrams with reliable radiocarbon dates to enable others to be dated approximately by correlation. The diagram from Fen Bogs may be used as a standard for the region (Fig. 1.1). It was first published by Atherden (1976), but the top few metres have recently been reworked by Chiverrell (1999). The pollen diagram covers most of the Holocene and illustrates well the extent of alteration to the ecology which had already occurred by A.D. 1000. Signs of human impact go back to the Mesolithic period but the first major clearance of the local woodland occurred in the Iron Age/Romano-British period, when most of the higher ground was converted to moorland or grassland. Whilst there is plenty of evidence that trees can regenerate on to moorland today, it appears that grazing pressure has prevented this from happening over most of the area during the past two millennia. Fluctuations in the tree and shrub pollen curves since the Romano-British period probably reflect changes in the woodland cover in Newton Dale and other valleys rather than tree colonisation on the plateau top.

The beginning of the last millennium can be fixed approximately by a radiocarbon date of 1060+/-160 B.P. at a depth of 1.15 metres. The large error on this date means that the true age could lie anywhere in the late Viking or early medieval periods. The dated horizon is a clearance phase (FB8) following a Dark Age phase of woodland regeneration (FB7). In A.D. 1000, trees and shrubs contributed less than 30 *per cent* of the pollen rain at this site, as compared with 70–80 *per cent* in mid-Holocene times, showing that woodland was by no means the dominant habitat in the landscape. The most significant tree/tree shrub species were hazel and birch, both characteristic of secondary woodland or scrub. The bulk of the pollen rain is from open ground plants but heather makes up a relatively small proportion, not exceeding 10 *per cent* except at the beginning of the clearance phase. By far the most significant plants were grasses, which contributed up to 80 *per cent* of the pollen rain. There is a wide range of agricultural indicators, including cereals and weeds indicative of both arable and pastoral agriculture, but the emphasis is on the latter. The farmland will have included some grasses, so it is not possible to make an accurate assessment of the area covered by farmland. Thus, the pollen diagram for this site suggests an early medieval landscape with grasslands and a little heather dominating the uplands, small amounts of scrub woodland and some farmed land in the valleys.

The end of the clearance phase is fixed by a date of 390 +/-100 B.P., placing it approximately at the end of the medieval period. The following zone (FB9) shows a regeneration of trees and shrubs, mainly birch and hazel again, and a gradual increase in heather. Grasses contribute much less to the pollen rain, declining to 10–15 *per cent* of the total. Other indicators of agriculture, including cereals, continue with little change. Therefore, the picture in the post-medieval period is one of regrowth of scrub woodlands on the dale sides, a change from grassland to heather moorland on the higher ground and continuing agriculture on enclosed land. The last zone on the pollen diagram (FB10) is not dated but is distinguished by a massive increase in heather pollen. Records for grasses and agricultural indicators continue, with a slight rise in ribwort plantain and *Potentilla* (probably tormentil), suggesting an increased emphasis on grazing. Trees and shrubs are reduced to very low proportions, generally less than 10 *per cent*. It is likely that this zone represents the last 200 years, when heather moorland came to dominate the landscape. A slight rise in pine and records for spruce pollen at the very top of the diagram indicate the presence of modern coniferous plantations.

Other pollen diagrams from the North York Moors also cover the last 1,000 years, *e.g.* four sites in the eastern-central part of the region (Atherden 1979). Although none of them has radiocarbon dates for the period, they may be correlated to the diagram from Fen Bogs. All show a clearance phase thought to be medieval in date, followed by a regeneration of trees and shrubs in the post-medieval period and an expansion of heather moorland in the modern period. As expected, the medieval clearance and subsequent woodland regeneration are more marked at sites near enclosed land and less significant at sites on higher ground. Chiverrell (1998) reworked some of these sites and added others. His diagrams show more detail for the rise in conifers at the top of the peat profiles. They also include charcoal records and a peak for these is seen on several diagrams in the modern period. Interestingly, two of the diagrams also show a peak in charcoal records around the period A.D. 1000–1100. The diagrams for May Moss and Yarlsey Moss include radiocarbon dates for the medieval period, assisting in the correlation between sites.

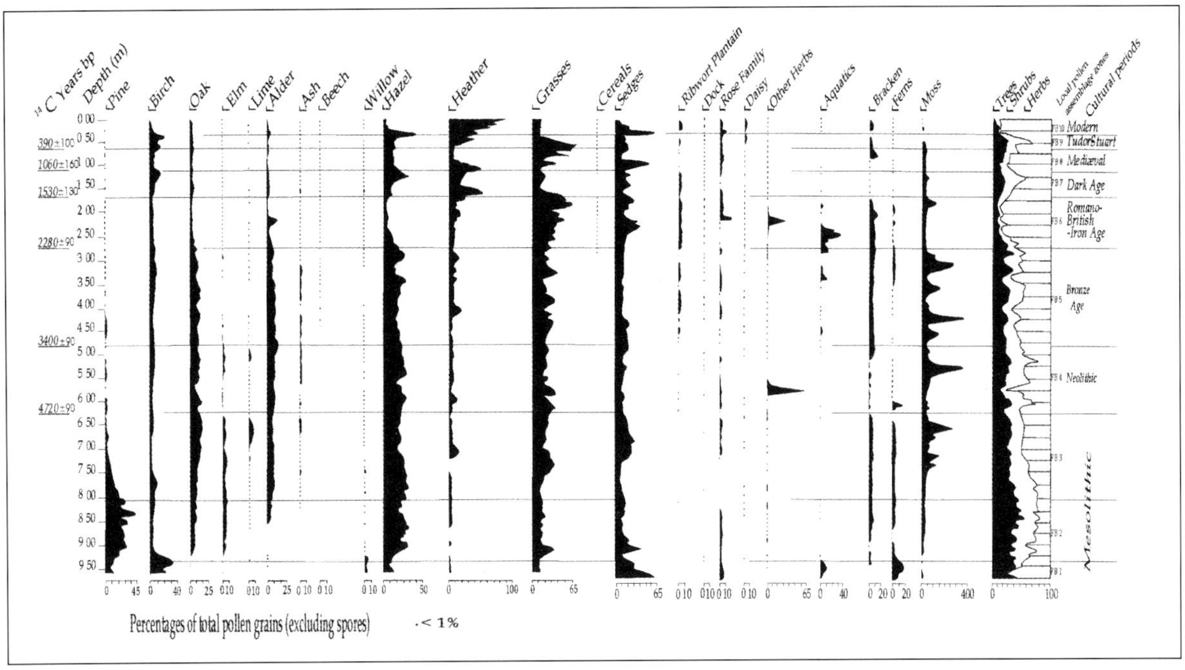

Fig. 1.1. Simplified pollen diagram from Fen Bogs (after Atherden 1999).

Thus, pollen analysis enables a broad reconstruction of the main changes in vegetation cover on the North York Moors during the past millennium. Some changes in soils may be inferred from the vegetation, particularly a trend towards podzolisation alongside the spread of heather moorland. Periods of deciduous scrub woodland regeneration would have reversed this trend in the soils of the valley sides but, as the moorland tops probably remained unwooded, soils there would have become increasingly acidified through time. This led to a secondary trend towards the build up of raw humus and the development of a surface peat layer, seen in many moorland soils today. Beneath the peat is a bleached A horizon and lower down often an iron pan and redeposited organic matter in the B horizons. Soils in the dales, by contrast, retain features of brown earths with only limited evidence of acidification and leaching.

SCIENTIFIC EVIDENCE FOR CLIMATE CHANGE

Peat cores may also be used to yield information on climate change (Barber 1981). Techniques include measurement of the degree of humification of peat, the study of plant macrofossils and reconstruction of the water table depth by the study of testate amoebae. Most research has concentrated on sites in the high rainfall areas of northern and western Britain (*e.g.* Barber *et al.* 2000) but Chiverrell (1998, 2001) has successfully applied some of these techniques to the drier region of the North York Moors. The research depends on the use of various proxy measures to reconstruct regional precipitation patterns from water levels in peat bogs. Whilst rainfall is probably the main variable involved, temperature and wind also affect water levels through evaporation rates. Results are usually expressed as shifts towards wetter/cooler or drier/warmer climate. It is important to select sites where the water table will accurately reflect changes in regional climate rather than local hydrological changes, so watershed sites are preferred. Chiverrell used information from May Moss and four other sites in his research (Chiverrell & Atherden 1999).

The degree of humification of the peat is assessed by measurement of the percentage light transmission through a liquid extract of the peat, using a photospectrometer (Blackford & Chambers 1993). The more humified (and therefore dark) the peat becomes, the less light can be transmitted through the liquid extract. In times of drier climate, the bog surface dries out and more humification occurs, so the percentage light transmission acts as a proxy measure of the wetness of the bog surface and thus of regional precipitation. There is a long-term trend in all peat bogs towards greater humification with time, which must be removed from the analysis in order to discern the variations due to climate. Once this has been done, a series of directional changes in the curve through time reveals shifts towards wetter/cooler or drier/warmer conditions. Plant macrofossils preserved in the peat bogs also reflect surface wetness. Increases in remains of plants such as heather or the moss *Hypnum jutlandicum*, indicate drier conditions, whilst increases in aquatic species, such as *Sphagnum* mosses, indicate wetter conditions. Individual species of *Sphagnum* can be identified from their leaves and give more precise information about the water table, as different species grow on hummocks and in pools (Barber *et al.* 1994). Testate amoebae are microscopic rhizopods with 'tests' (hard shells) that are well preserved in peat. They live near the surface and different species occur according to the depth of the water table. Studies of their modern ecology have enabled transfer functions to be developed, so that the percentage of different species can be used to estimate the depth to the water table (Woodland *et al.* 1998; Charman *et al.* 1999).

By combining these three techniques, Chiverrell was able to identify a series of wet and dry shifts, dated by a series of radiocarbon dates. The results varied between cores and the radiocarbon dates were only accurate to within 100 years at best, but some interesting overall trends emerged. There is evidence for drier/warmer weather from *c.* A.D. 1000 to 1200, followed by a more variable climate from *c.* A.D. 1200 to 1400. A major shift towards wetter/cooler conditions is indicated around 1400, followed by a drier phase at the end of the fifteenth century at some sites and another wet shift *c.* 1600. A short dry phase is seen at May Moss *c.* 1750–1800 and then another change to wetter/cooler conditions at *c.* 1800, which is maintained until *c.* 1900. Another site on the North York Moors, Harold's Bog, was studied by Blackford and Chambers (1999). Using humification analysis and evidence from pollen, fungal spores and charcoal deposits, they identified four shifts towards wetter/cooler conditions in the last 1000 years, the last of which was dated to between A.D. 1480 and 1590.

The research on the North York Moors may be compared to that from other parts of Britain. The dry phase from 1000 to 1200 corresponds in general terms to the beginning of the Medieval Warm Period (Lamb 1977) and also to the major clearance phase noted on the pollen diagrams above. From about 1200 to 1400, the North York Moors' climate seems to have been more variable than that in southern Britain. The major trends to wetter conditions on bog surfaces, at *c.* 1400 and 1600, correlate with shifts in many other parts of Britain and north-west Europe to the cooler/wetter conditions of the Little Ice Age (Grove 1988). On the pollen diagrams, a regeneration of scrub woodland is seen, probably reflecting a decrease in grazing pressure on the higher ground in the less clement climate.

DOCUMENTARY EVIDENCE FOR CLIMATE CHANGE

Another line of evidence for climate change is provided by documentary sources. Menuge (1997) studied 400 records to compile a climate database for the North York Moors. These records included chronicles, ecclesiastical histories, monastic charters, estate and Royal Forest records, tithe documents, court records, farming diaries and manuals, school log books, personal diaries, newspapers and local meteorological records. Some of these provide direct evidence of climate change, *e.g.* instrumental records, references to extreme weather events; others provide indirect evidence, *e.g.* references to poor harvests, famine or changes in land use. The early records are all general sources (*e.g.* Bede; *The Anglo-Saxon Chronicle*) but these may still be useful, for instance *The Anglo-Saxon Chronicle* for 1115 mentions heavy rains in the autumn and winter and a shortage of beech mast. However, they do not allow the climate of the North York Moors to be distinguished from that of the rest of northern England. The only pre-twelfth-century source which is specific to the North York Moors is the Domesday Book, and this gives little useful information on climate.

From the twelfth century onwards, there are sources which give a great deal of information on land use but relatively few which provide evidence for climate. However, documents from the thirteenth century suggest a climate with cold, wet winters and hot, dry summers, which fits in well with the scientific evidence for a more variable climate after A.D. 1200. There are also documentary references to augment the scientific evidence for colder/wetter weather after 1600, *e.g.* references to very wet and cold weather in 1621–23 and very cold winters in 1641–42 and 1782–83. The first meteorological records for the area date from the 1790s and confirm that this was a cold period. Further references to cold, wet weather occur in the mid-nineteenth century, and the first half of the twentieth century also seems to have been cooler and wetter in this area than further south. This fits in with the scientific evidence for a wetter climate continuing from *c.* 1800 to the top of the peat cores. Thus, documentary evidence provides some corroboration for the climate changes outlined above and also illustrates some of their effects on the landscape and land use of the area.

DOCUMENTARY EVIDENCE FOR ECOLOGICAL CHANGE

There is a wealth of documentary evidence for settlement and land use on the North York Moors, from which ecological changes may be deduced. Harrison and Roberts (1989) provide a useful synthesis of the medieval material while McDonnell (1989) discusses the post-medieval period. Approximately half the present-day settlements are recorded in Domesday Book but the vast majority of them are peripheral to the central moorland, concentrated in the lower dales or along the coast. Many had decreased in value dramatically between 1066 and 1086, as a result of the Harrying of the North, *e.g.* Pickering (held by the king) had decreased from £88 to 20*s* 4*d*, despite having land for twenty ploughs and controlling many outlying settlements. In contrast, some of the settlements in surrounding areas had increased in value, *e.g.* Coxwold had doubled from £6 to £12, suggesting a relocation of population and agriculture on to the better land. In Eskdale, the only notable settlement was Danby. Thus, enclosed farmland was scarce on the North York Moors in the eleventh century and confined to a few, mainly lowland, peripheral areas.

However, most of the rest of the area was exploited in some way, particularly as pastureland or woodland. The southern part of the North York Moors was managed from settlements along the spring line at the northern edge of the Vale of Pickering. Parishes typically included marshy meadowland in the Vale, arable land and woodland on the dip-slope of the Tabular Hills and rough grazing land on the high moors to the north. Some moorland grazing land was common to two or more parishes, *e.g.* Fylingdales Moor. Even on the modern Ordnance Survey map, place-names like Pockley Moor and Allerston High Moor are found 8 and 12.5 miles (13 and 20 km) north of their respective settlements. It is impossible to estimate stocking densities on these moors but they would certainly have been sufficient to prevent woodland regeneration on the higher ground. In the dales and on the dip-slope, on the other hand, woodland was a valuable commodity. Gledhill (1998) has mapped the extent of woodland in the medieval period. Much of it was concentrated on the Tabular Hills or in Eskdale and the other dales.

The twelfth and thirteenth centuries saw a substantial growth in many settlements in the area and the foundation of others, as in Bilsdale. By the end of the thirteenth century, many dales were well populated, *e.g.* Farndale (Harrison & Roberts 1989). Pressure for agricultural expansion led many landlords to clear more land as intakes and then let it to their tenants, but there is little evidence in this area for the peasants clearing land themselves, except where land was held freehold, *e.g.* between Guisborough and Whitby (*ibid*). Other land was granted to the large monastic houses. The lack of settlement in the central North York Moors facilitated land acquisition by the monasteries and, by the end of the twelfth century, about a third of the whole area was under their control. Several large foundations were involved, including Cistercians (*e.g.* Rievaulx, Byland), Benedictines (Whitby), Carthusians (Mount Grace), Augustinians (Guisborough) and many smaller priories and hermitages. The Cistercians, in particular, established many outlying granges, vaccaries or sheep cotes (*e.g.* Carlton Grange, Malton Cote). The scale of monastic agriculture was impressive and included arable farming in the dales and vast sheep walks on the uplands. This substantial grazing pressure accounts for the great expansion of grassland indicated on the pollen diagrams in this period, as grasses gain a competitive advantage over heather under heavy grazing. By contrast, the relatively light level of grazing pressure today produces heather moorland in most cases.

Another major land use in the medieval period was Royal Forest. About a third of the North York Moors was under Forest Law, including Pickering, Spaunton, Westerdale and Danby Forests and the private forest belonging to the Abbot of Whitby (Counsell 1988–9). The king only hunted in his forests occasionally; they were mainly a source of venison for the royal court or sometimes venison tithes for monasteries. Poaching of game was frequent and often involved aristocratic families or monasteries, as well as the local peasantry. Not all parts of the Royal Forest were densely wooded but it is clear that they contained substantial areas of woodland in the medieval period. Tenants often had rights to underwood and other forest products and rights to pasture animals in the forest, and these rights gradually changed to grazing licences by Tudor times. Enclosures were frequently made in the forests, too, and payment of a fine usually resulted in the person concerned being allowed to keep the land. A particularly fine set of records survives for the Royal Forest of Pickering, edited by Turton (1894–97). This includes many references to trees, often in relation to court cases for thefts of timber. Most of the references are to oak but a wide range of other trees is also mentioned, including alder, hawthorn, ash, holly, birch, elm and lime.

As a result of grazing pressure, illegal assarting and thefts of timber, woodland within the Royal Forests declined through time, as shown by surveys in the seventeenth century, such as those by John Norden, 1619. Surviving woodland was concentrated on inaccessible areas, such as the steep sides of Newton Dale, and sheep outnumbered deer. As well as Royal Forests, there were numerous private parks. The Mauleys of Mulgrave Castle established deer parks in the four corners of their estate: Julian Park in the south-east, Butter Park in the south-west, Newbiggin Park in the north-east and Cukewald Park in the north-west (McDonnell 1989). There were about thirty parks on the North York Moors, including Blansby Park and Duncombe Park. These were private hunting areas and, like the Royal Forests, they are likely to have been largely free of woodland by the end of the medieval period. Very few survived as parks beyond the sixteenth century (*ibid.*). Documentary evidence shows that most land on the North York Moors was enclosed by agreement or by Decree of Chancery, rather than by Parliamentary Enclosure. Only fourteen parishes had arable land enclosed by Act, whilst twenty-six had pasture or moorland (McDonnell 1989). Some land in the dales was enclosed piecemeal as intakes from the moor, sometimes reverting to moorland in times of economic recession. When such areas were abandoned, or grazing pressure was reduced on the high moors, trees and shrubs were able to regenerate in favoured spots, as seen on some of the pollen diagrams in the post-medieval period. Lay farmers taking over former monastic land or Royal Forest may have managed it less intensively, leading to the replacement of grassland by moorland and encroachment of scrub. There is little documentary evidence for a decrease in arable agriculture during the cooler/wetter period of the Little Ice Age. Indeed, the seventeenth century saw renewed land clearance, *e.g.* near Hutton-le-Hole, and in the eighteenth century some landowners attempted arable cultivation on former moorland, such as Turner in Kildale (*ibid.*). It is more likely, therefore, that changes in pastoral agriculture brought about the ecological changes seen on the pollen diagrams. Some former Royal Forest land was converted to rabbit warrens, which covered *c.* 6,000 acres (2,428 ha) on the Tabular Hills by 1817, according to Young. Large areas in the south-east of the North York Moors were managed as warrens, *e.g.* Dalby Warren, Allerston Warren, producing felt for the millinery trade. The modern Forestry Commission estate includes many remnants of the rabbit 'types' in which they were trapped (Spratt & Harris 1991).

There is ample documentary evidence to explain the expansion of heather moorland seen on the pollen diagrams in the last two centuries. The construction of the railway line from Whitby to Pickering in 1836, followed by lines from Whitby to Middlesbrough, Whitby to Scarborough and Scarborough to Helmsley, opened up the area and facilitated the growth of recreation. Regular rotational burning of moorland for grouse production dates from the mid-nineteenth century onwards and has produced its own characteristic landscape archaeology (Done 1999). Also in the nineteenth century, hardy varieties of sheep were bred that could withstand the moorland climate all year long. The dual economy of grouse and sheep dominated the North York Moors for most of the late nineteenth and twentieth centuries, only being replaced by tourism in the last few decades.

STUDIES OF MODERN VEGETATION COMMUNITIES

The North York Moors today are dominated by heather moorland on the plateau tops, with bracken encroachment on the more fertile soils. Deciduous woodland is concentrated on the dip-slope of the Tabular Hills and steep dale sides. Twentieth-century coniferous plantations cover a large proportion of the south-eastern quarter and significant areas in the northern fringe and south-western corner of the area. Enclosed farmland and grassland occupies the lower dales, part of the dip-slope of the Tabular Hills and glacially-derived soils near the coast (Fig. 1.2). Studies of some of these vegetation communities have also contributed to our understanding of the ecological history of the area and have added detail to the picture derived from other lines of evidence.

Deciduous woodland often hold clues to former management practices, such as coppicing or wood pasture. The vast majority of woods on the North York Moors show signs of former coppice management, *i.e.* multiple stems arising from a common stool. Hazel is the commonest coppiced tree and dominates the understorey in most woods, but other coppiced species include oak, birch, alder, lime and ash. From the size of the coppiced stems it appears that many woods were last coppiced just after World War I. The last generation of poles to regenerate from the cut stumps have competed with one another over the past eighty years or so to produce four or five large trunks, splendid examples of which may be seen in woods such as Cropton Banks Wood, near Sinnington. Single-stemmed trees are intermixed at some sites, indicating a former coppice-with-standards management system. In others, woods appear to have been clear-felled in the past, so no stands remain. Some woods apparently regenerated spontaneously, as in part of Garbutt Wood, near Sutton-under-Whitestonecliff, where a pure birch wood about eighty years of age is gradually giving way to a more mixed woodland today. Many coppiced woods in the area have rich ground floras, including typical indicators of ancient woodlands, such as herb Paris, early purple orchid, or lily of the valley. The presence of these plants is strong evidence for a long history of woodland on the site. An unpublished survey by the author for the Yorkshire Naturalists' Trust in the 1970s revealed some eighty ancient woodland sites on the North York Moors.

Signs of former wood pasture management are less frequent on the North York Moors. Some larger woods have areas within them which were obviously used as pasture at one time, alongside former coppiced compartments. Spring Wood, near Hawnby, is a good example, where the

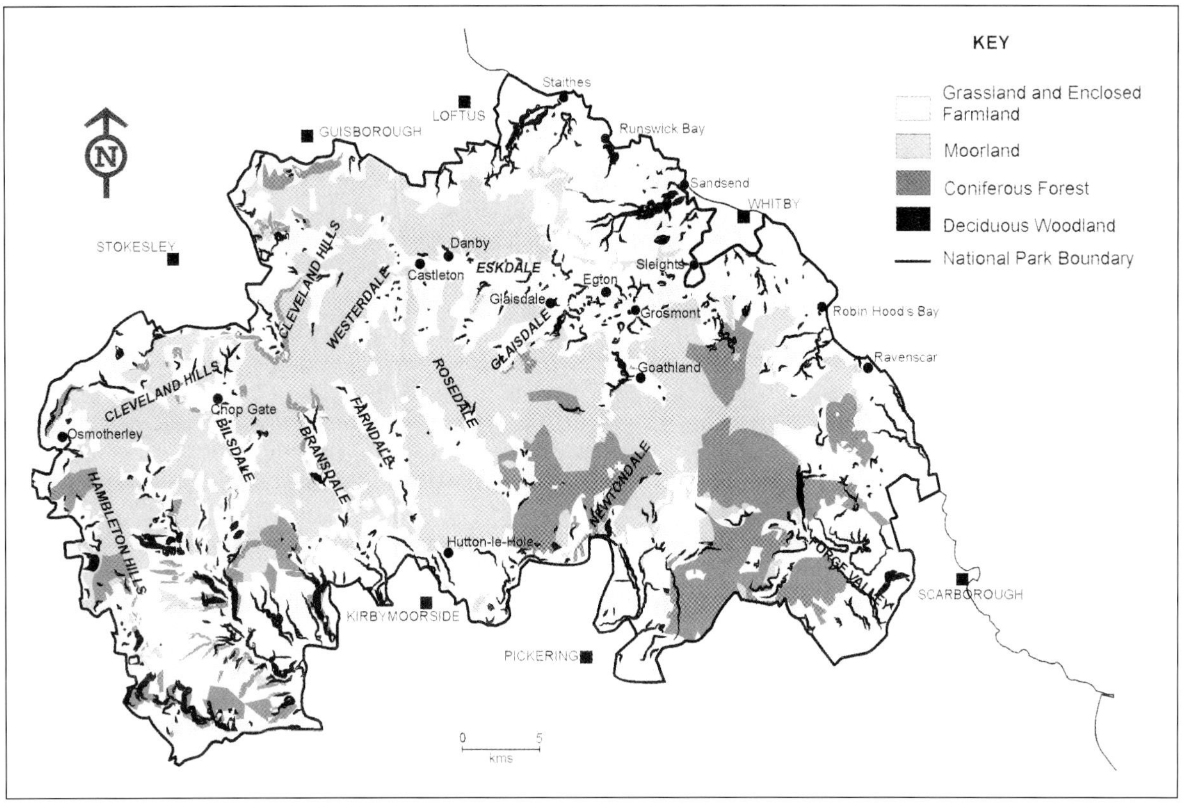

Fig. 1.2. Map of the major habitats on the North York Moors today.

former pasture section has trees which are mostly single-stemmed and a ground flora dominated by grasses and bracken. Other pasture woods include Birch Wood in Bilsdale and former parkland areas, as at the head of Bransdale and at Castle Hill on the Duncombe Park estate. These woods are dominated by very old trees, some of which have been pollarded in the past and have developed typical top-heavy structures. At Castle Hill, the trees include some excellent examples of small-leaved lime but the commonest parkland trees in the region are oaks.

From the modern woods, therefore, it appears that coppicing, with or without standards, was the commonest form of woodland management, and wood pasture was less frequent. However, the woods that survive today tend to reflect the most recent management systems. Documentary references from the North York Moors suggest that wood pasture was commoner than coppicing in the early medieval period. There are frequent references to pannage before A.D. 1200 and to wood pasture (*silva pastilis*) between 1200 and 1350 (Gledhill 1998). From the fourteenth century on, however, references to wood pasture are outnumbered by those to coppicing (*silva minuta*). This change has been linked by Gledhill to demographic decline in the fourteenth century and to a decrease in demand for pasture for livestock. Woodland names also give clues to former management systems. There are numerous 'hagg' names in the area, indicating coppicing (*e.g.* Greencliffe Hagg Wood), and also 'spring', especially after 1400 (*e.g.* Spring Bank Wood). However, other names recall the earlier wood pasture management, *e.g.* Ox Pasture Wood, Cowclose Wood, High Pasture Wood. Others reveal the key species, as in the names Nut Wood (hazel), Hazel Head Woods, Elm Hag, Ellers Wood (alder) or Hollins Wood (holly).

Thus, the evidence from modern woods complements the documentary and palynological evidence for woodland management in the area. Woods with ancient woodland indicator species or signs of wood pasture management indicate areas where woodland has probably survived from early medieval times, whereas evidence of coppice management usually dates from the later medieval or post-medieval periods.

Grasslands also preserve clues to former distributions and management practices. Sites with a very rich flora are indicative of long-established, extensive pasture management, without the use of inorganic fertilisers or pesticides. A survey of limestone grasslands on the Tabular Hills (Atherden 1985) identified ninety-one such sites. Many included species with poor powers of dispersal, the presence of which indicates a long history of pasture management on the site, *e.g.* clustered bellflower, bee orchid, burnt-tip orchid. Scrub invasion was a feature of some sites and most were small and vulnerable to agricultural change. Whilst their modern extent is a poor guide to their former coverage, their dispersed distribution suggests that pasture management was widespread on the calcareous soils of the Tabular Hills, whilst their species composition indicates continuity of management over several hundred years. It is likely that many of these sites have been used for sheep grazing continuously since early medieval times.

Modern studies of hay meadows have proved less rewarding as indicators of former management in this area. An unpublished survey carried out by the author for the North York Moors National Park in 1983–4 revealed that the vast majority of surviving sites were species-poor and agriculturally improved by the use of artificial fertilisers. Many former hay meadow sites had been converted to silage production. Very few fields remained in the area where traditional management was practised, with farmyard manure as the only form of enrichment and a late cutting date (usually July) allowing a wide range of wild flowers to set seed. Only four sites were identified as having a rich flora and meriting any conservation interest. Local people recall rich hay meadows in the past, for instance, sites in the Esk Valley in the 1960s included plants such as green-winged orchid and frog orchid, both indicative of stable management over many years. Sadly, the opportunity to learn more from modern studies of hay meadows appears to have been lost in this area.

The heather moorland communities on the higher areas of the North York Moors today tend to reflect the management for grouse production during the past 150 years. Margules (1984) classified and mapped the moorland plant communities and recognised nine vegetation associations. Most of the vegetation is characterised by the marked dominance of heather (*Calluna vulgaris*) but distinctive communities occur where bracken, bilberry, rushes, cotton-grasses or grasses are dominant over limited areas. Comparison of the present moorland communities with those described by writers from the early twentieth century shows a trend towards greater dominance of heather at many sites. An example is May Moss, which Elgee (1912) describes as being dominated by cross-leaved heath with heather as subordinate but where today the heather is much the commoner species. It seems that the degree of dominance by heather is a general guide to the intensity of moorland management, especially burning. Comparisons between sites which have been managed regularly and those which have not been burned or grazed in the past forty years show that heather can retain its dominance over other dwarf shrubs and herbaceous species fairly well but is gradually invaded by tree seedlings. These would undoubtedly shade it into a subordinate position in time. A good example of such a site is the former Ministry of Defence land near Fylingdales Early Warning Station, where, along with native species such as birch and rowan, there are well-established saplings of pine and spruce from local forestry plantations.

Today, most of the heather moorland on the North York Moors is burned and grazed, and in some areas this has led to soil erosion and increased decomposition of the surface peaty soil (North York Moors National Park 1991). Gullying on Levisham Moor shows evidence of several stages on erosion, the earliest of which is dated by pottery to the late nineteenth century (Curtis 1975). In other parts of the region, particularly severe erosion occurred after a series of uncontrolled fires in 1976, leading to the initiation of a programme of moorland reinstatement and experimental planting (North York Moors National Park 1991). Thus, there are signs that the rotational burning of heather moorland may not be sustainable. Alternative options for the future include cutting rather than burning of heather, a reduction in management intensity to produce a more mixed moorland plant community, or allowing scrub invasion to create greater diversity in the moorland landscape.

CONCLUSION

Research over the past few decades has elucidated many aspects of the ecological history of the North York Moors during the past millennium. Pollen analysis has allowed a reconstruction of the broad pattern of vegetation history; studies of climate change have revealed major fluctuations in climate; documentary searches have produced evidence of changes in land use, and studies of modern vegetation communities have furnished examples of how past management practices are reflected in the present-day ecology. Synthesis of these varying types of evidence leads to the following summary of ecological change in the area.

In the early medieval period, the North York Moors were more wooded than today, with substantial areas of mixed deciduous woodland in the valleys, on the Tabular Hills and along the coast. Much of this woodland was used as pasture for livestock and some was managed by coppicing. Other areas formed part of royal forests and were used for hunting with some secondary pasturing of animals and wood production. The higher areas were already largely free of tree cover and supported grassland communities with some heather moorland, maintained by a higher density of grazing than today. These areas and enclosed arable land in the dales were managed by monastic communities and lay farmers. The climate was slightly warmer and probably drier than the present one, facilitating a period of population expansion and agricultural development.

From the fourteenth century onwards, this picture began to change. Climate shifted on several occasions to a wetter/cooler mode, affecting the viability of upland farming systems. The decline of monastic influence led to a reduction in grazing pressure in some areas and allowed scrub to regenerate in the upper parts of the dales. On the plateau tops, the wetter climate and decreased grazing pressure favoured the expansion of moorland plant communities at the expense of grasslands. Lay farming continued in the lower dales. Many of the woodlands were converted to coppices; however, livestock numbers increased in the royal forests, reducing tree regeneration there. Illegal assarts and pressure on timber and wood resources also increased. From the Tudor period onwards, the royal forests were disafforested and parts were converted into rabbit warrens. In the nineteenth century, a dual economy of sheep and grouse production developed on the higher areas, leading to the gradual dominance of heather over other plants. Woodland continued to decline and was reduced to minimal levels by the end of World War I. From the 1920s onwards, the Forestry Commission began to reafforest former rabbit warrens and other areas, mainly with coniferous trees. The twentieth century saw the abandonment of traditional woodland management in most parts of the area, allowing former coppiced woods to grow up to form a higher canopy. Intensification of moorland management led to increasing dominance of heather, impoverishment of soils and problems of soil erosion. Changes in farming in the dales almost obliterated traditional hay meadow management and led to the agricultural improvement of many traditional pastures.

One can only speculate what the story of the twenty-first century will be. A decline in hill-sheep farming seems likely and possibly a reaction against blood sports. The dual economy of the heather moorlands seems set to change, probably producing a more varied upland vegetation cover and allowing the regrowth of scrub woodland. Global warming will probably accelerate this process, through a predicted combination of higher temperatures and higher winter rainfall. An increased emphasis on recreation and conservation may lead to the gradual conversion of some areas of coniferous forestry into deciduous woodland. Decline in the rural economy may result in the abandonment of farming in some of the dales, but heightened awareness of the ecological value of herb-rich grasslands and arable weed communities may produce changes in farming methods in others, resulting in increased biodiversity and a lower density of grazing. Indeed, the landscape of the North York Moors at the end of the twenty-first century may be more reminiscent of that in A.D. 1000 than that of the present day.

ACKNOWLEDGEMENT

I would like to thank Paddie Morrison for her assistance with the cartography.

Palaeoecology and political history: evaluating driving forces in historic landscape change in southern Scotland

Richard Tipping

ABSTRACT

The chapter reviews some of the problems involved in matching the evidence for environmental and landscape change obtained by environmental scientists with the data derived from historical records. To demonstrate how such evidence can be integrated, two case studies are developed from upland areas of southern Scotland: Swindon Hill in the upper part of the Bowmont Water in the northern Cheviot Hills analysed by Tipping, and Dogden Moss in the Lammermuir Hills analysed by Lisa Dumayne-Peaty. Some of the pitfalls of trying to match relatively precise but localised environmental evidence with broader historical trends in order to produce an understanding of landscape change are discussed.

KEYWORDS

Cheviot Hills, Lammermuir Hills, pollen analysis, climatic change, Little Ice Age, cultivation limits

INTRODUCTION

In the last few decades palaeoecologists have become a little more confident than before of 'plying their trade' within the historic period, when documentary and archival data have traditionally been of premier significance. Prior to the 1970s, and still prevailing in large measure today, were intellectual barriers seemingly separating the selection of research techniques appropriate to prehistory and those to be used in historical enquiry. The prehistorian willingly welcomed the contributions of the natural scientist in explaining socio-cultural change (*e.g.* Clark 1954; Butzer 1982) but this only tended to enhance within the disciplines the perceived differences between prehistory and history. There is still the suggestion that history is the preserve of the documentary historian.

This separation is largely irrelevant to the scientist because landscape change is a continuum. Broadly, the same environmental processes are active irrespective of time, although the twentieth century is sufficiently different that the same cannot comfortably be argued (McNeill 2000). The barrier in reality affects only the documentary historian, limiting enquiry beyond the shadowy world of proto-history, but has seemed to restrict equally or more the use within history of scientific techniques of environmental reconstruction.

One major barrier was, and remains, technical. Prehistorians, whether archaeologists or palaeoecologists, share the same inexactitude over their constructions of time. All disciplines use temporal controls such as radiocarbon (^{14}C) dating, and chronological imprecision affects everyone equally. This is not the case within the historic period, and the major stumbling block in using most techniques of palaeoenvironmental analysis is that scientists cannot work at the highly refined timescales of the archivist (Dumayne *et al.* 1995). This refinement has led to the assumption that documentary data are superior, but I will argue that deference to the written record in the writings of palaeoecologists and archaeologists is not appropriate or healthy for the discipline.

Notwithstanding this continuing problem of temporal precision, there are few other technical barriers to the use of scientific techniques, and considerable advantages, notably in the ability to establish records of landscape change which have temporal continuity for specific points in a landscape. Palaeoecologists can, depending on where they choose to work, particularly in upland landscapes, explore both temporal continuity and spatial patterning through correlating independently-dated sediment-stratigraphic sequences. Much of what I describe later will be work of this nature, in trying to derive dynamic models from an array of point-sources within a single upland landscape, in the northern Cheviot Hills of southernmost Scotland (Tipping 1999). Archivists cannot readily do this. Documentary records are patchy in what they describe, in both time and space. Historians overcome this patchiness by linking records from different locations and periods in what appear to be synthetic narratives, but few records are geographically specific for any sustained duration.

This chapter will not focus on the continuing technical difficulties because they are widely appreciated and are being overcome. Instead, this will be a more personal review of some philosophical difficulties in the linking of palaeoecology and history. In particular, I will describe and critically evaluate one approach to the interpretation of palaeoecological data from historical contexts which, I suggest, gives undue deference to one particular source, the written record, thus imbalancing interpretation. In doing so, I seek to define an environmental history in which different types of analysis are given more equal weighting, and in which a synthetic collaboration can be achieved (Tipping & Watson 1999).

CASE STUDIES FROM SOUTHERN SCOTLAND

This paper presents two case studies as illustrations, both from south-east Scotland (Fig. 2.1). The first is within the Bowmont Valley, draining north from the rounded mass of the Cheviot Hills. A detailed landscape archaeological survey (Mercer & Tipping 1994) was accompanied by a range of scientific approaches which considered landscape evolution over the whole of the Holocene period (Tipping 1992, 1994, 1996, 1997, 1998a, 1998b, 1999, 2000; Schweitzer 1997; Campbell, *et al.* 2002). A major focus of the palaeoecological work was the development of the historic landscape, summarised by Tipping (1999). This paper will present detailed analyses from one of the principal techniques employed, pollen analysis, in an upland landscape at Swindon Hill (Figs 2.2, 2.3) (Tipping 1997, 2000), as a 'worked' example of the method, to provide new data on the period, particularly on climatic change, and to provide a case-study illustrating many of the principal historic environmental changes in the valley. The second case study is a recent palynological analysis at Dogden Moss in the Lammermuir Hills by Lisa Dumayne-Peaty (1999), across the lower Tweed Valley from the Cheviots (Fig. 2.1), and is summarised here. The two sites are not directly comparable in terms of the landscapes they depict, but are examples of what may be seen as two different interpretative approaches to the same type of data.

SWINDON HILL IN THE LAST 1000 YEARS

Occupying a central position in the upland part of the Bowmont Valley at 365 metres (1,200 ft) O.D. (Fig. 2.2), Swindon Hill is a shallow, 1.5 metre (5 ft) deep, peat sequence that has infilled a small bedrock basin on a wide andesitic plateau (Pl. 2.I) over the last 5,000 years. The small diameter of the bog, at 60–65 metres (197–213 ft) mean diameter, indicates that at least 60–70 *per cent* of the pollen in the peat is derived from the plateau, from freely-drained peaty podsols (Muir 1956) now supporting very poor grazed *Molinia-Nardus* grassland (King 1960). For brevity, palynological techniques are considered elsewhere (Tipping 1995a, 1995b, 1997, 2000). Dating controls at this site are provided by a series of calibrated radiometric ^{14}C dates (Table 1: calibrated by the CALIB 3.03 program; Stuiver & Reimer 1993), constrained by the appearance in the pollen record at around 25

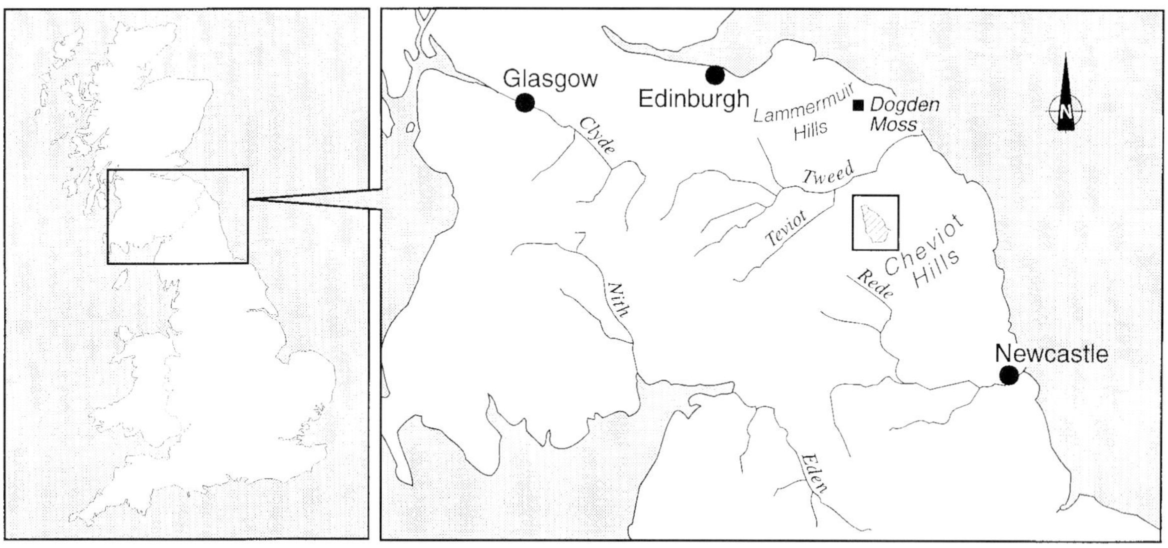

Fig. 2.1. South-east Scotland, showing the positions of the Cheviot Hills and the neighbouring Lammermuir Hills separated by the lower valley of the River Tweed, showing the location of Dogden Moss and within the box, the southern part of the Bowmont Valley depicted in Fig. 2.2.

centimetres (10 inches) depth of 'agricultural improvement' tree types like *Pinus* (pine), *Juglans* (walnut), *Ulmus* (elm) and *Fagus* (beech) (Fig. 2.4a: see Carter *et al.* 1997; Tipping 1997; Tipping *et al.* 1997), from which it is established that the last *c.* 1,000 years is recorded in the uppermost 80 centimetres (31.5 ins) or so of peat. Palynological changes in this period are depicted in Figs 2.4a and b which include all taxa (pollen types) represented twice or more in pollen counts of *c.* 300 land pollen: pollen sums are indicated on Fig. 2.3. The record is divided into five local pollen assemblage zones or subzones (hereafter lpaz) (lpaz C–E: zones A–B pre-date A.D. 1000 Tipping 1996). Above lpaz C, pollen spectra are temporally resolved at close to decadal intervals. This section briefly considers different aspects of landscape change (woodland; heath; upland grazing; the 'Little Ice Age') and evaluates some limitations and successes in the data, as well as indicates the interpretative approach taken in the analyses.

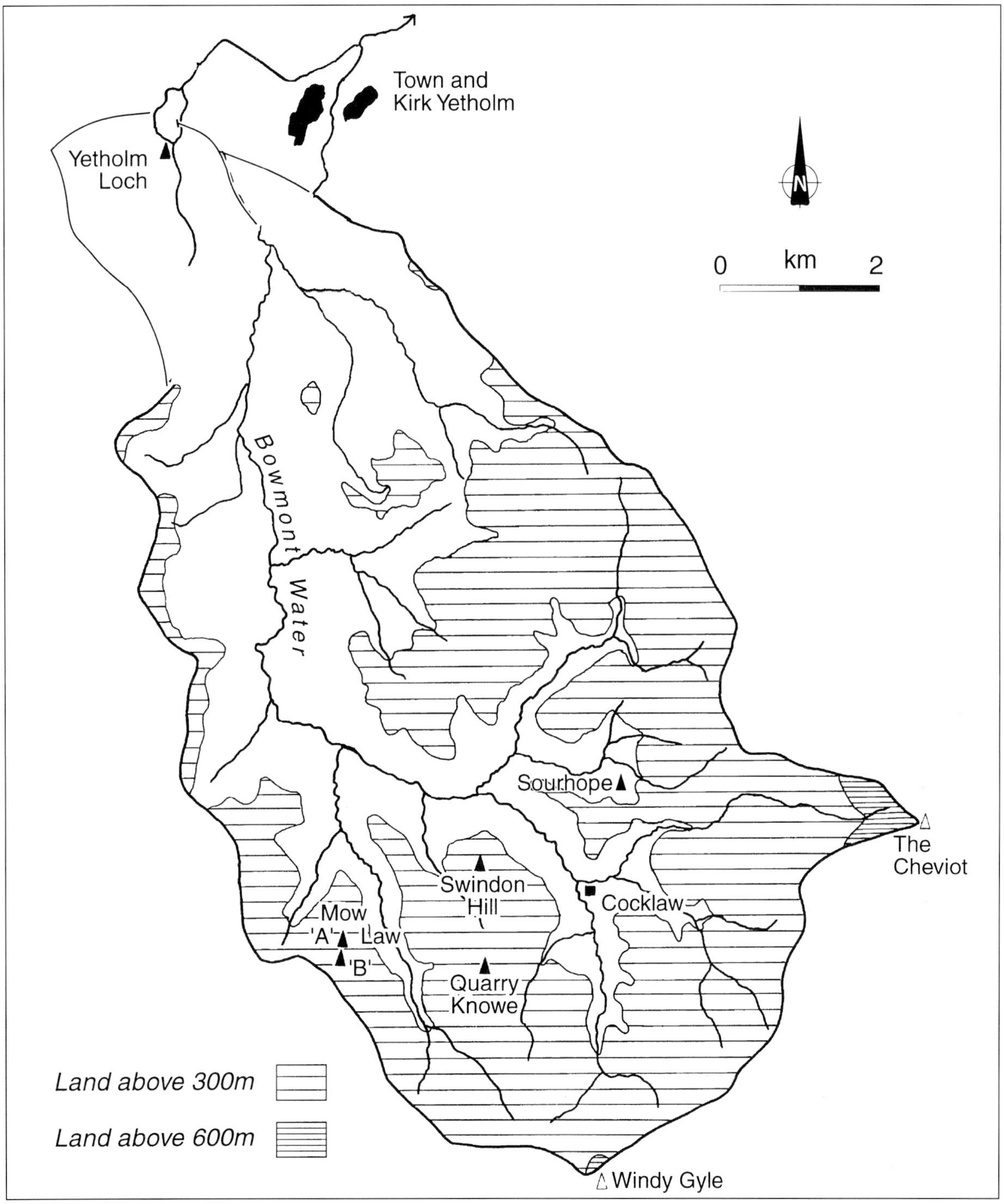

Fig. 2.2. The southern part of the Bowmont Valley in the northern Cheviot Hills, indicating the location on the plateau of Swindon Hill, the principal pollen site discussed in this paper and other sites in the valley considered in the text.

Plate 2.1. Photograph of the small peat basin at Swindon Hill, the dark patch of sedges in the centre, and the surrounding rough pasture of heavily grazed *Nardus* grassland, looking south beyond a band of post-WW II forestry planting to the border ridge at Windy Gyle.

TABLE 1: DETAILS OF THE RADIOCARBON ASSAYS FOR SWINDON HILL

LAB. NO.	MEAN DEPTH (cm)	SEDIMENT THICKNESS (cm)	^{14}C AGE BP	1σ	$\delta^{13}C$ (‰)	CALIB. AGE BC/AD & 1σ
GU-2493	26.5	29.0–24.0	modern		-26.5	n.a.
GU-2490	77.0	79.0–75.0	510	50	-26.0	A.D. 1398(1418)1437
GU-2491	95.0	92.0–88.0	1470	50	-27.0	A.D. 531(571)613
GU-2492	129.5	132.0–127.0	3100	50	-28.6	1442(1389)1321 B.C.
GU-2494	151.5	154.0–149.0	4720	110	-28.5	3640(3497)3380 B.C.

The comparative abundance of trees like *Alnus* (alder) and *Betula* (birch) between *c.* A.D. 1000 and 1100 (Fig. 2.4a: 1000–850 cal B.P.) does not represent the persistence from prehistory of native woodland, but the re-colonisation of a few trees, perhaps on the mire, following woodland loss throughout the valley in the late Iron Age (Tipping 1992, 1997; Mercer & Tipping 1994). Only within the confines of a hunting reserve around Cocklaw (Gilbert 1979) at the pollen site of Quarry Knowe (Fig. 2.2) did a dense scrubby woodland persist until the end of the seventeenth century (Tipping 2000). Medieval land grants in the valley specify managed woodland (Innes 1854; Jeffrey 1855), but only at Quarry Knowe is woodland seen to persist. There is a mis-match between the sparse archival and more abundant palaeoecological data, and although Tipping (1999) suggested that woodland in, for example, small copses might be hard to detect palynologically, it is probable that both data-sources are of equal interpretative value in this setting, and it is likely that well before the sixteenth century there were timber shortages in the Borders (*cf.* Anderson 1967; Tipping 1999). It would be highly informative to explore where these remaining woodlands were, and whether as early as the medieval period they were confined to narrow protected cleuchs or gullies (Badenoch 1997; Smith 1997).

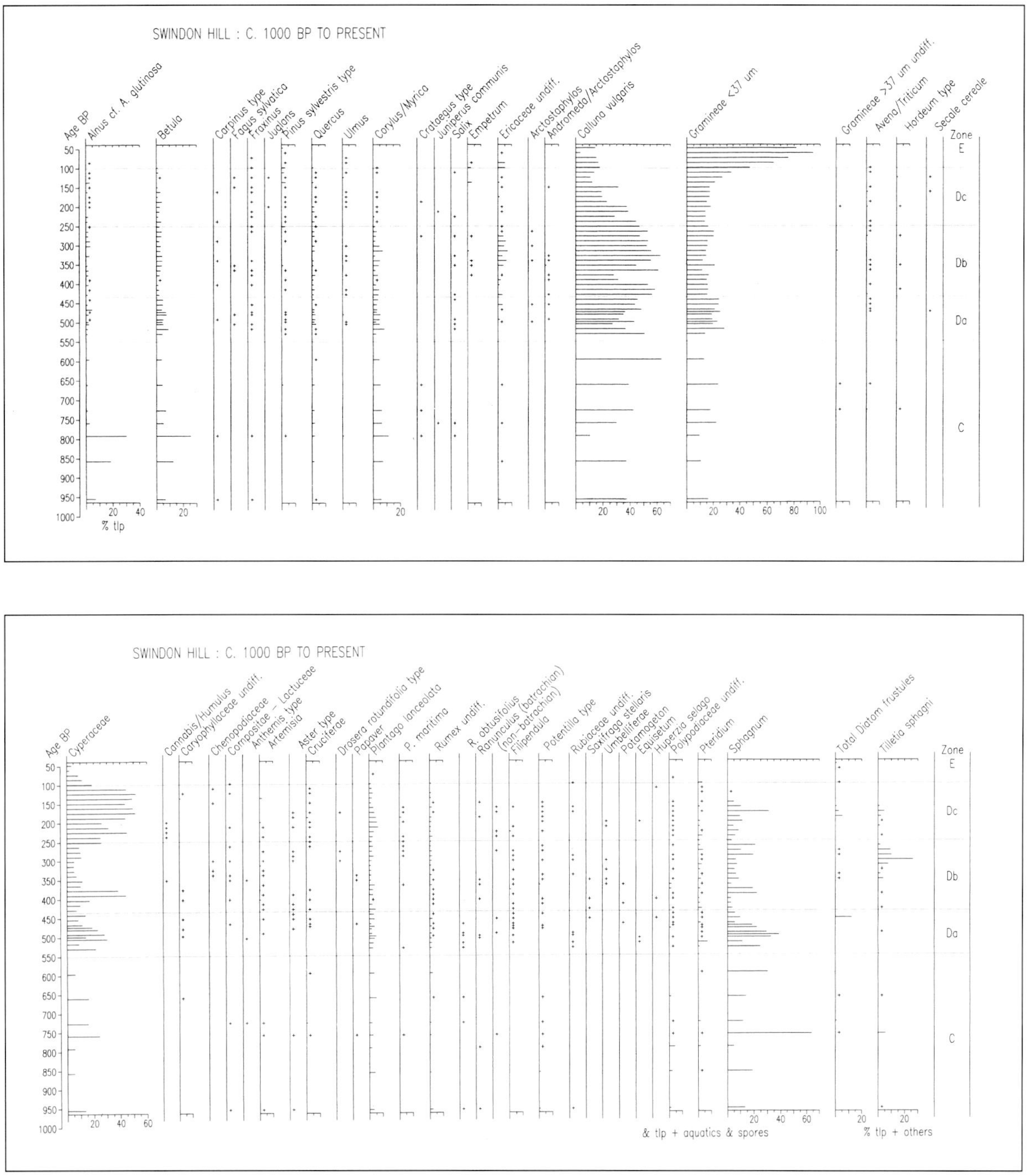

Fig. 2.3. Percentage-based stratigraphic record of selected taxa see text) from *c.* A.D. 1000 (1000 cal B.P.) to A.D. 1900 (50 cal B.P.) from the uppermost 80 centimetres of peat at Swindon Hill, plotted against calibrated years B.P. (Before Present). Crosses depict proportions <1 *per cent* of the sum: (a) trees, shrubs, heathers and grasses calculated as percentages of total land pollen; (b) other herb pollen types (*Cyperaceae* — *Umbelliferae*) as percentages of total land pollen, obligate aquatic types and spore-producing taxa (*Potamogeton* — *Sphagnum*) as percentages of total land pollen plus aquatics & spores, and miscellaneous components (undifferentiated diatom valves and spores of *Tilletia sphagni*) as percentages of total land pollen plus these two elements.

Calluna (ling) pollen percentages would suggest (*cf.* Evans & Moore 1985) that heath occupied only around 10–15 *per cent* of the plateau by A.D. 1000 (1000 cal B.P.), and species-rich heath did not develop around Swindon Hill until *c.* A.D. 1450 (500 cal B.P.), when *Arctostaphylos* (bearberry; Fig. 2.3a) was established. Now rare in south-east Scotland but found in poorly grazed Callunetum in Northumberland, bearberry can be encouraged by moor-burning (McVean & Ratcliffe 1962; Hobbs 1984; Hobbs, Mallik & Gimingham 1984). At other sites in the Bowmont Valley heath expansion is similarly late in the interglacial (Tipping 2000), and elsewhere in the Cheviots *Calluna* heath has not developed (Campbell *et al.* in press). There appears to be a link between livestock grazing and sward deterioration (Tipping 1999, 2000). The plateau around Swindon Hill was clearly grazed throughout the historic period, more intensively after 1400 A.D. (550 cal B.P.) when percentages of Gramineae <8 microns anl-D (wild grasses) increase, with abundant *Plantago lanceolata* (ribwort plantain) and both *Rumex* undifferentiated (docks) and *R. obtusifolius* (broad-leaved dock), the last indicative of high grazing pressures (Hughes & Huntley 1988). Comparable intensification is seen throughout the Bowmont Valley though at apparently slightly different times and to different intensities (Tipping 1997, 2000). However, what is meant by grazing 'pressures' is not at all clear, and we need to be much more specific as to process. High sheep stocking densities in the early mid-eighteenth century are very likely to have led in part to the demise of *Calluna* heath, the loss of many grassland herb species and their replacement by nutrient poor grasses, seen at Swindon Hill in lpaz Dc and E (Fig. 2.3: King 1960; Stevenson & Thompson 1993; Tipping 2000). It is unlikely that thirteenth- or fourteenth-century monastic sheep 'ranches' in the Bowmont Valley (Moffat 1985) were comparable in stocking densities to those of the last *c.* 250 years (Dodgshon 1976), although Tipping (1999) showed that sheep were more important than cattle in the Cheviot medieval agricultural system. Sheep were bred for different things at different times, of course (Ryder 1983), and large differences over time in food preferences, herding practice (Hunter 1962), seasonality of grazing pressures (Winchester 2000a), muirburn (Hobbs *et al.* 1984; Tipping 2000) and innumerable other factors add complexities to the relation between grazing animals and vegetation that we have collectively in no way defined. These, and other nuances in land management, are understood from the written record, although only patchily from the Bowmont Valley, and this richness of information makes current palaeoecological interpretations of land use seem at times clumsy, but equally the unlocking of the links, however weak at present, between land use and major vegetation and ecological change is only understood from scientific sources.

A useful illustration of the interpretative difficulties pollen analysts face is in the occurrence in a brief episode between A.D. 1700–1750 (250–200 cal B.P.) of *Cannabis/Humulus* (hemp or hop) pollen. Potentially very exciting as an insight into later historic land uses that locally went undescribed, this record may indicate either hemp or hop growing or neither. Hemp cultivation is identified by Tipping (1999) as a lowland medieval practice at Yetholm Loch (Fig. 2.2), as at other lowland sites in south-east Scotland (Whittington & Edwards 1990), and among other changes seems to mark an early differentiation of upland and lowland agricultural activities, but the record at Swindon Hill is significantly later and in the uplands. However, the numbers of pollen grains are too few to differentiate *Cannabis* from *Humulus* (French & Moore 1986; Whittington & Gordon 1987), and the pollen analyst in this instance cannot confidently define what the plant was or where it was growing, let alone its significance for the diversification of land uses in the eighteenth century.

More concern over the derivation, role and significance of cereal pollen (see Tipping 1998b) has allowed a more significant contribution in the re-evaluation of the long-term sustainability of cereal cultivation. Parry's (1975, 1978, 1981) model from the neighbouring Lammermuir Hills (Fig. 2.1) of an upland population vulnerable to climatic change within the Little Ice Age has been challenged by using the continuous record of crop-growing in pollen records from the Bowmont Valley. The Swindon Hill data-set is typical. Cereal type pollen (Gramineae larger than 37 microns): *Avena/Triticum* (oats/wheat), *Hordeum* type (*cf.* barley) and rarely, *Secale* (rye): Fig. 2.3a), is infrequently recorded in lpaz C and Da but abundant after A.D. 1450 (500 cal B.P.), and the record suggests the continued although not necessarily continuous production of cereals, presumably for subsistence, persisting to the end of the nineteenth century. There was no long-term abandonment of cereal cultivation in the Cheviot Hills during the Little Ice Age, and certainly no retreat from the uplands.

The impact of the Little Ice Age on the agricultural economy may have been over-estimated by workers in the past, but it seems likely to have been a factor in promoting 'natural' environmental change in the Bowmont Valley. Changes in the flood frequency/intensity of the Bowmont Water in the late seventeenth and/or early eighteenth centuries have been ascribed to the 'Little Ice Age' (Tipping 1994; Rumsby & Macklin 1996). These exceptional geomorphic events are not recorded by documents, although recognising the effects of increased flooding allows fuller explanation of post-medieval settlement patterns and routeways in the valley (Mercer & Tipping 1994). Effects on upland vegetation patterns of this climatic deterioration have rarely been recorded but in the Bowmont Valley these are most clearly recorded at Swindon Hill. There are two principal effects: a period of sustained waterlogging of the mire after *c.* A.D. 1400 (550 cal B.P.), increasingly common from southern Scottish mosses (Barber 1981; Barber *et al.* 1998; Charman, Hendon & Packman 1999; Mauquoy & Barber 1999), and also evidence, much less commonly reported, of the altitudinal depression of summit heath and snow-bed communities.

From *c.* A.D. 1400 (550 cal B.P.) the bog surface was considerably wetter, with less decayed peat increasingly colonised by Cyperaceae (sedges) and *Sphagnum* (bog moss) (Fig. 2.3b). Some pollen grains of *Andromeda/Arctostaphylos* may be of *Andromeda polifolia* (bog rosemary) colonising shallow pools within *Sphagnum*-dominated moss with batrachian (aquatic) *Ranunculus* (buttercup) species. *Equisetum* (horsetail) and later *Potamogeton* (pondweed), *Typha angustifolia* (lesser bulrush), *Sparganium* (bur-reed) and *Drosera rotundifolia* (common sundew) probably developed in shallow-water plant communities. Bands of *Sphagnum* peat are recorded and *Sphagnum* spores are prominent in several short-lived phases, *c.* A.D. 1550–1600 (400–350 cal B.P.) and *c.* A.D. 1675–1700 (275–250 cal B.P.), with *Tilletia sphagni* fungal spores (Dickson 1973) abundant here and *c.* A.D. 1775–1850 (175–100 cal B.P.), in which numbers of freshwater diatom valves are abundant. Waterlogging of the bog surface is probably linked to climatic deterioration, marked by discrete phases of greater intensity.

Around A.D. 1500 (450 cal B.P.), *Vaccinium* (bilberry) pollen is tentatively identified, as are two taxa frequently associated with Vaccinieta, *Cornus suecica* (dwarf cornel) and *Lycopodium annotinum* (Fig. 2.3). *Vaccinium* heath occurs today on the summit plateau of the Cheviot, above *c.* 800 metres O.D. in snow-bed communities (Ratcliffe 1977). Other heath taxa, *Arctostaphylos* (bearberry) and *Empetrum* (crowberry), are both arctic-alpine genera (Matthews 1955), and among grassland herbs *Plantago maritima* (sea plantain) grew locally after *c.* A.D. 1675 (*c.* 275 cal B.P.), a common plant on exposed mountain summits (McVean & Ratcliffe 1962), *Saxifraga stellaris* (starry saxifrage) occurred on Swindon Hill for a time after A.D. 1500 (450 cal B.P.) although it is today found locally only on the Cheviot summit (Ratcliffe 1977), and two spores of the arctic-alpine fir clubmoss, *Huperzia selago*, are recorded at this time. Their appearance together on Swindon Hill may be explained by altitudinal depression of plant communities during a phase of lowered temperature within the Little Ice Age. Taxa such as *Artemisia* (wormwood), Chenopodiaceae (goosefoots), Caryophyllaceae (pinks) and Compositae Liguliflorae (dandelion type) may at this time have colonised soils made unstable by freeze-thaw processes, although soil erosion did not affect the peat sequence directly. These high-altitude communities appear to be absent after *c.* A.D. 1700 (250 cal B.P.), suggesting that temperature depression was significantly less in the eighteenth century and after.

DOGDEN MOSS IN THE LAST 1,000 YEARS

Dogden Moss is a comparatively large raised moss on the south-east of the Lammermuir Hills, substantially lower in altitude than Swindon Hill at 207 metres (679 ft) O.D. (Fig. 2.1). The topmost 3 metres (10 ft) of peat was analysed for its pollen content and dated, as at Swindon Hill, by ^{14}C controls (Dumayne-Peaty 1999). It has a contrasting setting and different pollen recruitment characteristics to Swindon Hill, and there are fewer pollen spectra than at Swindon Hill in the period we are concerned with, the last *c.* 1,000 years in the uppermost 80–90 centimetres (31–35 inches). This period is subdivided into four phases comparable to the zones and subzones of Swindon Hill, defined from changes in the pollen assemblages, and notably from fluctuations in proportions of arboreal, tall shrub and herbaceous indicators of human activity (*ibid.*; table 2).

The area around Dogden Moss was more wooded than the Cheviot Hills, with abundant *Corylus* (hazel) and *Quercus* (oak) and lower amounts of wetland *Betula* (birch)/*Alnus* (alder) woodland. Although correlations with documented events are rightly seen by Dumayne-Peaty (1999) as tentative, as ever a consequence of a ^{14}C chronology, clear links are drawn to specific socio-political events described from the literature. For example, from *c.* A.D. 735 (1215 cal B.P.) woodland clearance and renewed crop-growing 'could be explained by the monastic settlement which increased between the Forth and the Tweed in the seventh century' (p. 131), possibly assisted by climatic amelioration in the early medieval period. The expansion of grasses continued until *c.* A.D. 1200 (750 cal B.P.) and woodland apparently continued to be removed, although Dumayne-Peaty infers agricultural decline from *c.* A.D. 1050 (900 cal B.P.) because some anthropogenic herbs are less common, and correlates these indicators with both 'the increase in English settlement and climatic improvement' (*ibid.*, p. 131) and political unrest.

Woodland regeneration from *c.* A.D. 1200 (750 cal B.P.) to around A.D. 1370 (580 cal B.P.) is associated with continuing political 'unrest between the Scots and English' (Dumayne-Peaty 1999, p. 132) but also the 'Black Death', harvest failures and deteriorating climate. However, from the late fourteenth century until the 1660s (*c.* 290 cal B.P.), significant woodland clearance and the development of a well-organised agrarian landscape, including probable *Cannabis* cultivation, is attributed to 'the peace which was initiated by the marriage of Margaret to James IV of Scotland in A.D. 1502' (*ibid.*, p. 132), and cemented by the Union of the Crowns in A.D. 1603, permitting a more confident agriculture within an ameliorating climate. From the mid-seventeenth century to the present, the vegetation around Dogden Moss reflected the post-'Improvement' landscape, although Dumayne-Peaty accounts for a decrease in proportions of anthropogenic indicator pollen types *c.* A.D. 1815 (135 cal B.P.) by economic depression following the Napoleonic Wars.

DISCUSSION: APPROACHES TO THE INTERPRETATION OF HISTORIC LANDSCAPE CHANGE

These case studies are not meant to draw parallels or contrasts in the way different parts of southern Scotland developed. They are rather examples of two emerging styles of interpretation, developing now because the application of scientific techniques to the historic period is quite new. They seem to define different ways of explaining landscape change that are particular to historic contexts, when palaeoecologists can use but can also be seduced by the precision and detail of the written record.

It is not my concern here to assess the technical difficulties of the discipline. Frank Oldfield, whose work in southern Cumbria (Oldfield 1969) should probably be seen as marking the earliest mature work in the UK, identified the issues that concern us to the present. Dating controls are central. ^{14}C-derived chronologies as at Swindon Hill and Dogden Moss are not solutions, and neither site is an example of the most rigorous application of dating techniques. Within the last several hundred years no single technique can be seen as inherently better than others, but the combination of many independent techniques to constrain age interpolations is providing significant advances (Clymo *et al.* 1990; Oldfield *et al.* 1994; Walker *et al.* 2000). More sophisticated dating controls will encourage us to pay more attention to the temporal resolution of our analyses. Some apparent shifts in the agrarian system at Dogden Moss are defined from single spectra (Dumayne-Peaty 1999), and Fig. 2.3 from Swindon Hill shows how less assured are interpretations in lpaz C because the time interval between samples is too large. There is no technical difficulty with improving this (Turner & Peglar 1988). Pollen analysts have achieved pseudo-annual resolution for understanding Mesolithic hunter-gatherer impacts (*e.g.* Simmons & Innes 1996) and yet the need to examine change at this resolution is probably more urgent in the historic period. Our failure to explore this suggests a lack of confidence, or that the questions are not sufficiently important which is surely incorrect. Precision in pollen taxonomy was demanded by Oldfield (1969), and the discussion at Swindon Hill concerning the representation of *Cannabis/Humulus* pollen was used to show how frustrating pollen data can be, but we are refining our identifications. On the other hand, the interpretation of heathland diversity at Swindon Hill comes from identifying a greater range of ericaceous pollen types than would be conventional (Oldfield 1959).

Swindon Hill and Dogden Moss sample the pollen from different areas around each site simply because they are different sized basins. Much effort has gone into defining pollen source areas with a view to identifying appropriate site types for specific problems (Jacobson & Bradshaw 1981; Jackson 1994), and in upland landscape mosaics the spatial scale of ecological and anthropogenic processes is probably most sensitively reflected from small basins yielding local records (Roberts, Turner & Ward 1973; Dumayne-Peaty & Barber 1998). There are, however, severe and continuing difficulties in demonstrating that pollen derives from local sources in open, non-wooded landscapes (Sugita, Gaillard & Brostrom 1999). Probably most critical is that many of our interpretations of land uses are too simplistic. For example, despite the overwhelming abundance of documentary data on woodland management (Rackham 1980; Smout 1997a) we have no models by which to demonstrate from pollen analyses the possibility that woods were managed, let alone the range of specific practices. We need to explore analogy more skilfully and adventurously.

To these technical issues, I would want to add interpretative issues of a more philosophical nature. Lisa Dumayne-Peaty's (1999) work was explored because geographically it is near my own research area in the Cheviots, because it is a welcome contribution to our understanding of the region and the period, but also because it seems to develop a specific relation to the documentary record. This can be defined as a 'confirmatory' approach, in that analysis of the pollen record seeks to establish correlation with the documentary record, but essentially only by confirmation. This approach can indeed be traced to Oldfield's seminal 1969 paper, where explicit correlations of the pollen record are made with a mix of economic and political events derived from secondary documentary sources. Later, the same approach characterised Barber's (1981) elegant exploration of historic landscape change around Bolton Fell Moss.

The concern to show that palaeoecology can be capable of contributing to historical understanding is uppermost in these analyses, but there are difficulties. Making correlations sometimes involves a selective reading of the written record and a reliance on general historical accounts. Thus, Dumayne-Peaty (1999) uses accounts by Millman (1975), Tuck (1979) and Parry & Slater (1980) to confirm agricultural expansion around Dogden Moss in the fifteenth–sixteenth century, although these descriptions are general histories with limited detail, and are not specific to this landscape. The willingness to understand the documentary record and go beyond the sole explanation of scientific data-sets is, of course, what makes these contributions special, but awareness that the archival record is patchy and generally operates by extrapolation at a rather amorphous regional spatial resolution demands caution in how the written record is used. A different approach was developed in the 1970s by, for example, Roberts *et al.* (1973) in Weardale in the northern Pennines. Here the documentary and pollen records were compared, and a palaeoecologist worked alongside a landscape historian, but comparisons were careful to use data that pertained to the same points in space, so that the same specific landscape was evaluated by different methods. In the Cheviot Hills, Tipping (1999) also used secondary archival sources, but did so only when they referred to the geographical area he sought to explain.

The effects of the Little Ice Age on farming communities in southern Scotland are still an important issue and are central to discussions in the Cheviot Hills (Tipping 1998, 1999, above) and at Dogden Moss (Dumayne-Peaty 1999). Pollen data in this paper have suggested the considerable effects on plant communities of temperature depression and the lowering of snow-beds to altitudes at around 360 metres (1,181 ft) O.D. on Swindon Hill, well within the day-to-day agricultural 'round'. Critically, pollen diagrams from the northern Cheviot Hills have been seen to be in conflict with existing historical paradigms, and have been used to question ideas of upland agricultural retreat (Parry 1975, 1978, 1981; Tipping 1998a). Dogden Moss in the Lammermuir Hills, where Parry developed his model, is at just over 200 metres (656 ft) Ordnance Datum and so below those altitudes argued to have been made agriculturally marginal by climatic deterioration (Parry & Carter 1985), although the lower slopes may have been impacted in turn by population displacement. Dumayne-Peaty has thus used Parry's model, but since Parry's chronology stresses upland abandonment between A.D. 1300 and 1600, his data are not 'in accord with the pollen evidence for increased clearance and agriculture' (Dumayne-Peaty 1999, p. 132). It is contradictory, and agricultural expansion probably occurred irrespective of climatic deterioration. This is of considerable significance but goes unnoted because it questions and challenges the documentary record, but it is in this conflict that the real value of independent but inter-disciplinary analyses emerges.

This 'confirmatory' approach means that there are no challenges to historical orthodoxy. The palaeoecological data are not able to speak for themselves, and there is no testing of either record. Pollen data for the last several hundred years are interrogated for slight deflections that might be capable of correlation with the documentary record, and this can be most objectively seen in the frequency with which workers have subdivided pollen records, the zones or phases in pollen diagrams. Oldfield's (1969) analyses of the last *c.* 2,400 years in southern Cumbria is subdivided into seven zones, but only the uppermost three of these, within the historic period, are further divided into subzones. The temporal resolution of analyses does not increase, however, to warrant this more refined interpretation. Similar patterns are seen at Dodgen Moss (Dumayne-Peaty 1999). The nature of interpretation thus seems to change from the prehistoric to the historic period. It is a moot point whether the historic period should be regarded as inherently more complex than later prehistory, and the provision of a seemingly high-quality documentary record should not make us assume that land uses were necessarily different to those in prehistory. It is more likely that we underestimate the complexity of land management in earlier times.

Our approaches to the explanation of landscape change derive from shadowy, often not clearly defined assumptions, and it is always useful to evaluate these. The paradigm introduced by Oldfield (1969) and maintained by colleagues since then seems to be of a rural economy responsive to almost any form of social or political instability. Thus the medieval woodland regeneration phase at Dogden Moss is seen as resulting from political and social unrest (above; Dumayne-Peaty 1999), but what the mechanism was remains unexplored. Detailed correlation with a largely political history is stressed but not necessarily the consequences of those changes for rural communities. My analyses (*e.g.* Tipping 1999) have implicitly assumed that agricultural change is only indirectly connected to large-scale but often short-lived and perhaps faddish socio-political developments. There is in this interpretation a 'distance' between political instability and agrarian practices. The upland landscapes of the northern Cheviot Hills were transformed on two occasions in the last *c.* 1,000 years: in the medieval period when, for poorly understood reasons, the systems of stock management promoted or allowed the establishment of dry *Calluna* heath, and again in the eighteenth century when system changes led to the destruction of that vegetation. These had large-scale causes in the rise of the monastic movement and agricultural 'improvement' respectively, but demonstrably through local ecological shifts induced by changes in the agricultural system. Equally, there were well-documented political convulsions such as the detailed pattern of destruction by the Earl of Hertford's raids into and through the Bowmont Valley in A.D. 1544 (Tough 1928), but lasting impacts on the agricultural economy need to be developed on a *priori* grounds and then tested rather than assumed.

Other patterns traced in the palaeoecological record probably have no expression in the documentary record (Tipping 1999). Nor should we assume them to have. What we identify in palaeoecological analyses are the elements of the landscape that mostly went without contemporaneous comment. It is a partial history, as is the written record. It is no lesser a history, however, and the argument in this paper has been that we need a science that maintains, within the historic period, an independence of thought, and studies that tell us something new about our landscapes, which are able to surprise and confident enough to challenge orthodoxies.

ACKNOWLEDGEMENTS

The views expressed in this chapter are my own. My work in the northern Cheviot Hills was supported by Historic Scotland, and I thank Gordon Barclay and Patrick Ashmore in particular for this. Roger Mercer, then at Edinburgh University and now at the RCAHMS, allowed me to explore the potential of different records in the Bowmont Valley, and he and Peter McKeague have helped in marrying archaeological and palaeoecological records. Gordon Cook and Gus Mackenzie (SURRC) provided support in developing chronologies. Bill Jamieson prepared the figures for publication. The paper benefited from a 'trial run' through the research seminar series of the Centre for Environmental History & Policy at Stirling and St Andrews Universities.

Moorland forests of medieval England

Angus J. L. Winchester

ABSTRACT

From the Cheviot Hills to Dartmoor, large parts of upland England had the status of 'forest' or 'free chase' during the middle ages. In theory, land protected as hunting reserves for feudal overlords, these areas were nevertheless exploited extensively for livestock production and as a frontier for settlement. In the face of the growth of stock farming in the medieval uplands, the boundaries of forests and chases retreated into the heart of the uplands. By the sixteenth century, many dales in the Pennines and Lake District contained settled hill farming communities and were forests only in name, but vestiges of true forest, retained in demesne by superior lords, remained as tracts of unsettled moorland waste. Despite attempts to enforce traditional forest rules, the numbers of deer dwindled in the face of competition from cattle and sheep.

KEY WORDS

Deer, forest, free chase, hunting, stock farming, upland colonisation, woodland

INTRODUCTION

The layman is often puzzled by the name 'forest' when it is assigned on the modern map to extensive areas of wide, largely treeless moorland. The deer forests of the Scottish Highlands are readily explicable as the creation of a nineteenth-century aristocratic hunting fraternity, but such names as Skiddaw Forest in the Lakeland fells; Lune Forest and Milburn Forest in the north Pennine moors; the forests of Pendle, Trawden and Rossendale in the brown, bare moorlands of industrial east Lancashire; or Clun Forest in the rolling hills of south-west Shropshire, leave many baffled. They are a legacy of the medieval centuries, when much, perhaps most, of upland Britain had the status of hunting forest or chase, the term 'forest' referring to their legal, rather than vegetational, character. The aim of this chapter is to attempt to identify those areas of the English uplands, which had this status, and to explore the legacy of forest administration in the institutions and landscape history of the uplands.

The wide extent of royal forest in medieval England, much of it in lowland areas, is well known (Young 1979, pp. 62, 152). Although the royal hunting grounds included some large upland tracts (Dartmoor and the High Peak, for example), most of the upland forests were private forests or, more correctly, 'chases' belonging to the lords of large baronial estates. Whether in Crown or lay ownership, most upland forests remained under the direct control of those holding the hunting rights in the middle ages, with the result that the management policies pursued by great lords determined the direction in which land use and settlement developed. Nowhere was hunting the exclusive activity in the uplands: almost all the owners of forests and chases saw their upland hunting grounds as potentially valuable reserves of grazing from which income could be raised. Demesne cattle farms ('vaccaries') were established in many forests; income was raised from 'agistment', that is allowing neighbouring communities to graze their stock in the forest; and some forests were opened up to permanent settlement (see Winchester 2000b; Fox 1994). The focus of this chapter is on the distinctive legal status of the upland forests, which lay behind their economic exploitation.

1. FOREST AND CHASE

Writing in the late sixteenth century, John Manwood identified four key features of forest status: first, 'vert', the preservation of woodland for the game; second, 'venison', the preservation of the principal game species themselves; third, forest law which upheld the lord's rights to vert and venison and replaced common law in forest areas; and, fourth, the appointment of foresters and other officers. The aim of this bundle of rights and institutions was to ensure that the forest was 'the better ... preserved and kept for a place of recreation and pastime meete for the royall dignity of a Prince' (Manwood 1615, fo. 18). It was the existence of forest law, which gave rise to the term 'forest' itself: a forest was an area set apart, outside (Latin *foris*) the reach of common law. As forest law only applied to royal hunting preserves, the private 'forests' held by lay landowners were technically not forests but free chases, that is areas over which a private individual possessed hunting rights. Manwood identified three differences between a forest and a chase: first and foremost, forest law did not apply to a chase, so offenders against a lord's privileges in a chase were punished at common law; second, a chase did not have the same officers as a forest, such as foresters and verderers, but only had keepers and woodwards; third, forest courts or 'swainmotes' were not held in a chase (*ibid.*, fo. 24). Despite these legal distinctions, many of the private chases of the uplands were termed 'forests' and were patrolled by foresters.

What, then, were the extent and number of these forests in the uplands? The gazetteer and accompanying maps (Figs 3.3-5), which form the second part of this chapter, attempt to list all those upland areas (defined as areas including land rising to over *c.* 300 metres) for which there is evidence of forest or free chase status during the medieval centuries. No fewer than seventy-four separate forests and chases have been identified, between them covering extensive swathes of each of the upland areas of England. A chain of forests ran down the Pennines from Cheviot Forest in the north to the forests of Macclesfield, High Peak, Leek and Alstonefield at the southern end of the range. Much of the Lakeland fells were forest, as were parts of the North York Moors. In the Welsh marches, each of the hill regions of southern Shropshire contained land that is recorded as forest, while the two principal upland areas of south-west England contained the royal forests of Dartmoor and Exmoor.

The forest status of the English uplands was paralleled in Scotland and Wales. Most of the southern uplands and the fringes of the Highlands are recorded as hunting reserves in the thirteenth century (Gilbert 1979, pp. 360-3), while Wales and the Marches contained numerous forest areas (no fewer than ninety-four in the southern half of the principality), most of which were private chases (Rackham 1986, p. 131; Davies 1978, pp. 120-6; Smith 1971, pp. 149-54). While forest creation is often ascribed to the Normans and the spread of feudal landholding, the roots of the forest rights found in the medieval uplands probably reach back into the pre-Conquest centuries. Hunting is well documented as a royal and noble pastime in the Anglo-Saxon period and the existence of 'hays' (Old English *haga*), enclosures of woodland for the preservation of deer, suggests widespread management of hunting reserves (Hooke 1989, pp. 123-9). More specifically, Domesday Book records evidence of hunting grounds in several upland regions later recorded as forest. The numerous 'hays' in southern Shropshire; the use of devastated land along the Welsh Marches as hunting grounds in 1066; and the description of wasted land in Longdendale, Derbyshire (later one of the divisions of the great forest of High Peak), as potential hunting territory all suggest that the tradition of the chase stretched back before the Conquest (Darby 1977, pp. 202-5).

It must be stressed that the simple listing in the gazetteer masks important chronological change. The principal evidence for the existence of private forests comes either from incidental references to a place being 'forest' or to a lay landowner's claim to possess the right of free chase, recorded in the Quo Warranto pleadings in the late thirteenth century. In many cases, the boundaries of forest areas are not recorded or, where they are, are only known from a late perambulation, as in the case of Macclesfield forest where the boundary was described in 1619. This is a significant limitation, since the areas of forest — both the legal areas and the areas devoid of settlement — shrank substantially between the twelfth and the sixteenth centuries. Nationally, disforestation in the thirteenth and fourteenth centuries reduced the royal forests substantially, many surviving as mere fragments, often wooded, of the twelfth-century forest (Young 1979, pp. 149-53). A similar retreat of forest boundaries is found in upland free chases. Whereas in some northern English baronies (such as the great Cumbrian baronies of Gilsland and Copeland), the lords appear to have claimed hunting rights across the whole of their estates in the twelfth century, by the end of the thirteenth, private forest rights were confined to more limited areas, usually located in the upland section of the estate (Todd 1997, p. 14; Liddell 1966, pp. 111-12). Where new subinfeudated estates were carved out of the fringes of the uplands, we find superior lords retaining hunting rights, confirming that the land being granted away had been deemed to lie within a forest. To take one example, when Austhwaite (later the estate called Dalegarth) in Eskdale, Cumberland, was granted by the lords of Millom *c.* 1200, they retained 'buck and hind and boar and wild sow', strongly suggesting that their hunting grounds extended at that period well beyond their recorded forest of Ulpha in the upper Duddon valley (Wilson 1915, p. 541; for Ulpha, see gazetteer below). A similar retreat of forest boundaries is also implied by the references to foresters in townships outside documented forest areas on the fringes of the northern and central Pennines (see gazetteer below).

In practice, as settlement extended into the uplands during the twelfth and thirteenth centuries, the areas of direct lordly control retreated to the unsettled upland core. In some of the better-documented forests, such as Exmoor and Copeland, a retreat of forest boundaries into the uplands can be charted, as Fig. 3.1 illustrates. Similar evidence of the retention of lordly prerogatives over unsettled wastes in the upper reaches of the valleys is found in the long-settled forest of Derwentfells in the northern Lake District, within which the effective forest consisted of no more than Gatesgarth Forest, a single bank of fellside at the head of Buttermere, by 1578 (Liddell 1966, p. 121). Similar was the retention of upper Redesdale and Tynedale in Northumberland as demesne pastures in the fourteenth-century (Winchester 2000a, pp. 86-7, 93). By the end of the middle ages, it is thus possible to draw a distinction between two types of upland forest. On the one hand, there were the settled dales, including many of the forests of the Pennines (Allendale, Weardale and Wensleydale, for example) and almost all those of the Lake District. On the other, there were unsettled tracts of moorland waste, such as Kidland, Askerton North Moor, Stockdale Moor (the last vestige of Copeland forest), Lune Forest and Milburn Forest in upper Teesdale, or the moorland cores of Dartmoor, Exmoor and Clee Forest.

2. FORESTS AS HUNTING GROUNDS

The clearest evidence for the presence of forest institutions designed to protect game for hunting is found, as might be expected, in the royal forests. Here, the full superstructure of forest administration often survived into the early-modern centuries and, with it, a continuing concern for the number and welfare of deer. In the royal forest of High Peak, for example, the bailiff or master forester was assisted by a forester in each of the three bailiwicks into which the forest was divided, four verderers, foresters of fee and woodwards (*VCH Derbyshire I* 1905, pp. 399-400). Even in the free chases teams of foresters are recorded in the thirteenth and fourteenth centuries: a head forester and 12 'foot foresters' (*forestarii pedit*) in Wensleydale forest in 1296; a head forester and nine under-foresters plus a pale-keeper (*palicarius*) in the

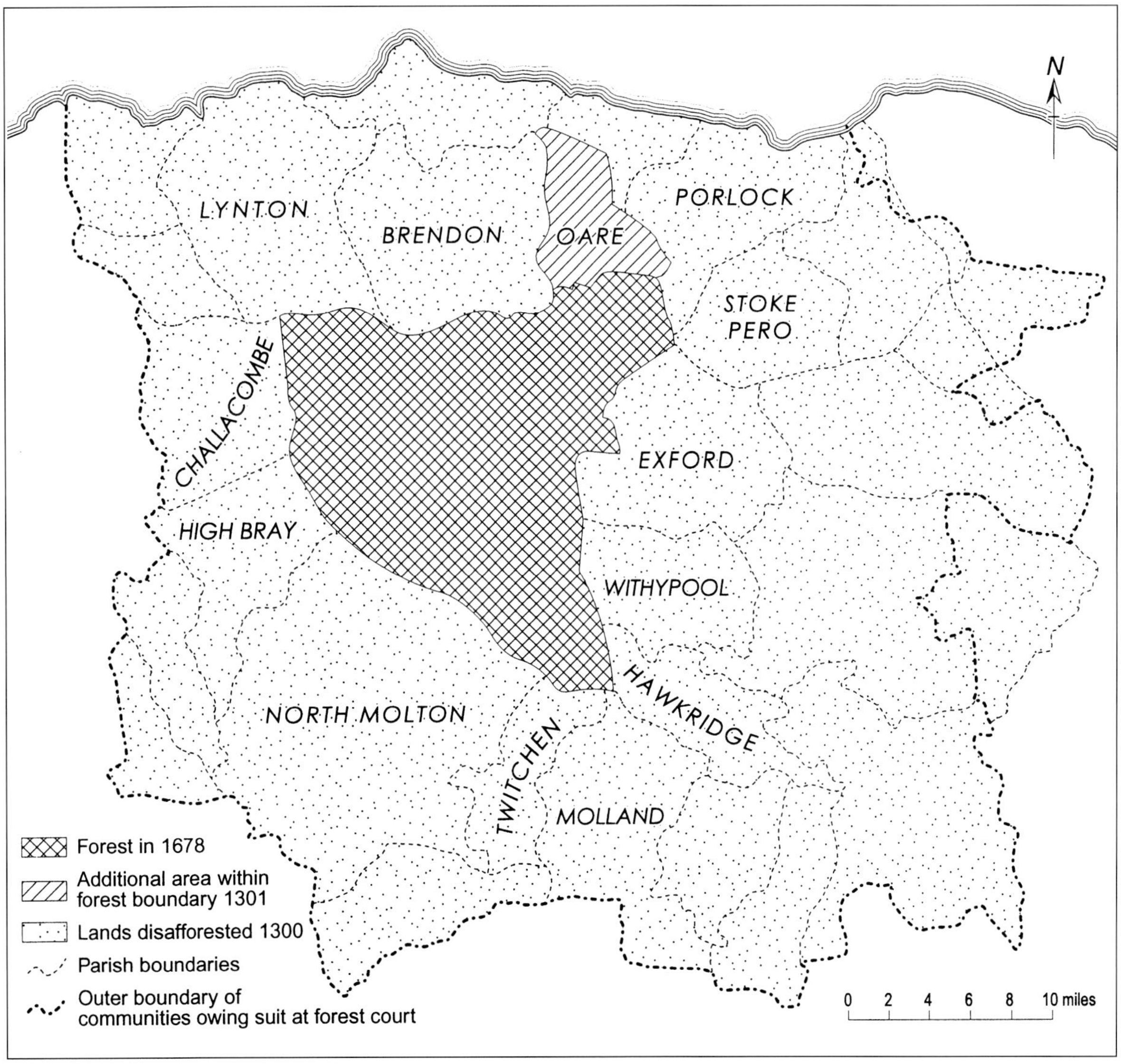

Fig. 3.1a. Exmoor forest: the retreat of forest boundaries (after McDermot 1973).

forest of Sowerbyshire in 1305; one salaried forester and four others paid on a weekly basis in the honour of Skipton in 1268; and three foresters apiece in the forests of Horwich and Mallerstang in 1282 and 1323 respectively.[1] Their role was to keep watch over the forest and specifically to guard the woodland and the deer, bringing to the forest court or 'swainmote' individuals who breached the lord's prerogatives of venison and vert. By the sixteenth century, salaries continued to be paid to foresters, even in forests such as Allendale and Derwentfells, which were densely settled and can have contained very few deer.[2] By then the role of the forester can have been little different from that of a manorial bailiff or reeve.

How much organised hunting and active management of game took place in the forests of the medieval uplands is difficult to assess. While presentments against illegal hunting are

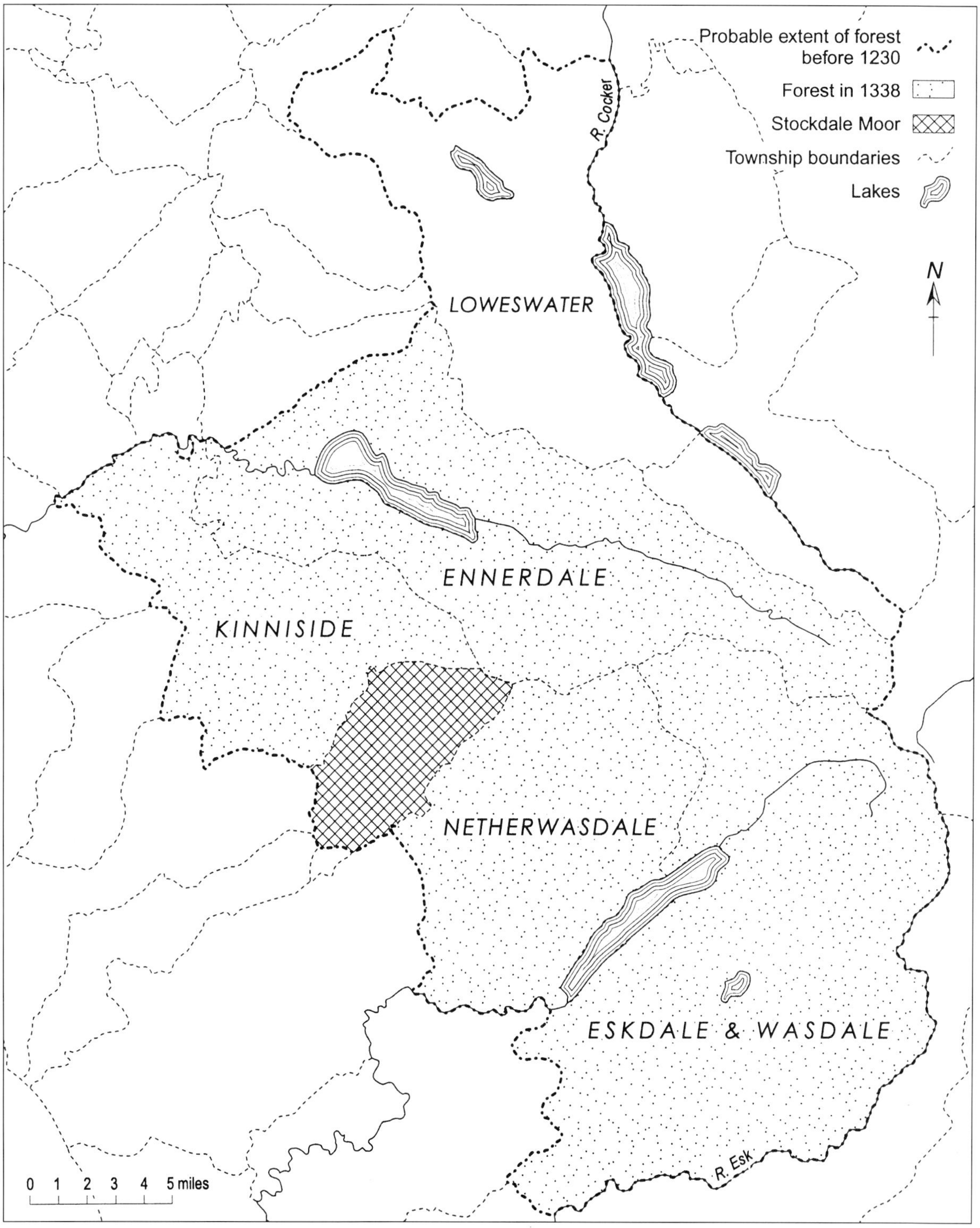

Fig. 3.1b. Copeland forest: the retreat of forest boundaries (after Liddell 1966).

numerous in the royal forests (*e.g.* in High Peak: *VCH Derbyshire I* 1905, pp. 401-9), evidence of hunting by the lords themselves is much more limited. We hear of 20 stags being taken from Exmoor for the king's use in 1315 and the bishops of Durham appear to have actively enjoyed the chase in Weardale Forest (McDermot, 1973 p. 29; Drury 1978, pp. 91-3) but direct references to hunting in the private forests are scarce. Increasingly, hunting appears to have been concentrated in deer parks or other enclosures in which game could be managed. In Macclesfield forest, for example, hunting appears to have been concentrated at the Coombs, where enclosures for the deer were recorded in 1291 and there was a hunting lodge by 1347 (*VCH Cheshire II* 1979, p. 183). In the chases of Blackburnshire, the great parks of Ightenhill in Pendle Forest and Musbury in Rossendale had been enclosed for deer before 1305 (R. B. Smith 1961, p. 8). In Weardale, the fallow deer protected in the bishop of Durham's great deer park at Stanhope became the focus for hunting from the early fourteenth century (Drury 1978, pp. 93, 96), while in Lune forest in Teesdale fallow deer were being taken from the park of Thringarth in 1412.[3] In Wasdale, in the Lake District forest of Copeland, the deer were protected in a wooded fellside, the 'New Frith', enclosed before 1578 (Liddell 1966, p. 128). By the sixteenth century the actual, if not the legal, extent of the hunting grounds in the uplands appears to have retreated and the foresters and forest courts were becoming increasingly anachronistic.

3. FORESTS AS GRAZING GROUNDS

Indeed, despite the administrative superstructures designed to preserve the upland forests as hunting grounds, the focus of seigniorial attention in these areas lay in the potential for income-generation offered by

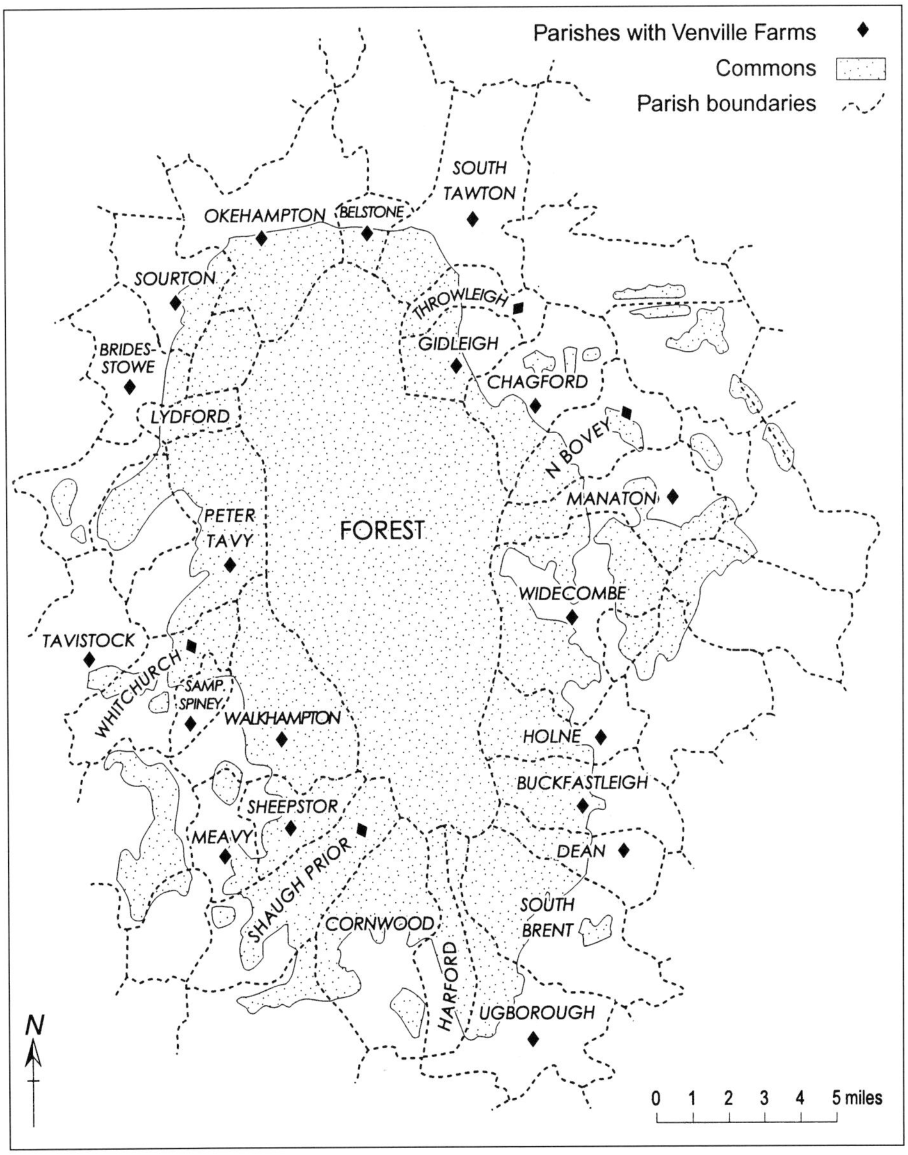

Fig. 3.2a. Dartmoor: intercommoning by surrounding settlements (after Gill 1971).

exploitation as grazing grounds. In part, this took the form of permanent settlement, whether through peasant colonisation or through direct exploitation by demesne stock farms, notably the 'vaccaries' and monastic stock farms, which are recorded in most of the upland forests in northern England by *c.* 1300 and were particularly numerous in the central Pennines (Winchester 2000b, pp. 76-81; Jennings 1992, pp. 28-9). By *c.* 1500, the demesne vaccaries, lordly parks and monastic stock farms of the thirteenth and fourteenth centuries had been leased and, in many cases, subdivided into smaller holdings, increasing the numbers of people (and, probably, the number of livestock) dwelling in hamlet communities in the forests. The century 1540 to 1640 witnessed considerable change in hill farming, including the growth of commercial livestock farming and the enclosure of pastures (Winchester 2000a). The cumulative effect of the process of settlement across the middle ages was the transformation of many upland valleys from hunting forest to a landscape of pastoral farming.

Even beyond the limits of permanent settlement, unsettled tracts of forest land were exploited for hill grazing, notably through agistment, where lords raised income by selling grazing rights to neighbouring communities. Such agistment grounds are encountered in most upland areas, from the shieling grounds of the Border wastes of Kidland and Askerton North Moor, to defined blocks of moorland retained as the lord's 'several pasture', such as Stockdale Moor in Cumbria, the last vestige of the forest of Copeland (Fig. 3.1), the 'gist-room' at the head of Arkengarthdale, or the side valleys of upper Weardale (Winchester 2000a, p. 94). Sometimes the whole forest formed a single agistment ground, as seen in the patterns of intercommoning recorded in the forests of Dartmoor, Exmoor, Clee and the High Peak. The parishes abutting on Dartmoor contained farms which had 'venville' rights on the forest, whereby a small fixed rent, recorded from 1296 but of greater antiquity, gave their tenants a pasture right on the forest (Gill 1971, pp. 95, 98; Fox 1994, pp. 156-62). On Exmoor, the 'suitors at large', inhabiting the parishes adjoining the forest, had similar rights (Riley & Wilson-North 2001, p. 92). Twenty-eight settlements in south Shropshire had common of pasture on Clee Forest, their inhabitants being termed 'strakers' and using traditional routes to drive their stock onto the forest pastures (Fig. 3.2) (Anon 1896, pp. 195-8; Rowley 1970, pp. 59-60). In Derbyshire, lands called 'wynlands' or 'wenlands', some on the edges of the forest of High Peak, others further afield, paid rents which appear to have been comparable to the venville rents on Dartmoor (*VCH Derbyshire I* 1905,

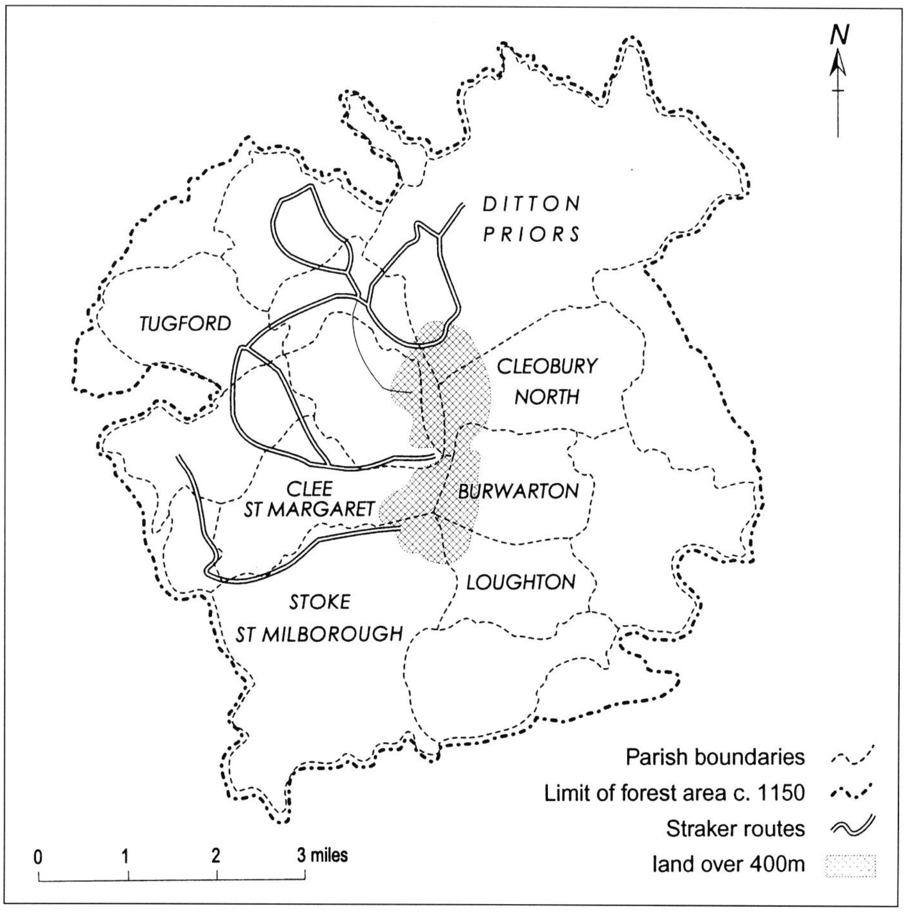

Fig. 3.2b. Clee forest: intercommoning by surrounding settlements (after Rowley 1972).

p. 408). The numbers of stock grazing on these uplands in the summer months were substantial: around 10,000 bovine cattle and an unknown number of sheep on Dartmoor *c.* 1400; 40,000 sheep, 1,000 cattle and 400 horses on Exmoor Forest in the later sixteenth century, for example (Fox 1994, pp. 161-2; Riley & Wilson-North 2001, p. 92).

Thus, by the sixteenth century, stock-rearing had long dominated over the preservation of deer, yet forest regulations were sometimes still enforced and, indeed, there was something of a resurgence in interest in the protection of game. Conflict was almost inevitable. The traditional forest prerogatives of 'venison' and 'vert' extended beyond forbidding illegal hunting and tree felling, to include customary rules placing further restrictions on the tenant communities. Preventing hunting extended to a ban on keeping 'unlawful' dogs, notably greyhounds, while providing browse for the deer extended beyond the preservation of woodland to a requirement that tenants should not make their hedges and fences so high that the deer could not enter to graze (*cf.* Weardale byelaws: Winchester 2000a, p. 166). The latter rule was stated explicitly by the Weardale court in 1607, when it ordered that no enclosures should prevent the passage of does and fawns and imposed the swingeing fine of 20*s*.[4] Deer were to have the freedom of the whole forest, including the tenants' farmland.

Yet these attempts to enforce traditional rules were too late in many upland forests: the balance between beasts of the chase and domestic livestock had tilted too far in the direction of the latter. The key to the survival of game lay in the preservation of woodland 'browse' for the deer in winter. The foresters who reported on the state of the deer in the royal forest of High Peak in 1527 identified the treeless nature of the terrain ('ytt ys a champion and playne place wherein no wood groweth') as the root cause of the loss of deer over recent severe winters, calculating that no more than thirty deer remained in the whole forest (*VCH Derbyshire I* 1905, p. 411). A generation later, in the 1560s, the Bowland forest court expressed concern over leasing, overgrazing and the failure to maintain the enclosures in which the deer over-wintered. In 1570, the jurors predicted the death of all the fallow deer for want of food, 'yf one evill winter or grett snawe cum', and the following year they recorded that 273 deer had died in the forest 'for wante of meate'.[5] In Weardale forest, it was said in 1595 that the pressure of grazing by cattle, sheep and horses in the frith in Stanhope park resulted in its being 'over eaten, so as the deare could have noe sufficient quiet stay or abiding'.[6] Once outside the friths and parks created for their preservation, deer were liable to wander and to be killed. As the deer departed in the face of competition from cattle and sheep, the role of the uplands as hunting forest became little more than a memory.

A GAZETTEER OF UPLAND FORESTS IN MEDIEVAL ENGLAND

The following gazetteer attempts to identify all those upland areas of England (defined as places in which the land rises to at least 300 metres) which had the status of forest or free chase in the middle ages. The numbers assigned to each forest refer to the key maps (Figs 3.3–3.5). Places where there are suggestions of forest status but no clear documentation of a defined forest territory are identified by letters, again referring to the key maps.

1. THE ENGLISH BORDERS (Fig. 3.3)

Large parts of upland Northumberland along the border with Scotland had the status of forest or chase. In the north lay the forest of Cheviot [1], covering the northern slopes of the hill of that name, south-west of Wooler. Recorded in 1182 as part of the barony of the Muschamps, a complex history of division and re-unification created two separate forest areas, known as Grey's Forest and Selby's Forest by the later sixteenth century (*NCH*, XI. 268-85). Immediately to the south, Kidland [2], a tract of extra-parochial waste covering the headwaters of the Coquet and Alwin rivers, was described as part of the forest belonging to the Umfraville lords of the liberty of Redesdale when it was leased to Newminster Abbey in 1181 (*NCH*, XV. 449). That implies that other land in Redesdale [3] liberty was also forest, as does the existence there of a 'Forster court' there, recorded in 1495 (*Cal. IPM ser II*, I, no. 971). To the east, much of the Simonside hills were included in the forest of Rothbury [4], granted with the manor of Rothbury in 1204 and later passing to the Percy earls of Northumberland (*NCH*, XV. 352-62). To the south of Redesdale lay the great liberty of Tynedale, held by the kings of Scotland from 1158 to 1296, within which lay Emblehope [5], at the head of the Tarset Burn, described as forest in 1330 (*Cal. IPM, VII*, no. 252). Further to the south lay the forest of Lowes [6], identified on Speed's map of Northumberland (1610) as lying north of Hadrian's Wall, between Haltwhistle and Sewingshields. Recorded from 1328, it was accounted part of the manor of Henshaw and was described in 1369 as a waste pasture containing three lakes, presumably the three 'loughs' (Crag Lough, Greenlee Lough and Broomlee Lough) from which the forest took its name (*Cal. IPM*, VI. 483; VII, no. 157; XII. 280).

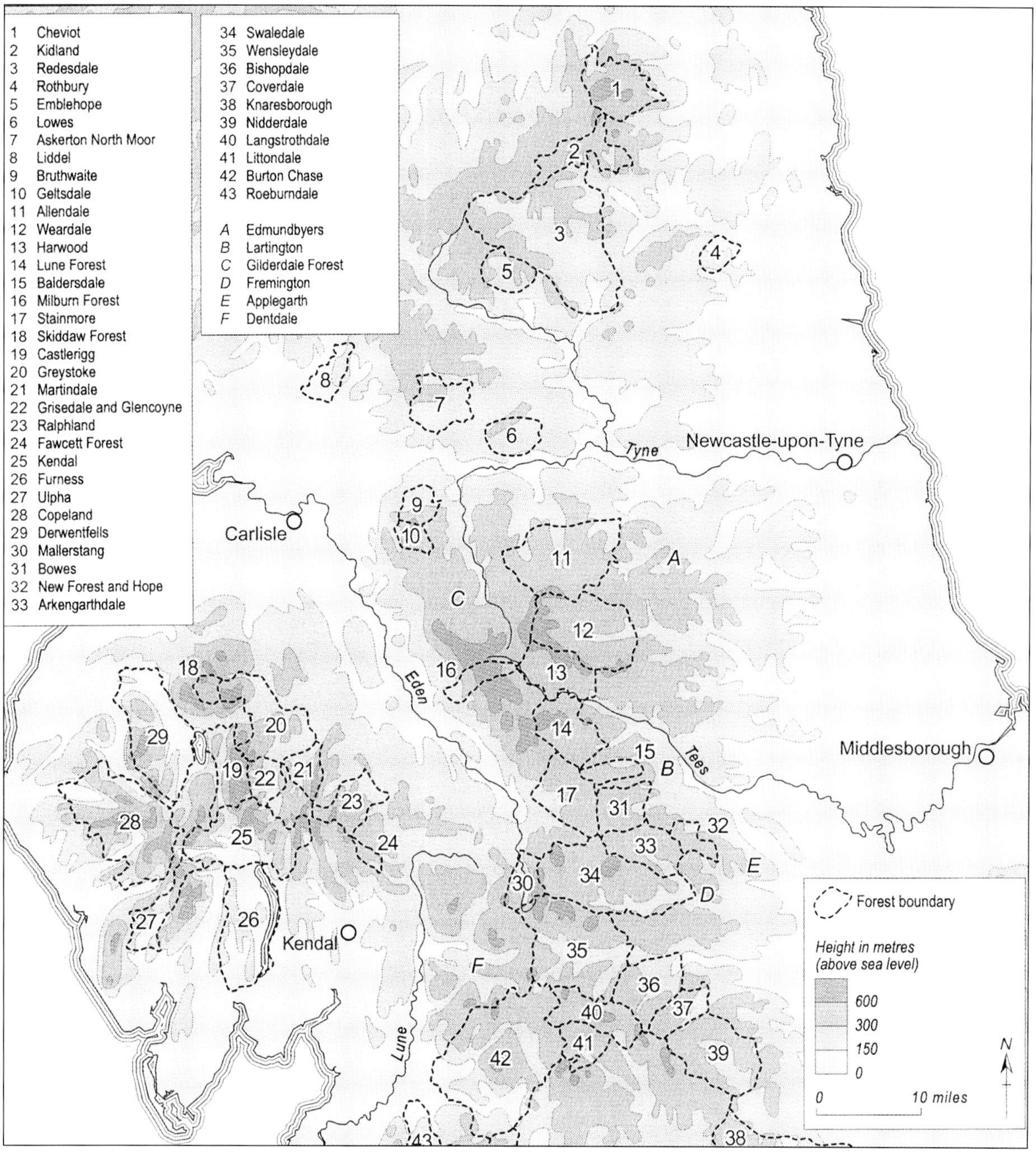

Fig. 3.3. The Forests of Upland Northern England I (Northumberland, Co. Durham, Cumbria and the North Riding).

Further west, on the border wastes of north Cumberland, the barons of Gilsland claimed free chase in Askerton North Moor [7] (the modern civil parish of Kingwater), described in 1295 as a great waste worth £24 a year, and 'Fulwode' in Askerton parish (*QW*, p. 126; *Cal. IPM*, III, no. 285). Finally, the higher parts of the barony of Liddel, hard against the Scottish border, formed the forest of Liddel [8], recorded in 1276, which had come to be known by its modern name of Nicholforest by 1300 (*Cal. IPM*, II, no. 195; PRO, C133/94/3, m. 2).

2. THE NORTH PENNINES (Fig. 3.3)

The upper reaches of almost all of the dales running down from the high moors of 'England's last wilderness' had the status of forest or chase. In the north-west corner lay the forests of Bruthwaite [9], or Tindaleside, and Geltsdale [10], two contiguous blocks of moorland waste belonging to the barony of Gilsland. Both were recorded as baronial forest in the early thirteenth century (Todd 1997, no. 25). Later in the century, the baron claimed free chase between the waters of Gelt and 'Cruyn', possibly the Black Burn, which forms the north-eastern boundary of Bruthwaite Forest (*QW*, p. 126; *cf.* plans of Geltsdale and Bruthwaite *c.* 1606: Durham Univ Libr, HN/C 713, nos. 12, 13). Allendale [11] was the forest of the archbishop of York's liberty of Hexhamshire. The forest is recorded from 1273 and appears to have covered the upper parts of both West and East Allendale (*NCH*, III. 72-8), though only the latter (which contained the grieveships of High Forest and Low Forest) was described as forest in 1608 (*NCH*, III. 95-8). Across the watershed to the south lay the bishop of Durham's High Forest of Weardale [12], recorded from the late twelfth century and covering the whole of the valley upstream from Eastgate, the entrance to the bishop's deer park, created between 1283 and 1311 (Drury 1978, p. 93). In upper Teesdale, there were forests on both the Durham and Yorkshire sides of the valley and where Westmorland straddled the watershed. On the northern side, the name of the township of Forest and Frith preserves the memory of the forest of Harwood [13], recorded in 1387 as belonging to the lordship of Barnard Castle (*Cal. Inq. Misc.*, VI, no. 347). On the Yorkshire side of the valley was Lune Forest [14], the bleak moorland between the rivers Tees and Lune, belonged to the Fitz Hughs' manor of Mickleton. It can be traced back to the late thirteenth century, when William de Greystoke claimed free chase at Crosthwaite in Teesdale, and Hugh son of Henry free chase 'in Mickleton within the water of Lune'. A separate right of free chase was claimed by Brian son of Alan in Baldersdale [15] in Cotherstone (English 1996, pp. 144, 155, 274, 277). Foresters continued to be appointed for the parks of Thringarth (in Lune Forest) and 'Peknyll' (in Cotherstone) in the fifteenth century (Durham RO, D/St/E.3/1/1). To the west, the Westmorland section of the north Pennine scarp was claimed as free chase by the barons of Westmorland: in 1292 John de Greystoke claimed hunting rights between Tees head and the Eden, from Crowdundle Beck to Swindale Beck near Brough (*QW*, pp. 786, 790), though within this lay the empty moorlands of Milburn Forest [16], which had been granted away in 1201 (Welch 1975, p. 141). Finally, to the south, lay the forest of Stainmore [17], belonging to the barons of Westmorland and attached to their manor of Brough. Covering the valleys of the tributaries of the Eden flowing down from Stainmore, it and the unidentified forest of 'Carreck' were referred to in the mid-thirteenth century (*Cal. Inq. Misc.* I, no. 436). In addition to these documented forests, there are hints that other areas may also have possessed forest status at an early date, including Edmondbyers [*A*] in the upper Derwent valley, west of Consett, where an order to a forester is recorded in 1370 (Booth 1889, pp. 97-8); Lartington [*B*] in lower Teesdale, where a forester made presentments in 1416 (NYCRO, ZPS 1/1); and Alston Moor in south Tynedale, where the name Gilderdale Forest [*C*] appears on the modern map.

3. THE LAKE DISTRICT FELLS (Fig. 3.3)

Much of the Lakeland massif consisted of private forests or chases belonging to the great Cumbrian baronies based in the surrounding lowlands. Their boundaries stretched into the heart of the Lake District to give each estate a section of the fells (Winchester 1987, pp. 17, 20-2). Running clockwise from the north, the following forests have been identified. Skiddaw Forest [18], a block of extra-parochial waste in the heart of the northern fells, still named on modern maps, was probably the free chase of the barons of Allerdale: it is recorded as a demesne pasture from the thirteenth century (PRO, SC11/730, m. 14v; CRO, D/Lec/29/1, m. 40). To the south, the lords of Castlerigg [19] manor, near Keswick, were said to have been granted a forest between 'Caltre' (unidentified) and the River Greta in the twelfth century (Wilson 1915, p. 492). This may have included the Thirlmere area, since there are references to forest in Wythburn manor in the seventeenth century (Cumbria RO, D/Van, Wythburn court baron, 1677). To the east lay the great forest of Greystoke [20], covering the upland half of that barony. Its boundaries, recorded in 1291, embraced all the land from the shore of Ullswater to the River Caldew behind Blencathra (*QW*, p. 119). In 1359, it contained two separate divisions, the 'forest of Grisedale' in the north and 'forest of Matterdale' to the south (PRO, C135/146, m. 9). On the Westmorland side of Ullswater the bounds of Martindale [21] forest were described in the mid-13th century (Ragg 1910, pp. 436-8), but the forest in this area also included Grisedale and Glencoyndale [22], described as forest in 1589 (PRO, LR2/212, fos 28, 31, 33). On the fells between Haweswater and Wet Sleddale lay Ralphland or Thornthwaite [23] forest (Noble 1901, pp. 8-9). Across the watershed south of Shap, in Kendal barony, lay the forest of Bannisdale or Fawcett Forest [24], recorded in 1310, covering the fells between Bannisdale and Borrowdale (Farrer 1923–4, I, pp. 231, 237). The bulk of the forest of Kendal barony [25] lay further west, the townships of Grasmere (recorded as forest in 1283); Rydal and Loughrigg (1274); Langdale (1274, 1283); Troutbeck (1272) and Ambleside (1437) forming a contiguous block of forest land (Farrer 1923–4, II, pp. 1, 20, 30, 40, 44; PRO, C133/5/10; C134/81/18). Lancashire North of the Sands contained the forest of Furness [26], granted to Furness Abbey in 1127 (Farrer 1902, pp. 304-5). It appears to have covered what later became the great monastic estate of Furness Fells, between

Coniston Water and Windermere. In south-west Cumberland, most of the western Lakeland fells and dales formed baronial forests. Ulpha [27] in the upper Duddon valley, recorded as forest in the early sixteenth century, appears to have been the last vestige of the forest belonging to Millom Seigniory; the great forest of Copeland [28] covered the western dales from Eskdale to Ennerdale and, before 1230, probably extended to cover Loweswater as well (see Fig. 3.1); and all the land between the Cocker and Derwent valleys formed the forest of Derwentfells [29] in the honour of Cockermouth (Winchester 1987, pp. 20-1 and sources cited there; Liddell 1966).

4. THE CENTRAL PENNINES AND BOWLAND FELLS (Figs 3.3 and 3.4)

At the head of the River Eden, in Westmorland, lay Mallerstang Chase [30], recorded from 1283 as a chase belonging to the barons of Westmorland (*Cal. IPM*, II, no. 478). It abutted on the east on the great forests of the honour of Richmond, which covered large sections of the Pennines in the North Riding. First, in the north, between the River Greta and Swaledale lay the forests of Bowes [31], the New Forest and Hope [32], and Arkengarthdale [33]. All appear to have been administered as one forest area by the end of the

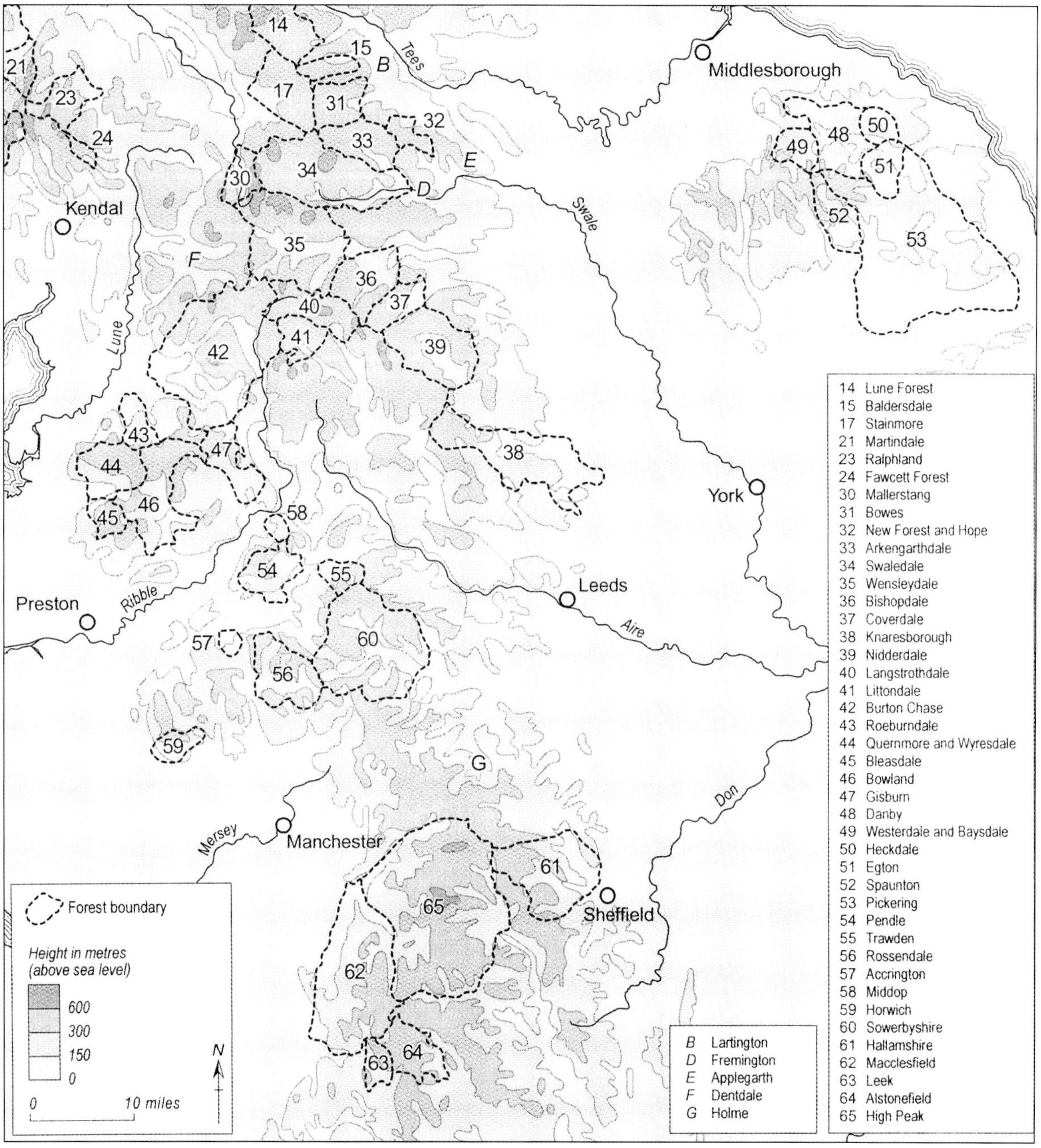

Fig. 3.4. The Forests of Upland Northern England II (the West Riding, Lancashire and the Peak District).

fourteenth century: in 1399 the under foresters responsible to the master forester of New Forest included two each for Bowes and Arkengarthdale. The forestership of New Forest and Hope is recorded in 1241, while in 1293-94 the earl of Richmond claimed free chase in Arkengarthdale, Hope and Scargill (*VCH Yorkshire North Riding I* 1914, pp. 37-8; English 1996, p. 266). The whole of Swaledale [34] west of Grinton and Fremington formed the manor of Healaugh, recorded as the forest or, more correctly, free chase of Swaledale from 1207 (Fieldhouse & Jennings 1978, pp. 37-8). A possible wider forest area is suggested by the references to foresters lower down Swaledale, at Fremington [*D*] and Applegarth [*E*], in the fifteenth century (NYCRO, ZJX 3/1/46, 3/1/53). All of upper Wensleydale [35] was forest, the earl of Richmond in 1293–4 claiming free chase through all Wensleydale west of waters of Thornton Rust and Askrigg. An earlier description of the boundary gave the eastern boundaries as the River Bain on the south and 'Merbek flowing from little Staggeswell' on the north. (*VCH Yorkshire North Riding I* 1914, pp. 200-1; English 1996, p. 266). The side valleys of Bishopdale [*36*] and Coverdale [37] were also claimed as free chases in 1279–81 (*QW*, pp. 189-90).

Most of the West Riding dales were also forest or chase. The royal forest of Knaresborough [*38*] included lower Nidderdale to the Clint and Washburn valley (Jennings, 1967, p. 47); while the upper reaches of the valley formed Nidderdale Chase [39], attached to the honour of Kirkby Malzeard and forming part of the extensive hunting grounds claimed by Roger de Moubray in 1279–81 (Gowland 1938, pp. 380-90; English 1996, p. 173). The headwaters of Wharfedale were embraced by Langstrothdale Chase [40], recorded from 1201 when forest rights there were disputed between the countess of Warenne and the owner of Buckden (*Curia Regis*, I. 469), and the forest of Littondale [41], part of Fountains Abbey's Pennine holdings (Lancaster, 1915, pp. 321, 451). To the west lay Burton Chase [42], the vast chase coterminous with the de Mowbray's honour of Burton-in-Lonsdale. This appears to have been a thirteenth-century expansion of smaller areas of free chase: it was said in 1293 that William de Mowbray had enlarged his chase after he purchased the estate around 1203–4, his predecessor's chases being restricted to the Forest of Mewith, on the northern fringes of the Bowland fells near Bentham, and Ingleborough, to the north (*QW*, pp. 218-19; English 1996, p. 226; Higham 1994). In the far north-western corner of the West Riding, the payment of salary to a 'forester of Dent' in 1373 and 1412 suggests that Dentdale [*F*] may also have had forest status (NYCRO, ZJX 3/2/7, 3/2/50).

Several distinct areas of forest can be identified in the Bowland Fells, covering between them most of that moorland block. As we have seen, the northern fringes formed the forest of Mewith in Burton Chase. Further to the west lay Roeburndale chase [43], recorded from 1199 (as the 'forest of Roger of Mountbegon') and forming a chase belonging to the lordship of Hornby (Farrer 1903–15, I. 29; III, 40). The western side of the Bowland moors contained the forests of the earldom of Lancaster, which, passing into Crown hands in 1399, became royal forest: Quernmore and Wyresdale [44], covering the upper reaches of the Conder and Wyre valleys, and Bleasdale [45] (Farrer 1903-15, I. 290; II. 26-31). The southern flanks, in the catchment of the River Hodder, formed the forest of Bowland [46], originally a free chase attached to the honour of Clitheroe or Blackburnshire, but later (from 1399) in Crown hands (Shaw 1956, p. 231). The 'forest of Chippingdale', recorded in 1258 (Farrer 1903-15, I. 217) may have been an earlier name for the forest, which later covered all the land west of the Hodder, upstream from Chipping. Finally, abutting the eastern margins of Bowland forest, lay the forest of Gisburn [47], a chase covering the catchment of Skirden Beck and its tributaries, which belonged to the Percy family, who granted the wood and grazing rights to Sawley Abbey in the early thirteenth century (McNulty 1933, pp. 16, 31; *Cal. IPM*, V. 313, no. 536).

5. THE NORTH YORK MOORS (Fig. 3.3)

Much of Eskdale, the long valley bisecting the Moors from west to east and running into the sea at Whitby, was forest. Four distinct areas can be identified. The forest of Danby [48], covering the western two-thirds of Eskdale, belonged to the lords of Danby and was recorded from the thirteenth century. From the later twelfth century, a forest in Westerdale and Baysdale [49] formed part of the Stokesley fee: it appears to be identified with the 2,500-acre block of extra-parochial waste called Stockdale Moor, recorded as forest in 1716. A separate forest of 'Heckdale' [50], also part of Danby manor, but lying down-valley in Lealholm, was recorded in 1272. Finally, further downstream, lay the forest of Egton [51] or Egton Wood. Settlements around Egton were said to have been destroyed by the earl of Albemarle in the twelfth century and a forest of Egton is recorded in 1222 (*VCH Yorkshire North Riding II* 1914, pp. 333, 343-4, 349, 413). Whether the Eskdale forests were the same as the forest of Whitby, recorded in 1311, is not clear (*Cal. Inq. Misc.* ii. no.104). On the southern side of the Moors, the land between the rivers Dove and Seven granted to St Mary's

Abbey, York, by Henry II, formed Spaunton Forest [52], recorded by name in 1335 (*VCH Yorkshire North Riding I* 1914, p. 524), and the land to the east of the Seven lay in the royal forest of Pickering [53] (Counsell 1988–9).

6. THE SOUTH PENNINES AND PEAK DISTRICT (Fig. 3.4)

South-east of the Ribble valley, the Lancashire moorlands were chases belonging to the great de Lacy honour of Clitheroe or Blackburnshire, until they passed to the earldom of Lancaster in 1311. In 1292 Henry de Lacy claimed free chase throughout his fee of Blackburnshire (*QW*, pp. 381-2) but in reality these rights appear to have been restricted to the four chases of Pendle [54], Trawden [55], Rossendale [56] (which included Hoddlesden Chase) and Accrington [57] (Tupling 1927, pp. 6-41; R. B. Smith 1961, p. 8). De Lacy had also claimed forest in the moor of Middop [58], west of Barnoldswock in 1279-81 (English 1996, pp. 180-1). On the southern side of the Rossendale fells, covering the moorland around Winter Hill, lay the forest of Horwich [59], referred to in 1282 and 1322, when it was attached to the manor of Manchester (Farrer 1903-15, I. 247; II. 56-7). Across the Pennine watershed, the upper Calder valley west of Halifax formed the large forest of Sowerbyshire [60], that part of the vast manor of Wakefield in which the earls of Warren claimed free chase. The forest covered the areas west of the Hepple Brook in the north and the River Ryburn in the south (Kendall 1926, pp. 85-107; Jennings 1992, pp. 18-27). Reference to foresters of Holme or Holmfirth [*G*] in the early fourteenth century suggest the existence of another forest covering the moorlands south of Huddersfield (Walker 1983, p. 57; Clay 1949, p. 252). To the south of these chases lay the chases of the lords of Hallamshire, covering the moors to the north-west of Sheffield. The forest of Rivelin [61] was said in the late thirteenth century to extend from Whitley Wood, north of Sheffield, to the Derbyshire boundary along Stanage Edge (Hunter 1869, p. 55; Hey 1991, pp. 24-5). An idea of the extent of the forest area can be gained from the existence of foresters for Bradfield, Rivelin and Greno (near Whitley) in 1442 (Thomas 1924, pp. 74-7), references to Ewden Chase and Agden Chase in the moors north of Bradfield (Hunter 1869, p. 459) and the list of 'several pastures in the woods and moors' in the manor of Sheffield in 1332, stretching from Ewden in the north to Fulwood in the south (*Cal. IPM*, VII, no. 470).

The whole of the western side of the Peak District formed a more or less contiguous block of forest, which extended into three counties. In the north west lay Macclesfield Forest [62], covering the east Cheshire moorlands, its boundaries recorded in 1619. Belonging to the earls of Chester, it was first recorded in the mid twelfth century, when it appears to have been linked with the earl's forest of Leek [63], across the county boundary in Staffordshire (*VCH Cheshire II* 1979, pp. 178-84). The exact extent of Leek forest is unknown but it included the townships of Leekfrith and Rushton Spencer and a hunting ground at Hollinhay (*VCH Staffordshire VII* 1996, p. 80). Further east in the Staffordshire moorlands lay the forest of Alstonefield [64], also known as the forest of Mauban and Malbank Frith. Recorded in 1227, it covered the townships of Fawfieldhead, Heathylee, Hollinsclough and Quarnford (*VCH Staffordshire VII* 1996, pp. 5, 6, 28, 29, 52). Finally, to the north, lay the great royal forest of High Peak [65], covering over 40 square miles and extending across the whole of the north-western corner of Derbyshire. Originally part of the honour of Peverel, it was forfeited to the Crown in 1155, passing to the duchy of Lancaster in 1372 (and hence back to the Crown by the fifteenth century). Its bounds included all the land from the River Goyt in the west (where it marched with Macclesfield forest) to the Derwent in the east, and from the River Wye, south of Buxton, in the south, to Longdendale in the north. For administrative purposes, the Peak forest was divided into three sections, Campana (that is the 'champagne' or open country) in the south-west, Hopedale in the east, and Longdendale in the north (*VCH Derbyshire I* 1905, pp. 397-413).

7. THE SHROPSHIRE HILLS (Fig. 3.5)

Large areas of Shropshire were forest or chase in the thirteenth century. The royal forest included wide swathes of settled lowland in the south-east of the county before the charter of 1301, which reduced its extent considerably, leaving only a few wooded remnants with full forest status (*VCH Shropshire IV* 1989, p. 46). The following list is restricted to the areas of true upland in the county. The Wrekin [66], the wooded peak south of Wellington, lay in the south-west corner of the forest of Mount Gilbert until disafforestation in 1301 reduced the forest to the hay of Wellington on the Wrekin's northern slopes (*ibid.* IV. 45; XI. 220). The moorland of the Long Mynd [67] and the hills to the east of the Stretton valley fell within the vast area covered by the Long Forest, which was again reduced to a few small woodland areas after 1301. The Long Mynd had an identity of its own, being recorded in 1212 as 'the king's forest of Long Mynd', but after 1310 it became a free chase of the earls of Arundel (*VCH Shropshire X* 1998, p. 96; Gelling 2001, p. 228). Along the far western fringes of the county, where the land rises along the Welsh border, were several tracts of forest. South-west

SOCIETY FOR LANDSCAPE STUDIES

SOCIETY, LANDSCAPE AND ENVIRONMENT IN UPLAND BRITAIN

Edited by Ian D. Whyte & Angus J. L. Winchester

(Series Editor: Della Hooke)

The landscapes of upland Britain have been the focus for a range of debates in recent years over issues such as access, afforestation, farming and planning. However, these landscapes have been neglected and misunderstood by contemporaries in the past and by modern historians. There has been a lack of research into the societies and economies of these areas and the landscapes they created.

Society, Landscape and Environment in Upland Britain presents a series of detailed, specially commissioned studies that help to redress this imbalance by examining a range of themes relating to the historic landscapes of areas from Cornwall to the Scottish Highlands. It provides a detailed, authoritative picture of how the upland landscapes of Britain have developed and demonstrates how rich, complex and multi-layered our upland landscapes really are. A detailed contents list is given overleaf.

Society, Landscape and Environment in Upland Britain is the second in a series of occasional volumes published by The Society for Landscape Studies. The first volume, *Landscape: the richest historical record* contains papers given at the Society's 21st annual conference, offering an exciting, sometimes controversial reassessment of landscape history by many of the leading authorities in the field. It 'summarises the study of landscape history as successfully as W.G. Hoskins' overview of 1955' (Professor R Dodgshon, President of the Society for Landscape Studies).

CONTENTS:

SOCIETY, LANDSCAPE AND ENVIRONMENT IN UPLAND BRITAIN *(188 pages)*
ISBN No. 0 9539711 1 2
LANDSCAPE: THE RICHEST HISTORICAL RECORD *(180 pages)*
ISBN No. 0 9539711 0 4

Both volumes are published by the Society for Landscape Studies. They are in A4 paperback format and contain colour and black-and-white illustrations.

ORDER FORM

To: Mrs Kathryn Brown, 38 Mill Road, Bozeat, Northamptonshire, NN29 7JA.

Please send me......copy(ies) of *Society, Landscape and Environment in Upland Britain* at £23.00 per copy inc. postage for members, £28.00 inc. postage for non-members.

Please send me......copy(ies) of *Landscape: the richest historical record* at £18.00 per copy inc. postage. (£15 if purchased with *Society, Landscape and Environment in Upland Britain*).

Cheques should be made payable to: The Society for Landscape Studies.

NAME:..

ADDRESS:..

....

Registered Charity No. 278393

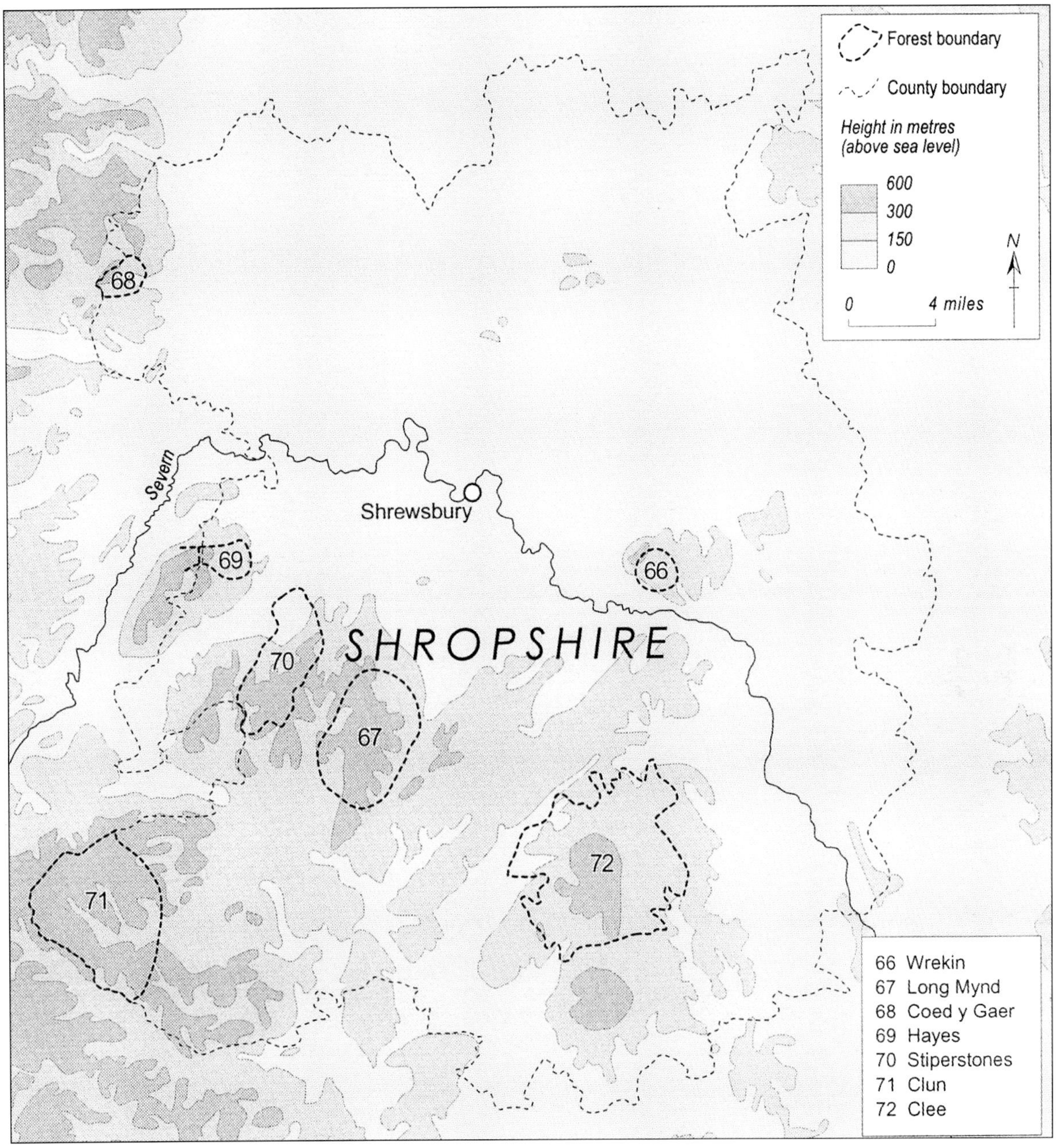

Fig. 3.5. The Forests of the Shropshire Hills.

of Oswestry lay the forest of Coed y Gaer [68], one of several forests in the lordship of Oswestry, which contained between them 1,500 acres (Smith 1971, p. 150). South of the rivers Severn and Vyrnwy, straddling the national boundary, lay the Forest of Hayes [69] (or Ffridd Cefn Digoll), a free chase covering Long Mountain, which lay largely in Wales but extended into Westbury parish, where the name of the township of Forest preserved a memory of its status (*VCH Shropshire VIII* 1968, p. 297). Across the valley of the Rea Brook was the forest of Stiperstones [70], a free chase granted to Robert Corbet in 1190 (when the name was given as 'Tenfrenstanes'), which included the vills of Shelve and Hope and also the woodland south of Minsterley, which came to be known as Hogstow Forest (*ibid.* VIII. 298; *QW*, p. 685). In the south-western corner of the county lay Clun Forest [71], a free chase covering the hilly western sections of the great marcher lordship of Clun (Salt 1887, pp. 248-61). Finally, away from the Welsh border, in the south-east of the county, Clee Forest [72] covered the Brown Clee hill and its surrounds (see Fig. 3.2). Originally royal forest, this was a free chase from 1155, attached to Corfham Castle. At the core of the forest lay the unenclosed waste of Brown Clee but the memory of the former extent of Clee forest was preserved in the rights of the 'out-commoners' who drove their stock up 'straker' routes to graze on the hill (Rowley 1970; 1972, pp. 52, 103-6).

8. THE MOORS OF THE SOUTH WEST

The two great moorland areas of south-west England were both royal forests from an early period. Dartmoor [73] (see Fig. 3.2) may have become a hunting ground for the kings of Wessex as early as the ninth century. After the forest was granted to Richard, earl of Cornwall, in 1239, it technically became a chase covering the moorland core and was coterminous with the parish of Lydford, excluding the borough of Lydford (Gill 1971, pp. 93-9). The status of Exmoor [74] (see Fig. 3.1) as royal forest also appears to stretch back before the Norman Conquest, as Domesday Book records that three foresters held land at Withypool in 1066. The forest was centred on the waste along the Devon-Somerset boundary, the area defined as forest from the thirteenth century consisting of the moorland around the headwaters of the rivers Exe and Barle on the Somerset side only, though settlements in Devon also owed suit at the swainmote courts (McDermot 1973, pp. 1, 17-18 and *passim*).

NOTES

1. PRO, SC6/1116/9, m. 5r; SC6/1087/6, mm. 3-5: Clay 1949, p. 252; Farrer 1903–15, I. 247; PRO, SC6/1044/6, m. 5.
2. Allendale, 1547: NCH, III. 75; Derwentfells, 1570: PRO, E164/37, fo.[56].
3. Durham RO, D/St/E3/1/1.
4. PRO, SC2/171/12.
5. Lancashire RO, DDHC1, box 86, Whitwell court rolls, nos 7-12; Shaw 1956, p. 237.
6. Durham Univ Libr, Archives & Special Coll, WCP 42.

ABBREVIATIONS

NCH	*A History of Northumberland*, 15 vols.
NYCRO	North Yorkshire County Record Office, Northallerton.
PRO	Public Record Office.
QW	*Placita de Quo Warranto*, Rec Comm.

Col. Plate I. *Grasmere and Fairfield from Helm Crag, Cumbria*

Col. Plate II. Mickleden, Great Langdale: striking contrast between valley in-bye land and fell grazings. (Photo. A. Winchester).

Col. Plate III. Watendlath, Borrowdale: an upland hamlet with a limited area of improved land. (Photo. I. Whyte).

Cornish uplands: medieval, post-medieval and modern extents

Peter Herring

ABSTRACT

The changing extent of the Cornish uplands from medieval to recent times is examined together with the processes that reduced and sometimes entirely removed areas of upland in the peninsula. The role of upland areas in the economies of medieval and post-medieval rural communities is considered. A detailed case study of the impact of these changes on Bodmin Moor is provided. Piecemeal enclosure caused increasing disaggregation of formerly coherent and extensive upland areas the perceptions of which steadily faded among local communities.

KEYWORDS

Cornwall, rural settlement enclosure, transhumance

INTRODUCTION

Although less than a quarter of its area is above 150 metres (492 ft) O.D. and Brown Willy, its highest hill, reaches only 419 metres (1,375 ft), Cornwall is usually considered to be part of Britain's Highland Zone (*e.g.* Rackham 1986, p. 4). Until recently, Cornwall's historic landscape, especially its dispersed farmsteads and largely anciently enclosed field patterns, was regarded as being typically 'Celtic', pastoral, and at least partly determined by an essentially upland topography. The settlement pattern and field systems may now be seen to be less clearly determined by either culture or geography (see below), but one of the aims of this paper is to reaffirm that Cornwall's countryside had, until modern improvements or homogenisations, a complex framework of which blocks of upland rough ground formed an important part. Other elements were the gently rolling lowlands, deep wooded valleys, long estuaries and, of course, the coast.

The Celtic Cornish language contains many topographically descriptive words, now mainly preserved as place-name elements. These indicate a full awareness in the early and later medieval periods of Cornwall's variety of landform. (See Padel 1985 for the six surviving place-name elements meaning 'hill', and the various words for downland, ridge, hillock, promontory, crest, peak, tip, hump, brow, *etc.*) Cornwall was certainly regarded by visiting topographers in the late medieval and post-medieval periods as a place containing extensive rough ground, including some particularly high places. John Leland in the 1530s noted the 'Hy Montaynes baren Ground … nerer to the North Part [of Cornwall] than to the Sowth' (Pearse Chope 1968, p. 11) and over 150 years later Celia Fiennes was unable to decide whether an unnamed hill near Dozmary Pool (possibly either Brown Willy or Roughtor?) was the, 'great mountain esteemed the second highest hill in England, supposing they account Black Combe in Cumberland the first' (*ibid.*, p. 133).

Appraisal or interpretation of past landscapes, whether done by local communities or by historians, is inevitably influenced by present or recent perceptions of an area's topography. In a country where uplands are not mountainous but are instead capable of effective transformation to 'lowlands' by enclosure and agricultural improvement, sight can easily be lost of former landscape structure, with consequent diminishment of historical understanding.

Historic landscape characterisation (HLC) and historic map sources confirm what is suggested by the proliferation within enclosed parts of Cornwall of place-names containing elements like *goon*, 'downland, unenclosed pasture' (Padel 1985, p. 108) or Down: that Cornwall's present upland areas are fragments of previously larger and more extensive downlands, and also that there were, in the later medieval period (and in some cases surviving well into the nineteenth and even twentieth centuries), many more upland areas. Uplands are defined here simply as blocks of unimproved rough ground higher than surrounding or adjacent enclosed farmland (see also Winchester 2000a, p. 5). As this paper considers differing but interrelated land uses in the upland rough ground and the lowlands, it is not proposed to enter into debate on more objective and modern definitions of uplands (for example, those based on altitude).

Those uplands that survive in Cornwall — mainly Bodmin Moor, Lizard/Goonhilly Downs, and the West Penwith downs, plus isolated areas of rough grassland and heathy, furzy or ferny hills from Kit Hill, Helman Tor and St Agnes Beacon to Hensbarrow, Carn Brea, Carnmenellis, Tregonning and Godolphin — tend to be the most marginal, mainly in terms of stoniness, steepness and exposure but also, especially on the Lizard and Goonhilly Downs, due to the poverty of their soils. Most of the other downlands have either been removed or greatly diminished by enclosure for new farms, smallholdings, or extensions to existing medieval farms, mainly in the eighteenth and nineteenth centuries. Smaller areas have been lost to mines and quarries while a large part of the Hensbarrow granite area has been replaced by nineteenth- and twentieth-century china-clay works.

The former, more numerous areas of downland not only helped provide greater visual and land-use variety in the Cornish countryside (along with the now almost entirely lost lowland marshes and meadows and the greatly diminished ancient woodlands), but they also broke the enclosed land into smaller areas, helping create a more fragmented Cornish landscape, each part more clearly topographically defined, and each with the potential to develop a distinctly local culture. The wider scattering of downlands probably also diluted the importance of the higher and more extensive upland areas like Bodmin Moor. In most parts of Cornwall, downlands would not have been as remote as they often now are; most settlements would have had upland rough ground near by and many downlands developed locally meaningful names — usually related to their attachment to particular farming estates and communities. It is probably significant in this respect that today's unifying names of Cornish uplands, like Bodmin Moor, West Penwith and Hensbarrow (the last often re-named the St Austell China-Clay Area) — names created not by farming communities but by topographers, map-makers and administrators — were not applied until the nineteenth or twentieth centuries. Earlier names like Foweymore (*i.e.* Bodmin Moor), given when their objects were extensive open areas used by larger numbers of communities, had largely lost their meaning, relevance and currency by the early post-medieval period. Instead, Foweymore had, by the later medieval period and by processes described below, become broken into numerous individually named areas. These processes on Hingston Down and in the Hensbarrow uplands have been presented elsewhere (Herring & Thomas 1989, map 7; Herring & Smith 1991, map 10, colour Pl. IV). Any associations of these uplands with wildness, remoteness and danger (for which see Altenburg 1999, p. 28) would also have been weakened by their settlement, fragmentation and familiarisation.

Giants, piskies, spriggans and other mythical characters of unease and fear that feature in the Cornish folk tales collected in the mid-nineteenth century (*e.g.* Hunt 1881) are usually attached to places removed from home and the working fields, places like rough ground, and usually uplands. Place-names with supernatural or disconcerting connotations also tend to be found in the uplands. The folk tales tend to be queer stories, often lacking clear narrative, reminiscent of those collected in the west of Ireland later in the nineteenth century. Although it is difficult to assess how old they are or to understand precisely what they mean, their very oddness lends authenticity and authority to the association of frightening creatures with the less well-frequented parts of Cornwall. If that way inclined, historians could suggest that such associations of uplands with worrying aspects of supernature might have been either used or even developed to structure and control use of these parts of the landscape; they may have been designed to help keep either people or permanent settlement off. If a conservative imperative is indeed seen for creating such stories and associations, then it was probably those users of the uplands who had the most to lose from their enclosure and fragmentation — those tenants who had various common rights on them — and who had the greatest interest in developing such off-putting tales.

DOCUMENTING CHANGE IN EXTENTS OF CORNISH UPLANDS

The 1994 historic landscape characterisation (HLC) of Cornwall, undertaken by the Cornwall Archaeological Unit with support from English Heritage (Cornwall Cty Counc 1996; Herring 1998), identified both extant and former upland rough ground, the latter mainly via the HLC Type 'Recently Enclosed Land' (that is farmland taken in from rough ground in the period after *c.* 1600 and mainly in the eighteenth and nineteenth centuries). It complements the evidence obtained from historic mapping, notably Thomas Martyn's excellent 1748 one-inch Map of Cornwall, the earliest countywide accurate, systematic and comprehensive map. This carefully distinguished between hedged and unfenced roads and thus indicated areas of open ground, which independent evidence always confirms was rough land, often 'uplands' (Fig. 4.2). Martyn also showed major hills in profile, often accurately portraying their shapes (Roughtor, Brown Willy, Kilmar and Carn Brea) (see Fig. 4.3). It is clear that only those hills that were then open rough ground were mapped, nicely reinforcing the point that once they are enclosed hills become significantly less visible in the landscape.

Martyn was mapping at the beginning of a period when there were significant intakes from upland rough ground. Hundreds of new smallholdings and farms provided food for an expanding population. Many of these, especially those on the granite, were associated with mining and other rural extractive industry but many others (*e.g.* on the north Cornish downlands) were part of a wider South-Western process of enclosure and improvement of the less marginal upland rough ground. Martyn's map, the 1994 historic landscape characterisation, the Ordnance Survey two-inch field drawings of the early 1800s, and the 1583 'Certificate of the Parkes and Commons in the Countie of Cornwalle' (PRO, SP, 12/162 no. 38; map prepared by Harold Fox: Fox 1971, fig. 4.1) enable early post-medieval extents of Cornish uplands to be established (see Figs 4.1, 4.2 and 4.3).

By adding coastal rough ground (the steeply sloping but still exploitable ground above the cliffs), towans (sand dunes), and medieval towns to the upland rough ground, what is left unshaded on a map is Cornwall's Anciently Enclosed Land. This is land taken in for farming by at least the late sixteenth century, and most of it by the ninth or tenth centuries (confirmed by the distribution of *tre*, *ker*, *bos* and other pre-Norman Cornish farming settlement names, and to some extent by the patterns of 'pasture' recorded in Domesday Book) (see, respectively, Cornwall Cty Counc 1996; Padel 1985; Thorn & Thorn 1979; Ravenhill 1967). Much had been enclosed by the later prehistoric period, as indicated by the distribution of the enclosed farming settlements known as rounds, although there seems to have been a significant reorganisation of field systems in the post-Roman or early medieval periods (Herring 1999a, 1999b). From this, it can be stated with some certainty that those early post-medieval downlands identified via HLC and map

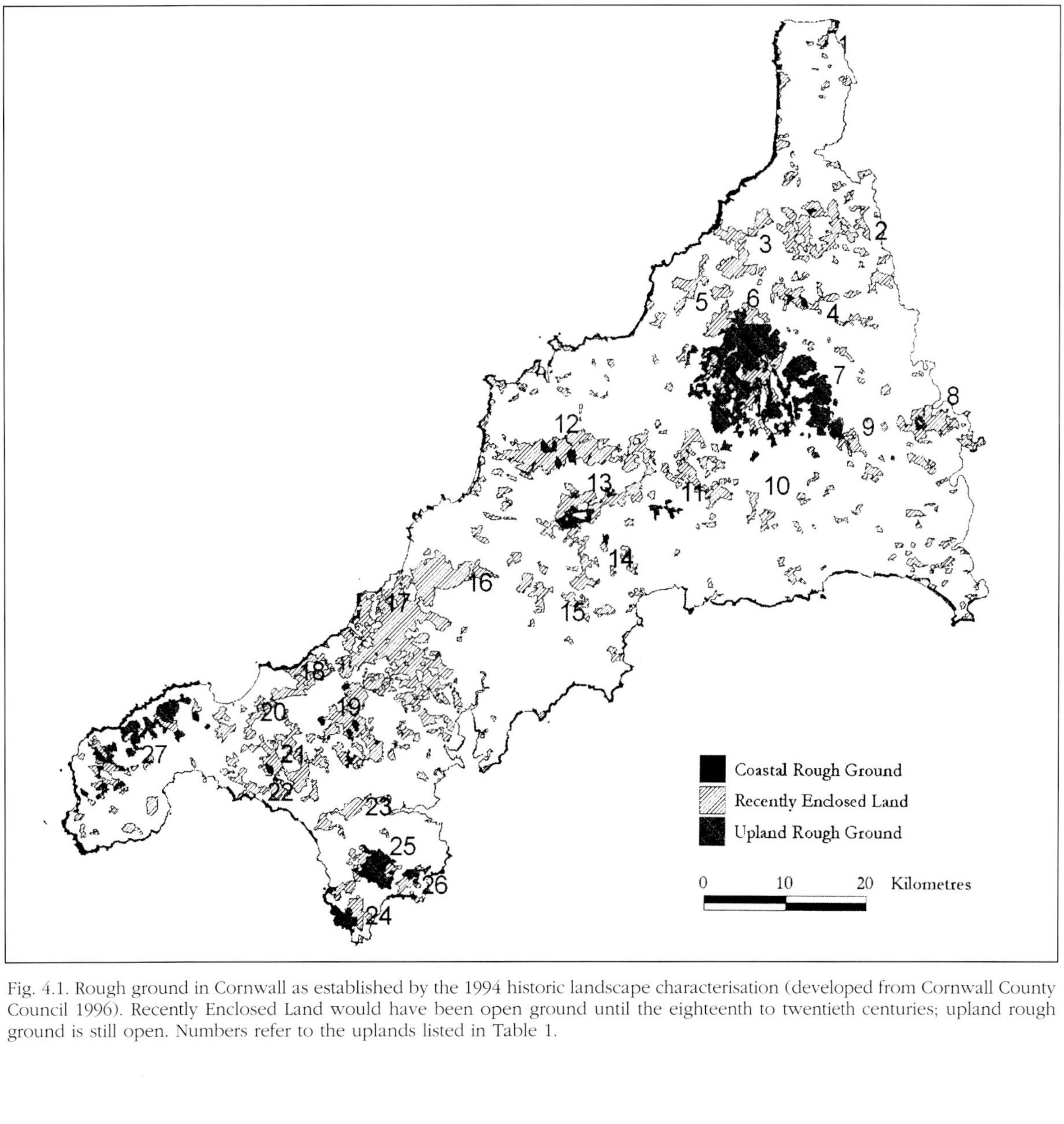

Fig. 4.1. Rough ground in Cornwall as established by the 1994 historic landscape characterisation (developed from Cornwall County Council 1996). Recently Enclosed Land would have been open ground until the eighteenth to twentieth centuries; upland rough ground is still open. Numbers refer to the uplands listed in Table 1.

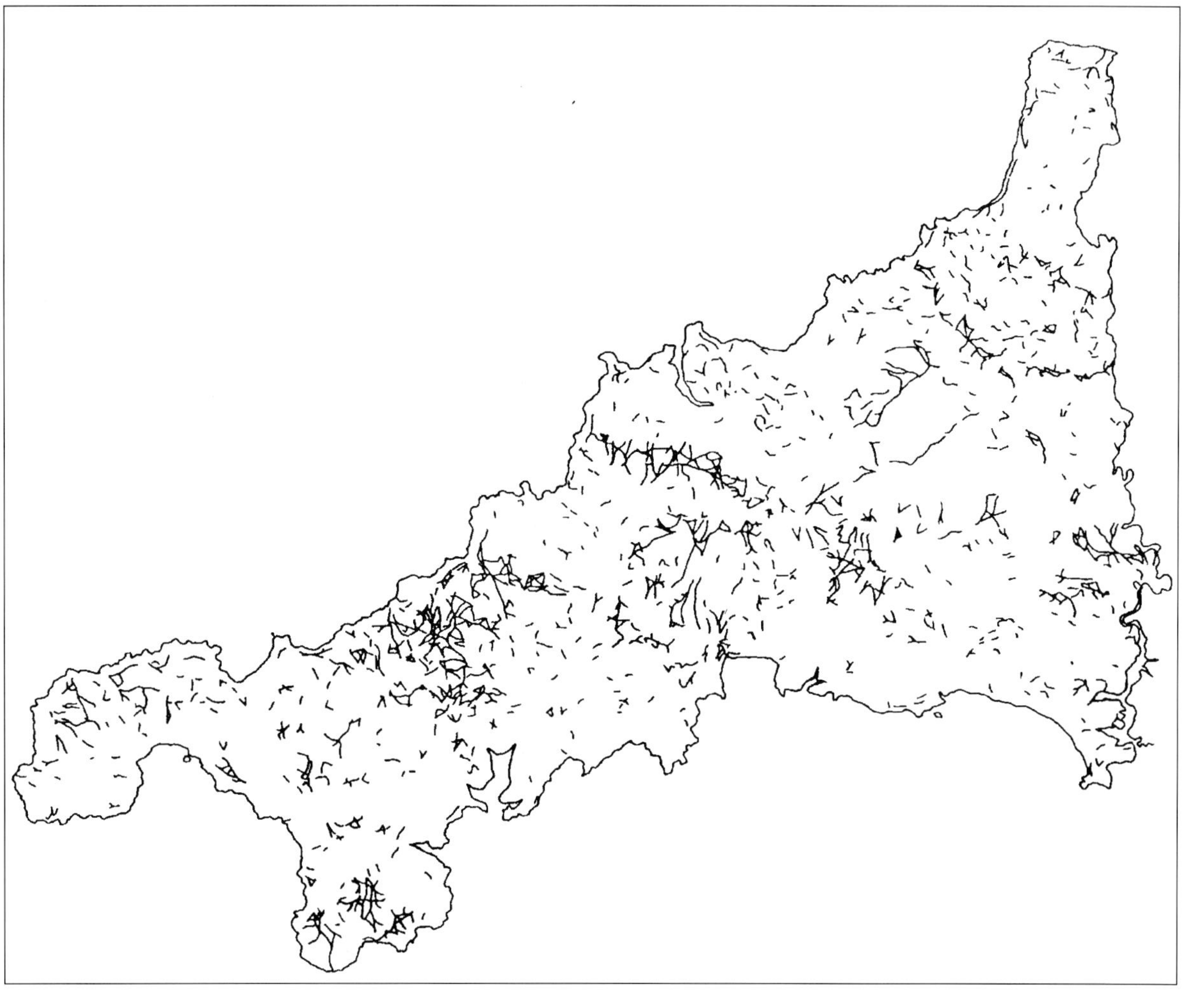

Fig. 4.2. Unfenced lanes (*i.e.* open land) shown on Thomas Martyn's 1748 map of Cornwall.

regression are also essentially those that existed throughout the later prehistoric and medieval periods.

Most medieval and early post-medieval Cornish farmers lived close to rough ground and waste, although those south of a line between St Erme and Pentewan, north of the St Breock Downs, or south of a line between Bodmin and St Mellion did not. The lost upland areas varied considerably in extent, altitude and cohesion (see Fig. 4.1 and Table 1). North of Bodmin Moor, in slate country, the rough ground was on rounded hills, and was often fragmented by medieval intakes although there were ridges of rough ground in Week St Mary and Egloskerry. East of Bodmin Moor, and close to the Tamar, is Kit Hill, the highest hill in Cornwall in terms of continuously rising ground (315 metres, 1,033 ft from Luckett). It was formerly part of Hingston Down, a relatively small granite and slate ridge. A much longer ridge of hills, including the St Breock Downs, runs from near the coast at Mawgan Porth through Bodmin town to Boconnoc. This was open rough ground until the early nineteenth century but nearly all has been enclosed in the last 200 years, a significant part of it since the Second World War, so that it no longer seems like an upland area. The ridge does create, however, a strong visual barrier between north and central Cornwall. In the latter area are the granite uplands of Hensbarrow, otherwise known as the St Austell China-Clay Area. Most of the hills here have been heightened and their forms altered by having waste dumps piled onto them, first finger-form tram-dumps, then conical sky-tips, and now massive ramped and terraced heaps. These dumps, together with ongoing industrial activity, help to make this area seem detached from Cornwall and its topography to appear artificial; many people would now be surprised to learn that this was the county's third highest upland area, after Bodmin Moor and Hingston Down.

Many more people would be surprised to learn that until the later eighteenth century the second most extensive uplands in Cornwall lay within the roughly triangular area with angles at Camborne, Feock and Goonhavern. With the notable exception of Carn Brea, the whole of this area is now enclosed and is busy country with many small villages and hamlets, most established to house mining families. There is a

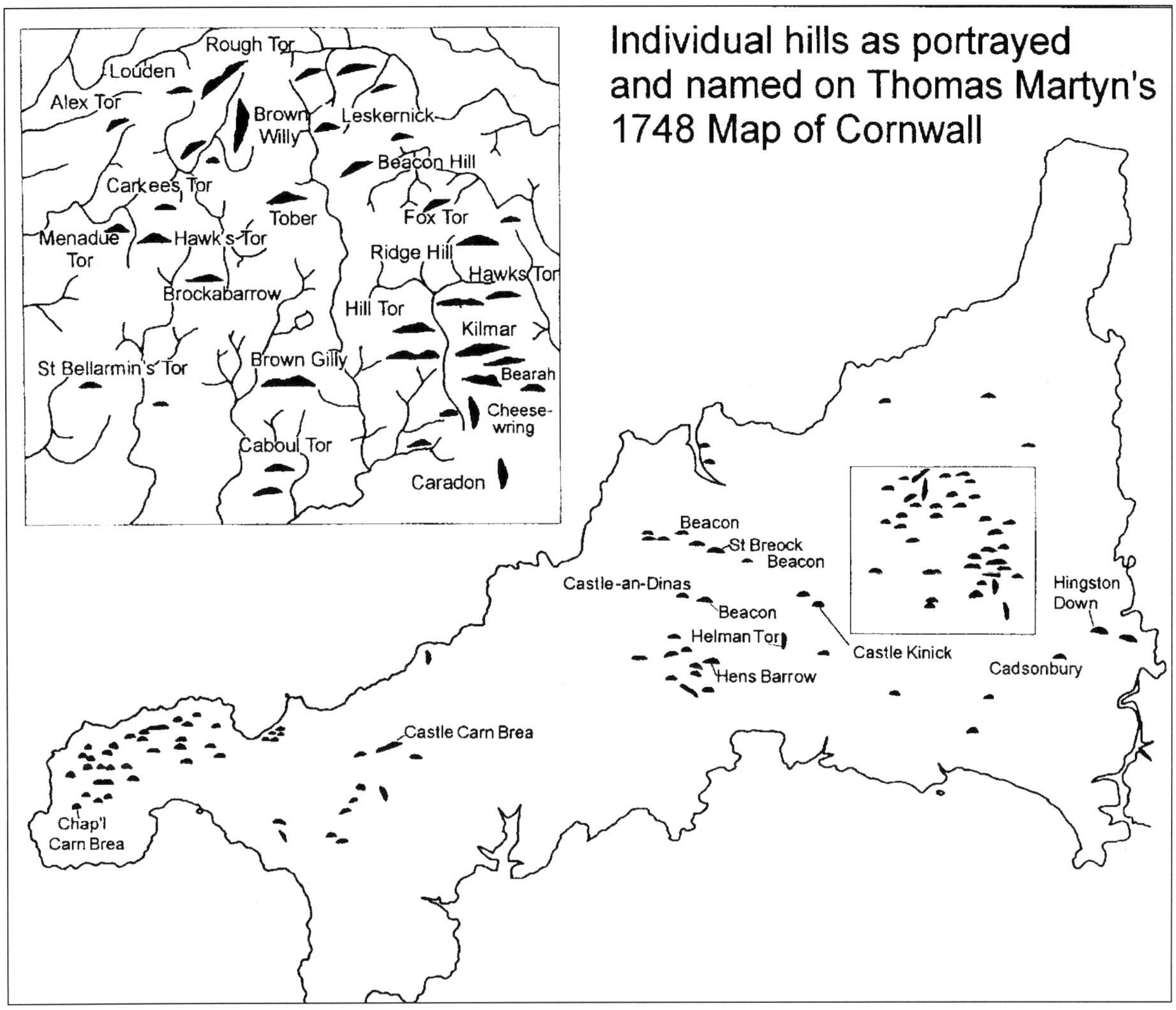

Fig. 4.3. Hills in profile as extracted from Thomas Martyn's 1748 map of Cornwall.

core area around Chacewater dominated by eighteenth-century smallholdings (all less than 10 acres in extent) and a larger area to the north where most of the intakes were in the form of 30–40-acre new family farms. Within this triangle of uplands there were small patches of anciently enclosed land, mainly in valleys, but until the late eighteenth century open uplands had been contiguous from east of St Newlyn East to west of Gwinear, a distance of 31 km (19 miles). When the extent of this former upland area was first fully appreciated during the 1994 historic landscape characterisation work, there was initial surprise that it had no known unifying name, but was instead made up of a large number of separately named commons, hills, downs and goons. Now we can see that this was typical of the post-medieval pattern of fragmented use and naming recorded on other extensive upland areas like Bodmin Moor and West Penwith.

In contrast to the area just described, the granite hills to the south of Carn Brea are more generally regarded as one of Cornwall's upland areas, and are now usually named from one of its largest hills, Carnmenellis. The HLC, however, has shown that this area had been much more fragmented by early enclosure than the land to the north, and that modern perceptions, influenced by the several extant areas of rough ground in the Carnmenellis area, distort understanding of the human geography of the recent past. Another important ridge of uplands, the Helston Downs, enclosed in the eighteenth and nineteenth centuries, worked in a similar way to St Breock Downs in that it helped to visually separate from the rest of Cornwall the Lizard and Meneage, contributing to the relative isolation of those parts of Cornwall. There were other important groupings of hills along the eastern side of Mount's Bay and in the southern half of West Penwith.

Palaeoecological evidence form Bodmin Moor suggests that the lower downlands there were supporting rough grassland communities containing plants typically associated with rough grazing by the end of the first millennium A.D. (Walker 1989, p. 184). In the absence of more extensive environmental evidence elsewhere in Cornwall we may at least model the existence of similar rough grasslands, with patches of

TABLE 1

No	Names (selected)	Extent	Altitude range	Geology	Topography
1	Shoreston, Woolley, Eastcott and Highborough Moors	4 (1)	180–220	Shales	Gently rounded
2	Greena, Brendon, Ogbeare, Wilsworthy, Haydon, Hornacott and Langdon Moors	24 (1)	120–170	Shales	Gently rounded
3	Tresparrett Downs, Otterham Down, High Down	16 (0)	140–260	Shales	Gently rounded
4	Wilsey Down, Kittow's Moor, Badgall Downs, Napps Moor, Laneast Downs, Tregeare Down, Red Down, Athill	12 (1.5)	150–280	Shales	Gently rounded
5	Hendraburnick Down, Vendown, Condolden	7 (0)	220–300	Slates	Gently rounded
6	Davidstow Moors	5 (3)	260–300	Slates	Gently rounded
7	Bodmin Moor (includes numerous Downs, Commons, Hills, Tors, Moors)	148 (112)	150–420	Granite	Tor-topped ridges; rounded downs
8	Hingston Down, Kit Hill,	19 (2)	70–330	Granite; slates	Rounded
9	Middlehill (Pensilva), Hammett Down, Herod Down, Cadson Bury Down, Amy Down, Viverdon Down, Golberdon	16 (1)	50–240	?	Rounded downs; some outcrops
10	Bofarnel Downs, Grey Mare Downs, Taphouse Ridge	7 (0)	100–160	?	Gently rounded
11	Penaligon Downs, Newdowns, The Beacon, Racecourse Downs, Cardinham Downs, Long Downs, Turfdown, Pinsla Downs, Tawna Downs	25 (0)	100–190	Slates	Gently rounded
12	Bear's Downs, Denzell Downs, Bogee Common, Trelow Downs, Rosenannon Downs, St Breock Downs, Pawton Downs, Hustyn Downs	44 (5)	90–215	Slates	Rounded
13	Castle Downs, Tregonetha Downs, Belowda Beacon, Mount Pleasant, Retire Common	18 (2)	100–220	Slates; granite	Rounded
14	Fraddon Down, Burthy Down, Rostowrack Downs, Longstone Downs, Trelavour Downs, Watch Hill, Hensbarrow Downs, Trenance Downs, Caerloggas Downs, Treskilling Downs, Carclaze Downs,	43 (3)	125–310	Granite	Rounded; few tors
15	Homer Downs, Ventonwyn, Treloweth Common	6 (0)	85–125	Slates	Rounded
16	Polgoda Downs, Newlyn Downs, Jenkyn Downs, Hendra Down	8 (1)	75–150	Slates	Rounded

No	Names (selected)	Extent	Altitude range	Geology	Topography
17	New Downs, St Agnes Beacon, Hurlingbarrow, Goonbell, Trevellas Downs, Four Burrows, Two Burrows, Mount Hawke, Allet Down	25 (1)	60–190	Slates, granite	Rounded
18	Tolvaddon Downs, Nancekuke Common, North Downs, Kerley Downs, Carnon Downs	32 (0)	50–120	Slates	Rounded
19	Carn Entral, Carn Brea, Carn Marth, Carvolth Downs, Carnmenellis, Crowan Beacon, Nine Maidens Downs, Rame Common, Butteriss Downs, Trannack Downs, Polcrebo Downs, Longstone Down, Prospidnick Hill,				
20	Connor Downs, Reskajeage Downs, Treswithian Downs, Magor Downs,			Slates	Rounded
21	Gwinear Downs, Polmenor Downs, Howe Downs, Burnt Downs, Binner Downs,	8 (0)		Slates	Rounded
22	Godolphin Hill, Tregonning Hill	4 (2)		Granite	Ridge and rounded
23	Carminowe Down, Helston Downs, Goonwin, Gweek Downs, Boskenwyn Downs	10 (0)	50–75	Slates	Rounded
24	Lizard Downs, Predannack Downs,	9 (6)	50–90	Serpentine	Gently rounded plateau
25	Goonhilly Downs	10 (8)	70–100	Serpentine	Gently rounded plateau
26	Crousa Downs, Main Dale	6 (2)	75–105	Gabbro, Serpentine	Gently rounded plateau
27	Trencrom, Trink, Trendrine, Zennor Hills, Beagleton, Amalveor, Carnaquidden Downs, Trewey, Treen and Bosporthennis Commons, Mulfra Hill, Carn Galva, Watch Croft, Chun Downs, Woon Gumpus, Carn Kenidjack, Bartinney Downs, Chapel Carn Brea	33 (21)	140–250	Granite	Tor-topped ridges; rounded downs

Notes to table

No	As on Fig 4.1
Names	Selection of names for component hills and downs
Extent	In hectares. Main figure is extent in early modern period; that in brackets is surviving open rough ground in 2001
Altitude range	In metres
Geology	Principal underlying rock types
Topography	Main character of topography

heather, furze (gorse) and ferns (bracken) and areas of exploitable peat (locally 'turf'), on the other upland areas by the early medieval period.

UPLANDS AND CORNISH MEDIEVAL AND POST-MEDIEVAL RURAL COMMUNITIES

Late nineteenth- and early twentieth-century cultural determinism led historians and geographers to propose for the isolated farms and squarish fields of western and highland Britain a Celtic origin, products of ancient enclosure and an ancient emphasis on pastoralism, separating them from the nucleated villages and subdivided open or common fields of those arable farmers, the Anglo-Saxons. An associated reawakening of Cornish Celtic culture reinforced such a scheme and as late as 1928 Cornwall's most influential historian, Charles Henderson, used the presence of strip fields around Cornish towns to confirm the towns' 'Saxon or alien origin' (Henderson 1935, p. 67). The shift from cultural/racial to geographical and environmental determinism in the 1920s replaced the questionable assumptions of the former with the respectability of the logical and functional basis of the latter, while leaving general models and their interpretations essentially unchanged. So an appeal to the logic of topography was made by A. L. Rowse when he suggested that while 'level and fertile corn-growing lands' in Cornwall may have been suitable for common fields, 'a country of hills and moors would obviously indicate scattered steadings' (Rowse 1941, p. 33). This, of course, would only have been obvious if Rowse's geographical determinism was actually still underpinned by the assumptions inherited from cultural determinism.

In the 1950s and 1960s, historical geographers demonstrated the wide distribution in medieval Cornwall of strip-based open fields and the hamlets of the small cooperative communities who worked them; not just on Rowse's level lands but throughout all land forms and soil types, from the Land's End coastal plateau through the slatey lowlands to the highest granite hills (*e.g.* Flatres 1957; Beresford 1964; Shorter *et al.* 1969, pp. 106-11; Fox 1971, pp. 21-74). Such patterns were confirmed by studies in landscape archaeology and history in the 1980s and 1990s (*e.g.* Herring 1986, II. 161-72, Johnson & Rose 1994, pp. 107-13; Cornwall Cty Counc 1996, pp. 140-3), and more recently a pre-Norman, but not necessarily Anglo-Saxon, origin has been suggested for the hamlets and strip fields of Cornwall, and for the communalism that created them (Herring 1999b). The Cornish strip-field systems typically contain around ten furlongs or cropping units, probably indicating a longer rotation than in midland England, and this and the antiquity of the practice of paring and burning turf from grass fields prior to their cultivation in Cornwall and Devon suggest that the fields were worked under a form of convertible or ley husbandry regime (Fox 1971, pp. 102-9; Herring 1986, II. 153-6). Such regimes are typical of mixed farming and there is ample evidence that the livestock element of medieval Cornish farming was as important as the arable.

Oliver Rackham suggested that Domesday Book (1086) indicates that around a third of Cornwall was then 'pasture' (Rackham 1986, p. 335). It appears likely from analysis of the ratios of ploughlands and plough teams recorded in the Cornish Domesday Book that the lands represented the enclosed land of Cornwall and the pasture the open rough ground. Rackham's estimate of the extent of this sits very well with the proportion (32.5 *per cent*) that the HLC suggests was unenclosed in the later medieval period (Herring 1998, pp. 40-1). It should also be borne in mind that under ley husbandry only a quarter or a third of a townland's fields would be under the plough at any one time (hence the pattern of ploughlands exceeding plough teams in Cornwall's Domesday Book), the remainder being under grass, suggesting that at least two-thirds of Cornwall would have been either grass or rough ground in the early Norman period.

Later medieval records from the Duchy of Cornwall and other estates indicate that many fourteenth-century peasants possessed herds of ten to twenty cattle (Hatcher 1970, p. 15), to some extent confirmed by the capacities (up to ten or twelve cattle) of some Bodmin Moor long-house shippons (Herring 1986, II. 79, 157). Fourteenth-century north-east Cornish dairies on the estates of Tavistock Abbey were equipped with buckets, pans, strainers, presses and butter crocks (Finberg 1969, p. 135). Cream was scalded, and therefore clotted, and the cheese made from the milk of both cow and ewe. Some of this cheese was sold, along with heavily salted butter made from the cream, in the local markets, the butter making about twice the price per stone as cheese (*ibid.*, pp. 135-44).

The arable cycle and its communal organisation of land and the associated tendency towards co-operation in farming practice influenced the use made of all parts of the country including the pastures and turbaries (see Herring 1986, I. 10-29). Cornish rural communalism probably shrank with the major demographic changes of the mid-fourteenth century; some hamlets were totally abandoned and their well-preserved remains survive on Bodmin Moor and elsewhere, but many more hamlets shrank, often to single farms. Other single farms developed throughout Cornwall from the reorganisation of communal systems: townlands were divided and isolated farms created within newly consolidated holdings, their names often having prefixes and suffixes like *Byghan*, *Wollas*, *Noweth*, Great, Little, East, West, Higher, Lower attached to the original townland name. (See Herring 1986, II. 208-10 for a discussion of the tensions between communal and individual interests in an increasingly commercialised regional economy that probably stimulated such reorganisations.)

AGRICULTURAL USE OF UPLAND ROUGH GROUND

Access to rough ground has been important to Cornish farming communities since at least the middle Bronze Age; lanes lead through fields to rough ground at second millennium B.C. Bodmin Moor sites like Craddock Moor and East Moor (see Johnson & Rose 1994, figs 30 and 42). The division of Cornish upland summer grazings between early medieval hundreds (themselves possibly developed from later prehistoric territories; Thomas 1964, pp. 73-4) has been previously noted (Herring 1996, pp. 41-2). Bodmin Moor, for example, was carefully quartered by Trigg, Lesnewth, and East and West Wivelshire hundreds (*ibid.*, fig. III.3). Many pre-Norman estates and the townlands or farmland of individual hamlets — especially those whose Cornish names bore the securely early medieval prefixes *tre* and *bos* — were laid out to incorporate blocks of rough ground, both upland and coastal (including towans). Parishes, which probably originated in the early medieval period as farming estates, divide the downlands of Bodmin Moor, West Penwith, St Breock Downs, Hensbarrow and the Lizard remarkably equitably and the early medieval townlands within Zennor and many other upland edge parishes form neat long ribbons with enclosed land at their centres and upland and/or coastal rough ground at one or both ends (Preston-Jones & Rose 1986, 141, and see Figs 4.4 and 4.5).

Rough ground was mainly used for summer grazing, the 'summer' traditionally extending from Mayday to Hallowe'en (Herring 1986, I. 115; 1996, 39); a deed of 1476 insisted that any beasts found wintering on *Fowaymore* (*i.e.* Foweymore, by then a western part of Bodmin Moor) were to be distrained (Maclean 1886, pp. 33-6). Summer grazing on wastes freed fields for hay and crops and made full use of available resources, thereby increasing farm productivity.

The organisation of later medieval and early post-medieval Cornish summer grazing is still poorly understood but it appears not to have been uniform. Wastes would usually have been common to hamlets, estates, or (as on West Moor and East Moor in Altarnun and the *Faweymore* of

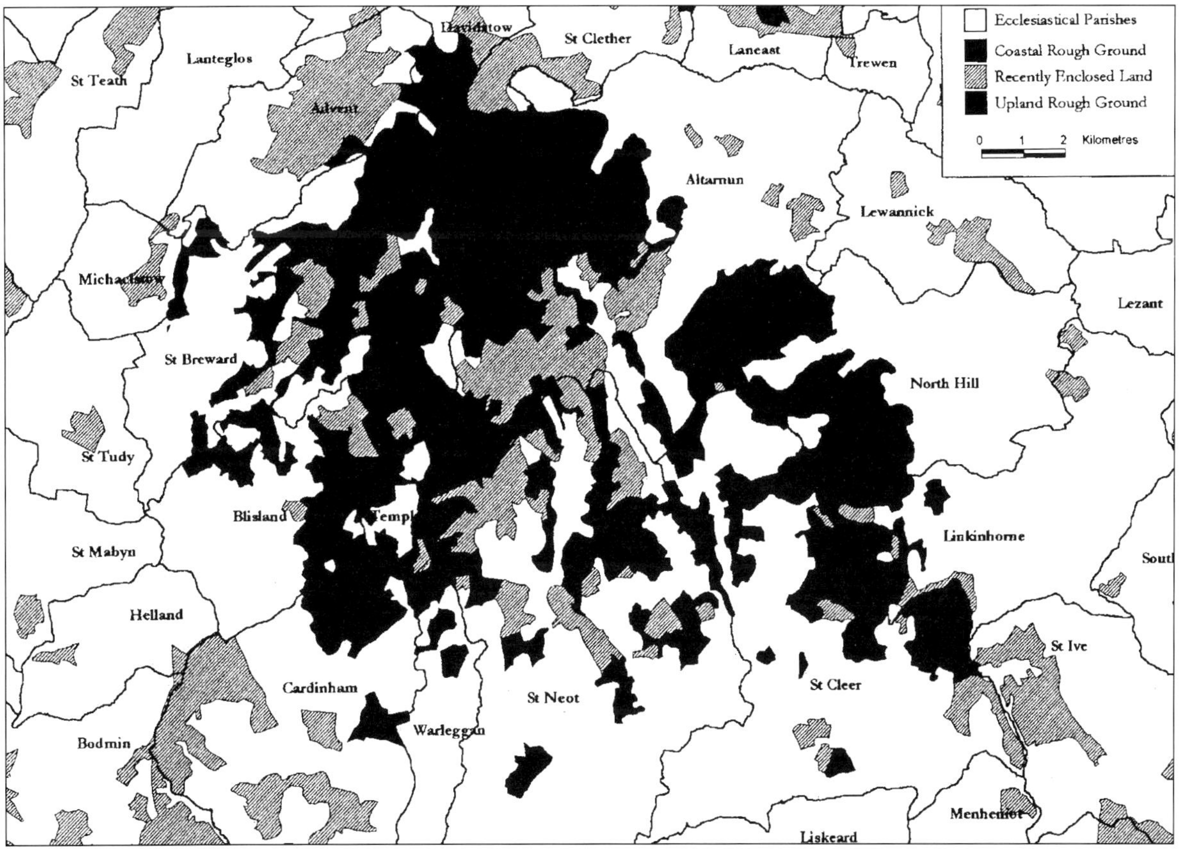

Fig. 4.4. Present and former rough ground on Bodmin Moor and adjacent uplands carefully subdivided between medieval parishes, probably originally agricultural estates, which required access to summer grazings and turbaries.

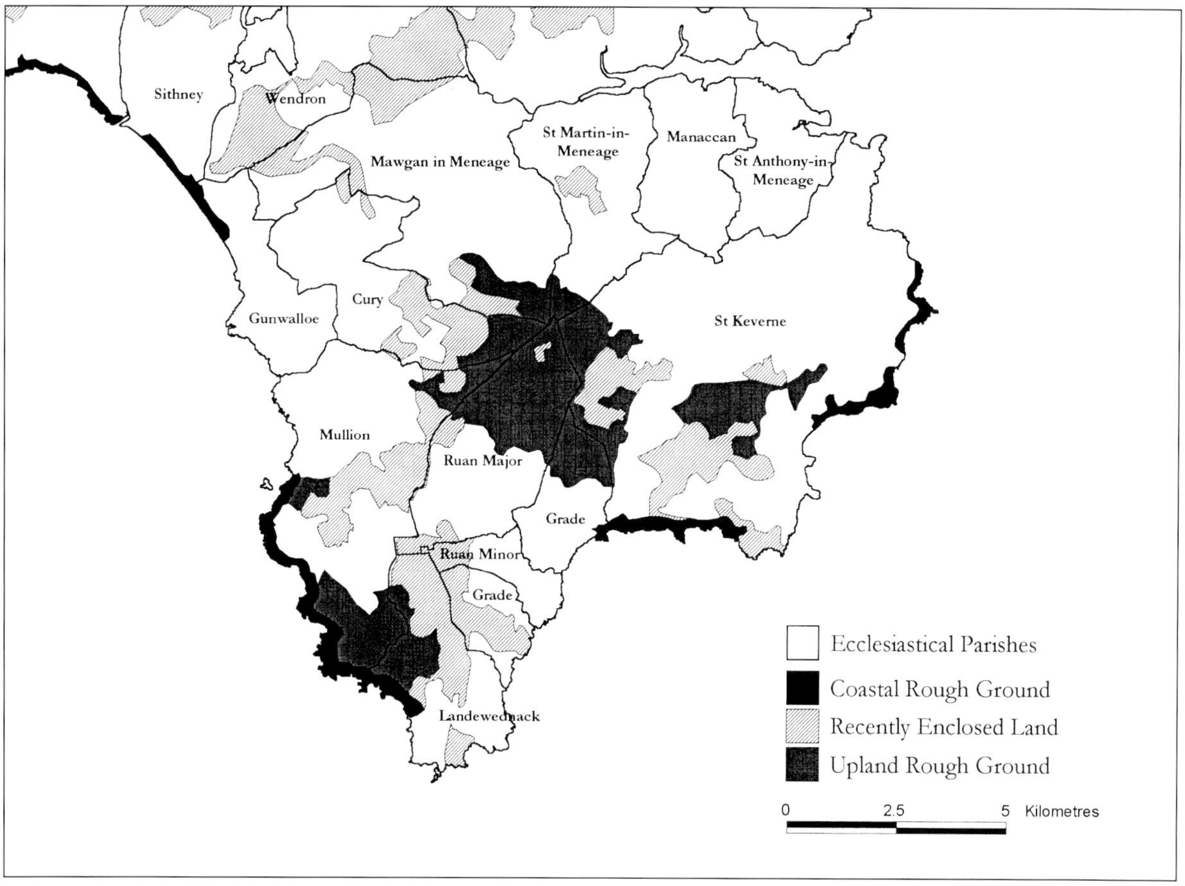

Fig. 4.5. Present and former rough ground on the Lizard and Helston Downs carefully subdivided between medieval parishes, probably originally agricultural estates, which required access to summer grazings and turbaries.

the 1476 deed) to groups of estates. John Hatcher has, however, shown that Duchy of Cornwall tenants had to lease rights to *terra vasta* or waste (Hatcher 1970, p. 23). Pasturing on Bodmin Moor in the post-medieval period was either on the basis of *levancy and couchancy* (*i.e.* only animals that could be wintered could be summered), as in eighteenth-century Hamatethy (RIC, GAT/B/6) and Helstone-in-Trigg (Potts 1974, p. 83), or without stint, as on Caradon Prior and Rillaton in the seventeenth century (Pounds 1982, p. 83). Rights to Twelve Men's Moor, however, were subject to stints in 1758, as indicated by a complaint heard at the Sheriff's Court in Lostwithiel which is also revealing of the range of livestock that were turned onto Bodmin Moor in the eighteenth century. Richard Luskey held two messuages at West Castick and through them had rights to pasture 400 sheep, 8 horses and 8 bullocks. He exceeded this spectacularly by running 10 bullocks, 40 oxen, 70 cows with their calves, 20 mares with colts, 60 rams, 50 weathers, 1,000 ewes with lambs, 40 he-goats, 300 she-goats with kids, 20 boars, 70 sows with young, 10 he-asses, 30 she-asses with foals, 30 mules and 700 geese with goslings (Spooner 1942, p. 53). Earlier references, however, suggest that control through payment may have been the more traditional method. The 1476 deed mentioned above also refers to pasturing tolls owed by tenants of several manors (Maclean 1886, pp. 33-4). When Twelve Men's Moor was carved out of Rillaton manor, in the later twelfth century, tenants from Caradon Prior had to pay the twelve men one penny per year to retain their shared use of these summer pastures (Henderson 1935, p. 127), and in an early seventeenth-century custumal, with back-references to 1413 (at least), the free and customary tenants of Blisland manor were shown to have common of pasture on the 'outmores' without stint upon payment to the lord's reeve, of a penny 'for every polle of their cattle' (Maclean 1873–76, Vol 1. 91-3).

Some of these arrangements may have developed from those associated with transhumance — the movement of selected members of household or hamlet to the summer grazings with the animals. There is good toponymical and archaeological evidence for transhumance in pre-Norman Cornwall (Herring 1996) but no clear evidence for it in the later medieval period, though it would be difficult to confirm, either on the ground or in documents. The coupling in 1284 and 1650, as manor and tithing, of places 10 miles apart in Lanteglos (by Fowey) and St Neot parishes — Lamellyon and

Hammett respectively — may be of interest in this respect as Hammett's name is derived from Cornish *havos*, 'summer dwelling', suggestive of the continued relevance in the later medieval period of transhumance relationships presumably developed in the early medieval period (Herring 1986, I. 108). There may have been, in the later medieval period, specialist herdsmen or women spending their summers on the uplands, as in post-medieval Cornwall (*ibid.*, p. 112). Inhabitants of the moor may have looked after some off-moor animals during the summer, as on Dartmoor in the fourteenth and fifteenth centuries (Fox 1994, pp. 158-9). Farmers may even have simply turned animals out onto those uplands on which they had grazing rights and then left them, as William Carnsew of Bokelly seems to have done in the later sixteenth century when he sent his cattle 8 miles away to Brown Willy in late April 1576 and visited them occasionally when the need arose (Pounds 1978, pp. 39, 41, 48, 50).

Some upland wastes were used as outfields in the medieval and early post-medieval periods, areas being temporarily fenced off from the surrounding pastures, de-turfed, beat-burnt, ploughed, divided into strips (if worked communally) and subjected to two or three years cropping before fences were removed and the ground allowed to return to rough (Fox 1971, pp. 164-205; Herring 1986, II. 148-57).

Away from the steep-sided valleys of southern and eastern Cornwall, timber and firewood would have been scarce from at least early medieval times (see Cornwall Cty Counc 1996, p. 165) and the upland peat and gorse (locally turf and furze) were critical sources of domestic fuel. Many medieval and post-medieval upland settlements would not have been viable without the turbary rights which allowed the three types of turf (valley bog, blanket bog and the thin hillside turf) to be cut and dried in the late spring or the faggots of furze to be cut in the early summer (see Herring forthcoming). In the two upland areas where turf-cutting remains are best preserved, Bodmin Moor and the Lizard, there are hundreds of turf 'steads', the usually sub-rectangular plats on which ricks of the dried turf were built to be left through the summer before being brought down to farmsteads in the autumn. Such steads appear to have been largely modern, developed when reserves of the better turf were exhausted, leaving only the more fibrous peat, liable to reabsorb water and thus needing ricking (*ibid.*). Attachments to turbaries would have been profound, and not just because of the need for the turf; the regular visits to cut, titch (turn while drying), rick and collect the turf would have reinforced familiarity with particular downlands and increased their personal and social meaning.

Turf and furze were also found other uses: turf for smelting tin; furze when laid on the ground beneath ricks kept hay, corn and bracken relatively dry, when stuck into gaps made makeshift barriers, when placed in trenches helped farmers drain wet ground; and when crushed made palatable horse fodder. Bracken (locally ferns) was important for bedding; and heather, as well as being important for grazing, may have been used in Cornwall as in other parts of upland Britain for thatching, rope-making, mattressing *etc.* Beehives would probably have been set up on heathland edges and the Cornish uplands would have been places were wild food was obtained by hunting, snaring, nesting, gathering, *etc.* Building and road-making stones and subsoil were obtained either from the surface or from quarries and pits. In addition, as has been extensively documented, minerals, rock and clay, when found in workable quantities, were streamed, mined and quarried on uplands (as well as in all other parts of Cornwall where the material was found).

Many of these communal uses of the larger open downlands — for grazing, as turbaries, and as sources of other resources — continued long after subdivided field systems had decayed from the thirteenth and fourteenth centuries onwards; some are still commons. Within the 'private' commons of townlands (for which see below), however, there was often a subdivision, from as early as the thirteenth century, of rough land between individual holdings, often enclosed and divided by stock-proof walls. In the western half of Cornwall this was usually in the form of fairly small irregularly-shaped enclosures usually named crofts (see Padel 1985, p. 71).

CHANGES TO GOEN BREN OR FAWYMORE, ALIAS BODMIN MOOR

Until around A.D. 1000, Cornwall's most important upland area, now known as Bodmin Moor, comprised a block of upland rough ground extending to roughly 200 square kilometres (77 square miles) (colour Pl. V). Transhumance was practiced in the early medieval period by tenants of estates around the Moor and grazing appears to have been controlled by the four hundreds which subdivided Bodmin Moor, trespassing animals being rounded up and confined in pounds (Herring 1996). Cornwall's hundred boundaries tend to follow natural features: ridges, streams *etc* (Thomas 1964, p. 70) and as construction and maintenance expenses would have exceeded benefits derived, it is unlikely that there were built boundaries (hedges *etc*) between the summer pastures of the hundreds. Early medieval Bodmin Moor would therefore probably have been open, all its land used as one, with stock from all four hundreds intercommoning and the area developing its own identity, as indicated in a twelfth-century reference, *Brentigie quoddam desertum est in Cornubia, et dicitur in nostra lingua goen bren, in lingua Saxonum Fawi-mor*, 'Brentigie which is a certain deserted place in Cornwall and said in our language *goen bren* and in the Saxon language Fawymore' (Curley 1982, p. 239). The Cornish name Goen Bren — *goon*, 'downland, unenclosed pasture'; *bren*, 'hill' (Padel 1985, pp. 31 and 108) — adds weight to the argument for Bodmin Moor being open pasture; the original meaning of the element *goon* appears to refer to downland pastured in common (*ibid.*, p. 108).

By 1086, certain estates had claimed rights to particular parts of the Moor (Johnson & Rose 1994, pp. 77-9), and it may have been when these subdividing claims were made that the first stock-proof boundaries were built across the previously open downs. Such boundaries might include those surviving either as relict banks or fossilised in post-medieval walls and Cornish hedges between, for instance, the manors of Hamatethy and Blisland, and Cardinham and Blisland. Old hundredal pounds seem to have been reused as manor pounds (*e.g.* Hamatethy and Blisland appear to have shared King Arthur's Hall), and new manorial drift pounds were built (*e.g.* Helstone-in-Trigg) (Herring 1986, I. 127-30). Disputes over estates' grazing grounds went to court; in 1358 the tenants of Helstone-in-Trigg tested Hamatethy's rights to Roughtor with a mass trespass of 500 beasts (Maclean 1876, p. 290). From the eleventh to the fourteenth centuries Bodmin Moor was resettled by people who lived mainly in hamlets. Their ring-fences enclosed both arable land (usually subdivided into strips) and rough pasture (see Austin *et al.* 1989, fig 6.3; Johnson & Rose 1994, pp. 100-14). As these ring-fenced townlands reduced the extents of commons, their inhabitants sometimes forfeited any rights to manorial commons, perhaps as a result of the 1235 Statute of Merton which set out the lord's obligation to protect the common rights of tenants. Henry Cauvel's failure in 1288 to establish common rights on the Hamatethy Commons out of which his new holding of Louden had been cut (Maclean 1873, 355) may have resulted from the lord of Hamatethy being torn between these obligations and a desire to intensify moorland exploitation and thus rental income. He may have denied Henry (and other similar colonising tenants) rights of common on the manorial waste in exchange for ceding to them the control of the rough pasture within their ring-fences. As the new settlements were usually hamlets the rough pasture within their ring-fences were effectively 'private commons', shared by the hamlet's several households. Organisation of the use of one of these townland commons can be explored in more detail.

Stock-proof boundaries enclose the medieval townland of Brown Willy with the assistance of the De Lank river and its tributary, separating the whole of Cornwall's highest hill from the surrounding downland and isolating from Fawymore a discrete block of land within which the establishment and development of a long-house hamlet and associated strip-field system and pattern of pastures and meadows could take place. Pasture boundaries split up the rough ground beyond the strip-field system but within the ring-fence (Herring 1986, II, fig. 37; Fig. 4.6). Two of these pre-date certain outfield groups attached to them and can thus be dated to before 1276 (see Herring 1986, II. 31-5 for justification). Another of Brown Willy's pasture-dividing boundaries is built up to both sides of a ruined beehive hut, post-dating it. Two similar beehive huts high up on the western side of the hill may also be regarded as pre-1276 in date (*ibid*, II. 33-5). Distance from medieval tin-working suggests these huts were not tinners' shelters; the western two, nearly at the summit, would be particularly ludicrously sited for use by tinners (see Greeves 1981b, p. 168, for beehive huts immediately adjacent to streamworks on Dartmoor). The panoramic views of pasture commanded by all three huts and their careful positioning, obtaining the maximum shelter possible for such exposed spots (Nowakowski & Herring 1985, pp. 193-4), suggest that they were shelters for people tending stock on the rough pastures in the period before the pasture-dividing boundaries were built. Their smallness makes it unlikely that the huts were anything other than refuges in inclement weather for herdsmen living in the long-house settlement; they could emerge occasionally from the huts to check the animals and move them on to preferred grazings.

The dividing boundaries which post-date the huts break the hill's rough pasture into large blocks that appear not to have been associated with separate farmsteads. Instead, the attachment of subdivided outfield groups to two of them indicates that the land was still held in common by the several households in the hamlet, the rough pastures parcelled by mutual agreement to give the community the potential to control the grazing animals with stock-proof boundaries rather than with full-time, communally supported, herds. One system of communal stock control appears to have been replaced by another. In the later medieval period, possibly by the late thirteenth century, Brown Willy's communal farming system broke down and was replaced by three separate farmsteads, each with its own enclosed rough pastures, often reusing the earlier communal pasture boundaries (Herring 1986, II, fig. 75). The medieval pasture boundaries, where not refurbished, vary in construction according to the availability of materials but would, of course, have been stock-proof. Despite being redundant for up to 650 years they are still substantial, being either stony banks generally over 1 metre high or earth banks

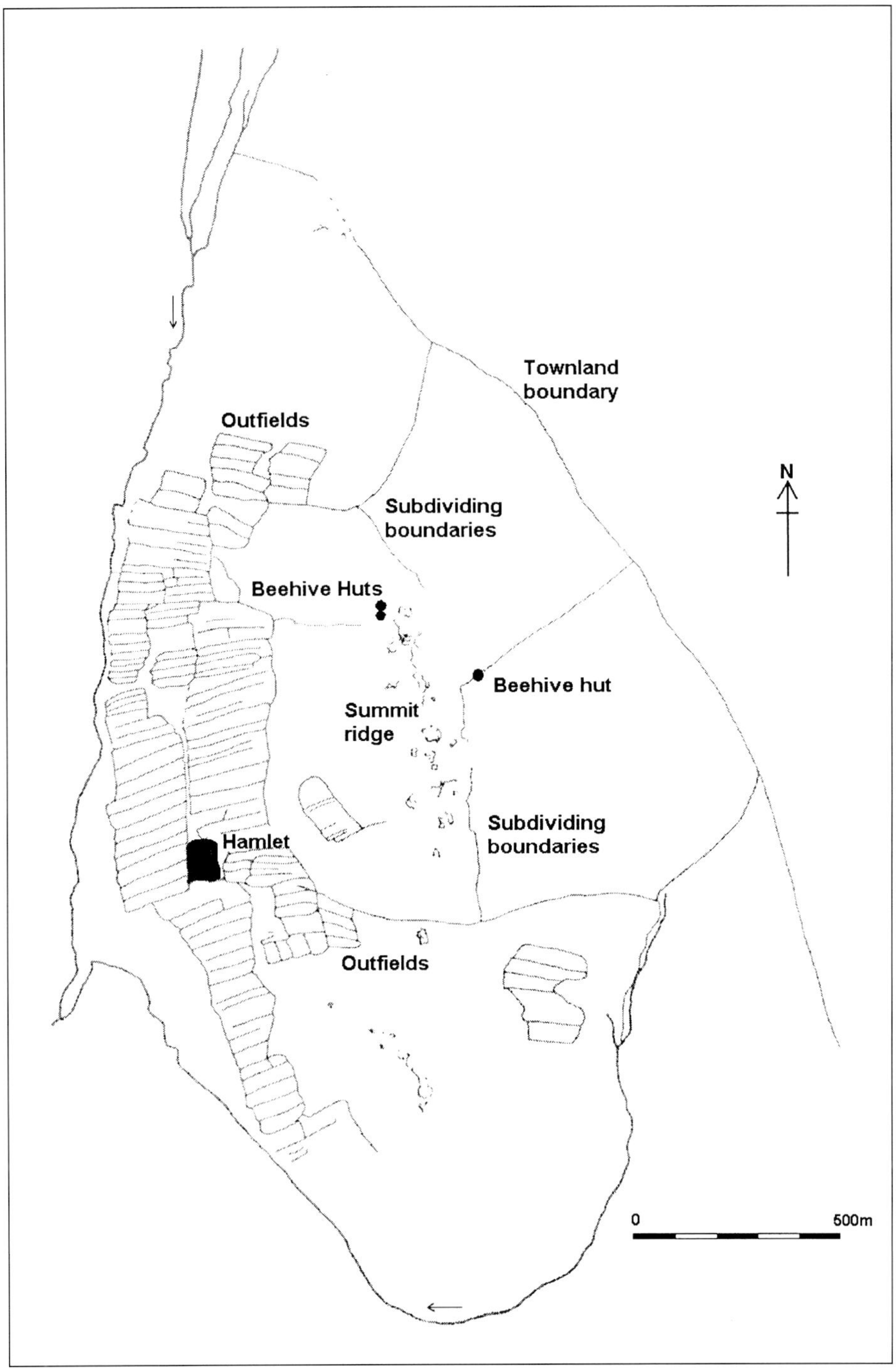

Fig. 4.6. Brown Willy, Cornwall's highest hill, isolated from commons by a medieval ring-fence and rivers and with its own rough ground subdivided by later medieval pasture boundaries.

possessing wide deep ditches (now around 1.7 metres (5.5 ft) wide and 0.4 metres deep (1.3 ft).

Other medieval pastoral boundaries serving similar functions to those on Brown Willy can be identified in the north-west of Bodmin Moor. Townland ring-fences around rough ground attached to hamlets, and presumably grazed in common by the several households, are well illustrated at Fernacre, Garrow, Leaze, Ivey and Carkees. Boundaries subdividing a townland's private common, as at Brown Willy, are found less frequently but can be seen at Codda and Casehill. Wide tracks, rather like drove roads, separated the enclosed private commons of Louden, Fernacre and Garrow but gave tenants of other farms further south continued access to the northern third of Hamatethy Commons (see Johnson & Rose 1994, fig. 66).

The effect of these enclosures was the piecemeal alienation of parts of commons from the other tenants, and the fragmentation of previously extensive tracts of undivided uplands. The recorded history of the name Fawymore, from the late twelfth century onwards, essentially coincides with that of the area's re-settlement and can be summarised as a gradual loss of relevance as a result of this fragmentation (see Herring 1986, appendix 2 and fig. 29).

Fawymore's survival into the sixteenth century as a name for the whole upland area was due mainly to its adoption in 1201 (when its pastoral basis was already dwindling) as the name of the eastern Cornish Stannary (see Smirke 1843, p. 9). By the later sixteenth century the name's pastoral relevance had virtually evaporated as the moorland settlements divided the uplands into small individually named commons, often separated by built boundaries. The name Fawymore became confined by the early eighteenth century to a small knoll at the southern end of High Moor, immediately to the east of Brown Willy, where the River Fowey rises at Fawy Well. Numerous leases of holdings in Altarnun, Davidstow and St Clether refer to rights of common of pasture and turbary in High Moor, Fawymore, and Buttern Down (for example that of Trevivian in 1770; RIC, GAT/3/13).

In the nineteenth century, Bodmin Moor was further fragmented by the establishment of new small farms usually with 30 or so acres of inbye land and rights to nearby turbaries and common pastures. Fields had perfectly straight boundaries of turf or dry-stone construction, typical of the recently enclosed land of Cornwall (see Herring 1998, pp. 86-8). These new farms tended to be confined to particular blocks of land, as landlords were important players in their creation, either increasing returns from long-held land in the case of the Duchy of Cornwall in Advent parish, or exploiting newly acquired land in the case of the Rodd family of Trebartha in the Pridacoombe and Tolborough area. Houses, barns and boundaries were built by tenants to specifications set out by the lord in their three-lives leases. On their expiry the property reverted to the lord who could then re-let at more favourable rates (see Herring & Giles forthcoming).

CONCLUSION

The extent and visibility of upland rough ground, a vital element of Cornwall's economic landscape since later prehistoric times, have been profoundly altered in the last seven centuries or so by waves of piecemeal privatisation of formerly communally organised downlands, and by associated enclosure. Perceptions, as hinted at by changing namings and imprecisely located folklore, reflect the increasing disaggregation of formerly coherent and extensive uplands like Foweymore, distancing recent and present communities from the experiences and values of their predecessors. The loss of easily readable historic meaning or relevance of such substantial and dramatic elements of the countryside illustrates well how easily the poorly documented past of the more modest sectors of rural society can be obscured. Detailed recording and analysis can help restore lost landscapes and recreate lost lives, allowing us to appreciate again the dynamics of the rich and varied relationships that medieval and early post-medieval people had with their world.

ACKNOWLEDGEMENTS

My colleague Nicholas Johnson created an earlier unpublished paper version of Fig. 4.1 to illustrate the present and former extents of Cornish uplands. Thanks to Neil Craze and Bryn Tapper for help with the figures. Oliver Padel of Cambridge University helped with the translation of Cornish and Latin words.

ABBREVIATIONS

HLC	Historic Landscape Characterisation
NMP	National Mapping Programme
PRO	Public Record Office
RIC	Royal Institution of Cornwall (housed within the Royal Cornwall Museum, Truro)
SMR	Cornwall and Scilly Sites and Monuments Record
URG	Upland Rough Ground (a HLC Type)

Col. Plate IV. (see ch. 4). Hingston Down in east Cornwall, with the surviving rough ground of Kit HIll in the foreground and Calstock common's nineteenth-century enclosures transforming the rest of this small granite ridge into farmland merging with that in the adjacent lowlands, transforming perceptions of this upland (Photo. Steve Hartgroves, Cornwall Cty Counc, F64/166, June 2004, © CCC).

Col. Plate V. (see ch. 4). Ancient semi-natural grassland on the slopes of Leskernick Hill on Bodmin Moor, maintained by grazing for over 3,000 years since the Bronze Age fields visible on the higher slopes were established. In the distance is the east side of Brown Willy, Cornwall's highest mountain (Photo. Peter Herring, April 2004).

Col. Plate VI. (see ch. 5). Aberedw Hill, Radnorshire (Powys): the common from the south with the Wye valley to the west (Photo. © Clwyd-Powys Archaeol Trust, CS99-36-12).

Col. Plate VII. (see ch. 9). Peat scales: half-way storage huts between the peat banks and the main farmstead (Photo. I. Whyte).

The Commons and the Waste: use and misuse in mid-Wales

R. J. Silvester

ABSTRACT

The uses of commons within the historic county of Radnorshire are considered from medieval to recent times. Lack of documentation makes it impossible to reconstruct precisely the extent of those commons in medieval times but landscape evidence of medieval farmsteads and larger nucleations helps to establish the limits of settlement at this period. More historical sources from the sixteenth century onwards provide a clearer picture of the uses of wastes and commons and the pressures on them. The seasonal use of upland pastures and the impact of enclosure are examined and a wide range of uses of the commons in the nineteenth century is considered.

KEYWORDS

Wales, Radnorshire, commons, medieval settlement, transhumance, enclosure

INTRODUCTION

'How infinitely more pleasing must the appearance of enclosures and plantations be to the eye of the speculative traveller than the present dreary aspect of the forlorn wastes'. Thus wrote Walter Davies, cleric, poet, antiquary and agriculturalist in his report on farming in north Wales at the beginning of the nineteenth century (Davies 1810, p. 268). Commentators and surveyors from John Norden in the early seventeenth century (Slack 1951, p. 19) had expressed similar reservations of the open uplands of Wales and the adjacent Marches, and it was echoed much later, though usually for self-interested reasons, by many who gave evidence to the Royal Commission on Land in Wales and Monmouthshire in 1895. Witness after witness to the inquiry spoke of the possibilities if the wastes were enclosed and improved. Walter Jones of Dolberthog, for instance, was 'of the firm opinion that it would be a great advantage to us to have the hills enclosed and for this to be compulsory. We who hold sheep farms suffer great losses annually where the sheep have to remain on the mountains summer and winter' (Royal Commission 1895, III. 991). Taken at face value these statements could suggest to the uninformed observer that the commons and wastes were useful only for what they might be, rather than for what they were.

There is, inevitably, an alternative view of those open uplands, one that has crystallised in recent times as, paradoxically, the centrality of the commons in the overall agrarian scheme has diminished. Frank Emery wrote in 1967 that 'whatever the size of their farms, most Welshmen were acutely dependent on open common grazings' (Emery 1967, p. 155); and Angus Winchester (2000a) has recently emphasised in relation to other hill ranges, those of northern England and the Scottish border, that the open uplands were absolutely essential to the pastoral way of life followed by many generations of farmers.

In past centuries, the open uplands of Wales, and of England, were immense, vast tracts of land that inevitably had a fundamental significance to those who lived close to them, and even within the last fifty years it has been estimated that across Wales there were at least 50,000 hectares (123,555 acres) of rough grazing, much of it open upland (colour Pl. VI). Legally and often socially, a distinction needs to be drawn between the commons and the waste, the two standard terms that historically are used to describe the open uplands. In Alan Everitt's precise phraseology, 'although all commons were in law the "waste" of some particular manor or group of manors, not all "waste" was necessarily "common" ' (Everitt 2000, p. 215, see Straughton, this volume). But while the open lands having common rights on them have been distinguished from the remaining wastes, at least for statutory purposes (Hoskins & Stamp 1963, p. 227), in any examination of their past history the two generally merge and the distinction is glossed over. Today, the boundaries between the commons and the waste may be identifiable only as a line on a map with little or no physical manifestation on the ground; in the past the distinction is likely to have been even less tangible.

The focus here is on one of the historic counties of central Wales (Fig. 5.1). Radnorshire was established in 1536, at the time of the Act of Union, and four and a half centuries later was subsumed as the central portion of modern

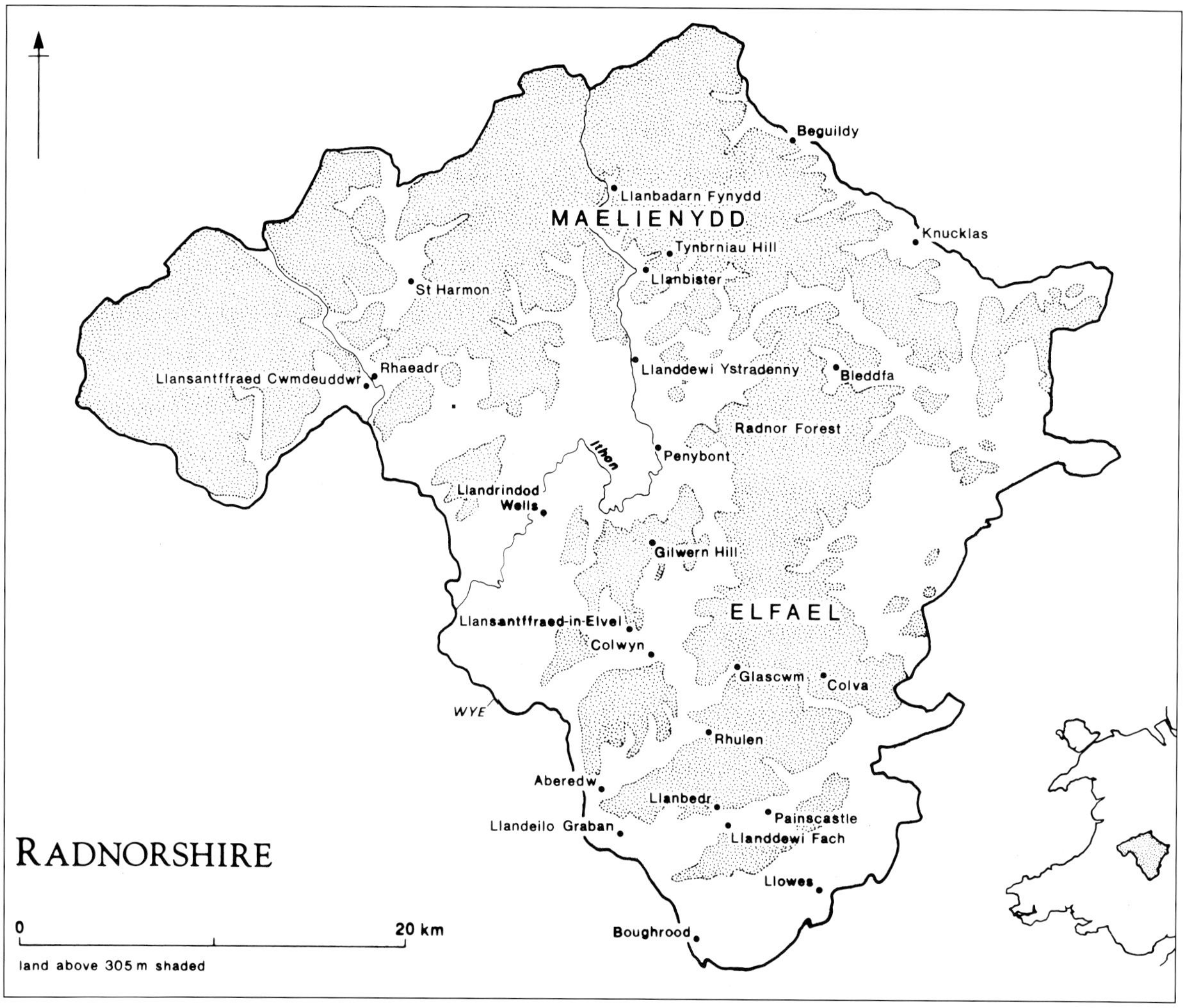

Fig. 5.1. The historic county of Radnorshire, indicating places mentioned in the text.

Powys, though for many living locally its identity remains. A border county running with Herefordshire, it is to most outsiders one of the more anonymous of the historic divisions of Wales. Its population is small, and indeed Powys as a whole is the most sparsely populated county in England and Wales (Slater 1988, p. 11). Like several of the Welsh counties, past and present, much of its land can be classed as hill and mountain land with more than 50 *per cent* of its 1,213 sq km (476 sq metres) over 305 metres (1,000 ft) above sea level (Howse 1949, p. 13), and much of that hill country is or was open land. Davies (1815, p. 73) divided its wastes (and commons) into three: the northern and western hills, the flat wastes of the interior and the outskirts of the mountainous range of the Forest of Radnor, and the other commons to the south and east. We can, however, simplify these divisions. Ignoring the low-lying valley of the River Wye, which constitutes the natural boundary of the county on the south-western and part of the south-eastern side, and the River Teme which fulfils a similar function on the north-east, Radnorshire's terrain can be broadly classified into two parts. Arching across the 'top' of the county are the northern hills, from the upland plateau around the Elan Valley reservoirs eastwards to the Kerry Hills, land that rarely falls below 300 metres (984 ft) O.D. The central and southern parts of the old county are different, more fragmented with their hills discrete topographical units separated by deep valleys, and almost central is Radnor Forest, the largest plateau and the only part that rises above 600 metres (1,968 ft) O.D. This physiography signals Radnorshire's unusual character with a large number of smallish tracts of upland; where not enclosed these would be classed, perhaps, as rough grazings, and many, though by no means all of them, as commons.

Because Radnorshire no longer exists as a political unit, modern assessments of the extent of unenclosed land are difficult to establish. In 1970 the area was still around 47,000 ha (116,141 acres) (MAFF 1970), while at the end of the eighteenth century it was estimated that the open upland extended over more than 80,000 ha (197,688 acres) or two-thirds of the county (Sylvester 1969, p. 58). The commons constitute only a portion of these uplands: there are now sixty-seven of them listed under the Commons

Registration Act of 1965 covering about 16,5000 hectares or 14 *per cent* of the land area, and ranging in size from less than 1 ha to 2,780 ha (2.5–6,870 acres) (Penfold *et al.* 1990).

This paper[1] is primarily an examination of the landscape of the Radnorshire commons and waste, but it is impossible to assess their significance without recourse to written records. Documentation relating to these uplands is reasonably prolific for recent centuries, though uneven and biased towards those owned by some of the larger estates. For earlier periods, particularly prior to the second half of the sixteenth century, there is a sparsity of local records, particularly court rolls,[2] the type of document so tellingly used by Angus Winchester to reconstruct the patterns of upland exploitation in northern England and the Scottish border (Winchester 2000a). This inevitably hampers our understanding of how the uplands were utilised in the medieval centuries, but the physical evidence does provide some compensation. Indeed, the documents and the material remains offer rather different perspectives on the commons. Many, though not all, of the former witness the open uplands under stress or pressure, generated through conflicts that led one party or another to seek redress from the manorial courts charged with administering justice. It is these conflicts that were committed to paper and, hence, the appearance of the waste in manorial or government records. Yet they are selective and inevitably offer only a sample of the events that influenced life in the uplands. In contrast, the physical remains represent a manifestation of persistent activity on the commons: they are less eloquent than the documents and the personalities are missing, but they are also less biased. Nowhere is this better seen than in the small warrens that developed during the later eighteenth century (see below). The documents tell us of no more than two or three of these enterprises, because by and large they were of little concern to landowners, interested only in the rents that accrued from the warrens. Yet there appear to have been upwards of forty in Radnorshire, almost without exception undocumented. The two types of evidence complement each other usefully.

UTILISING THE WASTE: THE MEDIEVAL CENTURIES

There can be no doubt that prehistoric man visited and settled in the uplands of Radnorshire. It is the same for almost all of the uplands in the British Isles, not necessarily signalling a preference for higher altitudes, but rather the enhanced survival of prehistoric monuments in environments less disturbed by later agricultural activity (Darvill 1986). Bronze Age cairns and standing stones and Iron Age enclosures, and even perhaps their Romano-British successors, are to be seen on more than a few of the surviving commons in Radnorshire (see, for instance, Pl. 5.II).

However, this examination properly commences with the uplands early in the medieval centuries. But what do we know of them? The answer is remarkably little. That open land was considerably more extensive before the great enclosures of the eighteenth and nineteenth centuries is indisputable, but there is no method for defining their extent (see Chapman, this volume). It is more profitable to consider how the uplands were viewed early in the medieval era, though there is little modern commentary on this aspect and, perhaps not surprisingly, an apparent absence of contemporary comment. It seems certain that, as a resource, the uplands were not under such pressure or by extension such hierarchical control, as in later centuries. The renowned Welsh historian, William Rees, conceptualised the development of the early community with its settlement and its clearances for cultivation. On the fringes of the clearings the waste was left for communal grazing with common rights developing through usage, 'this at a time when the uncleared land, unoccupied and unclaimed, and possessing little value in the modern sense, far outran the requirements of the limited population' (Rees 1966, p. 3). The waste was viewed as part of the commote to be used by freemen without hindrance; settlements expanded and the waste was cleared where necessary, for the ownership of the commons was vested in clan groups, while the more remote wastes, not claimed by any community, fell under the control of the local lord or prince (Lloyd 1911, p. 311; Smith 1972, pp. 23, 107, 363).

After the Norman Conquest, the Marcher lords undoubtedly asserted what they considered to be their rights over the open pastures and waste (Davies 1978, p. 121). This control is attested in 1297 when the men of Maelienydd (northern Radnorshire) on payment of £500 were 'confirmed in the right to hunt over the wastes of the *cantref*, except in the lord's demesne lands of Knucklas and in his wood of "Swydd", and in certain of the lands of Abbey Cwmhir' (Rees 1924, p. 114). Forests were created as hunting preserves, encompassing large tracts of the waste (Linnard 2000, p. 41), but they were used too for pasturing the lord's own flocks and herds, and were rented out for pasturage to local communities. Radnor, Colwyn and Knucklas Forests are well known and Painscastle seems to have had no less than three, the New and Old Forests and Forest Richard (Rees 1924, p. 110). In all there may have been at least nine forests in the area (Rees 1932). But, with the solitary exception of the mountainous Radnor Forest, which remained largely waste well into the nineteenth century and whose boundary was mapped, albeit roughly, on at least one occasion, defining these forests in the modern landscape is an impossible task. Local place-names around Colwyn Castle reveal where a part of the forest lay below the heights of Aberedw Hill, but are not sufficiently prevalent to identify the whole area that it covered and, indeed, distinguishing its bounds was a problem as far back as the Elizabethan era (Evans 1949–50, p. 385). The creation of these forests inevitably resulted in conflicts of interest, as Davies (1978, p. 125) pointed out in relation to a compromise effected in the lordship of Elfael (southern Radnorshire) where the lord's control of the forest pasture was limited to the period from May to September.

Uplands were also prone to alienation to monastic houses, and perhaps not surprisingly large tracts of western Radnorshire passed to the Cistercians. The Strata Florida grange of Cwmdeuddwr, west of the River Wye, was estimated at 8,500 ha (21,004 acres) in extent (Banks 1880, p. 32), the Golon Manor of Cwmhir Abbey, to the north-east of Rhaeadr, at over 7,200 ha (17,791 acres) (Williams 2001, p. 181). Subsequently, however, some granges were leased back to secular lords, particularly in the fourteenth century: the Beauchamps, for instance, took over the lands, granges and perhaps the flocks of Cwmhir in Elfael (Davies 1978, p. 117).

The creation of seigniorial forests, the acquisition by the Cistercians of extensive upland tracts as sheepwalks, and the development of vaccaries by secular lords were all practices common to many of the uplands throughout England and Wales (Hey 2000, p. 194). Only the last of these is poorly evidenced in central Wales.

It will never be possible to define with any accuracy the extent of the upland grazings and waste in the medieval era, whether in Radnorshire or elsewhere in Wales. Even allowing for the fact that the dynamics of farming and settlement must have resulted in a variable level of intake in different areas over the medieval centuries, there is still virtually no tangible evidence of the scale of medieval enclosure. Some features, however, offer indirect clues. The nature of medieval agriculture in Radnorshire has received minimal attention. Sylvester (1969, p. 224) gave little credence to the concept of co-aration and open fields in the region, but there can be little doubt that long narrow strip fields (or quillets) did exist around many of the villages. Relict systems could still be recognised around the Wye Valley settlements of Boughrood, Glasbury and Llowes in the mid-nineteenth century, Boughrood's abutting its common. The tithe maps show that other communities, such as Llanddewi Fach, away from the main valleys and at higher altitude, had their quillets right on the edge of the common, while the pattern of fossilised strips in Llandeilo Graban reveals similar early activity. Impossible though it is to establish where post-medieval rationalisation has wholly erased recognisable facets of this earlier agriculture, the visible change from strip fields to the less regular block fields and intakes of post-medieval date provides a preliminary guide to arable farming in the medieval landscape, and from these can perhaps be deduced the edge of the common grazing.

Generally, land enclosed in the medieval centuries would have continued in use in the post-medieval era, even assuming an intervening period of arable contraction. But there are also at least three places where medieval cultivation spreads onto what is now unenclosed common, enabling us to identify where agricultural holdings of medieval date have contracted. Two of the three are of comparable form: on Aberedw Hill, strip fields run up onto the common from the valley slopes below, and similar traces occur on Cnwch Bank 8 km (5 miles) to the north-east. The third example is rather different. Penybont Common survives as one of the lowest tracts of open land in the county, never rising above 275 metres (986 ft) O.D. In a sheltered valley on the east side of the common are the remains of a medieval farmsteading, consisting of several platforms and a wedge of cultivation ridges in strip fields (Fig. 5.2). Aerial photographs display similar strip fields in at least two other places on the common. Penybont Common thus offers a picture of medieval farming dispersed across lower ground that unusually remained unenclosed, probably because of the local assertion of common rights in later centuries.

A second range of evidence can be advanced for the extent of the medieval commons: the earthwork platforms prevalent around the periphery of some commons, normally those that have been examined in detail. Such platforms, with their long axes set down the slope, have been recognised as the earthwork stances for medieval dwellings since the fieldwork of Aileen and Cyril Fox in the 1930s (*e.g.* Fox & Fox 1934), although in practice platforms of this type continued in fashion through to the seventeenth century. The first to be excavated, on Gelligaer Common in Glamorgan, were considered to be the sites of permanent habitations (Fox 1939), but there is now a wider belief, first articulated by Iorwerth Peate, that the Gelligaer platforms were occupied on a seasonal basis (Peate 1944, p. 128; Locock forthcoming). Access to the extensive summer pastures could be controlled from the edges of the commons, whilst providing views over the enclosed lands below, a not unimportant consideration given the basic instability of the Marcher regions in the medieval period.

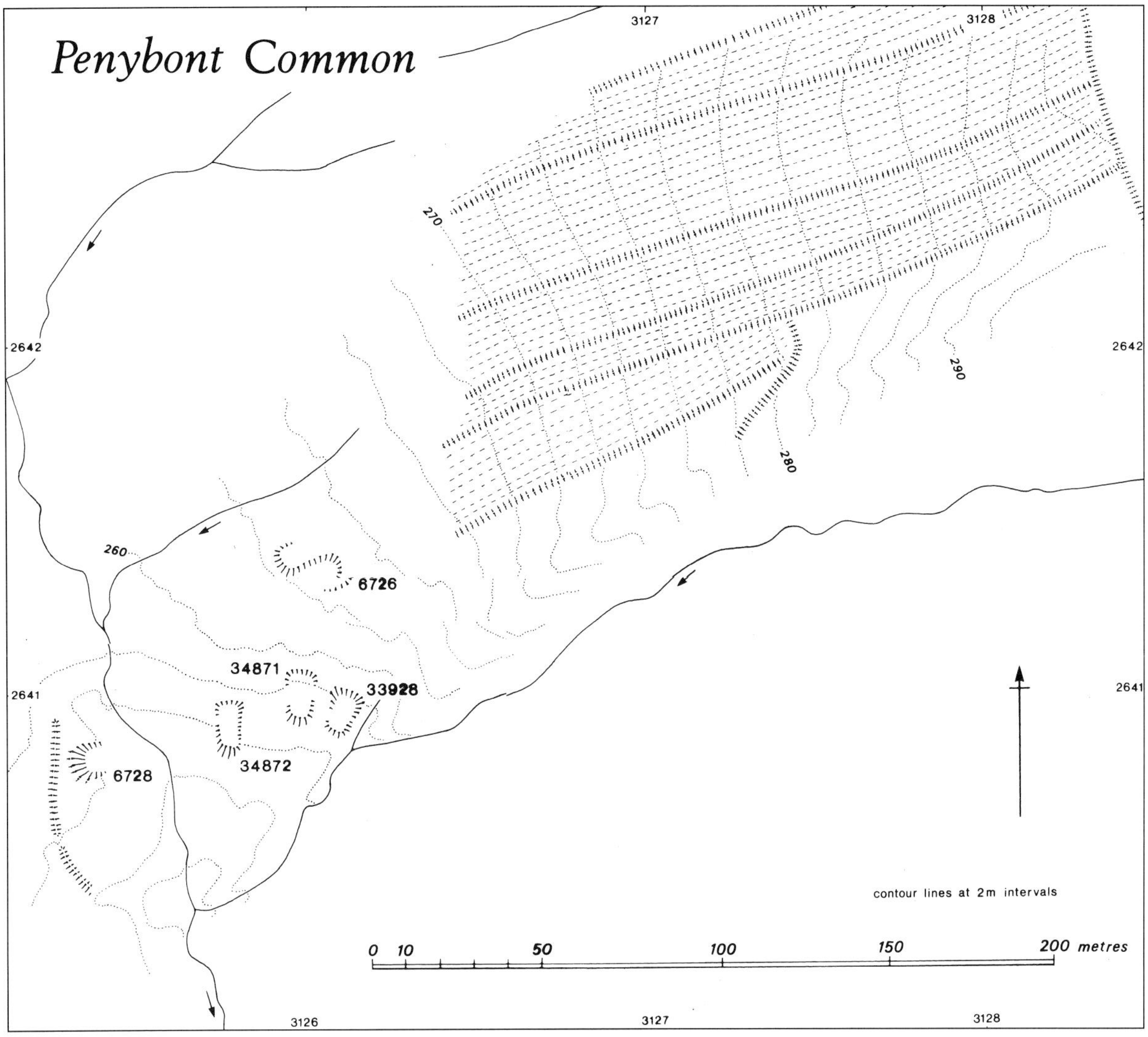

Fig. 5.2. A medieval steading on Penybont Common in central Radnorshire.

It is a hypothesis that can be extended to many of the unexcavated and undocumented platforms on the Radnorshire commons, which share morphological traits with those further south in Glamorgan, lacking both traces of associated fields or complex enclosure systems. The siting of the Radnorshire platforms is not regular, but they are often found within 100 or 200 metres of the boundary of the common on which they lie. On occasions this contiguity may appear to have a topographical explanation, but the locational association generally seems firm, implying that the boundary functioned as the edge of the common in the medieval era. Conversely, the absence of such platforms might reveal where a common boundary has been pushed back by later encroachment, although this remains to be confirmed, for only in Aberedw, noted above, is corroborative evidence immediately available.

Several nucleated complexes have also been recognised on the edges of commons. The classic site of Beili Bedw near St Harmon in the west of the county was partially excavated in the 1960s, the work suggesting settlement activity in the fifteenth century, or possibly even later. It lies just within a former common that was enclosed in the mid-nineteenth century and comprises a group of over a dozen platforms, some with appended enclosures. It has been suggested that this was a nucleated and permanently occupied settlement of free Welsh origin (Courtney 1991, p. 250), a plausible view given the proximity of the early medieval 'mother church' at St Harmon as a focal point no more than 900 metres (2,952 ft) away. But it is not inconceivable that Beili Bedw was an exceptionally large group of seasonally occupied sites. Other, similar if smaller, nucleations occur elsewhere in Radnorshire, as on the Begwns, a large common in the south of the county, where recent fieldwork has revealed a complex of house platforms with appended enclosures, at Pentre Jack, and on Cefn Wylfre, south-west of Glascwm. Whether these sites were used on a permanent or seasonal basis — and debate is likely to continue for some time to come (see Ward 1997, p. 106) — is less significant in the context of this study than the presence of a growing body of archaeological evidence for the exploitation of the commons in the middle ages. The medieval centuries witnessed a gradual intake of lands from the commons and waste, but while the seasonal use of the hills may have been extensive, this activity has left few landscape traces. The following centuries had a more dramatic and tangible impact.

EXPLOITING THE WASTE: THE POST-MEDIEVAL ERA.

A steady increase in documentation from the sixteenth century allows a broader assessment both of the utilisation of the wastes and commons and the pressures on them. With the Act of Union in 1536 the waste became truly part of the manor and local lords began to take more heed of what was in their ownership (Rees 1924, p. 127). However, 1536 should not be singled out as a watershed. Climatic deterioration and plague in the fourteenth century, and Glyndŵr's rebellion at the beginning of the fifteenth century, had had a drastic impact on both stability and population, and must inevitably have resulted in settlement contraction. But even assuming that there was a hiatus in the expansion of settlement and farming on to the waste, it is unlikely to have lasted for more than a few generations, and does not necessarily mean that the upland grazings were abandoned, rather perhaps that the patterns of utilisation altered. Written records, especially those concerning disputes over the waste, may point to the sixteenth century, but it can reasonably be assumed that there were pressures and a greater demand for land even in the fifteenth century.

Throughout the centuries that followed, different social and economic groups regularly signalled their interests in the open lands, interacting and at times confronting each other in a particular area: the landlords — and for large parts of Radnorshire this meant the Crown — the freeholders and their tenants, those with rights on the commons (not always necessarily the same as the freeholders), and the squatters and cottagers, to whom might be added on occasions representatives of the communities themselves such as overseers of the poor and parish vestries (see Howell 2000, p. 84; RCAHMW forthcoming, p. 123).[3] That the commons and waste were of crucial importance to many there can be little doubt. Thus in 1577 the lessee of the Crown's Forest of Colwyn clashed with those settled on its edges over what the latter claimed as their common rights (Lewis & Conway Davies 1954, p. 528); and a few years earlier, in 1561, jurors at an inquisition on the manors of Arwystli and Cyfeiliog in adjacent Montgomeryshire had refused to acknowledge the rights of the lord of the manor to the wastes of their commote (Evans 1949, p. 26). Just how seriously these issues were taken is indicated by the involvement of central government, forced to adjudicate on what were, essentially, local issues: the Court of Augmentations ruled on the case of Richard Thomas of Talgarth (Brecknock) in 1542, who had enclosed and cultivated 30 acres of common on nearby Cefn Llanelieu, claiming it as his own by inheritance (Lewis & Conway Davies 1954, p. 19); and about 1573 the freeholders of Radnorshire and Montgomeryshire petitioned the Council in the Marches of Wales because 'most of the land in these two counties consists of mountains, hills and other waste ground on which the freeholders have had as far back as can be remembered Common of Pasturage all the year round ...' but these were now being overgrazed as a result of agistment (Flenley 1916, p. 105).

The use of, and the pressures on, the uplands that spanned the sixteenth to the nineteenth centuries appear in a variety of forms, some becoming more emphatic as the period progressed. Overgrazing, enclosure, encroachment, the utilisation of the hills' other resources and recreation all played a part, though not all at the same time, nor in equal measure. Most, however, have left some degree of physical impression on the landscape.

Stock pasturing had always been ubiquitous, but the upland grazings became an increasingly valuable resource. Such activity, though, leaves few physical manifestations. Rather the exploitation emerges in negative terms, as communities strove to retain their upland grazing grounds, and rigorous attempts were made to confine common rights to local residents. The same general trends are encountered in virtually every region where common land or waste was prevalent, though we can be certain that in its details the exploitation of the commons and waste varied from place to place. Pressures already apparent in the sixteenth and seventeenth centuries increased considerably over the 200 years that followed, although on the limited evidence from Radnorshire and areas adjacent the conflicting uses on the commons seems to have gathered pace in the last two decades of the seventeenth century.

In one of its manifestations stock pasturing seems to have created few concerns. For western Radnorshire, west of the Wye Valley, there is a suite of references to summer pasturing and summer houses (*hafodydd* and *lluestai*) in the sixteenth century and later. A deed of 1523 referred to a tenement called 'Maes-yr-hafod' in Cwmdeuddwr (Banks 1880, p. 40) and a lease of 1598 for the same area notices the messuage of 'Bryth comb ygha' together with a summer house on Clettwr Mawr (PCC/R/D/Lew/2/237; see also RCAHMW forthcoming, p. 120). From almost a century later in the valley of the Wye is a lease on Nannerth with a cottage or 'somerhowse'

(PCC/R/D/Lew/2/245-6). Minor place-names, again from north-western Radnorshire, evoke this summer usage, initially *hafod* names, and later *lluestai* [4] which were used first as summer shepherding stations but then became permanently occupied steadings (Davies 1980, p. 8); the further west the more likely *hafod* and *lluest* are to appear as names on the tithe and later maps. Equally significantly, the remote valleys of north-western Radnorshire, in Cwmdeuddwr and adjacent parishes, frequently display the ruins of small stone-foundationed, rectangular huts that were almost certainly used only in the summer. Some of these could be of an antiquity stretching back into the medieval period, but many are probably later, the only physical traces of this transhumant practice (see Silvester forthcoming).

It is in the seasonal use of the uplands that the dichotomy of Radnorshire's post-medieval landscape emerges most clearly. For much of Radnorshire, east and south of the Ithon valley, documentary references to *hafodydd* and the like are absent. Exceptional is a claim of 1550 relating to cattle grazing on Radnor Forest that mentions also the payment of an annual fee for a custom called 'hauard', a reminder so it appears, of this earlier seasonal activity (Lewis & Conway Davies 1954, p. 513), as is a reference to summer houses by the jurors in their presentment to the Colwyn court leet in 1618 (Evans 1949–50, p. 388). Stone-built long huts on the larger commons are generally absent and significant place names — such as Hen Hafod in Beguildy — appear only intermittently. The absence of documentary and other evidence throughout the border zone implies that the tradition of summer pasturing, exemplified in earlier centuries by the platforms edging the commons, was already dying out by the sixteenth century, in contrast to those areas further west that edged the Cambrian Mountains where it continued well into the eighteenth century (Davies 1984-5, p. 79).

Regardless of this dichotomy, the landscape of the Radnorshire uplands was changed but little by seasonal activity. The imposition of seasonal dwellings usually on a valley floor or slope, sometimes with the creation of a small appended enclosure, perhaps for hay making (RCAHMW forthcoming, p. 121), establishes the low level of the impact. Occasionally, a favoured spot might later be adapted for a more permanent dwelling, particularly as cattle gave way to sheep and Suggett cites the example of the remote *lluest* of Clettwr Mawr which by the early nineteenth century had become the permanently occupied farm of Lluest Abercaethon (*ibid.*, p. 121). Generally, this seasonal activity has left little mark on the landscape.

More pervasive was enclosure, and in terms of area this had the greatest impact on the open hill grounds. Early references tend to be sporadic to an activity that became increasingly widespread as individual farmers expanded their holdings by taking in additional land, not always with the lord's agreement. New steadings might be constructed on these enclosures, but many reflected no more than the expansion of existing land holdings. Indictments of the like of Edward Burton, named in a report of 1758 on Maelienydd encroachments for having taken in 100 acres of waste at Llanddewi Ystradenny about ten years previously (NLW/Harpton/1773), only hint at a wider truth. By the nineteenth century, some courts leet seemingly dealt with little else other than enclosure and encroachment. John Chesement Severn of Penybont Hall, for instance, was undeterred by regular fines in the court leet of the Manor of Swydd between 1813 and 1849 for encroachments on Rhosswydd Common in the vicinity of Penybont (Davies 1949-50, p. 77); but as one of the principal beneficaries of the massive Llanbadarn Fynydd award in 1857 (Chapman 1992, p. 147; and see below) such fines probably meant little to him. Not all enclosures were so illicit. When in 1677 David Lloyd tried in Chancery to prevent the private enclosure of waste in Llansantffraid-in-Elvel, the defendants argued that they had agreed with the lord of manor to

> 'belt', burn, plough and sow and grain part of the common on the basis of one stang for every 20s a year in land which they held. A few acres were put aside for the maintenance of the poor, and 200 acres to be enclosed, and there remained sufficient common of pasture and water for the cattle of all commoners (NLW/Mayberry/5184).

The reason behind Lloyd's objections is unknown, but it is significant that the defendants took pains to stress that the common grazing rights would not be compromised by their actions. This form of enclosure, by agreement, was probably quite common, certainly more so than the surviving records reveal (Everitt 2000, p. 228).

On an altogether larger scale was enclosure by Act of Parliament, which for Radnorshire generally came late. The county witnessed more Acts than any other in the Principality (Chapman 1992, p. 23), impacting on about two-thirds of the fifty-two historic parishes, but none pre-dated the beginning of the nineteenth century, and the majority were passed after 1850. Where parliamentary enclosure occurred, large expanses could be affected: that for Llanbadarn Fynydd extended to 7,000 acres, for Bleddfa 5,000 acres. New farms might be created as a result of these enclosures though often the enclosures simply enlarged existing farms. The lateness of this enclosure allows easy detection on nineteenth-century maps, and the regularly laid-out intakes are immediately recognisable.

Notional enclosure also emerged with the creation of sheepwalks linked to specific farms. A mortgage deed of 1624 from Llanwrthwl on the Brecknock side of the River Wye, referring to 60 acres of waste or common as part of the holding, may presage the concept of the sheepwalk and indicate that the common could be identified as disposable property (PCC/R/D/Lew/2/119-120); it can probably be assumed that the development occurred as sheep became more important in the local economy, probably in the eighteenth century. In 1811, debate within the manorial court of the lordship of Cyfeiliog (Montgomeryshire) focused on the rights of freeholders to create exclusive sheepwalks without the lord's consent (Conway Davies 1944, p. 75). Boundaries rarely seem to have taken physical form, except inasmuch as natural features might be adopted to delimit such areas (similar in many ways to the identification of the parish boundaries across the open commons and waste). Nevertheless, the sheepwalks were zealously guarded, and Walter Davies claimed that a sheepwalk could be of more value to the farmer than the farm itself (Davies 1815, p. 164).

Few tithe maps distinguish the sheepwalks, but exceptionally that of *c.* 1842 for the townships of Golon and Cefn Pawl in Llanbister parish divide the waste around the village of Abbeycwmhir into fifteen named sheepwalks designated to nearby farms. Four, on a single, relatively small hill, were allocated to farms around the periphery of the hill. All these sheepwalks lay close to the Clywedog Brook which flowed through the village, and its tributaries. Further north in the parish, where holdings were sparser and the upland grazings considerably more extensive, there were no designated sheepwalks, an indication of less pressure on the land.

Enclosure, in whatever guise it occurred, severely reduced the extent of the commons and waste. Officially sanctioned parliamentary enclosure was extensive and its effects have been well documented (see, for instance, Howell 2000, p. 8). Enclosure by agreement such as that in Llansantffraid-in-Elvel or by illicit expansion is altogether less easy to quantify, but the scale can be judged by examining the field patterns in that parish. An intuitive analysis of the landscape using field boundary and track patterns and rights of way, together with field-names recorded in the nineteenth century allows a partial picture to be constructed (Fig. 5.3). Four areas of common, one of them close to the church, remain into the present, though cottage holdings have encroached in several places. Furthermore, post-medieval intakes of open upland have been extensive, suggesting that less than half the parish was enclosed at the beginning of the period.

Equally ubiquitous was encroachment, whereby new cottages and steadings were created on the commons, with, or more frequently without, the lord of the manor's permission. The late medieval era had witnessed changing patterns of land tenure and settlement in the wake of the catastrophes of the fourteenth and early fifteenth century; by the second half of the sixteenth century, inroads on the commons in many parts of upland Wales were causing concern to the Crown, to manorial lords and to the commoners themselves (Thomas 1967). In contrast to the activities of the community in the middle ages, new settlement types emerged as farming expansion occurred, with dispersed farmsteadings (*tyddynnod*) set in their own fields (Griffiths 1989, p. 233). The process can be recognised on some Radnorshire commons that harbour distinctive sets of settlement earthworks. The partially excavated settlement at Beili Bedw near St Harmon offers a starting point (Courtney 1991). The group of medieval platforms constituting the settlement was superseded by a later farmstead set within its own enclosures (Silvester forthcoming), occupied probably in the late sixteenth century or early seventeenth century. Aerial photography and fieldwork have documented, in recent years, comparable examples of farms encased by small enclosures on the commons. Though similar to the encroachments that were to come later, they are of distinctive appearance with a house platform or long hut at the centre of two or more enclosures, and are usually established a short distance from the edge of the common. Fron Top is a typical example where a two-roomed hut has small, contemporary enclosures on its south-west side and a larger enclosure filled with cultivation ridges to the east (Pl. 5.I); it was one of two such settlements on Tynbryniau Hill which had been abandoned by the time of the tithe survey in the mid-nineteenth century (Silvester: forthcoming). The Garn Fawr settlement (still marked on modern Ordnance Survey maps) on the south-eastern flank of Gilwern Hill, north of Llansantffraid-in-Elvel, comprises a deeply terraced platform approached by a track running between its enclosures. The settlement lies towards the higher end of land now enclosed, but its location and the absence of any association with the surrounding field boundaries implies that originally it lay beyond the fields rising up from the valley. The Garn Fawr settlement is an indicator of the changing and expanding pattern of enclosure on the commons, and other such settlements await discovery.

Later encroachments are much more obvious, both in the archaeological record and in the documentary record, the result primarily of the poor and the landless carving holdings for themselves from the waste. Recognised

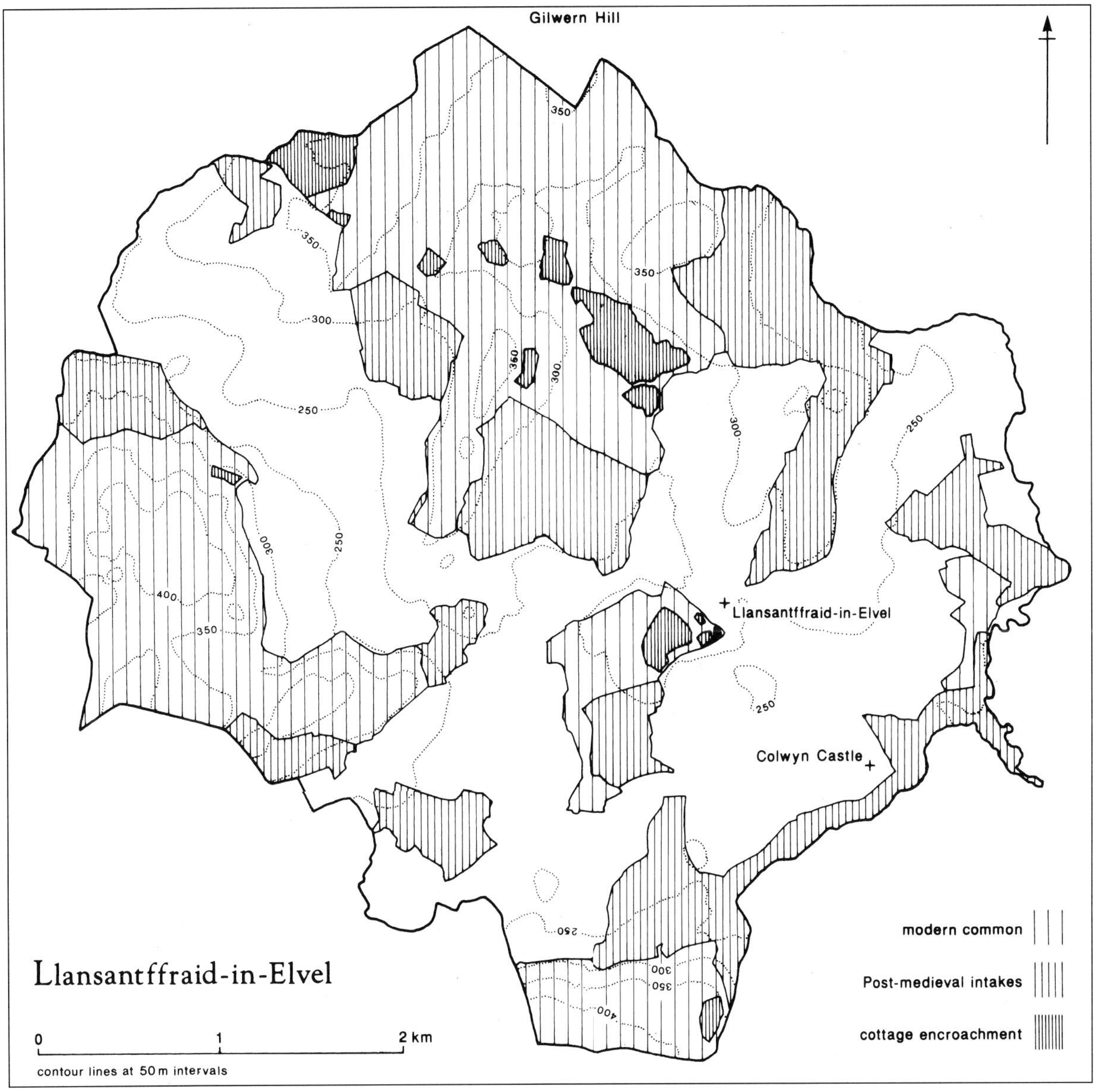

Fig. 5.3. The parish of Llansantffraid-in-Elvel showing the modern commons, earlier encroachments and possible intakes.

throughout Wales, the '*ty unnos*' or one-night house (but in Radnorshire also known, more poetically, as the 'morning surprise': Royal Commission 1895, p. 915) was the primary construction, a cottage or hovel as they were often described on contemporary maps. Normally of turf or timber (Peate 1944, p. 40), the *ty unnos* would be supplemented by small enclosures and ultimately the roughly constructed dwelling would be replaced by something more permanent.[5] In 1573, drawing on past custom, the Council in the Marches of Wales directed that without the lord of the manor's permission, the only common where a cottage or hovel could be erected by a freeholder was within his own township; and that such a cottage could be inhabited only between 15 May and 15 August, a clear throwback to the seasonal use of the hills. Interestingly, during the later part of Elizabeth's reign the Council was not called upon to adjudicate on encroachments on the commons (Flenley 1916, p. 17), perhaps signalling that it was not yet deemed to be a problem. But the situation was worsening, partly, it has been argued, because of the decline of the manorial courts as a result of the Act of Union in 1536 (*ibid.*, p. 18), and subsequently it became acute. In 1734 a survey of encroachments on Crown wastes in Maelienydd listed 784 such illicit activities, 421 involving the erection of a cottage and extending over 678 acres, 363 where only land was taken, a total in all of 1,475 acres. Howse (1955, p. 29) calculated that overall 760 different people were involved. The lease of the Crown wastes in 1758 by Richard Austin generated a flurry of activity as his agents were sent to look for illegal encroachments: an

Plate 5.I. Fron Top, Llanbister. A steading encroachment on the common (© RCAHMW).

account for that year for the several lordships in Maelienydd recorded that in one lordship alone 203 cottages had been erected on the commons of several parishes during the previous twenty years (NLW/Harpton/1784 & 1773). Included were several made by 'occupiers' who lived not in the parish but in Huntington in neighbouring Herefordshire.

Common to virtually all of the cottage encroachments on the commons was the small size of the associated holdings; the lists such as that of Maelienydd compiled for the Crown in 1734 (see above) shows that over 80 *per cent* of the 420 cottages had two acres of land or less (Howse 1955, p. 29). Many acquired names that seem now either ironic or naively optimistic: Cropshort in Bryngwyn, Golden Grove, Windy Hall and Hope's Castle, all in Beguildy. But such encroachments could aggregate with small groups of cottages and their fields; some continued and today constitute small settlements such as Moelfre Castle in Llanbister.

Legalising the encroachments by granting leases to the squatters was one response. Thus, the range of leases agreed by the Reverend Rice Powell, the new lord of the manor of Colwyn, in the 1680s was but one element in his determination to assert the rights that came with his purchase of the lordship (Silvester forthcoming). By the second half of the eighteenth century, the increasing pressure on landowners resulted in greater attention to money-making schemes and encroachments were afforded considerably more attention (Davies 1815, p. 69). Manorial papers and those of central government reflect the increasing conflict between those who wished to protect the rights of common, those who were intent on exploiting the common for their own ends, whether by encroachment or agistment, and those landowners who perceived them as a potential and valuable source of revenue. By the later eighteenth century this was no minor consideration, and court leet documents from neighbouring southern Montgomeryshire reveal the illegal use of the commons as the major concern in the last quarter of the eighteenth century (Lewis 1944). However, encroachment could be positively encouraged on occasions (Howell 2000, p. 82). A petition to the Crown in 1703 referred to the freeholders and inhabitants of Beguildy permitting a labourer to build a cottage on the waste, for it removed the need for the parish to subsidise his impoverished family though the local poor rate.

Enclosure and encroachment normally resulted in the permanent alienation and reduction of open upland, the impact being greatest on the smaller commons that were ringed by settled valleys. There were other events, more transient, yet which still left a mark on the landscape. The commons could be converted, if only temporarily, to arable. Conventionally, this has been viewed as a practice restricted to the Napoleonic Wars, when grain was in short supply (Thomas 1963, p. 7; Hey 2000, p. 204). This ignores the evidence of a much wider practice. In his presentation to the Royal Commission on Land in 1895, Sir Joseph Bailey of Glanusk, one of the great Brecknock landowners whose holdings ran into Radnorshire, referred to the practice of 'betting', whereby, in the mid-nineteenth century, two or three 'white' crops were taken and then the ground was 'let go back to the mountain' (Royal Commission 1895, p. 761). Occasionally, too, it surfaced in the manorial courts, and centuries earlier, in 1602, John Norden had noted the occurrence of 'betting' in the lordship of Oswestry in Shropshire (Slack 1951, p. 87). The degree to which these temporary cultivations had the agreement of the landowners cannot be established. In neighbouring Montgomeryshire, Edward Davies of Malgwin was presented, unusually, at the manorial court of Arwystli Uwchoed in 1786 'for cutting and burning a stang of betting upon Brunant Common' (Lewis 1944, p. 186). It has been argued for central Montgomeryshire that though an offence, cultivation of the manorial waste was regularised by payment of an annual fine (Griffiths 1949, p. 44). Cultivation ridges show up widely on the commons of Radnorshire. Coed Swydd near Llandegley is covered with cultivation furrows forming blocks lying at different angles (Pl. 5.II). Used for a few years and then abandoned, they were simply another way that those living close to, or on, the common could make a living from agriculture.

The emergence of small rabbit farms on the commons can be attributed to the eighteenth and nineteenth centuries, in the main on the initiative of those who had settled on or beside the commons rather than by the landowners. Certainly there were manorial warrens: that on the southern edge of Radnor Forest was often referred to in the Harpton Court estate documents towards the end of the eighteenth century; the construction of a warren house there can be linked to the warren being restocked in about 1793 with 400 'couples' of rabbits (NLW/Harpton/825). Warren House itself remains, and on the higher ground above are five pillow mounds, the long elongated earthworks deliberately constructed to encourage the rabbit population (Williamson & Loveday 1988).

Plate 5.II. Coed Swydd, near Llandegley: visible are several pillow mounds, extensive traces of temporary cultivation, and in the distance a small enclosure, perhaps of late prehistoric date (© RCAHMW).

What the lord of the manor could do on the Radnor Forest upland, so could others on the commons. Small groups of pillow mounds signal rabbit farming on a remarkable scale. Documentary references are again rare, but agents of the lessee of Crown lands in Maelienydd in 1760 were directed to a hill in the parish of Llanddewi Ystradenny where 'a warren was dug for the keeping of rabbits, without licence or authority' and ordered to destroy it (NLW/Harpton/1785). Over forty groups of pillow mounds have now been identified, dispersed across the small commons in central and south Radnorshire. At the head of the Milo Brook on Aberedw Common, the remote and abandoned holding of Pen-blaen-milo has half a dozen pillow mounds on the slopes facing it slightly higher up the valley, and the warren must have been worked from the house. One group per common is the almost invariable rule, implying local initiative to provide meat and fur, for which there would have been a significant demand in the eighteenth and early nineteenth centuries (Sheail 1971, p. 78). We can assume that they were more than subsistence initiatives, more mechanisms for commercial profit at a local level. When the messuages of Graig and Vron in Beguildy were leased in 1789, it was to a skinner from Herefordshire and a butcher from Worcestershire; they then sub-leased the land, presumably to a local man, to maintain a warren (PCC/R/D/MB/1/61-2).

The commons and the wastes were sources of raw materials other than the grass of the unenclosed grazings. Walter Davies (1810, p. 370) noted that a couple of centuries earlier wood had been the most common fuel, even in parts of the mountains. While the common right of estovers existed for some communities, and some commons still carried woodland at a later date, it is impossible to quantify this as a commodity. By the time of Davies's travels around Wales at the beginning of the nineteenth century, the decline in the amount of natural woodland had led to the increasing exploitation of the only other readily available fuel, peat (Welsh *mawn*). Those who did not have access to a turbary had to purchase peat, and in 1774 the claim that 'Raydar [Rhaeadr] people cannot live without the turf of Cwmtyddwr hill' (NLW/Harpton/c/26) was not mere hyperbole. Documented examples from Radnorshire, ranging widely in location and time, indicate the near ubiquitous importance of this material for fuel, both in the countryside and also in the town. In 1573, freeholders close to Radnor Forest complained that the 'farmer' who had acquired the lease from the Crown was preventing them from cutting peat (Owen 1969, p. 144), a concern that was resolved in subsequent leases (Lewis & Conway Davies 1954, p. 519). Two centuries later 'foreigners' from outside the manor of Arwystli in Montgomeryshire were regularly fined for cutting and removing peat from Pencerrig Common near Llanidloes, twenty-eight of them in 1786, forty in 1787 (Lewis 1944, p. 186). In the early nineteenth century the county historian of Radnorshire, Jonathan Williams (Davies 1905, p. 160), noted that the lowland turbary of Rhosgoch was exploited through the payment of an annual fee to the lord and produced fuel almost as good as coal: Rhosgoch still survives as a common with continuing rights of turbary (Penfold *et al.* 1990). Later it was not uncommon for a turbary to be set aside at the time of enclosure for the use of the poor of the parish, no doubt formalising practices that had existed for many years previously.

Peat cutting can leave significant traces. Turbaries are recognisable on the extensive wastes and commons to the north of the Elan Valley lakes in the north-western part of the county, where the linear depressions left by the peat cutters can be readily picked out on aerial photographs, though less easily on the ground. For many an isolated farm in those valleys its abandoned turbary is still visible on the hill above, usually 500–1,000 metres (1,640–3,280 ft) away, confirming Walter Davies' comments that every farm had its appropriated turbary (Davies 1810, p. 370). More extensive cuttings on Crugyn Ci about 5 km (3 miles) to the west of Rhayader and at least 2 km (1.2 miles) from any habitation, must result from communal activity.

On the commons of south and east Radnorshire, relict traces of peat exploitation are less obvious, perhaps because peat growth was less pronounced. Mawn pools remain on Aberedw Common and nearly a dozen other Radnorshire commons; some of these may be drowned peat cuttings, though an alternative explanation sees them as the equivalent of dew ponds (Penford *et al.* 1990, p. 10). Cuttings are visible on Llanbedr Hill and it was probably to these that the Reverend Francis Kilvert, immortalised through his diaries, referred, when he accompanied the incumbent of Llanbedr to fetch his '*mawn*' in 1872, in his description of 'the low conical heaps of peat turf scattered about among the heather' (Plomer 1977, p. 200).

Stone quarrying on the commons and waste was widespread, and on some commons the right to remove stone stills exist (Penfold *et al.* 1990, p. 9). Typical are a series of small surface quarries just within the circuit of Aberedw Hill which provided stone for facing the earthen boundary of the common, and perhaps material for building elsewhere as well. In 1737 Roderick Gwynne of Glanbrane asked permission of Thomas Morgan, lord of the manor, to quarry stone on common land in Merthyr Cynog (NLW/Tredegar/117/328), and there are other examples of Morgan being paid for this facility on the Breconshire Commons. In 1770 William Thomas was fined for 'raising stone on Borp

Common (Davies 1948, p. 74), and in 1703 'Thomas Roberts [was fined] for that he did not fill up the holes and open places which he digged in the Common of [Norton] and wee further present that the same is a great annoyance to the inhabitants ...' (Howse 1944, p. 48).

Harvesting the other resources of the commons and wastes has left fewer manifestations in the archaeological record, and even written records are sparse. But, just as in northern England (Winchester 2000a, p. 123), we can be certain that local communities utilised whatever the commons could provide: reeds, bracken, moor grass and even gorse. Edward Lhuyd reported at the end of the seventeenth century that in the parishes of Colva and Glascwm turf, gorse and heath (heather) were all used for fuel (Lhuyd 1909, p. 33). A penalty of 10 shillings was levied on people from outside the manor of Norton with no right of common who 'cut fern or stock gorst' (Howse 1944, p. 48), and in St Harmon fines were levied at the manorial court in 1793 for cutting 'trouse' or brushwood (Lewis 1944, p. 193). In Arwystli, in neighbouring Montgomeryshire, Elizabeth Morgan was presented at the manorial court for mowing and carrying away six dray loads of fern from a common near Llanidloes in 1786 (*ibid.*, p. 186). Clarke (1971, p. 34) remarked on the cutting of moor grass for hay in the Elan Valley region in the inter-war years, and even today common rights enable bracken to be baled on the Begwms and Llanbedr and Aberedw Hills, as bedding material for stock.

If there was a single component in the exploitation of the uplands that did not feature prominently in Radnorshire, it was the mineral resources, unlike adjacent counties such as Cardiganshire (Bick & Davies 1994; Morgan 2001, p. 132). Lead and zinc were mined at Cwm Elan in the vast parish of Cwmdeuddwr, for nearly a century from 1796 (Hall 1993, p. 80) and lead, too, came from workings further east near Llandrindod Wells (*ibid.* 1993, p. 82); trials are still visible in or two other places. But when in 1855 the sale particulars of the Boughrood Charity (established by the same Reverend Rice Powell who was so industrious in establishing leases in the late seventeenth century in Aberedw), which owned upland grazings in a number of Radnorshire parishes, made reference to lead and copper being worked in adjoining manors, we may suspect this to have been primarily a selling pitch (NLW/BRA 1977/64). Prospecting for coal appears to have been even less rewarding, although trials have been recorded north-west of Crossgates at Rhiwgoch and on Weythel Common to the south of New Radnor (Bick 1991, p. 69). In general, those parts of the Radnorshire wastes affected by mining were remarkably small.

The open uplands were also used for pleasure. In 1768 the agent to the lessee of the Crown's waste in Maelienydd forbade 'the unqualified to sport upon the hills belonging to Cantremelenith and the gentry to forbear for two years till the game was more plentiful' (NLW/Harpton/c/133). Some commons were used for shooting. Butts, no earlier than the later nineteenth century on the basis of general trends in game shooting (Carr 1981, p. 484; Newman *et al.* 2001, p. 119), are recorded on several commons. Llanbedr and Gascwm Hills has a history of game shooting and today are still owned by a shooting consortium; a recent field survey identified more than 130 butts on these commons, most of them in lines of eight or nine.

Llandrindod Wells with its mineral springs represents a special case, a town that developed on common land. Its growth was a cause of some concern in the second half of the eighteenth century because of the number of people who resorted to the springs and their impact on the area (NLW/Harpton/c/153), but it was with the Enclosure Act of 1862 and the arrival of the railway six years later that the real growth of Llandrindod commenced (Jones 1973).

Parliamentary enclosure in Radnorshire declined by the 1880s. In the following decade, attempts to enclose the vast Crown commons of Llanbister and Llanbadarn Fynydd were abandoned, for it proved too expensive (Royal Commission 1895, p. 917). A large part of western Radnorshire beyond the Wye came into the hands of Birmingham Corporation in the 1890s (and ultimately passed to Welsh Water) with the Elan Valley reservoirs lying at the heart of an extensive estate, much of it open upland which has remained in the same condition. By and large, the twentieth century witnessed greater stability on the commons and waste. Enclosure did not entirely cease, but the level declined markedly, while some other developments did have an impact, if only minor, such as the golf course constructed on the common at Rhayader in 1924 (PCC/R/D/Lew/2/616-7). Afforestation masked some former wastes, particularly around Cwmhir, but the impact of plantations in Radnorshire is less than in some neighbouring counties. During the Second World War some commons were cultivated. The southern portion of the Begwns, now part of the National Trust estate, was ploughed up, as was much of Newchurch Hill. Traces of this transient activity are sparse, yet the general appearance of these commons reflects the smoothing process of cultivation.

The commons and waste are now primarily grazing grounds. They are or can be utilised by those who still have rights: bracken is still cut on Aberedw Common; turbary rights are still in place for Beacon and Pool Hills (Penfold *et al.* 1990, p. 10). Some unfortunately are dumping grounds for machinery and old cars. But, as a result of legislation and voluntary practice, the pressures on the commons and the waste are arguably now less than in previous centuries.

CONCLUSIONS

Throughout this paper the terms 'commons' and 'wastes' have been used to describe the open uplands. Neither, however, is really adequate to describe the extensive upland pastures with their invaluable suite of resources available to the communities that lay in the valleys below them. The open uplands offered both the environment in which those communities operated and the resources that were utilised. Impossible though it is to gauge their extent before the middle of the nineteenth century, there can be no doubt that the open uplands originally constituted considerably more than half of the land area of the old county, and that for many they represented the primary means of livelihood.

The resource was utilised and exploited in diverse ways by different social and economic groups, and increasingly the attempts led to tension between those with an interest in, or a design on, the commons and the waste. There was, though, a change in emphasis over time. In the medieval centuries, the scale of utilisation was smaller, less diverse and to a certain degree it was, to use topical terminology, sustainable. Furthermore in some of its manifestations — the intake of cultivable land from the common adjacent to existing settlements and the establishment of groups of platforms around the periphery of the common — it was communal activity. But in the post-medieval centuries there was a shift with individuals exploiting the commons, and with this resources were consumed rather than sustained.

For many the commons were simply there to be used: by the commoners as a resource, by the land-less and farmers as a source of land, and by the landlords as a source of profit and occasionally sport. The commons and the waste were ubiquitous but were worthy of mention only where there was dispute or dissent, or where the resources that they proffered came under pressure. These areas were vital to the people who lived in the valleys around. Their economic value is impossible to measure, but they were of incalculable value to many; their use may be largely invisible to us but, as Alan Everitt (2000 p. 210) has noted, they underpinned the whole rural economy. No one visiting the small historic settlements of Rhulen or Glascwm, hemmed in by hills on all sides, can be in any doubt of the significance of the uplands to nearby communities. And while Radnorshire's wastes do present some unusual elements, the overall picture that emerges of both use and development can be seen as a microcosm for the open hills and commons across the Principality as a whole.

NOTES

1. This paper reflects the writer's interests developed over several years of working in mid-Wales. Five commons have been studied in some detail through systematic fieldwork in recent years, four by the Clwyd-Powys Archaeological Trust, one by the National Trust. My thanks are due to Ian Whyte for the invitation to produce the paper; to a number of landowners who have permitted access to their uplands; to Richard Suggett of RCAHMW for providing me with a copy of part of his volume on Radnorshire houses in advance of publication, and for useful discussions on some of the issues raised in this paper; and to Bill Britnell for commenting on a draft of this paper.
2. The sparsity is revealed in *Welsh Manors and Their Records* (Watt 2000, p. 58). The material listed for Radnorshire in the Welsh Manorial Records Database reveals there are few manorial records, whether medieval or later.
3. The cottaging phenomenon is one that merits treatment in its own right, and much social detail and discussion is available. See David Howell whose volume on the rural poor is a mine of detail, and Richard Suggett who has developed a framework for Radnorshire, and also points to the increased viability of cottage encroachments as the potato became a staple food of the poor (RCAHMW forthcoming, p. 124).
4. The parallel, and in places sequential, development of the *hafod* and the *lluest* is not straightforward, varying through time and by place. This is not the place to consider the various strands. E Davies established the general picture in a series of papers founded on place-name evidence (1984–5), and others, notably Anthony Ward (1997), have developed the picture. See also RCAHMW forthcoming, p. 120.
5. The concept of the *ty unnos* is deeply embedded in the social history of Wales. (See Sayce 1942; Wiliam 1988; and now RCAHMW forthcoming, p. 124.)

ABBREVIATIONS

NLW	National Library of Wales
PCC	Powys County Council (Archives)
RCAHMW	Royal Commission on the Ancient and Historical Monuments of Wales

The Scottish Highlands before and after the Clearances: an ecological perspective

Robert A. Dodgshon

ABSTRACT

The ecological basis of traditional Highland farming is examined and the changes brought about by the Highland Clearances considered with particular attention on stocking patterns and grazing levels. Traditional Highland farming was valley-based and oriented towards crop production with only limited use being made of the hill ground. The new systems of commercial sheep farming maximised the use of resources across all sectors of Highland farms, including the high ground. One result of this was pasture degradation with a reduction of heather moorland, and a shift from species-rich to species-poor grassland being commented on by the mid-nineteenth century.

KEYWORDS

Highlands, Clearances, stocking densities, grazing regimes, sheep farming

INTRODUCTION

The Clearances have been much studied as a social and economic transformation of the Highland landscape. However, we still need an ecological history of this transformation that defines the landscape ecology of farm production prior to the Clearances, including the main patterns of resource use and their ecological effects, and then explores how such patterns and effects were changed by the spread of commercial sheep farming. In recent years, an increasing amount of debate has been directed at the ecological impact that the Clearances may have had on Highland pastures. However, without being viewed against pre-clearance conditions, or being related to precisely what the Clearances involved as regards changes in stocking patterns, we cannot begin to understand how they changed the use of resources and the impact which this may have had on the landscape ecology of the region. This chapter will try to contribute to this debate by taking this sort of long-run perspective.

THE ECOLOGY OF FARMING IN THE HIGHLANDS

By way of background, we need first to understand the particular problems facing stock production in a region like the Highlands. Most traditional agricultural systems in Britain had to cope with a local diversity of ground conditions and, therefore, a diversity of potential output. What contrasted upland townships with lowland ones was the fact that the differences created by variations in soil quality, drainage, etc, were compounded by topographic variations, so that the typical upland township had to contend, not only with more extreme variation in ground conditions, but also with extreme variations in slope, exposure, growing season, frost and snow cover within its resource framework. This created two important differences between upland and lowland township ecologies. First, whereas many lowland townships could, physically, crop a high proportion of their ground, restricting the amount only for agricultural reasons or to preserve a sufficient arable:pasture balance, upland townships faced severe physical limitations on how much they could crop. Second, whereas most land within lowland townships was subjected to broadly the same climatic regime, with a relatively subdued range of variation between the different parts of the township, this was not the case with upland townships. Dominating the farming strategies of all upland townships was the need to accommodate exaggerated variations in seasonal output from one part of the township to another.

These distinctions are important because of the impact that they had on the strategies of resource use employed by upland townships. In particular, their limited amount of low-lying, sheltered ground led to a potential conflict between the needs of arable and those of livestock. The very land that communities needed for arable, their lower slope and low-lying valley or lochside grounds, was also that which had most value as meadowland or sheltered winter grazings. These land uses could more easily be kept segregated in a Lowland context, simply because townships there had a higher proportion of suitable land to choose from. In an upland context, such land uses invariably competed for the same limited space. Of course, given a low-input/low-output system, their competing demands need not have conflicted, but once either arable or livestock production was intensified, as they were in the Scottish Highlands by the eighteenth century, then the conflict became very real. Though the increased stubble provided some compensation by way of more manure, the expansion of arable reduced the capacity of townships to produce the hay needed to sustain stock over winter. Any such reduction in their capacity to over-winter stock invariably meant that they could not maximise their summer use of the hills. Conversely, any attempt to expand the acreage of hay meadows and winter pasture so as to fully exploit their summer grazing potential inevitably meant that less arable was available for subsistence. At some point in their expansion, Highland townships had to make a choice over whether land and labour should be directed at emphasising the grain output of arable at the expense of hay and livestock production, or vice versa.

THE PRE-CLEARANCE TOWNSHIP

When we look at Highland townships prior to the Clearances, most appear to have chosen the first of these options. Indeed, if we had to summarise the character of the pre-clearance township economy in a phrase it would be that they were effectively lowland economies squeezed into upland ecologies, most maintaining a significant output of arable but at the expense of their livestock output. Overall, the amount of arable per township was greater in the west, on Hebridean islands like Tiree and the Uists, than on the mainland. In the case of the former, it was possible to find townships with over 300 acres (121 ha) of arable, whereas a figure of less than 100 acres (41 ha) was nearer the norm in the case of the latter (Dodgshon 1998b, p. 136). These areal differences reflect variations as much in the overall size or density of townships as in the nature of resource endowment, with townships in the Hebrides tending to be fewer in number but larger in area. In both areas, though, we not only find sizeable arable acreages in areas suitable for cropping (*e.g.* Lawers), but we also find cropping in marginal areas (*e.g.* Rannoch).[1] A significant proportion of the grain produced would have been for on-the-farm consumption, since many townships carried a mix of runrig tenants, sub-tenants and cottagers and would have had a substantial on-the-farm demand. Much of the remainder would have been taken up as rent and marketed by landlords, or marketed by farmers themselves.

This significant grain sector meant that many pre-clearance townships cropped a substantial proportion of their better land. The scale of cropping involved is manifest from estate surveys like that for Harris or Netherlorne.[2] The recently published survey of Menstrie Glen in the Ochil Hills, though out of the Highlands *sensu stricto*, gives some idea of the extent of land formerly cultivated in upland areas. At least one of the farms in the area surveyed was reported to have had no arable in the sixteenth century yet appeared to have been extensively cropped since, with the presence of rigs of different types suggesting a gradual phasing of this build-up. More significantly, the rigs present suggest that this was for grain or potatoes, not for re-seeding pasture. Such sites show that not only was arable important in Highland townships but also that the amounts involved may have increased in the century or so prior to the Clearances (RCAHMS 1991).

The scale of arable cropping had consequences for stock management. The more land that was cropped, then the more it acted as a check on the amount of stock that could be carried over winter and the more it restricted the exploitation of the summer grazing potential offered by hill ground. Three aspects of the problem need to be considered: stocking levels, stock composition and the grazing strategies employed by townships.

Traditionally, a township's stock numbers were computed in terms of a standardised livestock unit called a *soum* that weighted horses, cows, sheep and goats according to their different demands on grazing. As well as determining stocking levels, the number of soums assigned to a township was also used to help determine its rent liability. Because of this, lists of stocking per township are sometimes available in rentals, either as the total number of soums allowed or in terms of the number of each stock present. Both forms enable us to calculate stocking levels. In one of the earliest indications of stocking levels, a seventeenth-century rental for Tiree indicates that not only were townships each rated as a *tirunga*, to which a fixed amount of sowing was attached, but each had 144 soums attached to it.[3] Such uniformity may have existed elsewhere, particularly where we find local townships bearing the same rate of land assessment. However, by the seventeenth century, when detailed soum data becomes available for other areas, the tendency was for townships to carry a varied range of assessments and an equally varied range of soum rates. Putting together early/mid-eighteenth-century soum data for 400 townships across parts of the mainland and Hebrides, the average soum rating per township was 78, but only 72 if we exclude the six exceptionally large townships that carried 300–400 soums each. The latter were probably held by dealers or specialist stock farmers and may represent an early response to the market in Highland cattle that developed over the seventeenth century.[4]

Though the modern concept of Livestock Units (LU) is based on the same principles and proportions as soums, converting soums into LU/ha data poses problems. First, pre-clearance cattle and sheep tended to be smaller in bodyweight to those of the nineteenth century and later so that any LU/ha index based on seventeenth/eighteenth-century data cannot be treated as directly equivalent to a LU/ha index based on nineteenth-century data (Gibson 1988). To equate the two in terms of grazing need, we would need to scale pre-nineteenth-century LU/ha data down by anything between one-third and a half. Second, many pre-clearance townships relied on the grazings within their bounds plus a share of what were often extensive common grazing (Bil 1990). By the time we reach the nineteenth century, though, most common grazings had been shared out between farms. The only way to derive a standard measure of extent is to assume that the nineteenth-century acreages provide an indication of what pre-clearance townships had access to, both within their own bounds and as a share of common pasture. Even using this assumption, though, there are few townships for which a reliable pre-clearance LU/ha index can be derived. The nine Perthshire townships for which this can be done produce stocking densities of between 0.1/ha and 0.2/ha, uncorrected for the smaller size of stock, so presumed corrected levels might be 0.05/ha and 0.1/ha (see Table 1). However, we need to correct the figures in the opposite direction to allow for the fact that the acreages used are total acreages, and make no allowances for areas of blanket bog, rock outcrops or enclosed woodland that existed on these farms. If we discount 25 *per cent* as unusable for grazing, then the average pre-clearance stocking levels range between 0.0625 and 0.125 LU/ha.

What is more difficult to establish is whether changes in stocking levels took place even before the Clearances. Two sets of relevant data are available. That for Tiree shows that whilst change did occur in some township soum ratings between 1541 and 1768, there were still townships that bore the same soums rating (=144 soums per tirunga) in 1768 as in 1541.[5] Data for the second area, Glenorchy, provide a glimpse of change across thirty-one townships between *c.* 1630 and 1730. They suggest more change, but it was not consistent change. Altogether, only five townships experienced an expansion of numbers whilst thirteen recorded significant decreases (>20 *per cent*).[6]

A township's soum rating was related to how much stock it could 'soum and roum' or over-winter. In part, this was calculated by how much feed (*i.e.* harvest stubble, hay meadows, etc) and sheltered land a township had available for stock over winter. However, townships also saw it in terms of how much manure was required for the arable. Clearly, this was a positive aspect of the relationship between stock and crop, one that integrated them in a reciprocal, mutually-supporting way. For a region like the Highlands, it was also a critical aspect of their relationship. Indeed, there is every reason to believe that in arriving at the stocking level for a township, the number of soums set may, initially, have had a direct relationship to the amount of arable. On Tiree, townships were said to comprise a tirunga of land or 48 mail lands, each tirunga having 144 soums and 72 bolls of sowing, giving two soums for each boll of sowing.[7] What subsequently happened to stocking and cropping over the seventeenth and eighteenth centuries can be read in different ways. At a township level, the exact statistical correlation between soums and the number of bolls sown that existed in 1541 had, by 1768, given way to a looser correlation.[8] Yet, when graphed, the 1768 data shows that whilst a small number of townships had significantly more soums for each boll of sowing,

TABLE 1: STOCKING DENSITIES IN NINE PERTHSHIRE TOWNSHIPS: Increases in LU/ha levels pre- and post-clearance

	1727	1730	1839	1870s(?)
Leadihary	0.93/ha		0.25/ha	0.375/ha
Laig Beg		0.031/ha	0.225/ha	0.337/ha
Larig More		0.031/ha		
Catnish		0.056/ha	0.225/ha	0.337/ha
Molay		0.0125/ha		
Ednavannich	0.175/h		0.35/ha	0.525/ha
Inishcharach	0.075/ha		0.387/ha	0.58/ha
Corrydarick		0.068/ha	0.225/ha	0.337/ha
Innerachan		0.025/ha		
Cunerosk	ND		0.362/ha	0.54/ha

the majority of townships still only had between 1.5-2.5 soums for each boll of sowing (see Fig. 6.1). In fact, when we take an aggregate or island view, the average number of soums was still only 2.32, compared to 2 in 1541. This was despite the fact that the island's total soum rating fell, from 2,880 to 2,490 between 1541 and 1768 following the loss of machair pasture through wind erosion.[9]

Data on the relationship between cropping and stocking are also available for other areas. The relationship on Islay (1722), Netherlorne (1730) and, to a lesser extent, South Lochtayside (1769) was similar to Tiree, with a small number of townships, presumably specialist stock farms, having a noticeably greater number of soums for each boll of sowing, but the majority of townships having between 1.5 and 3 (see Fig. 6.1). We cannot say whether the balance between arable and pasture in these areas was originally fixed at two soums per boll of sowing, as on Tiree, but arguably, the broad comparability between townships suggests that about two soums per boll may once have been the customary rate in other areas. If so, then it would suggest that most townships in these areas were still stocking in relation to the needs of arable rather than the opportunities offered by their summer pasture. There are other areas, though, for which available data may suggest a slightly different conclusion. In the case of Mull (1662) and Glenorchy (1730), the number of soums per boll of sowing was more variable between townships (Fig. 6.1). Not only is the impression given that a greater number of townships had started to move away from any standard relationship between stocking levels and arable sowing, assuming that one had existed, but also, their higher average number of soums per boll of sowing suggests that townships in these areas had started to relax the relationship between stock and arable.

However, a second factor shaping stocking levels was the supply of winter feed, for townships could only maintain what they could winter. Given that their potential summer capacity was far greater than their wintering capacity, the latter acted as a bottleneck. If we take the data available for pre-clearance townships for the years around 1800, they show a very strong contrast between the central Highlands and the western part of the region as regards the amount of green pasture available, with the former still having significant amounts but the latter having as little as 20 *per cent* of their land under green pasture. (Dodgshon 1998b, p. 226). A similar contrast is evident from the data for meadows. Indeed, in the far west, there are signs that townships made little use of meadows prior to the 1730s (see Fig. 6.2). Townships in the central Highlands made far more use, though local differences are apparent even here. This whole question of pre-clearance meadow requires careful handling. Descriptions of pre-clearance arable make clear that, quite apart from what grew between the rigs, the

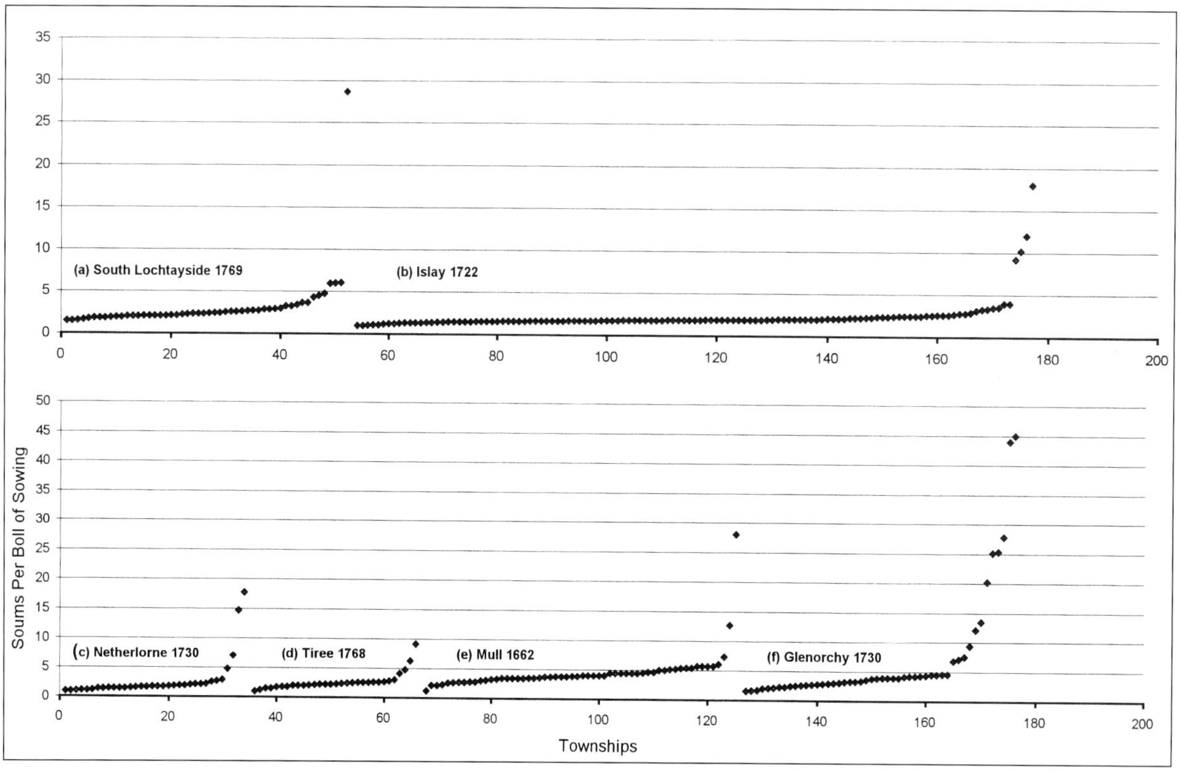

Fig. 6.1. Soum-arable ratios for selected areas.

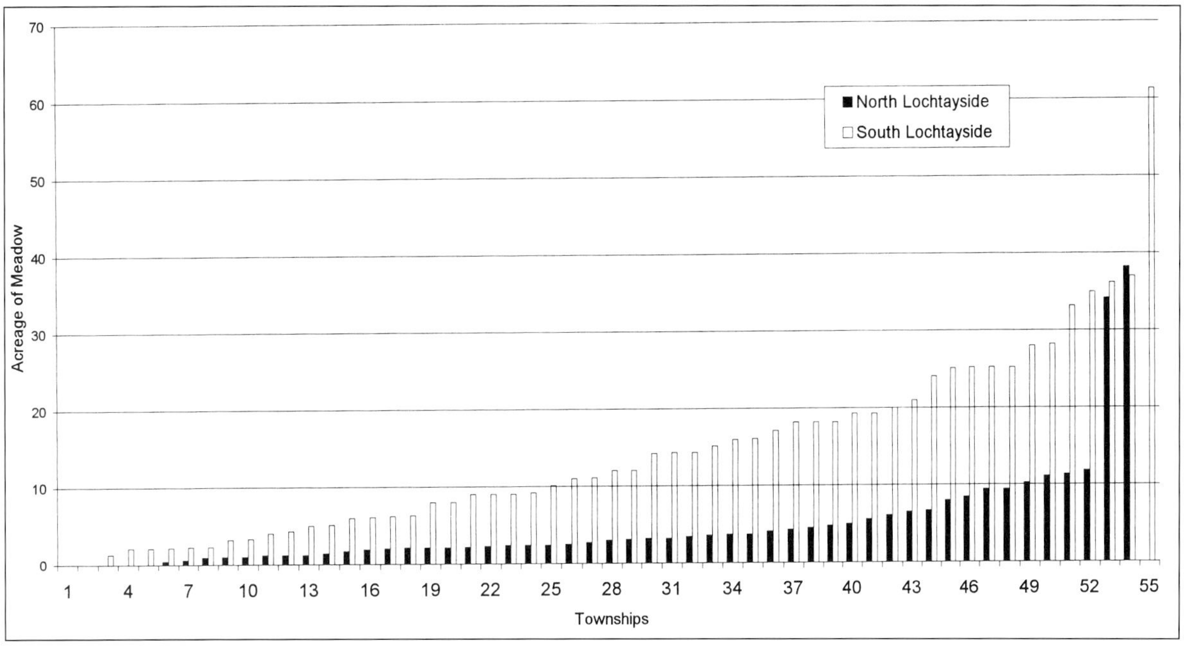

Fig. 6.2. Acreage of meadows in townships on Lochtayside, 1769.

standing crop itself was herb rich, an arable ecology encouraged by the relatively thin sowing of some pre-clearance arable. On Tiree, Duncan Forbes, writing in September 1737, put the crop:weed ratio on arable at 1:10.[10] He was probably exaggerating, but there is a sense in which the difference between arable and herb-rich pasture may have been one of degree, rather than an absolute distinction in pre-clearance times.

Turning to the question of stock composition, some commentators, possibly in an attempt to emphasise the transformative effects of the Clearances, have represented pre- and post-clearance stocking as a contrast between cattle and sheep. In fact, such a simple contrast is wrong. Prior to the clearances, most townships maintained a range of stock: cattle, sheep, horses and goats (see Fig. 6.3). This is important to keep in mind as the ecological effects of mixed grazing were quite different to those of mono-grazing owing to the different grazing habits of stock. Mixed stock grazing favours species-rich pasture, whereas mono-grazing by sheep does not. The latter can lead to species-poor grassland owing to their selective grazing and close cropping of herbage, with species like *Nardus* and *Molinia* tending to replace *Festuca*, *Agrostis* and *Calluna*.

Detailed township-level data on stock composition are available for parts of both the Argyll and Breadalbane estates for the late sixteenth to the early seventeenth century. They show cattle as a significant, but by no means dominant, demand on grazing. As well as being a source of manure, their customary use was for milk, cheese and butter with relatively little use being made of their meat, at least by ordinary tenants. Herds were inevitably organised around breeding cows with an annual calving rate of one for every two cows.[11] The importance of arable meant that horses also represented a significant claim on grazings, with mainland townships making more use of horse-drawn ploughs than parts of the west. In the latter though, the Uists and Tiree maintained a notoriously heavy number of horses owing to their use for carting seaweed.[12] In some cases, such as on islands like Mull and in the extreme north-western Highlands, horses or garrons were also bred for use in the Lowlands.[13] Though sheep and goats were numerically important, they played a lesser role in the livestock economy when weighted as a claim on grazing.

Overall, two adjustments are detectable to this pattern of stocking in the century or so before the Clearances. First, from the early seventeenth century onwards, we find lean beasts being driven out of the region on an increasing scale (Dodgshon 1998b, pp. 133-4). In response, a small number of townships began to specialise in cattle.[14] By the early eighteenth century, three or four decades before the Clearances began, there are even signs that local areas close to the southern margins of the Highlands had started to specialise in cattle. Viewing the region as a whole, though, the typical pre-clearance township still maintained cattle, sheep and horses. Second, by the early eighteenth century, some estates banned the keeping of goats because it conflicted with their growing concern for the economic potential of woodland.[15]

Some of these broad areal differences in stocking and in the use of meadows were underpinned by differences in farming strategy.

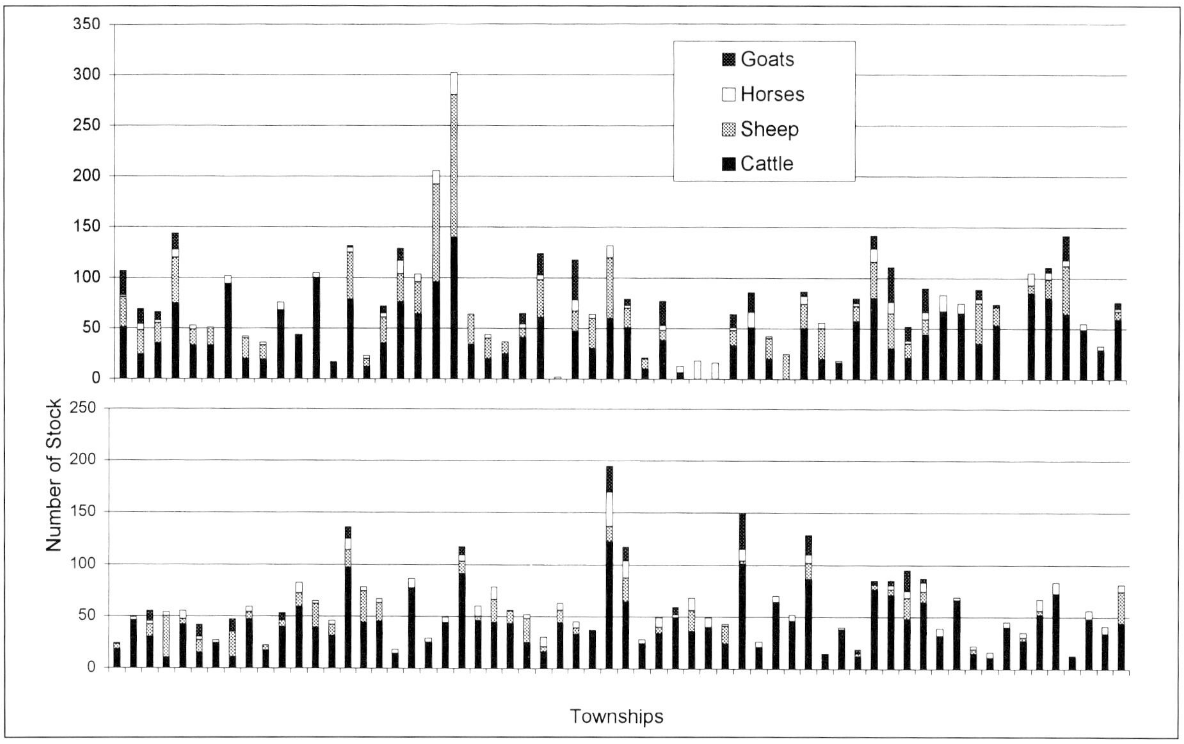

Fig. 6.3. Livestock in Highland townships: Lorne and Knapdale, 1609.

In the main body of the Highlands, the attention given to arable meant that — whatever their role as a source of meat, dairy produce or raw materials — stock had value as a source of manure. Apart from the reuse of thatch, or the turf cut at the expense of pasture and incorporated into house walls and dykes, such areas had no other form of manure. Their dependence on stock manure is really underlined by the fact that the mainland was characterised by infield-outfield cropping, a system that combined the use of winter manure (=infield) with the use of summer manure (=outfield). In addition to the manure produced by the grazing of the harvest stubble, the former relied on the indoor wintering of stock, with the manure produced over winter being composted with roof thatch and turf and spread over the infield in spring. Such a system created a demand for winter feed. The post-harvest grazing of stubble and the grass that lay between rigs provided only a partial solution to this problem.[16] Further, the higher frequency of low temperatures and snow meant that whilst available good pasture may have offered sheltered ground, it did not offer much in the way of winter feed. For much of the winter, stock had to rely on what had been cut for hay as well as what might be gleaned from wood pasture, including young growth, bark and leaves as well as the under grass.[17] Not surprisingly, these are the areas for which evidence of meadows and hay production is most abundant, and for which early evidence of longhouses for indoor wintering is most abundant (Smith 1988; Stewart & Stewart 1988).

Yet despite the established use of hay as a winter feed in mainland areas, its supply was probably not sufficient. Local reports suggest that stock were so routinely underfed that many had difficulty walking to the fields in spring.[18] There were a number of reasons why feed was scarce. When compared to alpine systems, in which high pastures as well as low ground meadows were used, Highland hay production was limited. This was partly because Highland pastures, especially in the extensive wet heathland areas of the north-west and west, were not as productive of hay as Alpine pastures, but also, because other pressures were acting on the availability of hay meadows and on the labour needed to manage them. The fact that these were the areas that developed outfield systems is relevant here. Outfield depended on the summer manure provided by the nightly folding of stock on that part due to be cropped the following summer. Though providing the basis for an extension of arable, tathing created as many new problems as it solved at least from a grazing point of view. The very land used for outfield cropping was that which might otherwise have been used for hay production. Its cultivation, even for three or four years out of every nine or ten, probably reduced the output of the green pasture involved by as much as 40-50 *per cent*, if we allow for the slow natural recovery of the sward.[19] More serious, not only did tathing draw stock away from hill pastures at the very time of year when the grazing yield of such pastures was at its peak, it also drew labour away from the management of hay meadows.

Yet despite their limited capability for supporting stock over winter, some townships seem to have increased their stocking levels in the years immediately prior to the Clearances. They could only have done so by juxtaposing two extremes: exploiting the summer surge in grazing potential, with its rearing of lambs and vital output of milk, cheese, butter and wool (Gibson & Smout 1995, pp. 226-9), but allowing stock to waste over winter through a dearth of winter provision, a dearth brought about by the expansion of arable at the expense of better pasture. Even today, upland stock experience large seasonal fluxes in weight, losing anything up to a third in body weight between autumn and January/February, but these fluxes may have been exaggerated in pre-clearance times (Maxwell 1983; Russel 1983, pp. 221-2).

However, the range of stock maintained by townships and the relatively low stocking densities involved would have ensured a balanced ecological impact. Besides, other factors were probably at work to ensure that the pre-clearance use of hill pasture was a low-input/low output system. Undergrazed because of the relatively low stock numbers carried forward from winter, upland pastures would probably have yielded less, in terms of both biomass and what was digestible by stock, than if it was well grazed.[20] Not only were stock numbers low, but the organisation of grazing around the needs of arable (as in the outfield folds) and those of the shieling (for milking) prescribed the movement of stock and the time they were on hill pasture. However, the nightly herding of stock around shieling sites meant that there were areas where grazing was of greater intensity and where the enrichment of hill pasture through continuous manuring would have led to their greening (Miller 1967).

Townships further west, particularly in the Hebrides, followed a different strategy but it was still one in which the link between arable and pasture had ceased to be supportive. On many islands, a grass-arable system was combined with what, down to at least the early eighteenth century, was a system of outdoor wintering for stock.[21] Outdoor wintering stemmed from two factors. First, communities had access to seaweed as a manure, so that their reliance on livestock manure and indoor wintering of stock for this purpose was less.[22] As a manure, seaweed enabled the balance between arable and grass to be altered, so that Hebridean townships could crop more of their green pasture, a factor that explains why the local ratio of arable:green pasture leaned so much in favour of the former. Second, winters were milder so that more autumn and early spring growth was possible, especially on the machair. The very fragility of machair as an ecosystem and the heightened risks of erosion that followed any disturbance of its sandy soils made townships cautious about the cultivation of such ground, even during times of population pressure. Beyond what the machair provided,[23] supplementary feed for Hebridean stock was scarce. A commonly used fodder supplement was seaweed but little effort was made to cut hay prior to the 1730s.[24] Wood pasture was also limited, restricted to islands like Mull and, even there, increasingly barred to all stock and not just animals like goats.[25] On other islands, like Skye, reports speak of townships allowing stock to roam freely, foraging for themselves, throughout the winter months, a practice that limited timber re-growth.[26] Not surprisingly, these same reports also stress the extent to which stock were underfed, as on the mainland.[27]

THE CLEARANCES

The Clearances have been too easily presented as a sharp break in the social and economic history of the region. For some west Highland and Hebridean townships, those cleared late in the process, this was certainly the case. However, in many parts of the central and eastern Highlands, the areas that ultimately saw by far the greatest build-up of sheep numbers, the Clearances were a more gradual affair, whose impact on land use and whose ecological effects unfolded slowly.

We can substantiate this point in a number of ways. First, the scale of capital required to stock sheep farms was such as to make it difficult for tenants to raise the capital required. In part, this was why some tenancies were taken by sheep farmers from southern Scotland who had already adjusted to the capital needs involved. Another solution was for some early sheep farms to be let to more than one tenant, as with earlier runrig townships.[28] For these townships, the term clearance clearly needs to be used in a qualified way.

Second, early clearances in the southern and eastern Highlands did not lead to the wholesale transformation of land use. Where we can reconstruct the farm economy after clearance, we find that many continued to maintain a significant grain sector, much of the grain still being marketed. Even after being constituted as a sheep farm, for instance, Ledcharry and Edravinach in Glendochart grew sufficient grain to maintain the families of its two tenants and to sell 20 bolls of barley per year; the same was true of Duncrosg in Glenlochy.[29] Seen another way, the continuation of grain cropping on such a scale meant that many sheep farms did not — at first — use their arable to maximise the stock carried over winter by cropping for sown grasses and turnips, at least not on the scale that would have released the full summer carrying capacity of their hill ground.

Third, when we look at the post-clearance stocking of farms, we find that many in the southern and eastern Highlands still pursued mixed stocking policies. Sheep flocks were certainly increased in size, but we also find farms continuing to maintain cattle herds, or folds of cattle. For instance, in 1810, some years after their clearance, Ledcharry and Edravinach still maintained 24 milch cows and an equal number of followers, whilst Duncrosg maintained 25 and their followers.[30] If we note their sizeable arable sectors, with its ongoing need for draught horses, the range of stock present on these post-clearance farm would not have been radically different from that of the pre-clearance township.

Fourth, the Clearances involved more than the replacement of one kind of stock with another. They also involved increases in stocking density. Because of changes in the layout of farms, establishing comparable pre- and post-clearance stocking levels is not straightforward, but it can be done for a small sample of farms in Perthshire. These show post-clearance stocking increases over pre-clearance levels on the majority of farms as averaging nearly 200 *per cent* in terms of their soum weighting (see Fig. 6.4). However, some of the pre-clearance data used in the calculation are from the early eighteenth century and excludes any increase in stock numbers that may have taken place in the decades prior to the clearances. At the same time, some of the farms involved were those that show a higher level of stocking in the early seventeenth century when compared to the early eighteenth, so that part of any subsequent increase, whether pre- or post-clearance, might simply have been a recovery of levels already seen in the early seventeenth century. Seen in terms of LU/ha, the increases took levels from between 0.01-0.06/ha up to between 0.25-0.38/ha in the nine Perthshire townships for which this calculation can be made (see Table 1). But given that, in percentage terms, these townships probably did not experience the largest post-clearance increase in soum levels, these figures should be seen as probably representing an underestimate of average levels of post-clearance stocking densities.

There were a number of ways in which increased stocking densities were sustained. Better winter feed, through the use of sown grasses and fodder crops and the laying down of former outfield to permanent pasture, would each have contributed to an increased winter carrying capacity which, in turn, would have enabled more of the summer potential to be utilised. Certainly, many townships would have gained good pasture from the laying down of former outfield but, as noted above, the introduction of sown grasses and fodder crops spread slowly, with many sheep farms still cropping grain until the collapse of grain prices at the end of the Napoleonic Wars in 1815.

More gains would have been possible through structural change, with many estates combining high exposed farms with ones offering good wintering land within a single lease, so that their contrasting capabilities were used to better advantage. We need only work through rentals to see how quickly such pairings emerged in the decades that followed the early clearances.[31] Another particularly significant change was effected by enclosure. Good hill pasture grazed rotationally is substantially more productive of biomass, and more productive of that part of herbage which is of value to stock, than land grazed in an uncontrolled way (Russel 1983, pp. 21-38). There were obvious ways in which such control could be achieved. The physical enclosure of land was a prime means. Because the region was characterised by large estates, the *legal* enclosure of waste between different proprietors was not a prerequisite for its physical enclosure. Prior to the Clearances, though, many hill pastures and mountain ground were shared between townships within particular estates. Their division between

Fig. 6.4. Stocking levels on the Breadalbane estate: pre- and post-clearance.

different townships or farms, a process carried out by the estate and underway before the Clearances,[32] was essential if more intensive use was to be made of grazings via their subsequent physical enclosure. This physical enclosure was underway with the first clearances if not before. As a high-cost improvement, it was a slow, drawn-out process rather than a rapid one, progressing more quickly when profits were high, such as during the Napoleonic Wars, but slowing down when prices and profits fell.[33] Of course, for full advantage to be taken of enclosure, grazing practices also had to change. Though its documentation is not straightforward, the undifferentiated herds and flocks of the pre-clearance township gave way quickly to a more active use of hirsels, with flocks divided functionally.[34] More importantly, the pre-clearance organisation of stock movement around the constraints of outfield folding and shieling huts now gave way to a routine that emphasised the grazing needs of stock, so that stock were grazed more widely and for much longer on hill pastures and with more regard to the rotational grazing of land.[35] As they were brought together, all these changes would have contributed to a marked increase in the carrying capacity of hill land.

Yet though stocking densities were not yet maximised, and though stocking was still based on mixed flocks and herds, we already start to detect some ecological effects. One or two reports suggest that, across the southern Highlands, heather moors were in retreat by the 1790s.[36] The problem with these reports is that such a decline might be rooted in pre- as much as post-clearance change. Palynological work has suggested that the extent of heather may have been fluxing even in the century or so prior to 1800 (Stevenson & Birks 1995). Regular collapses in stocking levels as a result of winter storms,[37] or market-driven shifts in the local composition or density of stocking, could have played a part in this flux. Heather moor is a seral, not a climax vegetation, one that emerges between the clearance of forest and its recovery. However, if managed by both grazing and burning so as to ensure the constant re-growth of young heather, it can be stabilised. Its sustained presence in the pre-clearance landscape was due to such management. References to the burning of heather, 'making muir burne', can be extended back to at least the fifteenth century. The fact that it involved ordinary tenants acting on their own behalf is a sure sign that it was carried out as part of a grazing strategy, increasing the availability of fresh heather growth in spring, quite apart from any benefits that it offered for game birds.[38] But as an ecosystem, heather moor is sensitive to too much as well as too little grazing (Gimingham 1995, pp. 9-19; Armstrong & Milne 1995), and we cannot rule out the possibility that the changes in the extent of heather moor detectable by the 1790s were because the early clearances led to the local grazing out of heather by sheep.

CHANGES IN SHEEP FARMING DURING THE MID-NINETEENTH CENTURY

To understand how sheep farms in the Highlands continued to change, we need to understand the changing economic context of farming. The early spread of the clearances reflected the rising demand for sheep, a demand that had first affected the Southern Uplands and which, by the 1750–60s, had spread to the southern edges of the Highlands. Ultimately, though, what shaped land-use change was not simply the rising price of sheep and wool *per se*, but also their profitability relative to other items of farm output. What helped the switch into sheep in the 1750s and 60s was the growing profitability of sheep and wool relative to cattle. Had this not been the case, then, farms might have switched more and more to specialised cattle production as some were already doing so by the 1720s and 30s.

By the 1790s, the market for sheep and wool rose even more dramatically. However, the impact of increased prices was moderated by the fact that grain prices also rose. Farmers gained as much from cropping oats and barley, as from putting land under sown grasses and turnips. The collapse in prices that followed the end of the Napoleonic Wars in 1815 saw a significant degree of sectoral shifting, as farms concentrated increasingly on stock production and as more arable was devoted to stock maintenance and more grassland became sown. As part of this switch to improving winter feed, far greater was made of away-wintering, with animals being taken to nearby lowland farms for wintering,[39] enabling the more exposed farms to carry forward a much greater number of stock from winter to summer and enabling far higher summer densities of stock to be kept on the hills.

Another significant shift in profitability came in the 1860–70s, when sheep, lamb and wool prices all rose sharply (Dodgshon 1998a, p. 31). This had the effect of encouraging a still greater concentration on sheep farming, with many farms in the southern and eastern Highlands especially abandoning their residual interest in cattle production and concentrating exclusively on sheep (Macdonald 1872, pp. 45, 52). The combined effect of this, coupled with the greater use of arable for fodder that had developed over the 1820–50s, brought about a sharp rise in sheep numbers, one that was particularly apparent in those counties that ultimately experienced the greatest build-up of sheep: Argyllshire, Perthshire, Inverness-shire, and Sutherland. In each of these counties, sheep numbers more than doubled, 1850–70s (*ibid*., p. 65). Such scalar increases in stocking suggest that farms had effectively addressed the winter constraints on summer, either because they were now using arable for fodder or because they were wintering stock on lowland farms. Once such solutions were in place and prices rose, farmers could maximise the output of their hill ground. However, though sheep numbers doubled, it does not follow that levels of LU/ha also doubled in step. On many farms, part of the increase — probably as much as 50 *per cent* — was achieved by replacing cattle with sheep, so that we can only assume that the remaining 50 *per cent* stemmed from increased stocking levels. On this basis, LU/ha probably increased to between 0.3–0.6 LU/ha by the 1870s. Again though, the farms involved in this calculation did not see the highest levels of post-clearance stock increase and may provide only a lower estimate of the increases that had taken place in LU/ha by the 1870s.

Such scalar increases in stocking suggest that farms had managed to remove the constraint or bottleneck formerly imposed by their limited over-wintering capacity, either because they were now using their arable for fodder or because they were actively wintering stock on lowland farms. Either way, hill farms could now maximise their summer carrying capacity. The Clearances brought in larger breeds in place of native or indigenous breeds. Using weight data for Highland native breeds and for stock like the Blackface and Cheviot, we can assume as much as a 100 *per cent* increase in grazing need from this factor alone.[40] When we combine this weight gain with the growth in numbers, the increased grazing need over pre-clearance levels was between four and eight times. There were also critical changes in the age at which stock were sold. Progressively, the decades from the 1830s down to the 60s and 70s saw a fall in the age at which animals were sold off the farm. In the 1820s and 30s, it was common for animals not to be sold until they were four and five years old. By the 1860s and 1870s, animals were being sold by the time they were two years old, intensifying the turnover of stock.[41] Arguably, this increased the pressure on hill pasture since the annual weight gain of sheep is greater up to maturity than once maturity is reached (Black 1983, p. 33). Combined with the increase in sheep numbers, the intensification of output would have meant that significantly more nutrients were being extracted from hill pastures in say 1870 than in 1770.

CONCLUSION

In terms of land use, the growth of sheep production over the 1850s–70s completed the transformation started by the first wave of clearances back in the mid-eighteenth century. In place of a system that was essentially valley-based and geared more for arable output, with only limited use of its hill ground, it was now a system that maximised resource use across all sectors of the farm, high ground as well as low ground, in the interests of sheep production. Furthermore, the endemic conflict that had existed between the summer needs of an over-expanded subsistence arable sector and the winter needs of an under-resourced stocking sector was now resolved. Arable, supplemented more and more by off-farm wintering, was used to sustain the year-round capability of the farm's stocking capacity. Such a shift in the agro-ecology of farm production, with its more intensive use of sectors that had previously been only lightly exploited, was bound to have ecological effects. If the late eighteenth century provides the first references to the contraction of heather moor, mid-nineteenth century reports provide the first local references to a shift from species-rich to species-poor pasture (Latham 1883, pp. 185-6).

Such pasture degradation has been interpreted in different ways. One view is that it reflected changes in the nutrient status of upland pastures that had been brought about by the overgrazing of sheep. Recent research, though, suggests that the level of key nutrients like nitrogen and phosphorus that were extracted by sheep is more than outweighed by what is added to pastures through dry atmospheric deposition (Innes 1983; Smout 2000, pp. 125-6). Yet that said, we need to keep in mind that the amounts added by dry atmospheric deposition have increased significantly over the past century or so (Smil 1990). Prior to 1850, the levels involved and therefore the balance between the input by dry atmospheric deposition and what was extracted by sheep would have been different. Another explanation for pasture degradation lies in the grazing characteristics of sheep and cattle. Changes in LU/ha on the scale experienced by the Highlands during the Clearances are more than capable of changing the floristic composition of hill pastures simply because of the way cattle and sheep graze land (Dennis 1999, pp. 38-40). Once grazing levels reached 0.5 LU/ha, especially where such levels also involved mono-grazing by sheep, they were more than capable of reducing species-rich to species-poor pasture. Given that the increased sheep numbers of the 1860s and 70s appear to have produced stocking levels in excess of 0.5 LU/ha, and given that these levels were associated with the abandonment or reduction of cattle folds on many farms, we need not be surprised if this is the point when reports of pasture degradation appear in the contemporary literature.

ABBREVIATIONS

BBP *Report of the Commission of Inquiry into the Conditions of the Crofters and Cottars.*

SRO Scottish Record Office (National Archives of Scotland).

NOTES

1. The extent of cropping in Glenorchy is conveyed by lists of sowing in SRO, Breadalbane Muniments, GD112/16/13/2/1, Rental of Glenorchy, 1730.
2. The small islands off the southern and western coasts of Harris illustrate the degree to which every available patch was being cropped. A 1772 survey estimated that 15,000 out of 24,950 acres on the seven islands adjacent to Harris had been cultivated, see Dunvegan Castle, 1/466/24, Description and Survey of Harris, 1772. Data for Netherlorne is provided by Breadalbane Muniments, GD112/9/1/3/43, Calculation of the value of the farms of Netherlorne, 1730.
3. Inverary Castle, Argyll papers, Box 2531, Memorandum Anent Tirie; *ibid.*, Memorandum of the Rentall of the East End of Tirii, 1662.
4. Smith 1896, appendix; SRO, Breadalbane Muniments, GD112/9/1/3/43, Calculation of the Value of the Farms of Netherlorne, 1730; *ibid.*, GD12/16/12/3/1, Rentall of Glenorchy Showing the present rent ... Holdings and Sowings, 1730; McArthur 1936, pp. 75-207; SRO, RHP 8826/2, General Description of the Island of Tirie, 1768; Brodick, Arran Estate Office, John Burrel, vol. I, 1766–1773, pp. 144-6.
5. Tiree soum data can be found in McNeill (1897, VII. 647-8; Inveraray Castle, Argyll Papers, Box 2531, Rentall of Tirie 1680; SRO, RHP 8826/2, General Description of the Island of Tiriy, 1768.
6. Figures based on a comparison between SRO, Breadalbane MSS, GD112/12/1/2/1, The Soums of Glenorchy in Sir Duncan's Time; *ibid.*, GD112/16/13/2/1, Rentall of Glenorchy, 1730.
7. Inverary Castle, Argyll papers, Box 2531, Memorandum Anent Tirie; *ibid.*, Memorandum of the Rentall of the East End of Tirii, 1662.
8. The correlation in 1680 was +0.94 and in 1768, +0.74.
9. The drift from 2 to 2.32 soums could be explained by the fact that the island had fewer bolls of sowing in 1768 than in 1541, largely because arable, including an entire township, had been destroyed by coastal storms, with some land being completely eroded and other land being buried under blown sand. Indeed, 10 *per cent* fewer bolls were sown on the island in 1768 compared to 1680. However, the drift in correlation at a township level was also because of the way a small handful of landholders had accumulated soums at the expense of other landholders.
10. Contained in a letter on the condition of the Duke of Argyll's estate on Tiree, Morvern and Mull, 24 Sept, 1737, that was published in BPP 1884, pp. 32-9, 389-92. An equally graphic description of how much fields were as much about weeds as about the growing crop is also well made by Marshall's description of the problem in the central Highlands. 'Oats', he wrote, were 'universally, hid under a canopy of weeds in blow; the wild mustard and the corn marigold predominant; the spurrey, corn scabious, and the thistle were next in prevalency; with a numerous tribe of minor weeds ... Some of the oats ... overcame the weeds and, in their turn, overtopped them; thus gaining the appearance of a tolerable crop' (see Marshall 1794, pp. 38-9).
11. This is put explicitly by a note on Coigach, with the value of farms being ascertained 'by the number of Milk Cows it can maintain thro' the Year, as the Following to these are generally understood being one Calf for every two Milk Cows, so whatever number of Milk Cows the farm keeps they Rear half that number of Calves, so that the Stocking of Black Cattle on the Farm, are year olds, two years olds, three year olds, & four year olds with what Horses, Sheep & Goats are necessary for such a Farm': SRO, Forfeited Estates Papers, E746/166.
12. Macdonald Trust, Armadale, RH2/8/24, John Blackadder's Description and Valuation of Lord Macdonald's estates of Sky and North Uist, 1799 and 1800, p. 122, refers to 'the grazing of so many useless Horses on every one of the Farms' on North Uist; SRO, RHP 8826/2, General Description of the Island of Tirie, 1768.
13. *Old Statistical Account of Scotland*, 6 (1791-99), p. 285.
14. Breadalbane stocking figures for 1727 suggest that some parts of the estate, mainly on either side of Loch Tay, may have concentrated their soumings on cattle, plus the horses needed to work arable (see Dodgshon, 1998b, p. 179).
15. The banning of goats in Morvern in 1733 was typical, see Inverarary Castle, Argyll MSS, Bundle 663, Instructions by his Grace the Duke of Argyll to Mr. Campbell of Airds, factor of Morvern, 1733.
16. The value of grass that lay in between arable rigs is highlighted by a Skye source that carefully regulates how much stubble a person leaving a tenancy was entitled to, and then laid down the scale of fine if such a person breached the regulation 'by the cutting of grass in the furrows'; see SRO, Mackenzie Muniments, GD403/40/1-2, Meeting of the Justices of the Peace for Skye, 1788.
17. We do not find references to stock being fed harvested leaves or bark, though such foddering must have been practised, but we can find many references to stock eating young tree growth, leaves and bark where they had access to wood pasture. For instance, a 1783 report dealing with Inveriger, beside Loch Tulla on Rannoch, talks about sheep being 'Great Enemys to trees of very kind & eat up every young firr that appears'. The same report talks about stock on the farm of Degnish having some young oaks 'Stinted in their growth by Cattle eating & croping them', see, Breadalbane MSS, GD112/16/10/2/3, Report of the Situation of Lord Breadalbane's Woods in Argyllshire, 1783. References to sheep and cattle destroying woods also occur in GD112/16/10/2/20, Survey of Woods and Plantations, 1792, whilst a report on woods in Glenorchy, 1793, still reported wild goats as 'peeling' trees, see GD112/16/10/2/23. For relevant comment on the problems created for stock by the enclosure of woodland over the mid-eighteenth century, see Smout 2000, pp. 57-8.
18. Reports of stock being carried to the fields and the high death rate of stock during winter were, of course, closely connected. Grant estimated that one in five farm animals died through starvation over winter (Handley 1953, p. 69). See also, Sinclair, ed, *Old Statistical Account of Scotland*, 8, 1791-99, p. 338, and its story that one landowner in Glenorchy lost over 200 cattle through starvation in the bad winter of 1744.
19. Of course, the manure provided through tathing would have left some residual enrichment for the pasture phase of the outfield cropping cycle.
20. This point is made by Russel (1983, pp. 21-38 but especially p. 225). The key to its maximum exploitation was a regular cycle of grazing and rest. Traditional communities must have understood the basic principle here for grass was hained, but not on a cyclical basis. See, for example SRO, John MacGregor Collection,

GD50/136/1 Court book of Menzeis aand Rannoch, which, in 1660, bound tenants at Weem to 'keep ther tath grass for ane monethes speace': this must have been common for outfield-based cropping systems.

21. For instance, Inveraray Castle, Argyll MSS, Vol. 65, Observations on Tiry by Doctor Walker, 1764, reported that cattle range the fields all year round 'having neither Stables or Cow houses, collect no Dung'; see also, SRO, RHP 8826/2, General Description of the Island of Tiriy, 1768. Walker also made it clear that horses and cattle were out-wintered on Skye also (see McKay 1980, pp. 208-9). On Lewis, Donald Monro reported that 'thair is mony scheip' and that they 'ly furth evir on mures and glennis, and enteris nevir in ane house' (see Munro 1961, p. 87). Even parts of the west coast mainland, wintered stock outdoors. In Barrisdale, for instance, it was said 'Their Black cattle & Sheep feed in the hills all the year round', SRO, Forfeited Estates Papers, E788/42, Report on the estates of Barrisdale and Kinlochmoidart, *c.* 1755.
22. Walker provides abundant reference to the early use of seaweed as manure (for example, McKay 1980, pp. 55, 65, 77 and 88).
23. McKay (1980, p. 75) has a fine description of the productivity of machair on South Uist. The most graphic description of its fertility though, is provided by an anonymous late sixteenth-century report on the Hebrides. Talking about the extensive machair of Tiree, it describes it as so productive that cows were 'milkit four times in the day'! See, 'The description of the Isles of Scotland', in Skene 1980, vol. 1, appendix iii, p. 438.
24. See, for example, Martin 1982, p. 269; he talks about the cattle and horses on Tiree being 'of a very low size ... being in the Winter and Spring-time often reduc'd to eat Sea Ware'. In his discussion of adjacent Coll, Dr Walker describes seaweed as the 'Article of the principal Sustenance of the Cattle in Winter' (McKay 1980, p. 173). Other references occur *Old Statistical Account of Scotland*, 13 (1791–99), p. 301; 14 (1791–99), pp. 121 and 340; and 8 (1791–99), p. 368.
25. Mull especially, had more woodland than most Hebridean islands, but the Lochbuie estate became very careful to control their use by the late eighteenth century, particularly by stock. See SRO, Lochbuie Papers, GD174/827, Interrogatorys to be put to the Tenants, 1782.
26. An Act of Parliament was passed in 1686 requiring all townships to regulate or herd their stock over winter but Highland communities, especially, were notorious for not herding down into the eighteenth century.
27. See, for example, Macdonald Trust, Armadale, RH2/8/24, John Blackadder's Description and Valuation of Lord Macdonald's estates of Sky and North Uist, 1799 and 1800, p. 15 and 77-8; GD221/4440/1, observations on an expedition to the island of Sky, 1799; GD221/4222, Memd. about the State of Skye, 1808 (McKay 1980, p. 187).
28. Examples are provided by SRO, Breadalbane MSS, GD112/16/13/4/9, Report Relative to Sundry farms belonging to the Right Honourable the Earl of Breadalbane By Robert Reid Surveyor, 1810.
29. SRO, Breadalbane MSS, GD112/16/13/4/9, Report Relative to Sundry farms belonging to the Right Honourable the Earl of Breadalbane By Robert Reid Surveyor, 1810.
30. *Ibid.*
31. A good illustration of the resource-based restructuring that followed the clearances is provided by Blaravon and Ardvrecknish in Glenorchy, which had the pendicle of Auchlader called Derrybeg given to it 'for wintering'. see SRO, Breadalbane Muniments, GD112/9/3/3/29 Rental of Earl of Breadalbane Estates in Argyllshire 1798–9. See also, *ibid.*, GD112/110/2/4/46, Note of Particulars regarding Farms on the Breadalbane Estate, 1840.
32. A good illustration of this process is provided by Arran. Tacks issued in the 1790s, like that for East Loch in 1795, required moors 'occupied in common' to be divided, Brodick MS, Printed Tack Agreement, 1795. The division of the common grazings in Trotternish and from Portree to Loch Sliaghan are documented by GD221/4208/1, Memorandum Lord Macdonald to his Chamberlain, 1806.
33. The physical enclosure of land in the Highlands has received surprisingly little comment. Youngson (1973, p. 168) estimated that barely one-tenth of all arable had been enclosed by the 1790s but does not hazard a guess as to how much pasture, including hill pasture, had been enclosed by then.
34. Some indication of the post-clearance organisation of sheep is detailed by NLS, Sutherland MSS, 313/993, Misc. estate management papers, 1808–1816.
35. The rotational grazing of grassland, with pastures rested on a 20-30 day rotation, is thought to increase digestible biomass by as much as 10x.
36. See, for example, *Old Statistical Account of Scotland* (1791–99), V. 465; *ibid.*, X111. 83. In some cases, the signs of decline were only apparent by the early 1840s, see, *New Statistical Account of Scotland* (1845), X. 310.
37. The general belief was that winter storms capable of devastating sheep flocks occurred with a frequency of one every twenty years.
38. The earliest reference is in a 1457 Act of Parliament, *Acts of Parliament of Scotland*, 11, p. 61. The regulation of muir burn was also a feature of local courts, such as the 1621 act issued by the laird of Glenorchy through his courts binding tenants 'to mak muirburne at na tyme in ony yeir cuming bot yeirly in the moneth of March, conform to the Act of Parliament, and that upone the Mount upon grass only, saffand hedder and young wood outwith the hills ...' (see Bowrie 1855, p. 352; see also Whyte 1979, pp. 96-8).
39. The use of off-the-farm wintering can be traced back to the decades immediately following the clearances. The farm of Benmore (Perthshire), for instance, was reported in 1810 to carry 2,100 sheep, as well as cattle, and was said to winter all its hoggs away, see SRO, Breadalbane MSS, GD112/16/13/4/9, Report Relative to Sundry farms belonging to the Right Honourable the Earl of Breadalbane By Robert Reid Surveyor, 1810. By the 1850s, such seasonal movement was widespread. Two 1857 surveys of ten sheep farms in Perthshire and highland Argyllshire, for example, named seven as wintering stock away, mainly hoggs and young sheep, see *ibid.*, GD112/16/14/7/8, Memorandaum Grazing Farms on the Breadalbane Estate out of lease 1857; *ibid.*, GD112/16/14/7/29, Note of the Particulars of Grazing Farms in Breadalbane to let, Whit. 1857. A listing of thirteen sheep farms, drawn up in 1863, reported ten of them as wintering their hoggs and other sheep away: thus, Lochs in Glenlyon, 'a very dangerous winter farm', needed, 'in addition to the hogs, a great part of the older sheep ... to be provided for off the farm during winter', GD112/16/14/8/13, Grazing Farms to let in Breadalbane, 1863.
40. Strictly speaking, there were two stages to this weight gain: one taking place when the old Hebridean or Highland sheep were replaced by the Blackface or Cheviot and the second, when the Blackface was replaced in some mainland areas by the still heavier Cheviot. The former began in the mid-eighteenth century but was an ongoing change that continued to occur down into the early nineteenth century as the clearances spread northwards and westwards. The latter was a shift that tended to occur more in the nineteenth century (see Gibson 1988, p. 169).
41. The shift in the balance of flocks towards ewes plus younger stock is well conveyed by a census of 'Forest' farms on the Breadalbane estate in 1861. Altogether, it listed 4,634 ewes, 186 tups, 57 four-year-old wedders, 17 three-year-old wedders, 1,066 two-year-old wedders, 1,539 one-year-old wedders, 53 tup hoggs, and 3,168 hoggs as well as 15 bullocks and 14 cows. See SRO, Breadalbane Muniments, GD112/16/14/8/3, Inventory and valuation of live and dead stock, 1861.

Parliamentary enclosure in the uplands

John Chapman

ABSTRACT

Parliamentary enclosure in the uplands has attracted relatively little research. The distinctive reasons behind enclosure in the uplands are examined, particularly the pressures facing the management of upland commons. The extent of parliamentary enclosure in upland areas of England and Wales is then assessed. The particular problems facing enclosure commissioners in upland areas are discussed and the extent to which enclosure actually led to land improvement.

KEYWORDS

Parliamentary enclosure, commons, enclosure commissioners, land improvement

INTRODUCTION

It is something of a cliché to begin any discussion of parliamentary enclosure in the uplands by lamenting the lack of previous work on the topic. Searle (1993), for example, does so in his article on Cumbria, and the current author made similar comments some thirty years ago in an article on the North York Moors (Chapman 1976). In reality, more research has been carried out than is often acknowledged. Some of the pioneer researchers in the early twentieth century made reference to it, notably Gonner (1912), and later studies cover areas as widely scattered as Cumbria (Dilley 1972; Searle 1993; Whyte 2000a), North Yorkshire (Chapman 1961, 1976), the West Riding (Crossley 1955), Derbyshire (Eyre 1957), and North and South Wales (Edwards 1963; Chapman 1972 and 1991b).

Having said this, there is little question that the topic has received less attention than it deserves. A disproportionate amount of the literature has focused on the enclosure of the open field arable, leaving common and waste as very much the poor relation (Chapman 1987; Kain, Chapman & Oliver 2004). Where due attention has been paid to the enclosure of the commons, for example by Neeson (1993), this has tended to focus on the lowland commons of midland England, and some of the conclusions reached reflect this bias.

Parliamentary enclosure, by definition, concerns only enclosures carried out under the direct authority of an act of parliament, either an individual private or local act or one of the general acts of the nineteenth century. It therefore excludes the large amount of enclosure carried out, legally or otherwise, without such authority. Non-parliamentary enclosures are beyond the scope of this chapter, but the author has recently offered an indication of the extensive nature of their significance (Chapman & Seeliger 2001; Kain, Chapman & Oliver 2004) and there can be no doubt about their impact in some upland areas. It is sufficient here to note that encroachment by local farmers contributed greatly to upland enclosure in some regions, and that the resulting patterns of small irregular fields form a characteristic feature of our upland landscapes (Chapman 1961, map 6).

Defining the 'uplands' from the point of view of parliamentary enclosure is not easy. It must be noted that Scotland is excluded, since the different legal system means that parliamentary enclosure, as normally defined, did not operate there, but both England and Wales were affected. In both, it was normal practice to cover all the open and common land in a manor, parish or township by a single act, thus reducing costs, but this often resulted in the incorporation of widely-differing types of land in one enclosure. Parishes, and even townships, were often large in northern England and in Wales, and might stretch from sea-level to the tops of neighbouring moorlands or mountains. The enclosure of Allerston, in the North Riding of Yorkshire, included lowland marshy commons and meadows alongside the River Derwent, a classic open field system grouped round a compact village, and a large area of wild common moorland. Similarly, that for Nevin in Caernarfonshire encompassed both small coastal commons and the mountain of Yr Eifl. Attempting to disentangle the 'upland' and 'lowland' elements in cases such as these can result in only a crude approximation, at least until every award has been examined and the detail extracted. Such a procedure is, in any case, open to methodological objections. Allerston's fields and meadows in the Vale of Pickering formed as much a part of a single agricultural system with its moorland commons as did, for example, the open fields of Westerdale, high in a moorland dale and ringed by heather-clad moors. 'Uplands', in this context, can therefore refer only to the general region within which the enclosure took place, and not to the situation of the individual pieces of land concerned.

The reasons why it was felt necessary to enclose the uplands differed significantly from many of those advanced for the enclosure of open fields. The abolition of fragmentation was not an issue: indeed, the enclosure of large moorland areas often led to increased fragmentation of many farms, since it was physically impossible to locate allotments adjacent to the existing farm unit. Similarly, the shortage of pasture quoted in some lowland acts, stressed by Turner (1980, pp. 135-51) as a major reason for early enclosures in the midlands, had no relevance here. On the other hand, a feeling that the great tracts of moorland were a wasted resource, and one that urgently needed to be exploited, was undoubtedly in the forefront of the minds of contemporaries. Those taking a broad national view saw it as essential that Britain should increase its productive acreage, both to provide extra food for the growing population and to provide extra work in the rural areas; local landowners and farmers saw increased profits from reclaiming the land and putting it to more intensive use. The former often had highly optimistic views on the potential reclaimable areas: the author of the Board of Agriculture Report for North Wales felt that 35,000 acres (14,164 ha) could be reclaimed in Merioneth alone (Davies 1813), and a Commons Select Committee (House of Commons 1844, p. iii) stated that 'it appears, by the evidence of competent and experienced Witnesses, that a large portion of the Waste Land of the Kingdom is capable of profitable cultivation or other improvement'. The latter made careful calculations of the likely profits. The Crown agent at Cloughton and Scalby, Yorkshire, produced a detailed valuation of the predicted Duchy of Lancaster allotments of field land and common waste, and foresaw an increase in the rental value of the estate from £302 per year to £856.[1] Similarly, Peter Nightingale, lord of the manor at Dethick, Lea and Holloway, Derbyshire, calculated that the enclosure of the commons would leave him with an estate worth £2,539 after paying £200 as his share of the expenses.[2]

There were potential uses of the enclosed uplands, other than purely agricultural, which must have encouraged some landowners, especially in the nineteenth century. Forestry was increasingly seen as a profitable use of such areas, but was impossible to carry out effectively unless stock could be excluded. More significant still in many uplands was the rising popularity of grouse shooting. The social and political significance of being able to invite influential guests to a private shoot was initially far more important than the commercial value to be obtained by letting out the rights, but in neither case was much benefit to be gained unless the owner had the sole rights to take game. The significance of this is apparent at Lockton Moor, where grouse shooting had become a free-for-all due to the lack of clearly-defined common rights, causing one irate landowner to write to demand a speedy conclusion of the enclosure in order to put a stop to it.[3]

There were other, more negative, reasons why enclosure might seem attractive to the legitimate right owners, for there is ample evidence that many were gaining little or nothing from their existing rights. John Tuke, a highly-regarded contemporary observer, notes of the North York Moors that

> the pasturage of these moors and pastures, while they are common, is in general monopolized by a few individuals, some of whom occupy but small farms, consequently their right upon the wastes ought to be in proportion to them. These people, about Midsummer, go to the fairs in the north, where they buy large flocks of Scotch wethers, to turn upon the commons, which they so effectively eat up, that the regular breeding stocks of the country cannot be maintained to advantage, and therefore have greatly declined (Tuke 1800, p. 198).

The right owners of Kirkbymoorside had been complaining about such problems since at least 1592, when they petitioned the Crown, as lord of the manor, to take action against squatters who were settling on the common and making use of its resources,[4] and they were by no means alone in their concerns. Such incidents were widespread in both time and space.

More overtly threatening or violent incidents were also widespread. Charles Mickleburgh of Montgomery, a well-known enclosure commissioner, asserted that sheep-stealing was prevalent on the open moors in his district, whereas it was rare on enclosed land (House of Commons 1844, p. 179), and that enclosure would therefore greatly reduce the problem. The practice of 'dogging', using dogs illegally to drive animals off the commons, was another problem which occurred widely on open moors. The Revd Thomas Williams reported this from Ystradgynlais, admitting that his own herdsman indulged in it on his behalf and the Revd Carus-Wilson recorded its use in Westmorland and in the Yorkshire Pennines. The sheep were often driven many miles away in the wrong direction, and might be injured, lost, or even killed in the process. Though much of this activity was by legitimate right owners acting against illegally depastured stock, this was not always the case. Some individuals deliberately dogged the stock of legitimate owners, and were quite prepared to use terror tactics to discourage other users.

Williams recorded that when one of the perpetrators was caught in the act, the stock-owner was too terrified to prosecute, and a Mr Elam noted that when a tenant of his at Dent caught a man dogging his sheep the incident ended in fight (Commons Select Committee 1844, pp. 124-41). These problems were given as a major reason why such upland commons needed to be enclosed, and it was stressed that it was small farmers, without the resources to keep a constant watch on their stock, who were being deterred from using them. Williams admitted that he was getting more than his fair share of the grazing because he could afford a herdsman, and that his share at an enclosure would be less.

Other rights were often of less value than might at first appear, especially compared with their lowland equivalents. The picture painted by the Hammonds (1911, I. 24, 102) and others of cottagers and the landless casually gathering brushwood for fuel may possibly be valid for some lowland commons, but it certainly did not apply to all upland ones. Quite apart from the firm prohibition imposed on some manors (as will be discussed later), the distances involved, and the difficulties of the physical environment, placed severe restrictions on those without substantial resources. At Lockton the peat deposits were a minimum of 3.5 miles (5.6 km) from the village, and reaching them involved a steady climb of 300 feet (91 metres), followed by a very steep descent of 200 feet (60 metres), the whole journey to be repeated in reverse laden with the fuel. Quite how anyone without access to carts and a good team of horses could exploit such resources is difficult to see. Such difficulties were, of course, not universal in all upland communities, but nor were they unique. Contemporaries from many upland areas speak of the worthlessness of fuel rights to the poor due to the same factors (House of Commons 1844, pp. 128-33).

In the circumstances, it is hardly surprising that the stereotype of the lord forcing through parliamentary enclosure in the teeth of opposition from the tenants and small landowners does not hold good.[5] Searle (1995) strongly supports the view that the customary tenants took a leading role in the initiation of parliamentary enclosure in Cumbria.

As a general rule, it is fair to say that upland parliamentary enclosures tended to occur towards the later stages of the movement, during the nineteenth century. For this there were at least two reasons. Firstly, the potential value of much of the land involved was relatively low, and the problems of both enclosing and reclaiming it relatively high. As a consequence, for any given region, upland enclosures tended to lag behind those of lowland, and particularly open field, ones (Chapman 1987, pp. 32-5). Secondly, the parliamentary enclosure movement tends to show a diffusion process, spreading from a core in Leicestershire and Northamptonshire. Since the uplands, by and large, are concentrated in the north and west of the country, this in itself would tend to ensure that the idea of parliamentary enclosure would reach them relatively late in the process. However, it must be appreciated that parliamentary enclosure was never subject to any central planning, and that it was always initiated by those with a direct stake in the community concerned. The pattern is therefore not entirely logical. In Northumberland, for example, six of the eight enclosure acts before 1760 were concerned solely with common and waste, and one of the other two, Gunnerton, enclosed more common than field. Much of this common and waste was upland, and in three of the parishes involved, Hexham, Simonburn, and Haltwhistle, there was open field land that was enclosed by much later acts.

The total amount of land affected by parliamentary enclosure in England remains a matter of controversy, so that putting a precise total to the proportion lying in the uplands is impossible. Apart from the problems of definition already discussed, such figures as are available are not to be trusted. The inaccuracies of the estimates given in the acts and awards are well known (see Chapman & Harris 1982), and these apply with particular force in the uplands, where many of the moorlands were not measured accurately until late in the nineteenth century. As a result, figures for large areas of common waste are the least likely to be accurate, and are the most likely to omitted completely from the preambles to both acts and awards. At Mochdre, Montgomeryshire, the actual amount involved seems to have been just over half the estimated 20,000 acres (8,093 ha), while conversely at Hope, which straddled the English-Welsh border, Turner (Tate & Turner (1978, p. 78) gives a figure of 6,000 acres (2,428 ha) and Evans (1983–4) 4,053 acres (1,628 ha), against only 3,500 acres (1,416 ha) in the act. Missing figures are often very large. The act for Llanarmon-yn-Iâl, Denbighshire, was doubtless accurate, but hardly precise, in estimating that the commons to be enclosed were 'of considerable extent', and at Llanymynech, where no comment at all was made, the actual area turned out to be 22,770 acres (9,214 ha).

In these circumstances, working from the act or award estimates is particularly dangerous. In the very large northern English or Welsh parishes, it is often difficult to tell whether any of the land concerned could reasonably be described as upland, or to make any acceptable guess at the amount. For these reasons, use has been made of a 10 *per cent* stratified random sample of all parliamentary awards, totalling every single allotment and noting its location, as far as the maps and documents allow.[6] While this method has its own problems, and the documentation is not always as accurate or complete as one might wish, it does allow a distinction to be made between upland and lowland enclosure, and direct comparison between them on a consistent basis.

From this it would seem that fifty-one of the 535 English enclosures sampled fell within what might be somewhat subjectively defined as 'The Upland Regions', and sixteen of the twenty-four Welsh. Taking the English figures first, the numbers of individual enclosures give a misleading impression, for though the fifty-one upland enclosures account for less than 10 *per cent* of the sample, they make up 22.38 *per cent* of the sample acreage. This would imply that something of the order of 1.7 million acres (687,952 ha) of the land affected by parliamentary enclosure could be classified as falling within the uplands. Of this, just over 3.2 *per cent* appears to have consisted of common field or common meadow, and therefore may be presumed to have fallen within the valleys or other lowlands within the region, though there is a need to be wary of terminology in such cases. Any land physically fenced off from the open moor, but still subject to common rights, was liable to be described as 'a common field' in north Yorkshire and Cumbria, and probably elsewhere as, for example, in the description of Raw Pasture in the Fylingdales Enclosure Act so it is possible that some of this land was at a high level, and was in no sense common field as understood in midland England. As for the common and waste, which made up almost 97 *per cent* of the total, (2,350 acres, 951 ha), or 1.37 *per cent*, can be specifically identified as lowland pasture, but the overwhelming majority of the rest seems to have been open moorland, though not necessarily at very high altitude. Given the potential sampling error, this small area of lowland common can be ignored for all practical purposes: the sampling error is discussed in Chapman (1991a).

For Wales, it is possible to make a rather more direct calculation of the totals, since almost all the extant awards have been examined and the remainder estimated with, it is hoped, some precision (Chapman 1992). Again, definitions are somewhat subjective, particularly along the border with England and in the Clwydian Range in North Wales, where enclosures tend to cover a considerable height range, but a total of just under 443,400 acres (161,760 ha), or just over 84 *per cent* of the land enclosed by act in Wales may be regarded as falling within the upland parts of the Principality. In total, therefore, about 2,150,000 acres (870,057 ha) of land within the uplands of England and Wales was affected by the parliamentary movement. The Welsh total consisted almost entirely of common waste. Although common field was not lacking in Wales, much of the field enclosed by act lay in lowland Monmouthshire, and less than 0.01 *per cent* of the land in the upland areas seems to have consisted of field and meadow. To all intents and purposes, therefore, this can be ignored. As for the proportion of 'lowland' common included in the total, this is probably a little higher than that for England, but again, is not of such size as to seriously affect the results.

The precise terms under which any parliamentary enclosure was carried out were determined by the local parties involved, for it was they who drew up the individual private act and incorporated such clauses as they felt appropriate. Parliament increasingly introduced rules to combat various abuses of the process and to accord with changing views as to the rights of the general public over common land, but made no attempt to enforce a standard pattern until 1845. In that year they passed a General Enclosure Act setting up a central Inclosure Commission, with responsibility for approving and overseeing all new enclosure proposals, but even then limited local variations were permitted (see Straughton, this volume).

This freedom to modify the details of the enclosure process was of special importance in the uplands. The sheer size of many upland commons, and their hostile physical environment, encouraged adaptations of the conventional parliamentary enclosure process. The promoters were often aware that attempting to swallow up the whole moor at a single gulp might defeat them, and that parts might prove uneconomic to tackle. As a consequence, either partial or permissive enclosures were sometimes adopted. In both cases, the whole of the area concerned was specified in the act, but the moor was to be divided into two areas, a 'better' and a 'poorer'. A value of three shillings per acre was normally set as the dividing line, anything judged to be worth less being regarded as of dubious potential for reclamation. In practice, the precision with which this division took place varied greatly. It was often based on traditional named areas, with the 'High Moor' being regarded *in toto* as of low value and the 'Low Moor' as worthy of compulsory action. In contrast, the maps for Pickering and Kirkbymoorside, both permissive enclosures, reveal complex divisions cutting across the various named areas, and showing all the signs of a serious attempt at valuation.

In partial enclosures, the commissioners were given powers simply to exclude from the division any land that they did not consider worth improving, and this was left subject to communal grazing, with specified stints for each legitimate owner (see Straughton, this volume). The creation of small communal pastures, to be shared by a group of smallholders, was not infrequent in the lowlands as a device to avoid the costs of fencing small and almost useless plots, and similar small-scale arrangements occur in the uplands. At Burton in Kendal, for example, the commissioners created two stinted pastures, of 96.5 acres (35 ha) for Burton and 68.75 acres (27.8 ha) for Holme, out of a total area of 1,489 acres (602.5 ha). However, what is significant in the uplands is its use for substantial acreages of open moor where the allotments would not have been small had the owners been given their entitlement. While this avoided forcing the owners to undertake major expenditure with little prospect of profit it left a twofold problem for the future. Firstly, its success depended on the ability of the commissioners to make an accurate valuation of land which had normally received little attention, and which might have suffered degradation due to misuse. Secondly, by the eighteenth century relatively little of the uplands of England and Wales were physically incapable of being upgraded. The judgement was therefore essentially an economic one, dependent on the state of farming when the assessment was made. Land unlikely to give an economic return prior to the Napoleonic wars might do so during them, for example, and land valued at under three shillings an acre immediately prior to the Wars might well exceed that figure ten years later. Owners could therefore find themselves in the position of wishing to reclaim more land but needing a second act of Parliament to overturn the decisions taken under the first. Such a situation arose, for example, at Middleton-in-Teesdale in 1805, where an earlier act of 1785 had enclosed 1,996 acres (808 ha) but left a further 7,228 acres (2,925 ha) as open moorland. The owners now wished to enclose parts of the latter, but needed a further act to over-ride the original provisions.[7] Similarly, the initial Lockton act of 1784 enclosed only those parts of the moor south of certain ancient metes and bounds, and a parliamentary order was necessary in 1866 to allow the proprietors to tackle the rest.

An answer to this problem was to allot all the land, but to make the enclosure of all or part permissive. The permissive area was stinted, and remained as common pasture, but each owner was empowered to enclose all or any part of his allotment when he wished, surrendering the appropriate proportion of his stints at the same time. The system was simple, flexible, and capable of being highly responsive both to changes in farming prosperity in general and to the specific financial circumstances of the individual. Why it was not more widely adopted is unclear. Some commissioners, such as the highly-experienced George Maxwell, argued strongly against it (House of Commons 1799–1800), but Maxwell's experience was restricted to lowland eastern England, where its benefits were less obvious. What is more surprising is that landowners and commissioners in upland areas failed to use it even when they must have been familiar with it from neighbouring parishes, or ones where they had interests or had worked. As has been noted elsewhere (Chapman 1976, pp. 8-10), only eight out of twenty-three parliamentary enclosures in the southern North York Moors made use of it, and landowners such as Sir Charles Duncombe were involved simultaneously in compulsory and permissive enclosures. The full extent of its use is difficult to determine, since it was not necessarily mentioned in the acts. The commissioners were usually left with the final responsibility for the fencing rules, and it was they, in consultation with, or under pressure from, local landowners, who were responsible for making fencing permissive. At Slayley, Northumberland, for example, the act makes no reference to permissive enclosure, but the commissioners determined that in certain named areas fences should not be compulsory. The idea was certainly used in North Wales (Edwards 1963), in Cardiganshire, and, in very different circumstances, for open field land in Berkshire, but it appears to have reached its maximum extent in the North York Moors.

Legally, once an act had been passed, or an order obtained, responsibility for the proper conduct of an enclosure rested with the commissioners, or valuers, as their successors under the act of 1845 were called. Other officials might be influential, notably the solicitor to the enclosure, or might carry out significant parts of the work, especially the surveyor, but it was the commissioners who were responsible for ensuring that the lands were fairly allocated in proportion to the valid claims. They were also normally responsible for deciding which claims were valid and which not, though their decisions were open to appeal, either to the Quarter Sessions or, sometimes, to arbitrators. The number of commissioners employed varied, but three became the norm during the later eighteenth and early nineteenth centuries, with later enclosures usually being entrusted to a single individual. Often one commissioner acted also as the surveyor, thus increasing their control over the process even more.

As was normal for the whole parliamentary enclosure process, the commissioners were drawn primarily from the local area, at least until the later nineteenth century. Thus, those operating in Cumbria almost all came from Cumberland and Westmorland, or from the immediately adjoining areas of the north Pennines in Yorkshire. Similarly, the commissioners in Wales were recruited largely from Wales itself or from the neighbouring English counties along the Welsh border. The local proprietors who nominated the commissioners were, not surprisingly, suspicious of people who they did not know, since they had no means of judging their fairness or competence. At Broughton-in-Furness, Lancashire, the proprietors voted 33 to 3 in favour of

John Slater, from nearby Hawkeshead, against the far more experienced Makin Durham of Thorne in south Yorkshire. The logic was not just that a local would be less expensive and his reputation more likely to be well known to the bulk of the proprietors, but that he presumably had some knowledge of the local customs and environment on which his judgements would have to be based. However, commissioners were not necessarily locally born and bred, nor did they specialise in upland enclosures as such. Two major commissioners in North Wales, Richard Wakeford Attree and John Maughan, both gained their initial experience in Hampshire and the Home Counties respectively, before taking up residence at Ruabon (Attree) and at Oswestry (Maughan).

The task facing commissioners in the uplands was often particularly difficult, not merely because of the sheer size of commons concerned. As with any common and waste enclosure, there was a problem of multiple usage and conflicting rights that did not normally exist with open field or meadow. Field land was held in known proportions by specific individuals, and all legal rights derived directly from this, so that there was usually no problem in deciding the specific shares due to each owner. Any given piece of common, on the other hand, might serve a whole range of different persons, each with different rights over the same area. The precise nature, extent, and limitations (if any) of such rights was a matter of local custom, and at enclosure the commissioners had to determine not only who was legally entitled to which rights, but also what proportion of the land to be allotted was a fair compensation for each type of right. An individual who owned half the pasture rights could not be given half the common if other individuals owned, for example, fuel rights over the same area.

The difficulties were often further complicated by the practice of intercommoning, whereby a given area of moorland was open to the stock of several parishes or townships. This was not unique to the uplands, but was far more widespread there, and the boundaries between the various townships, parishes, or other units were often not properly defined. Since rights were normally held to derive from property owned in a particular manor, the amount of enclosed land allotted to any individual would be determined by the total acreage of moor in that manor divided by the percentage of the total allowable claims from that same township. The way in which manorial boundaries were drawn could therefore make a significant difference to the amount any individual received, and the determining of these boundaries was often a commissioner's first task. The Wombleton, Nawton and Harome enclosure is a case in point, since the commissioners had to begin by making a formal division of the moor between the townships of Wombleton and Harome before they could decide how much land was available for division between the right owners in each.

Even if the outer boundaries were firmly established, there remained the question of establishing what was legally common. As has been mentioned, illegal encroachments were particularly frequent in moorland areas, and the commissioners were required to determine what was, or was not, legitimate. This was a highly contentious issue. The act usually stated the period of undisturbed occupance necessary to establish ownership, but it fell to the commissioners to determine as best they could just how long an encroachment had existed. The normal rule was that anything under twenty-one years should be regarded as part of the common, and should be allocated as such, but upland enclosure acts were particularly apt to extend the time period. At Slayley, for example, the limit was set at forty years, leaving the commissioners dependent on the memories of locals, possibly unreliable or biased, old enough to offer evidence. Encroachments were normally valued as if they were unimproved and it was common practice to allocate them to the occupier if he or she had a valid claim to that amount. If not, practice varied. At Slayley, the occupier was to receive the appropriate proportion of the encroachment, but elsewhere the option of buying the rest was often offered, the money going towards the costs of the enclosure.

The complexity of the task of establishing who had rights varied greatly from enclosure to enclosure. While some manors had made little attempt to enforce the rules, thus allowing a free-for-all, others acted fiercely against intruders, even if the moor was large and unstinted. The former steward at Helmsley gave evidence in 1882 that he had always removed any animals whose owners were not entitled to graze them on Helmsley Moor, including the inhabitants of Carlton, which lay in the same parish and had the same lord of the manor. He had also 'turned many a Carlton person off whom we found getting Ling for kindling'.[8] Such a policy was in sharp contrast to nearby Kirkbymoorside, mentioned above. Attitudes might vary even within a single parish, especially if different lords of the manor were involved. Edwards (1963, pp. 108-9) contrasts Coed Marchan and Efenechtyd commons, both in the parish of Llanfwrog, the former being very little encroached, whereas the latter was subject to much squatting. From the commissioners' point of view, previous strict enforcement of the rules made life a great deal easier, since they could rely on the existing situation as being the legally valid one, and could probably use manorial court records to decide any dubious cases. Where previous administration had been lax, they could be faced with a mass of disputed claims. County Durham seems to have had more than its fair share of disputes, possibly because many of its uplands were unregulated, and possibly, also, because of the potential mineral wealth which a successful claim might bring to the owner. Certainly, many Durham enclosures adopted the highly unusual habit of appointing a body of arbitrators, usually lawyers, to determine disputes (Winchester 2000a and Straughton, this volume).

Pasture rights were often the simplest aspect to deal with, since some commons were divided into 'stints', entitling each owner to depasture a known number of animals, which they were not allowed to exceed. Unfortunately, many were not, and this applied particularly to the upland moorlands. Though some *were* stinted, this had obviously appeared unnecessary with others, since prior to the eighteenth century there had seemed little likelihood of farmers owning enough sheep to cause a problem of overgrazing. There were therefore no known proportions to provide an easy basis for division, since existing usage might be subject to the abuses mentioned earlier.

An alternative way open to the commissioners was to use the proportions of enclosed land (and common field, if any) held by each individual. Most commons had a 'closed season' during which all animals had to be removed.[9] It followed that they had to be accommodated elsewhere, on the farmer's other land, and the number of stock which he could support in this way could be used as a measure of his entitlement to a share of the common. Some manors had a strict *levancy and couchancy* rule, as it was known, already in operation, but commissioners certainly adopted it as a rule of thumb even when this was not the case. Another option was to use the Land Tax as a basis, as at Little Ormside, Westmorland, where the tax for 1798 was used for an enclosure under an act of 1803.

Difficulties arose because by the period of parliamentary enclosure this neat and tidy linkage had long ceased to exist in many areas, if, indeed, it ever had. As Gonner (1912, p. 10) points out, lords had long made grants of rights independent of the amount of land held, and these 'common appurtenant' rights were as legally valid as any others. Certain 'ancient cottages' had acquired rights through long-established unchallenged usage; others had not. Again, it was normally the commissioners who were faced with the problem of determining which claims were valid and which were not, together with the complication of deciding the amount of land that was appropriate to genuine cottager claimants whose other land could clearly not support their customary number of stock during the closed season.

Other types of rights often played a rather more significant role in the uplands and tended to take a rather different form from their lowland equivalents, though there was, of course, no clear-cut division. Fuel rights, for example, were far more likely to involve specific rights to cut peat and turf, rather than the more nebulous and legally disputable right to collect brushwood. The problem of compensation for these produced a wide range of different solutions. Allocating a plot of land to each right owner was one obvious answer: this was done at Lynton, Devon, for example. The problem with this was that the monetary value of peat rights was very low, so the compensatory plot was liable to be extremely small, leaving the cottager who owned no other rights with the costs of fencing a tiny plot of little practical use. Cash payments were sometimes used instead, but left the owner with nothing of value in the long term. More useful for the small man was the practice of creating a common peat allotment, open to all existing right owners, but again there were problems. Since peat cutting is a destructive form of exploitation, the common turbary would have to be large if it were to last for more than a year or so, and this was only really possible if the moor was large, otherwise the allotment would seriously diminish those of the owners of grazing rights. It is doubtful whether the five acres allotted at Easington, North Riding, was of much value, in contrast to the 250 acres (101 ha) at Ebberston. Location was also a problem, and there was a danger that it would merely increase the problems of accessibility mentioned earlier, to the detriment of the very people most in need of the facility. Other solutions merely perpetuated another problem, namely that of multiple rights over the same piece of land. Several commissioners chose to allocate land to one individual, but allow to another peat-cutting rights over it, as at Harwood Dale and Horton in Ribblesdale.

Mineral rights were often of special significance in the uplands. The lord of the manor had a particular interest, for mineral rights over the common belonged to him, and the decision had to be made whether to relinquish them and take a larger allotment of land, or to retain them and take less. In some cases the answer was obvious, since known deposits existed. Thus at Brampton, Cumberland, the Earl of Carlisle insisted on a clause that no coal mines, minerals and metals were to be taken into account at the valuation, and that all such rights should be reserved to him. At Matlock, Derbyshire, the lord, Peter Nightingale, accepted a twenty-second part, surrendering his right to stone gathering, but retaining his rights to mine minerals, while John Colwell Roe at Lynton, Devon, received a sixteenth, retaining the metallic mineral rights but surrendering the rest. Compensating the various smaller right owners for their rights to take stone for repairs to houses and boundary walls was dealt with by a similar range of expedients to those used for fuel. At

Church Coniston, Lancashire, for example, the traditional right of all cattle-gate owners to dig slate was compensated for by creating a slate quarry in which all those concerned could continue to dig slate free for their own use, but not for sale. Any rents or royalties from commercial use were to be split amongst the owners in proportion to their cattle-gates. At Gunnerton, Northumberland, where the allotments to one of the four allottees, Stephen Kitching, contained no suitable stone, the award specified that he was to be allowed to dig freestone for building from Walter Blackett's allotment at Dunshell Burn Cragg.

Upland enclosures were particularly likely to raise the costs by the sale of land, rather than a levy on the owners. The large size of so many of them meant that the impact on the owners was minimised, especially as some of the poorest agricultural land was often an attractive proposition for the grouse or forestry mentioned earlier. At Mickleton the Earl of Strathmore snapped up over 1,080 acres (437 ha) of the land 'least capable of improvement', leaving only one other tiny plot needing to be sold to balance the costs. Some enclosures even made provision for individuals to opt out of the sale if they wished, taking their full entitlement, but paying a levy instead. In the sample awards twenty-two of the fifty-one English enclosures and no less than thirteen of the sixteen Welsh raised all or part of their costs by sales, and almost 14 *per cent* of the land available was disposed of in this way.

As with so many other aspects, the extent to which the enclosure of the uplands produced any significant 'improvement' has been much debated. Allen (1992, p. 275) makes the dismissive statement that 'some enclosures may have resulted in land reclamation', implying that this was of little significance. Much, however, depends on what is regarded as improvement. Most of the moorland areas concerned were never likely to become permanent high-grade arable land, and only the most wildly over-optimistic contemporaries thought they were. For many, the ability to make small-scale closes on the moor, where pasture could be improved, hay for winter fodder produced, and sick animals, pregnant ewes or young lambs given temporary protection, was a significant improvement in itself. It made the sheep-farming economy more manageable and more economic, especially when coupled with the clearly-defined grazing rights which replaced the often-chaotic earlier system. Units created in this way survived as independent farms with as little as 4 acres of walled-off fields into the 1960s in North Yorkshire. Edwards (1963, pp. 72-3) claims that many North Welsh enclosures were purely to create single-owner sheep-walk, and the land was never intended to be reclaimed.

There is also the question of the time period over which an improvement is to be judged. Much of this land has always been economically marginal for any form of 'improved' farming, and has been subject to a constant ebb and flow of the limits of cultivation since enclosure in response to changing economic and political conditions (Chapman 1961). Judging its impact at the height of the ploughing-up campaign after the Second World War produces a very different result from doing so in the depths of the depressions of the late nineteenth century or the 1930s. It is also possible to see an increasing farming logic gradually exerting itself over time. The first upland enclosures were not necessarily of the best land, nor the last of the worst. Farmers faced with the task of recouping the costs of a compulsory enclosure were tempted to improve as much land as possible as quickly as possible, often being forced into a retreat from the worst parts of their allotments some years later. Simultaneously with this retreat, neighbours in a later-enclosed parish might be frantically attempting to reclaim land of the same or poorer quality, driven by the same imperatives.

A detailed study of the North York Moors (Chapman 1976, pp. 13-16) illustrates the extreme variability in both the degree and methods of reclamation within a small area. At Kilburn, a compulsory enclosure with fifty-seven owners, almost 63 *per cent* of the moor had been reclaimed within twenty years, with a further 6 *per cent* under woodland, but only one new farmstead created. However, in the following decade over a quarter of this reclaimed land reverted to rough grazing. In contrast, at Sneaton the one dominant owner carried out a carefully phased programme of reclamation based round three new isolated farmsteads. Fifty years after the enclosure only one of these had reached its final form, one was built and with some fenced and reclaimed ground, and the final one was just beginning, with no farmhouse but a small acreage of reclaimed land. By 1856, the two parishes were showing completely opposite trends, with Kilburn in rapid retreat and Sneaton in the middle of an expansion programme. By 1950 much of the reclaimed land at Sneaton had, in turn, been lost, but by the early 1980s most was back to improved pasture once more.

The contrasts between compulsory and permissive enclosures emerge clearly in this respect. The latter tend to show a much more measured and cautious response. Owners frequently took in only a small part of their allotments initially, gradually building outwards if the experiment proved successful and resources allowed. In parishes where moors were divided into compulsory and permissive areas, the former were usually reclaimed almost immediately, whereas the latter were only partially taken in, and at a leisurely pace over many decades. Subsequent events frequently proved that this was not just a reflection of the perfect judgement of the commissioners in valuing the land, for reversion of compulsory areas then set in, while extensions to some of the permissive areas continued.

An example of this is provided by Pickering, where the enclosure act of 1785 gave rise to a division into compulsory and permissive areas. By 1817 almost all the compulsory area had been reclaimed, much of it within the first five years after the award, whereas in the permissive area little had been done, though the nuclei of most of the new farms had been established (Tuke 1800, pp. 204-14). A steady increase in the permissive area continued right up to the depression of the late nineteenth century, by which time parts of the compulsory area were reverting to rough grazing. Between 1856 and 1892 the former gained 420 acres (170 ha), while the latter lost 160 acres (65 ha). Many of these planned farms in the compulsory area remain today, though now largely as tourist-orientated facilities set in a sea of coniferous plantations, which have swamped the rest of the former moor.

Contemporary evidence supports the view that great variations occurred, and records the fortunes achieved by some, while others faced disaster through misfortune or misjudgement. Howlett (1781), for example, quotes figures from the Mendips (probably supplied by John Billingsley, a major enclosure commissioner in the area) to show that some 5,000 acres (2,023 ha) had been reclaimed over the previous forty years, with the average value rising from 3*s* 6*d* to 14*s* per acre. On the other hand, Marshall (1788, pp. 283-5) and Tuke (1800, pp. 202-3) record the sad tale of Sir Charles Turner, who ruined himself at Kildale in a grandiose and ill-judged scheme to reclaim Kempswidden, leaving nothing but the remains of his ditches and walls behind.

Attempts to produce a global figure for the amount of moorland actually reclaimed are inevitably crude, and sometimes misleading. Clements (1992, p. 34), for example, says that 'During this period two million acres of heathland vanished', but this figure appears to represent an inaccurate estimate of the commons enclosed in England by act of Parliament, rather than the actual amount of heathland lost to other uses. Williams (1970, p. 61) produces rather different figures for *all* waste reclamation, suggesting that the amount of waste fell from 21.3 *per cent* in about 1800 to 6.4 *per cent* in 1873, but the sources used, more particularly the Board of Agriculture Reports for *c*. 1800, must be regarded as highly unreliable, and the figures, in any case, do not apply to the impact of *parliamentary* enclosure. In reality, it seems unlikely that much more than 10 *per cent* of the upland commons enclosed by act was ever 'improved', in the sense of being converted to arable or temporary pasture, at any one time, with the possible exception of the Second World War. More may well have been subject to improvement at some stage, but not necessarily contemporaneous with what was happening elsewhere. A very much higher proportion was ring-fenced, and in the twentieth century a significant amount was afforested, but this must be distinguished from land reclamation in the strictly agricultural sense of the word.

Space does not allow detailed exploration of the implications of this study for some of the more controversial aspects of general enclosure theory, but it is appropriate to end by stressing a few significant points. Firstly, almost all landowners ended up with *larger* holdings than before, undermining the arguments of those, such as Cohen and Weitzman (1975), who postulate that they would be smaller. Even cottagers might acquire quite large acreages in the big moorland enclosures. Secondly, it cannot be taken as read that smallholders faced high compulsory costs. The widespread use of sales, coupled with partial or permissive enclosures, left many with land or a secure title to clearly-defined rights at no immediate cost. Thirdly, the upland enclosures throw a different light on the issue of the before-and-after value of the land to the poor (as portrayed by, for example, Neeson 1993). Quite apart from the question of strict application of the rules, distance and the physical environment frequently made the commons of little value, so those unable to use them before had nothing to lose, and those who had rights they could not use might even gain. Upland enclosures were not uniform in their characteristics, nor do they constitute anything approaching a majority, but the features of a sector making up almost a quarter of the whole movement need to be taken seriously when forming general judgements.

NOTES

1. PRO, DL41/72.
2. Derbyshire RO, D3585/1/1. His calculations give a gross value of £2,739, possibly suggesting that he would sell land to cover his costs.
3. PRO, DL45 10/6.
4. PRO, E134, 28 Eliz. 1592.
5. The validity of this stereotype in the lowlands is also highly dubious.
6. The sample was stratified by county (Chapman 1987). I am grateful to the ESRC, whose support made the collection of this data possible.
7. Turner (Tate & Turner 1978, p. 108) records the earlier act as 'Eggleston' and the latter as 'Eggleston and Middleton'. The new award actually allotted 9,464 acres (3,930 ha) and involved 9,552 acres (3,865 ha) in all.
8. North Yorkshire RO, ZEW VI/15.
9. At Pickering, for example, the closed season lasted from 21 November to 4 April.

ABBREVIATIONS

Derbyshire RO	Derbyshire Record Office
North Yorkshire RO	North Yorkshire Record Office
PRO	Public Record Office, London

Beyond enclosure: upland common land in England and Wales since 1800

Eleanor A. Straughton

ABSTRACT

A significant acreage of common land remains in the mountains, moors and fells of England and Wales; landscapes where parliamentary enclosure had incomplete and idiosyncratic effect. Looking beyond enclosure, this chapter asks for greater awareness of upland common land and common agriculture. The chapter argues for close analysis of 'communal' grazing customs and institutions existing within a changing cultural and political environment. Further, it is suggested that a global debate on 'common pool resources' informs analysis of upland commons and reaffirms their international importance.

KEYWORDS

Access, common Land, common pool Resource, common Right, conservation, grazing, land use, parliamentary enclosure, uplands

INTRODUCTION

The history of enclosure rightly occupies a central place in research on the evolution of the rural landscape, to the extent that there is a tendency to assume the elimination of common land, and common agriculture, as significant features in our landscape. Thus, E. P. Thompson: 'The commons and wastes shrank, in the nineteenth century, to the village greens (if such survived) and communally-shared custom shrank to the "calendar customs" and survivals collected by the folklorists' (Thompson 1993, p. 182). Yet over a million acres of common land exist in England and Wales today, much of it in upland regions. On open, uncultivated mountain and moor, fell and heath, common grazing is still a primary land use.

This chapter will argue that there is a rich modern history of common land and will clarify some of our misconceptions as to its use and character. We are perhaps at a critical point for both research and policy. Many upland commons today are subject to overgrazing (DETR 2000, p. 27) and debate continues over where power and control should lie — with government agencies, commons associations, or forums of wider interests. Moreover, the nature of rights is undergoing significant change. Problematic legislation, and a trade in grazing rights, is eroding a once-definitive tie between rights, land-occupation and community. With the increasing emptying of upland farms, an irreplaceable commons culture — local knowledge, memory, and practice — is at risk.

The first section of this chapter outlines acreage and distribution, the second clarifies the meaning of 'common land', establishing conditions of ownership, use and access, principally in relation to upland grazing. Accuracy is imperative. In his influential paper on 'The Tragedy of the Commons', for example, Garrett Hardin asked his readers to 'Picture a pasture open to all ...'; a pasture which would, in his view, fall to ruin through rational self-interest (Hardin 1977, p. 20). Yet this model can be shown to be based on a generally false premise that commons were open to all, as will be shown below. Moreover, the uplands present a more complex array of *communal* lands and land-use systems, which challenge, also, our view of enclosure. The third section provides an outline of changing legislation and values attached to common land since 1800, as a modern historical context. A concluding section situates the commons in global and theoretical debate where, in the last thirty years, interdisciplinary research has covered a range of common resources, from Atlantic fishing grounds to forests of the tropics.

I

Whilst acreages of parliamentary enclosure can be calculated approximately from acts and awards, the acreage of common land at any given time is hard to quantify. Contemporaneous measures are notoriously unreliable. As late as 1955, for example, the Royal Commission on Common Land was warned that existing estimates could be wrong by a million acres 'either way' (Hoskins & Stamp 1963, p. 96). L. Dudley Stamp's supplement to the Commission's survey, though insightful on local detail and distribution of commons (and a key source for this chapter), somewhat overstated their extent (*ibid.*). Today, figures are invariably drawn from county registers of common land, established under the 1965 Commons Registration Act, and though it cannot be assumed that registers reflect exact acreages of *de facto* common land — registration included manorial waste lands not subject to rights of common, for example — they constitute the best available source.

Some 1.37 million acres (554,409 ha) of land are registered as common, of which 0.91 million acres (368,257 ha) are in England and 0.46 million (185,152 ha) in Wales; combined, they amount to an approximate 4 *per cent* of the total land area (Aitchison 1990, p. 273). On a national scale, the concentration of common land in upland regions is striking. As Aitchison's map, Fig. 8.1, shows, common land is concentrated in a number of famous districts and national parks, including the Lake District, Pennines and North York Moors, the Brecon Beacons, Snowdonia and Dartmoor. The National Trust's Lake District estate, alone, is claimed as 'the largest area of common land in Europe managed as a shared agricultural resource' (National Trust 2001a). At county level, the local significance of common land, and its importance in upland locations, becomes even more apparent. Using registration figures, Aitchison found that common land accounted for above 25 *per cent* of the total land area of Breconshire (26.7 *per cent*) and Westmorland (25.5 *per cent*). Levels were above 10 *per cent* in Radnorshire (13.7 *per cent*), Cumberland (11.4 *per cent*) and the North Riding of Yorkshire (11.2 *per cent*) (Aitchison 1990, p. 274).

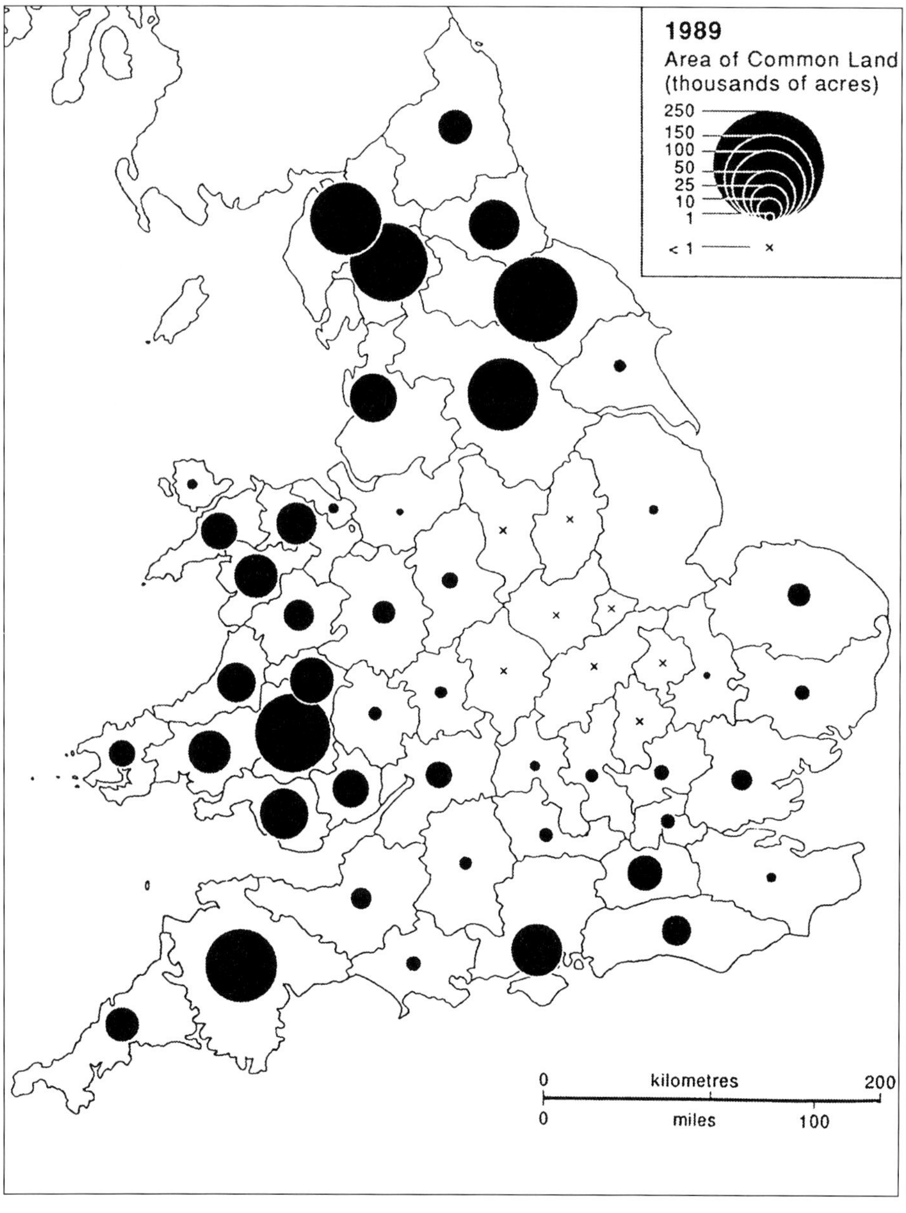

Fig. 8.1. Beyond enclosure: upland common land in England and Wales since 1800 (after Aitchison 1990).

Common land is registered in upwards of 8,600 units (see Aitchison 1990 and Rodgers 1999), but these units are not necessarily discrete in use or appearance. In upland areas, contiguous commons often produce vast common landscapes, broken only by manor or parish boundaries. The significance of boundaries varies: some contiguous commons are unfenced and subject to rights of vicinage (admitting neighbouring commoners' stock); others are fenced and subject to trespass fines. Aitchison and Hughes point to twelve 'clusters' of contiguous commons, each over 9,800 acres (3,966 ha), which account for over half the common land of Wales; and of Westmorland, Stamp claimed: 'it is possible to walk from one side of the county to the other without stepping off common land' (Aitchison & Hughes 1988, p. 98; Hoskins & Stamp 1963, p. 200).

These areas were once, by and large, common manorial wastes, with the topographical features and land qualities one would expect. The areas shown in Fig. 8.1 are closely related to regions of rough grazing mapped by the Land Utilisation Survey, Fig. 8.2, and on mountain commons only the hardiest breeds of sheep will survive. But this seemingly marginal agriculture has a wider cultural and environmental significance, supporting species and landscapes lost elsewhere to intensive cultivation (Pollard 1997 has made valuable study of the 'contribution', real and perceived, of such marginal lands). Thus, many commons have unique conservation value. To date, almost half of English common land is wholly or partly designated a Site of Special Scientific Interest; almost a third (31 *per cent*) lies wholly or partly within Areas of Outstanding Natural Beauty (DEFRA 2002). In Wales, also, common land is associated with SSSI sites and reserves, and five key AONBs account for over a hundred commons (Aitchison & Hughes 1988, pp. 106-7).

This chapter does not address the reasons why the surviving upland commons escaped

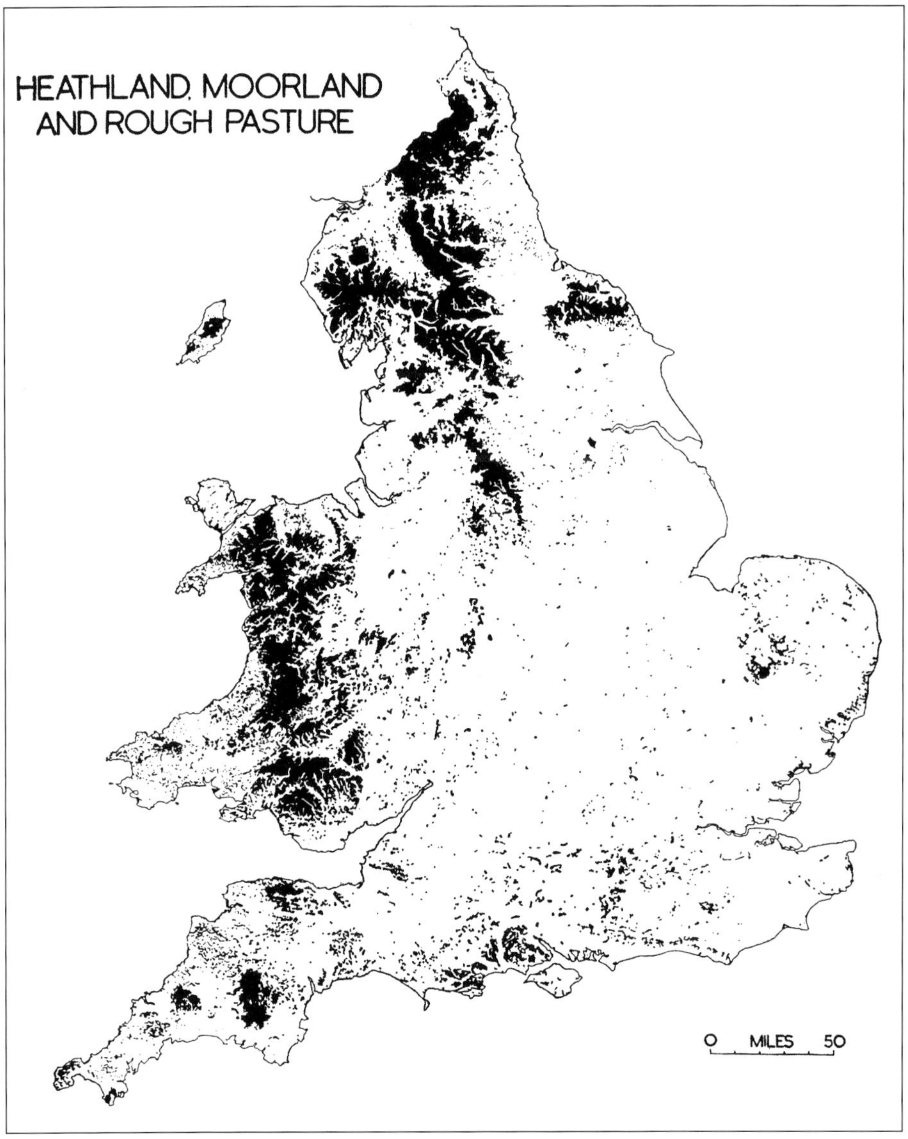

Fig. 8.2. Heathland, moorland and rough grazing in England and Wales (after Land Utilisation Survey of Britain.

enclosure. On the whole, upland rough grazing was unlikely to repay investment in enclosure bills, walling or improvement. There were few opportunities for changes in land use, though other motives for enclosure did apply: resolution of disputes, enfranchisement, or the creation of saleable assets. There are, of course, upland districts with relatively little common land, including the Peak District and Exmoor, and enclosed moors and fells occur in the midst of commons: the reach of enclosure — ancient and modern — is not explained purely by topography, land quality or regional trends. But the density of common land in historic counties such as Westmorland, highlighted above, does suggest a distinctive enclosure story. In the northern uplands of England, historians and geographers have indeed pointed to local patterns (see for example Chapman 1976, and this volume; Searle 1993; Whyte 2000a). This has yet to be exhaustively researched. It seems that research on enclosure *and* surviving commons requires a renewed engagement with upland environments and society.

II

W. G. Hoskins and L. Dudley Stamp were incisive on common land: 'The concept, if not the definition, of common land is clear enough' (Hoskins & Stamp 1963, p. xvi). Determining the status of common land in strict law is a curious problem. Common land has been the subject of statute law since the Statute of Merton of 1235, yet most inclosure and commons acts employ the term without qualification, or list classes of land 'subject to enclosure'. G. D. Gadsden considers the terms of the 1965 Commons Registration Act as the first *statutory* definition (Gadsden 1988, p. 11), and, today, only those lands found on the register are recognised as common. But statute law barely touches the realm of custom, or *lex loci* (Thompson 1993): traditionally, commoners looked to manor courts and communal memory for custom and practice (*ibid.*; Winchester 2000a). In this chapter, then, a balance has been sought between reference to general discourse, legal context, and custom typical of upland grazing.

In general usage, common land is privately owned land over which third parties have rights to a *profit à prendre* — in the definition favoured by Halsbury's *Laws of England*, a right 'to take or use some portion of that which another man's soil naturally produces' (Halsbury 1991a, VI. 197). The 'common' nature of the land stems not from commoners' collective use of it, but from the 'community of use' between landowner and commoner: whilst the landowner is owner of the soil and its minerals, and frequently also the timber and game, the landowner's share of certain products is subject to others' rights. Often, the landowner's interest is limited to the residue left after rights have been exercised (for more detailed exposition see Gadsden 1988, pp. 21, 59-63). This emphasis on a 'community of use' is not, however, recognised in statute law, which has a wider definition. Under the 1965 Commons Registration Act, common land is defined as, firstly, lands subject to rights of common (as defined in the Act), whether exercisable at all times or for limited periods, and, secondly, waste land of a manor not subject to rights of common. The Act's definition of rights 'in common', includes rights of sole or several pasture (see CRA 1965, section 22 in Halsbury's *Statutes of England and Wales*, 1991b, VII. 696), where the landowner generally has no interest in the grazing. Unsurprisingly, interpretation and application of this Act has proved difficult (Gadsden 1988; see also discussion of stinted pastures and 'sole right', below).

In general, common rights can be rights to pasture, turbary (peat or turves), estovers (woody or fibrous material), piscary (fish), pannage (acorns and beech mast for pigs), and to stone, sand or gravel. Products vary from common to common: manorial documents might refer to the cutting of holly, bracken and gorse, the collection of slate or juniper berries, or the cutting of coarse grass for kindling (Garnett 1912; Mabey 1993; see particularly Neeson 1993, ch. 6, and Winchester 2000a, ch. 6). The question of who has a common right is usually determined by habitation and property, with rights attached to specific fields, cottages and farms — even barns and inns: thus, though custom might admit a more general population for local purposes, statute law has never recognised an inherent common right of access to the public. The form of attachment is itself classified as 'appendant' or 'appurtenant', though manorial documents are sometimes inconsistent on this point (Gadsden 1988, p. 66). A common right appendant is a right attached to arable land, permitting animals used for ploughing and manuring to be depastured on manorial waste. These rights continue to stand even where the arable land has since been built on or turned over to pasture. A right appurtenant is also attached to land or buildings but is not restricted to arable lands, and can include animals not typically associated with tillage or manuring (such as geese and goats). Less frequently, common pasture rights are entirely unattached to property, being held 'in gross' as a share of the rights permitted on the common. Rights 'in gross' are more easily traded or let; they may, however, be allotted to particular officers, such as the priest or manor steward (for detailed classes of rights, see *ibid.*, pp. 66-72, and Halsbury 1991a, VI. 199).

A right does not signify unlimited or unconditional use of the common. While the manor courts were operational and effective, juries and their officers administered rules and fines, monitored and controlled grazing, and determined the exercise of rights to turves and estovers (Neeson 1993; Thompson 1993; Winchester 2000a). The manor steward and court jury would identify areas where turves could be cut each year, appointing commons shepherds and officers to maintain boundary walls. Crucially, manorial custom would also determine stocking densities on the common. Rather than a fixed numerical system, grazing was regulated on many upland commons by the rule of '*levancy and couchancy*': the commoners could only graze on the common the number of stock they could over-winter on produce from their own holding. Rights described in manorial documents as '*sans nombre*' were often regulated in this fashion ('without number' did not automatically signify an unrestricted right). Levancy and couchancy indicates a careful union of the in-bye land (the dominant tenement) and common waste land (the servient tenement), and as such reflects the ancient conditions of appendant and appurtenant rights. This is not to suggest that landless inhabitants, and those without common-right dwellings, were universally excluded, but their use of the common would fall within a structure of surveillance and regulation.

In certain upland areas, grazing of sheep on open land (whether common or not) is limited to a commoner's 'sheep heaf' or 'walk'. Again, this cannot be translated into fixed numbers, but suggests a framework for limitation and control. The sheep from a particular holding are 'hefted' (accustomed) to an area of the open land. A heaf might be depicted on old maps, and occasionally by markers on the ground, but often there is no proof other than use and memory. The Lakeland Herdwick is famously territorial, and hefting has been sustained in Lakeland through the custom of selling or letting a core flock *with* the dominant tenement (known to manorial tenants as the 'lord's flock'). The legal status of the sheep-heaf is complex, however. According to Gadsden, hefting on commons is a practicable use of common rights, but in law the rights remain 'ordinary rights in common' to the whole waste (Gadsden 1988, p. 96). Although not describing sheep-heaves, Harris and Ryan similarly suggest: 'it is inimical to the basic conception of common land that rights of common should be restricted to any part of it' (Harris & Ryan 1967, p. 61). The 1965 Commons Registration Act has greatly complicated this issue, since many farmers registered their rights to a heaf, rather than to a common as a whole.

Grazing may also be regulated through limiting stocking densities to a set number of 'stints' or 'gates' (often called beast-gates or cattle-gates), distributed among common-right holdings. Each holding has a fixed number of stints, but the value of the stint reflects the different grazing patterns of stock, and locally and annually variable conditions. Thus one sheep without lambs could equal one stint, five stints might be equated with four ewes with unweaned lamb or lambs, and so on (for upland stinting see Winchester 2000a, ch. 4; for stinting of lowland commons after 1700, see Neeson 1993). Stinting provides a more systematic means for levying of rates (for maintenance and shepherding), and opportunities for commoners to let their stints, where such is permitted. It is a tradition in its own right (Winchester found stinting to be 'part of the vocabulary' of the northern uplands of England before 1250: Winchester 2000a, p. 83), but it is also seen as a solution to grazing problems, and has been introduced on many commons in the modern period. Commons regulated under the 1876 Commons Act were given stinting schemes, for example. In 1958 the Royal Commission reported that stinted grazing accounted for 33 *per cent* of the total area of common land, with 46 *per cent* unstinted (Hoskins & Stamp 1963, p. 109), although this figure is likely to have included a number of enclosed stinted lands (discussed below).

Certainly, the existence of rules and courts, stints and heafs, was no guarantee either of benign control or compliance. The vacuum left after the demise of the manor courts in the eighteenth century must be a central concern. But this outline shows that common land is not, as a genus, the 'open pasture' assumed by Hardin's theory. As has been intimated above, practices such as stinting and heafing are features of communal land use, and are not restricted to common land. In the northern uplands of England, for example, Winchester points to examples of enclosed stinted pastures, or communal intakes, found on the lower slopes of moor and fell; lands which altered the shape of pastoral agriculture after the medieval centuries (Winchester 2000a, pp. 68-73). Gadsden also describes a 'stinted pasture', though legal classifications are not necessarily coterminous with historical ones. A 'stinted pasture' can be usefully subsumed under 'common land', and is registrable under the 1965 Act, as it is subject to a *profit à prendre*, but it is not strictly common land. The rights exercisable over it are known as sole or several rights (also 'sole profit' or 'sole pasture') rather than rights of common, as the landowner has granted away his or her residual grazing interest. Thus, though retaining landownership, the landowner has no 'community of use' or 'commonality' with the graziers (Gadsden 1988, pp. 12, 22-3, 91-3).

Perhaps of greater interest are the 'regulated pastures'. A regulated pasture (again, as named by Gadsden) is not common land, and legal argument continues over its registration (Gadsden 1988, pp. 37-9). It also involves stinted grazing, but the graziers are owners of the land itself: 'the grazing is directly related to the share which each person has in the land ownership' (*ibid.*, p. 27). Some regulated pastures can be assumed to have always existed as such; others are the product of more recent private enclosures or agreements. Some, however, became regulated pastures through parliamentary enclosure. Together with more familiar land-allotments, the 1845 General Inclosure Act allowed for enclosure with stints, formal management structures and field-reeves, enabling enclosure of grazing lands where physical division was impractical and undesirable (see, for example, Halsbury, 1991b, VII. 581-5). It therefore involved a quite different form of privatisation from that typically associated with enclosure regimes, but had a particular relevance to uplands grazing, where it is thought to be more prevalent. It is unclear how much stinted and regulated pasture there is across England and Wales: this perhaps underlines the fact that our interest in the true range of communal lands has thus far been limited.

Inevitably, the niceties of legal definitions can appear remote from local practice. This section concludes, then, with a case study which defies easy or consistent definition, found at Watermillock (Cumberland), near Ullswater. 'Watermillock Common' is named as such on Ordnance Survey maps today. It is on the commons register, and 'Watermillock Stinted Common' is listed in Hoskins and Stamp's volume, with 925 acres (374 ha) (Hoskins & Stamp 1963, p. 260). The exact acreage is inconsistent in documentary record — this is not unusual for common land. But of more interest is the existence of an enclosure award. 'Watermillock Common' appears in W. E. Tate's *Domesday*, as being enclosed by private act in 1829 (awarded in 1835) (Tate 1978, p. 88). The 1835 award shows that 4,591 acres (1,858 ha) of 'divers commons and waste lands' in the manor were physically enclosed, but a separate section of the award allowed for the laying together of allotments into a 'stinted pasture', of 883 acres (357 ha). According to the award, the lord of the manor and 'certain owners' asked that their allotments be laid together, 'and the same shall for ever hereafter be held used and enjoyed by the several proprietors according to the Stints specified in the schedule'.[1]

The Watermillock award describes stinting of 'the said Plot or parcel of Ground', and, from an early date, the somewhat ambiguous nature of this piece of ground becomes apparent: in correspondence, a herdsman's book and account book, dated between 1835 and 1951, it appears variously as Watermillock Common, Stinted Common, and Stinted Pasture. These documents reveal something else of immediate importance: the laying out and functioning of a communal system. The first herdsman's book details the tasks of the herdsman, including, for example, the herdsman's responsibility for taking 'a written Ticket' of the number of cattle each person is depasturing, signed by the owner of the stint; the herdsman was also to 'inspect the cattle twice every day for three months from the day of stinting and once each day afterwards — notice to be immediately given to the owner of any cattle that are unhealthy'. The account book shows, among other details, expenditure on ale for the herd-letting and income from payments for the privilege of shooting on the stinted pasture; the letting of mole-catching to one George Thompson, for fourteen years, from 1843; expenditure on a constable's 'two journeys to Penrith' on a case of trespassing, 1843; and a note of a case of trespass dealt with at Penrith county court in 1878.[2] The picture is therefore complex: financial and recreational interests, collective action involving both court cases and ale; a calendar which is both social and pragmatic.

Cases such as Watermillock do not meet our standard perception of either enclosure or common land, yet they are important examples of communal grazing. They suggest that themes typical of enclosure research can be discussed and compared in relation to changes in communal regimes: stinting for example, can be compared with a view to power and exclusion, labour and capital, across a range of lands. They suggest, further, that whilst analysis must recognise the significance of enclosure, and the particular conditions of common land, it must acknowledge, also, a relationship between upland community and environment — manifest in land use and custom — that transcends legal differentiation. A broader reading of *communal* land and agriculture is possible, perhaps essential, in the uplands.

III

In the wake of enclosure, common land has become a more complex cultural entity, an icon, even, in modern visions of landscape and land use. In the previous section, the assumption of public access to common land was corrected. Certainly, until the 2000 Countryside and Rights of Way Act, an inherent right of public access to common land had not been recognised in law. But the *idea* of access has been instrumental in shaping the modern history of common land, its use, meaning and survival. Equally, the rise of scientific conservation, and legal protection of landscapes, has brought about the rewriting of common land and rights in law.

An organised preservation campaign arose within the environs of Parliament itself. Parliamentary enclosure of open field arable, common and waste, was concentrated in the period between 1750 and 1850, with enclosure of common and waste particularly significant during and after the Napoleonic wars (Turner 1980). But purely in terms of legislative change, the nineteenth century was the more significant. The first half of the century saw the state extending its role as facilitator. As the century opened, each application for enclosure had to be won through a private bill; costly and slow, this was seen to be hindering enclosure, just when government wished to promote it. A series of general enclosure acts (particularly acts of 1801, 1836, 1840, and 1845) made enclosure swifter and cheaper, with little reference to Parliament other than an annual aggregate bill. There was, however, an inherent contradiction in nineteenth-century enclosure. Common land was condemned, yet upland wastes were often the very landscapes the new touring class was seeking: looking at trends across the eighteenth and nineteenth centuries, Keith Thomas detected 'a growing concern to preserve uncultivated nature as an indispensable spiritual resource' (Thomas 1983, p. 267). With the repeal of the Corn Laws, and with growth in international trade, political pressure for cultivation and improvement diminished rapidly. Concurrently, an expanding urban population raised fears over public order and health (see Smout 2000).

On its formation in 1865, the immediate purpose of the Commons Preservation Society (which counted MPs, peers, and social reformers as its members) was to make London's commons accessible to the public. The 1866 Metropolitan Commons Act made this possible. After 1866, the city's commons could be regulated for recreation and access, without the lord of the manor's consent, and with management invested in a board of 'conservators,' thereby signalling a new weighting of the public interest in common land. In the 1860s and 1870s a number of court cases and campaigns in and around London secured among others, Wimbledon Common, Hampstead Heath, and Epping Forest. Confidence also faltered in the rural enclosure regime. In 1869, a committee investigating the conduct of enclosure commissioners called a temporary halt to all enclosure applications, critical of how few acres had been set aside for recreation — far fewer than the terms of the 1845 Act had promised — and how few applications had been refused. Whilst the 1876 Commons Act permitted the resumption of enclosure, it was under more stringent terms, with an alternative — regulation — provided for in the provisions of the act, together with a stronger commitment to public access and recreation. Some thirty-six commons were regulated under this Act between 1876 and 1919, including large upland commons such as East Stainmore, Crosby Garrett, Winton and Kaber (all Westmorland), and Matterdale (Cumberland). The 1899 Commons Act allowed district councils to regulate local commons for the public benefit, an act responsible for many familiar commons of towns and cities. By the turn of the century, enclosure had become a rare occurrence (for a history of campaigns and legislation, see Shaw-Lefevre 1894; Eversley 1910; Gadsden 1988; Williams 1965).

Among early campaigners, preservation was more than protection or access. It was envisaged as a return to the land, and as the recovery of a national identity born of landscape. Thus in her essay on *Open Spaces*, delivered to the National Health Society in 1877, Octavia Hill (later a founder of the National Trust), described the regenerative effects of green spaces on an individual's health, moral character and patriotic feeling. Campaigners also sensed, and employed, the dialectic of city and country. Hill called on her audience and readers to 'Keep those fair, far, still places for your children, and your children's children,' for as the cities expand, 'the more man's soul will long for the beauty, for the quiet, which the city does not, cannot give' (Hill 1877, p. 151). In an urbanised population and rapidly changing environment, the sense of an archaic and unchanging landscape would indeed become a recurring, and perhaps reassuring, theme. In 1894, the founder of the Commons Preservation Society, George Shaw-Lefevre, described the open lands of England and Wales as having remained 'in their original state of nature from the earliest times' (Shaw-Lefevre 1894, p. 1). Some seventy years later, W. G. Hoskins described common land as 'still hardly changed from Anglo-Saxon times' (Hoskins & Stamp 1963, p. 3). In a consultation document of 2000, the Department of Environment, Transport and the Regions described common land as 'largely untouched', and as having 'served generations for centuries' (DETR 2000, p. 1).

Perhaps in view of this strong identification with common land, the twentieth century saw the growing myth that modern common land was, in fact, primarily a public and recreational resource: 'The use of a common now is regarded mainly from the point of view of recreation', wrote E. C. K. Gonner, in 1912 (Gonner 1912, p. 3). Access was not made comprehensive in law, but it grew, piecemeal. Since its formation in 1895, the National Trust has bought or leased vast common lands and made them accessible to the public. The Law of Property Act of 1925 made public access automatic to all commons lying wholly or partially within Urban Districts — as a result of the high populations in the Welsh valleys and around Windermere and Ambleside in the Lake District, this also enshrined access to unique areas of rural common land. In the National Parks, too, a heavy proportion of common land has public access. But overall, the effect has been limited: in 2000 a mere 20 *per cent* of common land had a statutory right of access (DETR 2000, p. 7). Only implementation of the 2000 Countryside and Rights of Way Act, more than 150 years after the Metropolitan Act, will bring public access close to a comprehensive right.

In the meantime, regulation and conservation have also come to the fore. Regulation under the 1876 Act invested Whitehall with a new supervisory role in management of commons outside London: stinting rates set by conservators of regulated commons required annual approval by the Board of Agriculture, and byelaws required approval by the Home Secretary. In 1908, a Commons Act was passed allowing a meeting of commoners to regulate grazing of uncastrated animals — it was designed to protect breeding lines rather than give commoners powers to regulate stocking numbers — and the state was involved here, too: the meeting called for the purpose required the sanction of the Secretary of State. But, as with access, these measures were applied on a case-by-case basis. The 1925 Law of Property Act provided the first general statutory protection, preventing all fencing, building or encroachment on common land, save by permission of the Secretary of State. More complex protection was hampered by a lack of accurate information: authors of the Land Utilisation Survey, launched in 1930, were prevented from identifying common land separately from other land types by threats of legal action from landowners. According to Stamp (director of the survey), identifying common land would have been 'clearly fraught with danger'. Attempts were frustrated again during and after the Second World War, when the requisitioning of much common land brought both opportunity and demand: according to Stamp, 'successive governments hesitated to handle what might prove to be political dynamite' (Stamp 1962, p. 479).

It was not until 1955, perhaps emboldened by the success of the national parks, that a Royal Commission on Common Land was formed, promising both careful survey and recommendations for law and management. The Commission surveyed at an unprecedented level of local detail, but it confirmed existing fears over the state of knowledge about common land, admitting particularly unsafe figures for Welsh commons. However, their findings revealed conclusively that common land was primarily used for grazing. Distribution was significant, as Stamp confirmed in *The Common Lands of England and Wales* (based on his work with the Commission). In the southern and Home Counties, some 64 *per cent* of common land was being used primarily as an amenity. But across England and Wales as a whole, only 10 *per cent* fitted this description, whilst almost 80 *per cent* was primarily used for grazing (Hoskins & Stamp 1963, p. 109). Categories and measures of 'primary' usage are certainly no indication of economic or cultural value, but from the heartland of amenity commons, a wider agricultural interest might perhaps have been less visible:

TABLE 1. LAND USE ON COMMON LAND (Adapted from Hoskins & Stamp 1963, p. 109)

Use/Type of Common Land	*% of Commons in England and Wales*
Grazing land: stinted	33.0
Grazing land: unstinted or otherwise managed	46.0
Forest and Woodland	1.9
Arable	0.3
Bog, fen, and marsh	0.6
Scrub and derelict	7.8
Amenity and Recreation	10.4

The Royal Commission was to prepare the way for a national management strategy, but only the first stage of the Commission's recommendation — a commons register — was implemented. Even as a first stage, the ambition and reach of the 1965 Commons Registration Act was unparalleled in the long history of the commons. Under this act, all common landowners and rights owners had to register their interest with their country council; after 1970, only land or rights found on the register were legally common, and land where owners could not be found, or proven, was vested in bodies chosen by Parliament (usually local authorities). Registration successfully secured the common status of lands and rights, and began to clarify the picture of Welsh commons, so long uncertain. But it did not secure 'the commons' in their existing form. Under registration, all grazing rights had to be registered as a number. In effect, this eliminated the principle of levancy and couchancy, and required registration of stints at maximum value (Gadsden 1988; Rodgers 1999; DETR 2000). The commons operate today within the legacy of registration. It is unclear how many mistaken land registrations have occurred, but gardens and houses were included. A 'Rectification of Registers' act was introduced in 1989 to amend mistakes discovered by that date; and registration of a number of regulated pastures remains a dilemma. In at least one case, at Tatham, Lancashire, the stint-holders of a regulated pasture subsequently challenged their own application for registration.

Registration of rights has proved the greatest challenge, however. Many rights were exaggerated or inaccurate at registration and are now enshrined in law. Moreover, quantification of grazing rights has facilitated the treatment of appurtenant rights as rights in gross. In the case of the Buttermere Commons (over 13,580 acres, (5,496 ha) and designated an SSSI), the National Trust claims that whilst all rights were appurtenant at registration, many have since been leased or sold away from the dominant tenement (National Trust 2000a). There are environmental consequences: where severance of some or all rights has occurred, a balance of dominant and servient tenement is irrecoverable, and the problem of agreeing stocking numbers, already complex, deepens. Environmental stocking agreements on many commons designated as SSSIs or Environmentally Sensitive Areas have therefore suffered a volatile mix of headage payment subsidies, inaccurate numbers, and severed rights (DETR 2000; National Trust 2000a; Rodgers 1999). The legality of severance has been in question wherever it has been found, but the House of Lords, has, effectively, settled the matter with a new precedent. In a landmark decision of May 2001, the Lords upheld a verdict by Bodmin County Court in the case of *Bettison v Langton*, which allowed the severance of a farm's appurtenant pasture rights to Tawna Down, Cornwall. Severance was possible, it was judged, because the pasture rights were expressed as a number (House of Lords, Judgements, UKHL 24 2001).

Christopher Rodgers has studied the legal and environmental consequences of the Registration Act in detail, and Susan Birtles has considered the effects of registration on Norfolk commons; Aitchison and Hughes have also considered the problems of using the register as a data source (Rodgers 1999; Birtles 1998; Aitchison & Hughes 1982). The effects of the registration process on the uplands have yet to be comprehensively studied, though Andrew Humphries, well versed in the workings of Cumbrian commoners, describes it as 'a legacy of chaos' (Humphries 2000, p. 52). From a historical point of view, however, it is perhaps necessary to see the commons register in context. If interest in access, preservation and conservation has grown in the wake of enclosure, it has been largely an engagement with the land itself. The register did not reflect a dynamic and local land-use system, or a living community and changeable environment. The commoner has had a particularly ambiguous role since the demise of enclosure, placed somewhere between local guardian and ever-present threat. Stamp, in fact, described commoners in Epping Forest as a severe restriction on management, with just one commoner having almost a power of veto: 'a power inherited through an accident of birth by a man who may be entirely illiterate and untutored' (Hoskins & Stamp 1963, p. 162). Such a drastic dissociation of commoners from common is not unusual.

Current policy-makers are perhaps moving towards a different outlook. Under the Dartmoor Commons Act of 1985, an association of local parties is charged with regulating grazing and balancing agricultural, conservation and recreational interests. Looking at prospects for new environmental laws, Rodgers sees a case for developing commons management associations with 'new statutory powers to regulate land use', and suggests that Dartmoor might form a useful model (Rodgers 1999, p. 248). Since the mid-1980s, bodies such as the Common Land Forum and Countryside Commission have advised new management strategies. The Department of Environment, Transport and the Regions has noted calls from farmers and commoners' associations for powers to regulate grazing, and has acknowledged the not insignificant problems of the register (DETR 2000, p. 29). Indeed, agriculturalists do not appear to seek a free-for-all, rather coherency in regulation of grazing. This debate has intensified since the foot-and-mouth disease outbreak of 2001. It is therefore possible that we will see new developments in the law of commons in the near future.

IV

The communal lands of upland Britain belong to a wider landscape history, in which ideals flow between continents. Globally, 'the commons' are a touchstone for histories of imperialism and cultural exchange, sites of ideological and sometimes bloody conflict over distribution and use of resources. E. P. Thompson and Richard Drayton have shown the connections between enclosure in England and Wales and restructuring of local land tenures across an empire (Thompson 1993; Drayton 2000); communal regimes have also survived and changed under community, state and colonial systems, through changing economies and political climates. Interdisciplinary researchers have studied, among other subjects, mountain meadows and forests from Switzerland to Japan; ancient 'water courts' in southern Spain and colonialism in irrigation of the Philippines; and lobster fisheries from Maine to Mexico. Studies of North Sea and Atlantic fish stock crises have shown the benefits of combining anthropology and social history, political theory and ecology — as, at macro-level, governments struggle to win supra-national protocols (see in particular Berkes 1989; McCay & Acheson 1987; Ostrom 1990).

The state of theory on communal regimes today has relevance to the management crises mentioned in the previous section. Analysts such as Elinor Ostrom are able to see a secure future for common resources lying wholly or at least partially with *local* management institutions (see Ostrom 1990). This does not necessarily mean the exit of the state, or the resolution of conflict. Singleton warns that formalisation of community management 'may harden existing inequalities or create new ones,' (Singleton 2000, p. 18) and, undoubtedly, there is a risk of idealising local practice. Equally, however, there is a danger of associating all commoners and commons with what E. P. Thompson perfectly describes as the 'glum' thesis — Hardin's predictions of remorseless ruin (Thompson 1993, p. 107). Commons tragedies are routinely predicted by the logic of rational choice theory and prisoner games. But commoners do not exist in the prisoner's isolation or stasis: a modern history, such as that outlined in this chapter, points to a range of cultural and legislative influences, changing the meaning and power structures of the commons, providing new crises and opportunities.

Refreshingly, Ostrom's commoners are neither innately co-operative nor inherently greedy; they are 'fallible, norm-adopting individuals', pursuing 'contingent strategies in complex and uncertain environments' (Ostrom 1990, p. 185). She does not prescribe unilateral self-governance, but she does explore the conditions for its success, and finds, at its centre, a responsive system of locally designed and enforced rules. The key challenge Ostrom's commoners face is maintaining commitment to these rules — sometimes in the face of substantial short-term benefits for those who break them — whilst fairly and effectively monitoring each other (Ostrom 1990, especially ch. 3). Commitment appears to be the heart of successful management, the condition on which future survival of commons world-wide will depend, yet is a profoundly difficult element to explain. In his analysis of decline and 'recommitment' to the commons of Asturias, Spain, Fernandez wonders how traditional communal practices made 'the obligatory desirable', and what causes such 'allegiance' to the commons to fail (Fernandez 1987, p. 267). As Andrew Fleming deduced from his history of the valley of Swaledale in Yorkshire (where commons management fell away before the twentieth century), maintaining egalitarian commons governance would have demanded 'regular hard work and attention to detail'. The history of the commons, says Fleming, 'is a sobering reminder of just how tough-minded, clear-sighted and well organised egalitarians need to be' (Fleming 1998b, pp. 55, 63).

But there is also, surely, in the consumption of ale at herd-lettings, a hint of the meeting of social and working life. This chapter was intended to propose a modern history and it has, it is hoped, provided context at the level of distribution, definition, legislation and theory; but even from this final global perspective, it points to something much more basic. As Thompson saw it, pre-enclosure custom took effect within 'the workaday routine of livelihood' (Thompson 1993, pp. 101-2). What is lacking in the post-enclosure era are local histories of social and working lives carried out in upland landscapes, on individual commons and communal lands, continuously (and sometimes chaotically) to the present day. Common land is safe from physical enclosure in England and Wales — a dramatic turn from 1800 — but the risk of losing the 'culture' of the commons, the indigenous knowledge, memory and commitment, should perhaps be a particular concern in the twenty-first century.

NOTES

1. Cumbria RO, Carlisle: Q/RE/1/17, Watermillock Enclosure Award, 1835.
2. Cumbria RO: DSO/146/1, Watermillock Herdsman's Book; DSO/146/2, Watermillock Cash Account Book. Untangling this shifting status is the subject of ongoing research.

ABBREVIATIONS

CRA	Commons Registration Act
Cumbria RO	Cumbria Record Office, Carlisle

Fuel economy and the uplands: the effects of peat and turf utilisation on upland landscapes

Ian D. Rotherham, David Egan and Paul A. Ardron

ABSTRACT

Although the nature of the Norfolk Broads as flooded medieval peat workings has been known for some time less attention has been given to the scale of peat removal for domestic consumption in upland areas and the impact of such removal on upland landscapes and ecology. The scale of upland peat removal is evaluated and its environmental impact discussed, and an assessment made of the effects on upland landscape and ecology.

KEYWORDS

Peat cutting, peat bogs, upland ecology, fuel

> Peat was the only alternative fuel to be had in any quantity. There is even more of it in Britain than in Ireland, despite the poets and the travel brochures; but it was too bulky to be carried far from its source. Peat burns readily; its merit is to smoulder without a blaze, though this makes for a smoky fire. The 'peat-reek' is pleasant at a distance, and a whiff of it is not unwelcome in one's Harris tweeds; but in a 'lum' cottage its pungency is dreadful. Peat has been 'coked' to destroy the reek, powdered, mixed with pitch or rosin, and compressed into bricks that were claimed to be better than coal. Lacking true peat, some burn turf, or parings of peaty soil with roots of heather and gorse (Wright 1964, p. 62).

INTRODUCTION

The interactions between peat and turf used as fuels, and other energy sources are complex and interesting, and the uses and periods of utilisation are pertinent to an understanding of the British uplands (Ardron *et al.* 1996b, 1998 and 1999; Rotherham 1999a). In particular, the fuel economy of upland environments is a neglected topic: this chapter is intended to raise issues, to consider and establish the scale and extent of impacts, and to identify triggers for and barriers to exploitation. We aim to give a broad overview of some of the relevant literature and to establish in general terms the scale and importance of these uses. This is supported by evidence from detailed site studies and other sources.

Many human impacts on upland environments are well documented. However, domestic and subsistence fuel economies of upland settlements, particularly peat and turf exploitation, have been substantially overlooked, particularly by ecologists. The environmental impact of this utilisation, especially since early medieval times, up to at least the mid-1900s, has been dramatically underestimated. In the 'Dark Peak' of the English Peak District for example, there was more medieval peat removal than from the Norfolk Broads at around the same time (Ardron 1999a). However, apart from occasional mention in more recent texts on regional archaeology (such as Barnatt & Smith 1997), it is generally either overlooked, or dismissed as of very limited significance (Anderson and Shimwell 1981, for example, in their meticulous account of the region's ecology, recognise its occurrence but suggest its impact to be unimportant). The peat workings themselves have been attributed to other causal factors such as air pollution or bad moorland burns. In practice the evidence is distinctive and incontrovertible. Recognised by many historians, but not on the scale of its true occurrence, and frequently overlooked by ecologists and land managers, this is a determinant factor in many contemporary upland landscapes. Omission from regional descriptions is surprising when the documentation in some areas is so well known. Winchester (2000a) for example, presents a very lucid account of the importance of such fuel rights in many northern parts of England and the Scottish Borders. The environmental and ecological consequences of this scale of usage are very significant.

The effects of peat cutting on the ecology and hydrology of the uplands are discussed by Ardron, Rotherham and Gilbert (1996b, 1998). Besides obvious and direct impacts of massive removal of organic matter and catastrophic disruption of hydrological systems are more subtle effects. Peat and turf cutting over many centuries has left ditches, drains and denuded surfaces, often covering many square kilometres. The hand of the peat cutter has left its mark across much of upland Britain.

There are important issues concerning the conservation of the upland palimpsest of peat-cut landscapes, and the fate of the last few domestic peat cuttings in upland England (colour Pl. VII). Peat cutting is generally perceived as the industrial-scale peat extraction of the late twentieth century, and a consequence is a reluctance to recognise or conserve the traditional and small-scale, domestic use or its landscape archaeology. The core of this study combines site surveys and mapping of case studies from specific areas, such as the Peak District and mid-Wales, with an assessment of impact across the UK uplands. Evidence is drawn from a diversity of sources including modern and earlier literature, local accounts (especially relating to agriculture, land use and industry), cartographic evidence, archives (court rolls, enclosure awards, estate archives, etc.), aerial photography, site surveys, and interviews with farmers and others.

LANDSCAPE DESTRUCTION AND EVOLUTION

Extensive destruction, abandonment and fragmentation of lowland heaths and commons, and raised mires in the UK are generally recognised (Gimingham 1972; Webb 1986). Research has focused on southern, lowland heaths (*e.g.* in Dorset, Hampshire and East Anglia) and mires in southern Scotland, and in both north-west and mid-west England. Lowland heaths and low-lying heather moors of midlands and northern England, and upland-fringe moors, blanket bogs and mires of England, Wales, and south-west Scotland receive less interest (Rotherham 1995 and 1996). The scale of peat cutting and associated exploitation of these is far greater, more extensive and permanent than generally appreciated.

The local fuel economy in upland environments, with the cutting of peat and turf, and the associated drainage of vast areas of hillside and hilltop, and also of upland, valley-bottom mires, has been hugely influential in affecting the present landscape (Rotherham *et al.* 1998 and Rotherham 1999b). The impact of peat and turf harvesting was compounded by extensive practices of cutting ling (*Calluna vulgaris*), broom (*Sarothamnus scoparius*) and gorse (furze or whin) (*Ulex sp.*), and gathering kindling and other materials for fuel and for other uses. Birch (*Betula sp.*) and bracken (*Pteridium aquilinum*) were extensively harvested for a variety of uses including fuel and for building materials. Turf and ling were widely used as cheap or free materials for buildings for people and livestock. These uses were discussed in detail for lowland heaths by Howkins (1999) and for other areas by Rotherham (1999b). Winchester (2000a) describes these uses in upland Britain. The use of peat as fuel for heating and cooking on domestic fires is well known (*e.g.* Hartley & Ingilby 1968). Whilst most accounts are cursory and anecdotal, some imply the huge scale of domestic peat cutting and its landscape impact.

Occurring over many centuries, largely on a localised, domestic scale but sometimes also on an industrial one (Ardron *et al.* 1996b and 1998), the effects on vegetation, soil and hydrology have been massive. It is surprising therefore that many key ecology texts overlook the implications of utilisation. For example, Tansley (1939), Pearsall (1950), Gimingham (1972) and Atherden (1992) give virtually no reference to this exploitation. This omission seems to be an upland phenomenon. Perhaps associated with recent histories, different scales of conservation management problems, and the lesser importance of burning for game conservation, lowland workers seem more aware of these impacts. Key writers on southern English heaths and commons (Tubbs 1986; Stamp & Hoskins 1963; and, more recently, Webb 1986) demonstrate this awareness. Webb for example, restricting himself to heaths below 250 metres, suggests that the ecological consequences of peat- and turf-cutting have been considerable, and that evidence of turbary exists for almost all heathland in Britain.

Detailed literature review shows a wealth of information on peat and turf cutting, and it is interesting how little has crossed into mainstream ecological work. Writers on ethnology and local history have described both the processes and the importance of the use of peat and turf to local communities in many areas of Britain. The pioneering works of Lambert *et al.*, (1961) and of Godwin (1978) on the ecological history of the East Anglian Broads and the English Fens are widely known. Accounts by Fenton (Gailey & Fenton 1970; Fenton 1986) in Scotland and by Jenkins and Peate (Jenkins 1965; 1969, Peate 1962) in Wales are notable. Writers on Ireland (*e.g.* Feehan & O'Donovan 1996) and on the Scottish Highlands and Islands also note the importance of this utilisation to the local economy. Smout (1997b) gives a useful and succinct account. TeBrake (1985) and De Vries (1974) confirm wider recognition of the economic and environmental impacts of peat and turf exploitation.

Yet an otherwise detailed and perceptive study such as Fleming (1997, 1998a, 1998b) makes little reference to uses of peat and turf influencing landscape evolution of upland Swaledale in northern England, and Muir (1997), writing on the landscape history of the Yorkshire countryside, makes no mention of it. This is despite the clear importance of peat fuel in the region. Winchester (2000a) gives a clear account of the significance of exploitation in both northern England and the Scottish Borders. He also describes in detail both the administration of the exploitation itself, and the archival resource available for researchers. This is perhaps the most full account of the system and it highlights the potential of meticulous research into manorial accounts and other archives to illuminate the human cultural impacts. In a similar vein, Woodward (1998) considers key aspects of human usage of landscape resources — for fuel, food and building materials. Woodward highlights the range of uses and the complexity of associated issues in the human utilisation of the countryside for materials of basic sustenance. In a collection of papers edited by Thompson, Hester and Usher (1995), drawing together key writers and research on the ecology and management of 'heaths and moorlands as cultural landscapes', short papers by Kirkpatrick, Scott and Macdonald, and MacLennan give some insight into the cultural history of these landscapes. Kirkpatrick and Macdonald (2001) develop some of these ideas further.

There are two main reasons for some lack of awareness of the scale of peat extraction and its effects. The first is that these uses have declined progressively over the last two centuries, and particularly during the late twentieth century. Many researchers and site managers are simply unaware that they ever occurred. The second reason is that the all-encompassing scale of exploitation has often removed the evidence of use from the landscape. Remaining clues may be in place, trackway or building names, and in documentation.

Studies such as that by Hartley and Ingilby (1972) in North Yorkshire and the Yorkshire Dales seldom provide quantitative information. However, in the Yorkshire Dales turf or peat has been recognised as being the chief fuel used for centuries, especially after forest clearance and even where local pit coal was available. It was cut in this area by isolated settlements, particularly at the dale heads, up to the Second World War (Hartley & Ingilby 1968). The quantities of peat fuel consumed by an individual farmstead varied with the type and quality of the available peat, the size of the building, its exposure, construction, the number and affluence of the occupants, and whether the peat was being used simply for heating or for other purposes as well.

To more fully understand the use of fuel in these landscapes it is important to assess the processes influencing the demand for the different resources available. Why were particular fuels used in certain locations and times, and for individual domestic and industrial functions? Competition between various available fuels, the problems of location, of harvesting, of processing, of transportation and issues of both sale and use are critical in this emerging picture.

UPLAND FUEL ECONOMY AND THE ENVIRONMENT

Understanding the peculiarities of the upland fuel economy is important in informing our concepts of upland landscapes and communities. Upland environments have distinctive features with respect to the fuel economy. High altitude is associated with colder, longer winters so that fuel consumption *per capita* is increased compared with the lowlands. The growth rate of vegetation, particularly trees, is slow in comparison with lowland areas. Grazing management systems may adversely affect vegetation, particularly woodland regeneration. Human impact and periods of cooler and wetter climate may limit woodland recovery and favour the expansion of blanket peat at the expense of other vegetation. Upland landscapes tend to have relatively low population densities although these have fluctuated significantly over time. Access to settlements was often poor, difficult and sometimes seasonal. This type of fuel use would demand local and accessible fuels rather than better quality materials from distant sources. Upland areas have often in the past been subject to seasonal occupation through systems of transhumance. It may be that intensity of fuel exploitation varied with the occupation of summer pastures etc. Extreme environmental conditions have also led to the careful use of available natural resources such as the cutting of holly as winter fodder, gorse for fuel and bracken for bedding.

THE RESOURCE AND ITS EXPLOITATION

The technology and techniques for the utilisation of peat and turf in Britain were present from before the Romano-British period. Wooden implements now interpreted as peat spades have been recovered from lowland peat bogs, originating from perhaps Iron Age or even Bronze Age activity (John Coles pers. comm.; Bryony Coles pers. comm.). Furthermore, the spade as a tool was developed substantially by the Romans (Gailey & Fenton 1970) and was indeed a significant aspect of Roman military technology. Peat bogs at lowland sites such as Askham in Yorkshire were used to supply fuel to the major Roman settlement of York (Fitter & Smith 1979). Of direct significance to our argument is that peat use and peat digging implements have been found associated with upland Roman settlements along Hadrian's Wall.

In upland Britain this fuel exploitation took

place in landscapes of peat and of thinner organic soils. These included lowland fens and mires; upland blanket bogs; upland and lowland raised bogs; other bogs; upland, wet, heather moorland; upland, dry, heather moorland; lowland heath; grass moor; grass and heath commons; broom and whins or furze. The 'peatlands' and 'commons' remaining in the twenty-first century are fragile, threatened environments, ranging from productive, lowland fens to low-nutrient, unproductive peat bogs, moorlands and heaths. In terms of 'cultural impacts', and particularly in terms of domestic use over long periods, many of these systems were quite robust. That said, it is clear from research by Fenton and others (*e.g.* Gailey & Fenton 1970; Fenton 1986), that some subsistence use in the Scottish Highlands and Islands was not sustainable. As the resource dwindled, then human suffering and even depopulation resulted. Similar trends are reported for the heaths and commons of southern areas such as Cornwall and Dorset (Pl. 9.I).

Historically these areas were often called 'wastes' and 'commons'. Many, though not all, were relatively unproductive, but they provided, fuel, food and building materials for human populations, and grazing for domestic stock sustainably over many centuries, and across much of the rural environment. The term 'waste' may reflect more a perception of the wealthier landowning classes that these areas were not productive for them directly and also, by the nature of their terrain, were seen as dangerous places. Usage for fuel ranged from small-scale domestic exploitation over long periods, or at sporadic intervals, to large-scale and intensive, industrial extraction. The latter was often associated with particular industrial demands such as for metal smelting.

IMPORTANT CULTURAL LANDSCAPES

Before the almost total destruction of lowland commons, heaths, bogs and peripheral moors through enclosure and 'improvement', or abandonment, a substantial majority of people relied on them for a diversity of products.

Whilst the effects of this loss of a vital resource on local communities are discussed elsewhere (*e.g.* Briggs 1994) the impacts of usage and its subsequent demise on the landscape are not fully appreciated. These would be more obvious if the evidence had not been almost totally removed from many areas by the sheer scale of enclosures and subsequent land improvement from around A.D. 1500 to the mid-1800s. Conversion of heath, moor, waste, and marsh, to arable and enclosed pasture, dramatically ended this landscape utilisation by the majority of the countryside population: the rural poor and the poorer commoners. More of this type of vegetation cover remains in upland Britain than in the lowlands, and domestic use has carried on longer. Some small-scale use of peat and turf lingered in remote areas,

Plate 9.I. Gathering fuel, Dorset, late nineteenth century.

particularly in the uplands. However, by the late 1900s almost all subsistence exploitation in England and Wales had died out. Domestic use in Scotland and Ireland is also in rapid decline (see Feehan & O'Donovan 1996 for example).

Even when landscape change has removed the physical evidence of utilisation, there may still be a legacy of place-names and surnames of local people. Place-names such as Peat Lane, Moss Side and Turf Moor are typical of former fuel extraction, while surnames such as Peatman and Mossman indicate its importance within society.

Peat and turf were not the only fuels from heath and common and the use of materials varied from site to site with the nature of the resource, ownership and rights, and the particular needs (Pl 9.II). Gorse was an alternative fuel when wood and peat were in short supply. It was also used as kindling or where a high temperature was required (such as for baking). Humphries and Shaughnessy (1987) describe the amount of gorse brought into and stored in Dublin in the seventeenth century as so great that there were complaints about the hazards of great stacks of it near the city walls, where they 'doe overtopp the said walles in height'. Gorse was also an important fodder for cattle and horses, particularly in winter when other crops would be in very short supply. Many commons also yielded underwood and timber (but not for fuel) and less so in the uplands. Bracken and heather were also used.

It is clear that fuel was both important and often scarce. John Evelyn (1729) writing about 'fuel' notes:

> ... But besides the Dung of Beasts, and the Peat and Turf which we may find in our ouzy Lands and heathy Commons) for their Chimneys, Cow-sheds, etc. they make use of Stoves, both portable and standing ... In many Places (where Fuel is Scarce) poor people spread Fern and Straw inn the Ways and Paths where Cattle dung and tread, and then clap it against a Wall till it be dry...(John Evelyn, *Silva*, 1729).

Plate 9.II. Harvesting rushes, Peak District, early twentieth century.

For many commoners and other peasants, peat and turf were the main fuels. Around Milnthorpe in north Lancashire for example, peat was the main fuel until *c.* 1800 (Bingham 1987).

The scale of use is highly significant and may relate both to domestic and/or industrial/commercial harvesting. It is possible to estimate peat or turf removal on site from detailed mapping, as in the case of the Peak District study. The other approach is to consider accounts of annual consumption. A farm with average unpretentious needs, using peat mainly for cooking and heating, would, if long-standing, remove a considerable quantity of peat. For instance a traditional Cornish farm burnt about 1,000 turves annually (Hamilton-Jenkins 1932). If occupied for 300 years, it would use about 300,000 turves (each *c.* 0.5 m x 16.5 cm), the equivalent of about 4,200 cubic metres of peat. Even greater consumption is recorded for north-east Yorkshire, where the moderately-sized farm of North Ghyll, Farndale, used 17,500 turves per year (Hartley & Ingilby 1972). Since turves cut in this Yorkshire area measured 15–18 x 5 x 4 inches, in a 300-year period, it would consume the equivalent of a 1-metre depth area of peat 400 metres x 100 metres. Even at this local scale these are significant impacts. Lambert *et al.* (1961) for example estimated the turf consumed by a single household for fuel, litter and other purposes as roughly at 8,000 turves per year. In Wigtownshire, Scotland, in 1792 six tons of peat was considered equivalent to one ton of coal (Mann, Old Statistical Account, 1993). The peat stacks were as big as the cottages they heated (Pl 9.III), and there are similar descriptions for North Wales up to the 1970s. At Martham in East Anglia, a household used 5–8,000 turves per year; at Scratby *c.* 10,000. This was mostly domestic use often with no records of peat bought or sold. However, it is clear from some interview returns that some domestically cut fuel from the peat moss was also sold on. Peat fires traditionally burnt all year round, never going out, and, needed for cooking as well as for warmth, they were central to life in the uplands.

Commercial exploitation of the Norfolk Broads, by Norwich and its Cathedral Priory, used around 400,000 turves per year during the 1300s and 1400s (Lambert *et al.* 1961). Similar use is described by TeBrake (1985) in Holland, and demonstrated by Ardron *et al.* (1998) for parts of the Peak District and South Pennines. Significantly in the upland context, there was more medieval peat cut from the South Pennines (*c.* 34 million cubic metres), than from the Norfolk Broads at the same time (Ardron 1999a). Most was in the early medieval period. Lower-lying sites were often exploited and progressively destroyed during the sixteenth,

Plate 9.III. Peat stacks outside cottages, Ireland, 1920s.

seventeenth and eighteenth centuries. This was associated with Parliamentary and private 'enclosures' of heath, moor, common, bog and 'waste'.

Indeed, the Revd William Harrison writing in the 1500s was concerned about the depletion of woods and the lack of fuel:

> Howbeit, thus much I dare affirm, that if woods go so fast to decay in the next hundred years of Grace as they have done and are like to do in this ... it is to be feared that the fenny bote, broom, turf, gall, heath, furze, brakes, whins, ling, dies, hassocks, flags, straw, sedge, reed, rush, and also seascale, will be good merchandise even in the city of London, whereunto some of them even now have gotten ready passage, ... Of coal-mines we have such plenty in the north and western parts of our island as may suffice for all the realm of England; and so they do hereafter indeed, if wood be not better cherished than it is at this present ... their greatest trade beginneth now to grow from the forge into the kitchen and hall, as may appear already in most cities and towns that lie about the coast, where they have but little other fuel except it be turf and hassock (Revd William Harrison, Withington 1899 and quoted in Wright 1964, p. 64).

An advantage of peat and turf was that they were often 'free' for the cost of cutting and transportation. They were also a valuable 'free' resource to help support vital and potentially expensive services such as the schoolmaster in Scotland: the schoolmaster, 'He also has his peats cut, dried, and brought home free' (Revd Mr James Dingwall, *Old Statistical Account*).

Writing about the Norfolk Broads in the late 1800s, Suffling describes the value of peat:

> ... this is turf, and its lower brother peat. This peat, or, as it is here called, 'hovers', is, when properly dried, a capital and economical substitute for coal. It gives off a blue smoke when burning, and this, as it rises from the cottars' chimneys, wafts a rather pleasant perfume in the air, which is a great improvement on the soot-laden, evil-smelling smoke of the metropolis. A peat-ground, properly managed, is a rather valuable holding, as may be gathered from the following statistics. The peat blocks, when cut are about 4in. square (shrinking by drying to about 3¼in.) by from 2ft. to 2½ft. long (the depth of the boggy surface soil). Each square foot, therefore, produces 9 'hovers', each yard 81, each rod 2450; and, consequently, each acre the enormous number of 392,000 hovers. As these are retailed at from 1*s.* to 1*s.* 6*d.* per 100, a good profit must be realised. (Suffling 1885, p. 72) [Value = £196–£294 per acre].

Although based on a lowland site this is a useful estimate of price at the time.

Hartley and Ingilby in their wonderful account, of traditional life in the North York Moors, state:

> Rights of turbary appear frequently in monastic charters and peat and turf were dug in more places than would appear possible now, including the Carrs of the Vale of Pickering almost to the coast near Filey. Until the seventeenth century, fuel used at Scarborough was mostly got from the moorlands north of it and from the extensive Allerston Moor near Pickering. Special areas were sometimes allocated on the moors for the use of the tenants of a manor, and the sale of peat and turf, regulated by manor courts often caused trouble and ill feeling. From the fourteenth to the nineteenth century, records show that this occasionally took the form of throwing down and burning of the stacks drying remote from the Company in the wide moors (Hartley & Ingilby 1972, p. 73).

Even into recent times, this domestic and sometimes subsistence utilisation was an important part of the annual cycle in many upland areas (Pls 9.IV and 9.V). At Lockton Village in North Yorkshire this use in the early 1900s is vividly recalled from interviews with local people in a book edited by Ruth Strong (2000).

The importance of peat fuel and the use of peat mosses in brought to life by the account of the work of Peter May, a land surveyor in north-east Scotland in the late 1700s (Adams 1979). His diaries and accounts demonstrate the issues involved in these areas and also the administration of matters relating to competing land uses and to the administration of fuel rights. These describe the activity in the 1700s but also, in noting that certain sites had become exhausted, indicate extensive cutting in the 100-150 years or so prior to his observations. The accounts relate to peat grounds both in the valley-bottom mosses, but also on the hillside too.

Along with domestic use, peat and turf were extensively cut for industrial purposes. Peat was exploited as fuel for iron smithing and smelting, probably converted into charcoal before use. This was more commonplace in upland areas than in the lowlands, and highland smiths are known to have used peat charcoal up to recent times. It was also widely used as a fuel for lead smelting, in some areas in large amounts. In the Pennine lead industry, peat was used locally and seasonally, but sometimes in great quantity. This was the case in terms of the earlier processes utilising hilltop locations for wind assisted 'bale hills' or 'bole hills' *c.* A.D. 1400–1500, and for later smelting, for instance at the Old Gang Mine in Swaledale. For the latter, a year's peat was cut during late May and June and then transported to a purpose-built storage shed 391 feet long and 21 feet wide (119 metres x 6.3 metres) (Raistrick & Jennings 1965). The Old Gang Mine in 1810 employed 111 people in the peat-getting process and is a well-quoted example of a large consumer of peat fuel. The lead-smelting mills of

Plate 9.IV. Cutting turf, North Yorkshire, mid-twentieth century.

Plate 9.V. Collecting peats, north of Dublin, 1920s.

the Yorkshire Dales in general, are known to have used enormous quantities of peat (Hartley & Ingilby 1968). Peat fuel was used extensively for tin smelting particularly on Dartmoor; indeed peat charcoal was the main fuel used in that area during the medieval period (Greeves 1981a, 1981b). It was also used for localised copper-smelting industries, notably in the Lake District. Donald (1955) indicates the scale of usage during the late sixteenth century, showing that twenty weeks of operation at a smelting site at Coniston required 4,800 horseloads of peat, costing £60. Collingwood (1912) presents detailed accounts of this industry during the period from around A.D. 1564 to 1577. These are extracted from company account books of the time and give locations of cutting grounds, amounts used, prices paid, competing fuels, and the locations of smelting sites. The interactions between peat fuel, charcoal, and fuelwood are discernible.

IMPACTS ON LANDSCAPE AND ECOLOGY

Domestic utilisation had huge impacts on landscapes in countries such as England, Wales, Scotland, Ireland, Holland and Denmark, and parts of Germany. Similar use of heathland areas has also been important in southern European countries such as in parts of Italy and Turkey.

In upland Britain, peat cutting and other exploitation have directly or indirectly changed much of the landscape. This is by widespread, visually obvious, vegetation change and by breaking-up the uniformity of the land surface. Ardron (1999a and 1999b) presents a detailed account of the impacts of large-scale upland peat removal on the ecology and landscape of the South Pennines in England. The vegetation change has most impact where dark-coloured blanket mire, typically *Calluna* with *Eriophorum*, is replaced by light-coloured grassland notably *Nardus*, on exposed mineral soils. In other areas *Calluna* and *Eriophorum* are replaced by *Molinia*, or by a coarse mosaic of plant species. Associated drainage of the wider landscape and subsequent land improvement, and even enclosure or tree planting, may mask the original driver of landscape change.

The research highlights the complexity of these interactions. There are particular phases of use in different regions, and competition between fuels. Matters of availability, accessibility, cost (financial and otherwise) and the quality of fuel for the required purpose, all influence the utilisation and hence the landscape impact. Availability of mineral coal had a major influence on the harvesting of peat and turf. Good quality sea coal would compete effectively where sites were close by the coast and transportation good. Inland and especially in upland areas, lower-grade peat and turf held their own for much longer. In parts of nineteenth- century Lancashire, even when coal had generally replaced peat as a fuel, in times of poor weather and difficulty of transport along bad roads, the farmers would once again cut the local peat bog for free fuel (Bob Middleton pers. comm.). In cases like this, the change in use and the environmental consequences occurred over a long transitional period. This extended back to perhaps the 1600s and 1700s as mineral coal became both widely available and more generally accepted as a domestic fuel, and then up to the late twentieth century.

In North Yorkshire and parts of Scotland, surface outcropping coal (sometimes called 'moor coal') was available but was itself a rather low-grade Jurassic material. Here again, this did impact on the use of peat, but in some cases such as at the Tan Hill Inn and neighbouring houses in North Yorkshire, the two fuels were mixed and burnt as briquettes (Hartley & Ingiliby 1982; Pontefract & Hartley 1934).

Other interactions include the relationship with the use of wood. It seems likely, in upland areas where wood was scarce from a relatively early date, that peat and turf were used as fuels. Wood was saved for other purposes. The availability of peat or turf in sufficient quantities would therefore have a further indirect effect on these landscapes through the relationship with associated woodland resources.

These potentially complex interactions require more robust datasets and a more thorough interrogation before final conclusions can be drawn. Costs, both real and relative, and case study examples for the use of peat and turf, and both coal and coppice wood are necessary to more fully inform the discussion.

CONCLUSIONS

THE SCALE OF UTILISATION

The research confirms the extent of utilisation as far greater than previously suspected. For example, well-defined peat cuttings around remaining blanket mire in the Peak District cover around 3,500 ha. Those on or around North Yorkshire moors are of a similar scale. Thin peats and turf on low level moors have also been stripped away. Many areas have had extensive 'turf-cutting' and 'paring and burning'. This was sometimes associated with land improvement for agriculture and the creation of in-bye land. Upland peat and turf cutting have greatly influenced the pattern and expansion of in-bye, which in turn has affected human settlement, particularly around the moorland fringe.

Shallow peat cutting, 'turf-cutting', and 'paring and burning' were extensive across upland landscapes. These included valley sides down to areas of cutting and utilisation in the lowlands. This affected valley mires, raised bogs and fens, and many lowland heaths and commons, mostly now obliterated from the landscape. Where suitable landscape remains intact, be it upland or lowland, the widespread occurrence of drainage features and other cutting infrastructure indicate that little if any 'peatland' was unaffected by the utilisation.

WHEN DID THE PRACTICE CEASE?

There are diverse reasons for the end of this use, and a wide range of dates for abandonment across Britain. In some cases, like the Derbyshire White Peak, exhaustion of reserves, combined with loss of land to enclosures and improvement, were likely causes (perhaps during the 1700s and early 1800s). Indeed the major cause of abandonment of these uses historically was probably major land-use change. This was largely driven by people and factors separated from the day-to-day domestic exploitation. In many regions it brought about massive change in landscape and utilisation (see Chapman, this volume). Land improvement and loss of common rights were key movers in this fundamental change. Some use did continue and some occurs even today. Abandonment of other cultural landscape uses often follows similar patterns.

In terms of fuel utilisation, the reason for change in some cases was competition from other fuels. These were either cheaper, more accessible, or of better quality. The *Old Statistical Account* of the Parishes of Anwoth and Girthon in 1792 notes that for coastal areas of south-west Scotland:

> Peats, the fuel used by the farmers and cottars, are dear, owing to the distance of the mosses, and, the bad roads which lead to them. ... Coals are the general fuel here. They are imported from Whitehaven, Newcastle, etc. and run from 30*s* to 40*s* a ton (*Statistical Account of Scotland 1792*).

In mid Wales, around Rhayader, the arrival of coal brought to the valleys by train in the 1860s /1870s, was the main reason. In the Yorkshire Dales, and the North York Moors, extensive cutting probably finished by the 1930s–1940s, as coal delivered by rail and road became more accessible.

Smith notes that in north-east Scotland:

> Peats are not used so widely as in former years. Prices are high normally £2 and over per cartload. Coal is brought to the door by motor lorry from Aberdeen and sells at the high price of £5 a ton for English coal and £4–15 for Scottish coal (Smith 1951, p. 96).

Loss of demand associated with either the collapse of specific industries (such as lead smelting in the Yorkshire Dales) or rural depopulation, are other likely causes. Exhaustion of supplies, the hard work of extracting and preparing the fuel, and financial considerations (especially the advent of cheap and easily accessed energy supplies from coal, electricity, oil and gas), are all important factors. Indeed the survival of the practice to the mid 1900s was often due to the peat fuel being cheap or even free. In some cases, the product from peat fuel was lower grade and of lower value than that from competing resources. Peat was then generally used when the others were unavailable. This applied to industrial use as well as domestic. Peter, discussing iron smelting around Silverdale in north Lancashire in the 1700s and 1800s, notes that:

> There was a plentiful supply of wood in this district to convert into charcoal for fuel. The tendency of timber supplies to become exhausted was a continuing problem for the iron producers at this period. Leighton was fortunate, however, in having an alternative fuel supply conveniently available in the peat obtained from the Arnside and Silverdate Mosses. When production was at its height, upwards of 8,000 cwts of peat a year were used at Leighton. The price of peat iron was low (ninety shillings a ton), whilst charcoal iron sold at seven pounds a ton. Occasionally quantities of peat iron had to be re-smelted (Peter 1984, pp. 42-3).

THE ECOLOGICAL IMPLICATIONS

Appreciating this impact is essential to inform both the conservation of this heritage, and the effective nature conservation of these areas. The domestic usage of these landscapes was very significant in terms of both micro- and medium-scale disturbance, and particularly in nutrient removal from the ecological systems. The importance to wildlife of both macro- and micro-scale disturbance is demonstrated by Ardron (1999a). Much contemporary eutrophication of remaining areas (especially lowland heaths) must in part be a result of these changes. There are serious and long-term implications of the cultural severance from domestic and often subsistence exploitation over perhaps 1,000–1,500 years. Long-term exploitation for fuel was important in maintaining low-nutrient status — essential for many specialist species. Abandonment has allowed a gradual but perhaps irreversible move towards eutrophication. This has profound long-term implications.

The most important conclusion relates to the fundamental scale of change in these landscapes. Firstly, the long-term use of these areas for fuel supply from A.D. 1200 onwards until the 1950s (but probably earlier too), and its impacts, have been grossly underestimated. Secondly, the separation of many landscape zones into lowlands and uplands may mask the human element. These peatland and former peatland areas are very much reflections of enclosed and unenclosed landscapes. The conversion of peatlands and other commons has had far greater impact in the lowlands. Enclosure, cutting and drainage and, finally, often catastrophic agricultural intensification or creeping urbanisation, have radically altered the lower ground, almost beyond recognition. However, whilst the upland areas have escaped this fate, the impacts of drainage, isolation, and fragmentation are huge. Not only this, but the domestic use of the peat and turf in many upland areas had influences beyond their immediate boundaries. Through the complexities of fuel economies in upland environments, and interactions with other managed natural resources, the availability and exploitation of peat and turf have affected much of the British uplands.

ACKNOWLEDGEMENTS

Thanks are due to our co-researchers and colleagues for their enthusiasm and encouragement, and to numerous others who have given freely of time and knowledge. Ian Whyte and Angus Winchester are thanked for their encouragement and for helpful comments on an early draft.

The landscape and environmental impact of mining and quarrying in upland Britain

Ian D. Whyte

ABSTRACT

Industrial landscapes often survive best in upland areas where they have been less disturbed than in the lowlands. The chapter looks at the landscape evidence for, and environmental impact of, mining and quarrying in upland Britain, focusing on the period from the sixteenth to the early twentieth century. The role of changing technology is considered together with the problems of generating power in remote upland areas and processing metallic ores. The transport problems involved in mining in such difficult environments are then reviewed and a range of environmental impacts caused by mineral and rock extraction are examined.

KEYWORDS

Mining, quarrying, lead, copper, iron

INTRODUCTION

The uniqueness of Britain's industrial history is widely appreciated. Industrial landscapes have often survived best in upland areas where they have been less disturbed than in the lowlands. In extreme cases, as with the slate quarrying landscapes of North Wales, a combination of large-scale extraction and a dramatic physical environment have created landscapes of 'terrifying grandeur' (Trinder 1982, p. 4). Prominent among industrial remains in upland areas are those of mining and quarrying. This chapter reviews the landscape evidence for, and impact of, an important set of activities that has profoundly altered large areas of upland Britain. The focus is on the period from the sixteenth to the early twentieth century, the peak of activity and landscape impact.

Four types of materials were involved: first, those which were stratified, where the deposits occurred over extensive areas relatively uniformly in terms of quantity and quality. They might be extracted widely on a small scale, as where shallow coal seams were worked by large numbers of shallow bell pits; or extraction could be concentrated at locations where access and transport were relatively easy, as with many quarries. Production from such deposits could be relatively continuous and geared to demand. This category includes limestone, sandstone, slate, coal and many iron ore deposits. However, some unstratified igneous rocks, such as granite, were more limited in their distribution.

Second were vein minerals, such as the ores of lead, zinc, and copper, which were more limited in distribution and variable in quality, veins often widening out into large ore bodies or dying away into thin strings. Such minerals were generally mined wherever they were discovered, regardless of transport problems and other difficulties. Third were minerals like tin and gold which might occur in veins but were also extracted from alluvial deposits. Finally, there were rare minerals, such as the graphite deposits in Borrowdale, where production was concentrated in a limited number of locations or even a single site. Different kinds of stone were quarried for various purposes depending on the local geology and the economy. Sandstone and gritstone, where it could be split thinly, was used for roofing as well as for walling and flooring, coarser gritstone for gateposts and lintels. Some sandstones were worked for millstones; rejects can still be found lying in some quarries (Barnatt & Smith 1998, pp. 106-7). Limestone, as well as being used for construction, was burnt to produce agricultural lime. Granite was quarried only from the nineteenth century with the development of steam-powered cutting equipment.

CHRONOLOGICAL SURVEY OF THE DEVELOPMENT OF MINING AND QUARRYING

Three broad phases of technological development in mining and quarrying in the British uplands can be identified, though they are blurred by the fact that many units of production remained small scale, with little mechanisation, until the late nineteenth century. Levels of technology and the scale of operation remained essentially medieval in character until the later seventeenth century though some water-powered machinery such as stamping mills for crushing ore had been introduced. From then until the later eighteenth century, improved technology, including the use of gunpowder, more effective water-powered lifting and pumping equipment and tramways, led to a substantial expansion in the size of some operations. In the nineteenth century, the increasing mechanisation of mines and quarries, with the introduction of powered drills and stone-cutting equipment, and steam railways generated further growth in the size of enterprises and their landscape impact.

Industrial landscapes were limited in extent before the eighteenth century. Nevertheless, the scale of prehistoric landscape modification through stone extraction could be considerable locally. The production of Neolithic stone axes from upland sites involved mainly the use of scree material but, in some cases, stone was quarried or even mined, as at Mynydd Rhiw in Caernarvonshire (Megaw & Simpson 1979, pp. 109-10). The stone axe production sites in the Lake District, working a particular band of volcanic tuff, occurred over a wide area of the central fells. At the most heavily-used sites stone was quarried as well as being picked up off the screes (Claris & Quertermaine 1989).

Tin was mined in the South-West from Bronze Age times (Gerrard 2000, pp. 15-16). Work may have been started in the valleys of upland streams where alluvial tin was close to the surface. Such activity may have been related to the removal of alder woods for charcoal. Some hut circles on Dartmoor, not evidently associated with fields, may have been inhabited by prehistoric tinners. Finds of tin slag from Iron Age settlements like Chysauster indicate that mineral extraction may have been part of the economy of what would otherwise have been identified as purely agricultural communities (*ibid.*, p. 19).

Under the Romans, mining expanded significantly. Gold was mined at Dolaucothi in Wales and lead in Derbyshire, North Wales, Shropshire, and Mendip. Finds of ingots from the Yorkshire Dales and the North Pennines indicate Roman activity, though no definite landscape remains from this period have been identified. Some small, weathered bell pits close to a Roman kiln site at Quernmore near Lancaster may be contemporary (Hudson 1998, p. 24). Copper was also mined in Shropshire, North Wales and Anglesey. In post-Roman times some deposits continued to be exploited. Norse settlers worked steatite deposits in Shetland at five different locations and carved the soapstone into vessels. At Catpund Burn the hillside is still covered in debris from Viking quarrying (Turner 1998, pp. 108-10). Field evidence of medieval mining is poor; documentary references are sporadic and rarely site-specific (White 1997, pp. 78-9). Fountains and Jervaulx abbeys are known to have worked lead in Nidderdale, Swaledale, Arkengarthdale and Wensleydale while Furness Abbey was involved in iron smelting in the southern Lake District.

The rise of mining in the sixteenth century was associated with the Tudor expansion of industry. The Society for Mines Royal, founded in 1568 to open up copper mines in the Lake District (colour Pl. VIII), had to bring in technical expertise from the Tyrol. Their smelter near Keswick may have continued operating down to *c.* 1650 (Collingwood 1912). A spin-off from this activity in northern England was a phase of prospecting in Scotland by English miners like Bevis Bulmer who opened up the alluvial gold deposits on Crawford Moor (Porteous 1876).

During the seventeenth and eighteenth centuries output grew substantially at some mines and many smaller workings were opened up. For the first time the scale of activity created extensive mining landscapes in upland areas embracing not just the extraction of minerals but the production of fuel, the generation of power, the transport of materials and the creation of specialised industrial settlements (Palmer & Neaverson 1998). Mining was often carried out at high elevation and the ore was frequently dressed at the mine to reduce the amount of waste transported. Smelting, on the other hand, often involved the collection of ore and fuel supplies from a wide area as well as requiring waterpower, and was usually located in valleys. The irregular nature of much production was due to the nature of the deposits and lack of knowledge of geology, though political events such as Civil Wars also caused interruptions. Improved technology in the cutting of shafts and levels, power generation, and ore processing, such as the introduction of charcoal-fired blast furnaces into the iron industry, increased the scale and efficiency of production. Some activities, however, like coal mining and stone quarrying, mostly continued into the eighteenth century as part-time, small-scale work. Even more than mining, early quarrying is poorly documented and surviving features on the ground can be difficult to date. Slate quarries at Stockdalebank, Longsleddale, in the eastern Lake District, can be shown to have been worked for a limited time, mainly in the 1720s. The small, intermittent rock faces that are visible emphasise the limited scale of production (David & Brambles 1992).

From the late eighteenth century, demand for many ores and rocks increased greatly, especially with the need for slate and paving stones for rapidly growing industrial towns. By the 1840s, the UK was the world's largest producer of lead with half of global output (Trinder 1982, p. 50). The production of copper from Cornwall trebled between 1750 and 1770. Mining greatly altered the landscape of many upland areas at this time, though the scale of operation at individual sites often remained small. New technology, such as the use of gunpowder, and steam power for pumping, winding and ore processing, also began to have a wider impact by cheapening the costs of extraction. By the nineteenth century, the scale of quarrying in areas like North Wales reached a point where upland extractive sites became major visitor attractions and objects of awe.

The mid-nineteenth century saw the peak of production in many mining and quarrying areas with the development of much larger units of production. The scale of slate quarrying in North Wales, which peaked in the 1880s and 1890s, probably represents the most striking modification of an upland British landscape by mineral extraction (Lindsay 1974). In the last two decades of the century, however, a rapid fall in production occurred in mining with a sharp drop in prices due to the opening up of overseas deposits, though output from quarries continued to grow. Many mines were abandoned and the scale of working was drastically reduced elsewhere (Barnatt & Smith 1998, p. 101).

In the twentieth century, some more profitable concerns continued to operate: the Greenside lead mines in the Lake District only closed in 1962. Elsewhere, however, activity often involved only the more efficient re-working of spoil to extract ores or minerals such as barytes and fluorspar for which new uses had been developed. Efforts to reopen some deep mines met with little success due to the flooding and collapse of the workings. The decay and sometimes deliberate dismantling of surface remains for safety reasons was only halted from the 1970s with increasing interest in mining and quarrying landscapes as heritage. The 1980s and 1990s saw the establishment of industrial museums and heritage centres in places like Nenthead and Wanlockhead, and the survey and consolidation of other sites by organisations such as national park authorities and the National Trust. The quarrying industry ran down in many areas too with changes to new materials and activity was increasingly concentrated in a few large-scale sites.

MINING AND QUARRYING TECHNOLOGY AND THE LANDSCAPE

The remains of early, small-scale workings can be difficult to identify and date. Such features are sometimes identified as 'Roman' by local historians without hard evidence but are probably mostly much later in date. The Siller Holes and Jeannie Barrie's Cave, near Carlops, south of Edinburgh, are a good example of mining features that, from surface evidence, are extremely hard to date (RCAHMS 1967, pp. 353, 355). In Furness some iron-working sites are assumed to be prehistoric due to their proximity to other, more easily-dated remains but such associations, lacking firm dating evidence, are dubious (Bowden 2000, pp. 12-14). Some early quarries can be associated with the extraction of stone for particular construction projects, like Bourjo quarry on the Eildon Hills which provided stone for Melrose Abbey (RCAHMS 1957 p. 323).

Patterns of extraction over space and through time were related to structures of landownership and the amount of capital and enthusiasm possessed by individual proprietors, as well as to wider market conditions. Ownership, as much as geology, could determine the scale and character of development. There are major contrasts in landscapes created by the small-scale working of individual miners' claims, as on Grassington Moor in the Yorkshire Dales, and areas dominated by large-scale, capital intensive working, as on Alston Moor (Palmer & Neverson 1998, p. 30). Manorial lords retained the right to minerals on their estates, even on land enclosed by parliamentary act in the eighteenth and nineteenth centuries. In different areas, mining claims were organised in different ways. In the Yorkshire Dales the discoverer of a vein of lead had the right to work it for two meres (a mere being, traditionally, the distance over which a hammer could be thrown), the claims being marked at the surface by mere stones. Changes of ownership could greatly increase the scale of operations, as when the Leadhills mining field passed by marriage to the Hope family in the early seventeenth century, leading to a marked increase in investment and output (Whyte & Whyte 1987, p. 44).

Prospecting for metallic ores was often hit or miss with much hard work and, frequently, no gain, as is evidenced in many mining fields by trial workings around the main veins where all that was evidently found was quartz, calcite or barytes. Prospecting for tin lodes by digging a series of shallow pits, often in straight lines, can be seen in the South-West at sites like Blackrock on Foweymore (Gerrard 2000, pp. 8-9). Veins might be located at the surface in outcrops, streambeds or by changes in vegetation. In a mining field, veins were often more or less parallel and could be intersected from underground workings by driving cross-cuts. Where the bedrock was under a drift cover, hushing might be employed. Thought to have been known to the Romans but much more frequently used in the eighteenth and nineteenth centuries, this involved damming water on a hillside, often diverting it from streams by artificial channels. The dam was then breached, releasing a flood that stripped away vegetation, soil and drift to cut a gully which eventually revealed the bedrock, allowing veins to be searched for. Mining could then proceed in the bed of the hush by opencast working, levels or shafts. Hushing was widely used in the Pennines (White 1997, p. 79), in the South-West and in the Leadhills area. The technique does not seem to have been used much in Lake District, apart from on the smooth slopes of the Skiddaw Slates, perhaps because surface outcrops were much more frequent than in the Pennines.

Tin mining involved alluvial streamworks and the exploitation of eluvial deposits on hillsides. Water was used to wash away the lighter clay and sand, leaving behind cassiterite tin ore. The velocity of the water needed to be carefully controlled by altering the volume of water and the gradient of the washing surface. Types of streamworks included hatchworks or small pits where water was fed directly from a leat, a technique used for small-scale working or prospecting. Cuesta works were spoil dumps with asymmetrical profiles created by dumping from wheelbarrows. Parallel works were linear banks up to 4 metres high with symmetrical profiles created using shovels rather than wheelbarrows. Eluvial streamworks exploited deposits in dry gullies above rivers where the ore had been transported from the lode but had not been sorted by fluvial action; the remains of such workings are often better preserved than alluvial streamworks as they have been less affected by fluvial erosion and deposition. At some sites, water for washing the alluvium was brought many kilometres by specially-constructed leats (Gerrard 2000, p. 47).

In some areas, gold was obtained by washing alluvial deposits rather than mining from veins. On the Elvan Water near Leadhills the remains of former opencast workings from which gold-bearing gravels were extracted are visible as hummocky topography. Some of the workings may date from the late sixteenth century (Lythe 1960, p. 76). On the Glengaber Burn in Selkirkshire, valley-floor earthworks extending for some 600 metres have been interpreted as large-scale sixteenth-century operations for alluvial gold (RCAHMS 1957, pp. 75, 124). In the Strath of Kildonan in Sutherland alluvial gold workings survive from the gold rush of 1868-9. The temporary camps that accommodated up to 600 prospectors have left traces in the form of levelled platforms on which huts were constructed as well as the excavations relating to individual mining claims (Pollard 2000).

Opencast workings for tin created narrow elongated gullies. Elsewhere simple stope workings occurred where veins of lead, copper or iron outcropping at the surface were worked horizontally and vertically creating shallow trenches whose bottoms were reached by wooden ladders (colour Pl. IX). Drainage was, inevitably, a problem. Good examples, probably dating from the seventeenth century, can be seen in the Red Dell valley at Coniston (Holland 1986, p. 31). Underground working was used by the Romans and seems to have begun again in some areas in medieval times. Where the topography was suitable, horizontal adits leading into the workings were preferable to shafts as they made for easier drainage. The introduction of gunpowder from the late seventeenth century made possible the construction of longer, wider levels draining extensive areas of underground workings. Where these carried tramways for bringing out the ore they were sometimes referred to as 'horse levels'. Shafts without adits needed equipment for pumping and for raising the ore. Before the introduction of gunpowder, adits and shafts were driven by hand, generally by hammering wedges into cracks or drilled holes. As a result, adits were made as narrow as possible and are often known as 'coffin levels'. Even with gunpowder, the holes for the explosives had to be bored by hand. Only in the later nineteenth century were compressed air drills and dynamite introduced. Deeper deposits could be worked by underhand and overhand stoping, where veins were worked downwards or upwards from a level driven horizontally into a hillside, some of the waste material being stacked within the mine rather than being carried to the surface.

Where seams of coal and sometimes other minerals lay close to the surface, bell pits were used into the nineteenth century. These were shallow shafts where the seam was worked for a limited distance around the base until drainage problems or the threat of roof collapse prompted a move to a new pit. Classic bell pits are surrounded by a ring of spoil but in some areas, such as Quernmore in Lancashire, where large numbers exist without spoil, there may be confusion between bell pits and ventilation shafts designed to serve more extensive underground pillar-and-stall workings (Hudson 1998, p. 43). In the Pennines, thin seams of poor coal among the Yoredale and Millstone Grit series were worked for local use before the coming of the railways. On the summit of Fountains Fell, at an altitude of over 600 metres, the remains of shafts, levels, coke ovens (Pl. 10.I) and access roads can still be seen. In the Tan Hill area, south of Stainmore, coal was worked from medieval times until the 1930s. Remains of hundreds of grassed-over bell pits can still be seen but later mining used mainly deeper shafts. Much of the coal was converted to coke in primitive ovens for lead smelting in Swaledale while coal was also carried by packhorse to local farms for domestic use.

Before the later eighteenth century most quarries were small, and are difficult to date unless linked to particular construction projects.

Plate 10.1. High and remote: coke oven on the summit of Fountains Fell.

When Lord Wharton had a new deer park created near Ravenstonedale, Westmorland, in 1561, a perimeter wall, which still survives to a height of ten feet in places, was constructed (Hoyle 1995). Stone was obtained from the moorland immediately adjoining the wall and the shallow hollows from which it was taken can only be distinguished from natural sinkholes in the limestone by their more elongated shape. A more readily datable class of quarries are those associated with the parliamentary enclosure of upland waste. Enclosure commissioners generally included provision of small areas for quarries to provide material for making the new public and private roads, as well as walls for allotments, and in some cases new farmsteads.

In some areas, by the later eighteenth century, the scale of quarrying was increasing. Problems with the disposal of waste from slate working arose from the fact that around 90 *per cent* of the rock that was quarried was unwanted and had to be backfilled into underground workings or tipped on spoil heaps at the surface. In the central Pennines around towns, like Darwen and Rawtenstall, horizontally-bedded gritstones were quarried on a large scale to meet the demands of the rapidly-growing industrial towns of south Lancashire (Ashmore 1982). In Cornwall, the china clay industry expanded rapidly in the mid-nineteenth century from small beginnings a few decades earlier (Trinder 1982, p. 224).

Slate quarrying, which expanded steadily in North Wales, the Lake District and Argyllshire during the later eighteenth century, grew dramatically in the nineteenth. The Penrhyn quarries at Bethesda and the Dinorwic quarry at Llanberis were the largest in the world, employing tens of thousands of workers. The Ordovician and Cambrian strata of Snowdonia provided the best slate but it was also worked in the other areas, like Llangollen, where the slate was less durable but was located closer to urban markets. The slate around Llanberis was worked at the surface using a series of open terraces 15–20 metres high. At Blaenau Ffestiniog the slate was mined underground as the beds dipped at 30 degrees to the horizontal. In between these two types of working were pits where the slate beds dipped vertically, as in the quarries around Nantlle. Underground workings sometimes required water- or steam-powered pumping equipment, as at the Dorothea Quarry, Dyfferyn (Lindsay 1974).

Limekilns were common in many upland areas with Carboniferous limestone. The lime was burnt to make quicklime using coal, peat, or wood as fuel and was used for construction and agriculture, especially with the enclosure and improvement of land (Cleasby 1994). Early kilns were simple clamps, piled-up mixtures of limestone and fuel that had to be destroyed to extract the lime. These are hard to identify in the landscape, often appearing as shallow hollows outlined by banks (Whyte & Whyte 1991, p. 225). Field kilns were small, single-chambered structures, adjoining or even built into the outcrop from which stone was worked. Larger commercial ones were built wherever cheap coal was available, along canals like the Leeds-Liverpool or beside railways.

Drainage was a perennial problem for all mines in a wet country like Britain. Adits connecting with the surface could be used for drainage. From the later seventeenth and early eighteenth centuries main drainage levels were cut, sometimes of considerable length, reaching the surface at the lowest possible altitude, to drain extensive areas of workings above. It was also easier to bring ore out along a level than wind it up a shaft. Gripps Level at Leadhills, driven in the 1790s and Deep Level at Coniston, dating from 1825, are examples. The Nent Force Level on Alston Moor, nearly 8 km long, was wide enough for 10-metre narrow boats to be used to carry out the ore.

POWER AND PROCESSING

Horse gins were used for raising water and ore, the horses walking in a circle with the rope being wound round a drum. Traces of them can often be seen on the surface beside shafts. Water was the main source of power in many mining fields until late in the nineteenth century, for winding, pumping, crushing, dressing, smelting, and ventilation. It was much cheaper to use than steam where coal had to be brought in over a distance. Waterwheels, sunk to half their depth in rectangular pits, could be very large (Pl. 10. II). One at the Barrow Mine, Newlands, near Borrowdale was 20 metres in diameter (Adams 1995, pp. 40-2). An equally impressive one survives at Killhope at the head of Weardale. An alternative was the water-bucket pumping engine, an example of which can be seen at Wanlockhead (Wickham-Jones 2001, pp. 135-7) (Pl. 10.III). It was used to pump water from a shaft and dates from the later nineteenth century. Simple, yet remarkably effective, it consisted of a beam, one end of which was raised and lowered by water pouring into a large metal bucket. The weight of the full bucket pulled one end of the beam down but the bucket automatically emptied when it reached the ground, causing the beam to lift again.

The amount of water available in small upland catchments, particularly in summer, was sometimes limited, requiring careful management. Water was sometimes brought considerable distances to particular dressing mills and smelters, as on Grassington Moor where a main clay-lined leat 11 km long was fed by series of reservoirs to provide power for series of mines and crushing mills. At Coniston, a series of channels carried water between the

Plate 10.II. Sources of power: water-wheel pit, New Engine Shaft, Red Dell valley, Coniston.

Red Dell and Paddy End valleys, the tail race of one waterwheel connecting with the flume of the next, at successively lower levels (Holland 1986, pp. 221-4). The limited amount of waterpower available in Cornwall, plus the ease with which coal could be shipped from South Wales, helps to explain why the county's mining landscapes are dominated by engine houses (Pl. 10.IV). Steam power was useful where there was coal on site (as in some Pennine lead-mining areas) or fairly close and transport not too expensive. Variations in the price of coal could cause switches from water to steam power and back again. At the Bay Mine, Wanlockhead, the base of a steam engine can still be seen. Dating from 1790, it was used for only a short period, burning coal brought from Sanquhar 20 km away (Whyte & Whyte 1987, pp. 49-50).

Smelt mills in upland areas were often located in the valleys rather than at individual mines, closer to sources of charcoal, and drawing on the ore from several sets of workings. Crushing and treating the ore involved several processes. The most simple was smashing it by hand to separate the ore from the country rock. Debris from such primitive activity can be seen beside seventeenth-century stope workings at Levers Water above Coniston (Holland 1986, p. 33). From medieval times, water-powered stamp mills were used to crush the ore. The remains of over sixty are known

Plate 10.III. Sources of power: water-bucket pumping engine, Wanlockhead, Coniston.

Plate 10.IV. Sources of power: steam engine house, Clintsfield colliery, on the edge of the Bowland fells.

from Dartmoor (Gerrard 2000, p. 115). A later development was the use of crushing mills with cast iron rollers. In tin-mining areas, ore was finely ground between millstones. Further washing in buddles, angled wooden troughs, and flotation in large tanks was also used; the specific gravity of metallic ores like lead and copper was higher than other associated minerals that washed out more easily.

Smelting was accomplished with various fuels. 'White coal' or kiln-dried wood was efficient but expensive. Charcoal was used more widely. The existence of large areas of broadleaved woodland in the southern Lake District was crucial in allowing the development of a major iron-smelting industry during the eighteenth and nineteenth centuries. In turn, the demands of the industry encouraged the conversion of a good deal of pasture in this area to coppice woodland. Sustainable exploitation by coppicing meant that the industry was not detrimental to local woodlands. Today, former coppice woodlands show evidence of past exploitation in the form of stone walls dividing the coppices into rotational units, circular platforms or pitsteads on which charcoal was burnt, the remains of temporary charcoal-burners' huts and the tracks by which the characoal was transported (Bowden 2000, pp. 27-35). Coal was sometimes available for smelting but its quality was often poor and it was not used for smelting lead until after *c.* 1700 (Palmer & Neaverson 1998, p. 50). In the Pennines and other areas, peat was often used for smelting lead. The scale of peat use is demonstrated by the 119 metre-long peat stores at Old Gang smelt mill at the head of Swaledale; heather thatched, they had open sides to aid drying (White 1997, p. 86). An indirect effect of mining in such areas was the widespread stripping of peat on surrounding ridges both as fuel for the smelters and for domestic use by workers who lived at or close to the mines. The amount of charcoal needed for a blast furnace could also be considerable. The Duddon Bridge furnace in the southern Lake District would, on a fourteen-year coppice rotation, have required the charcoal output of ten acres of woodland per week (Palmer & Neaverson 1998, pp. 21-2).

For copper, lead and tin, smelting on simple bale hills gave way to water-powered hearths in the sixteenth century and coal-fired cupolas or reverberatory furnaces in the early eighteenth, though in the Pennines hearths burning peat continued in use long after cupolas were widespread elsewhere. Where the higher smelting temperatures provided by charcoal were essential, ore was sometimes brought considerable distances to the fuel supply, as with the iron smelters established in the West Highlands of Scotland in the later eighteenth and early nineteenth centuries, like the well-preserved site at Bonawe, opened in 1753 by the Cumbrian Newland Company. Cumbrian iron ore was brought in by ship, smelted using local charcoal, and the iron sent back to Furness (Lindsay 1975). Slate required fewer surface buildings for preparation than lead, copper or iron. Blocks of slate were prepared by hand and later sawn mechanically. They were then split and dressed by hand. The growing use of gunpowder in the nineteenth century for both mining and quarrying led to the siting of gunpowder factories in some upland areas. A characteristic of such plants was the way in which the various buildings were widely scattered over the site to reduce the damage caused by accidental explosions, as at Elterwater in Langdale and Gatebeck south of Kendal.

TRANSPORT

The main form of transport for fuel, ore, smelted metal and other commodities in upland areas before the eighteenth century was by packhorse. The early influence that some mining activity had on road networks is emphasised by Fleming's (1996) identification of a Roman road and its medieval successor linking the Vale of York to the lead-mining area of Swaledale. Loads were often carried over extremely difficult terrain. In the early seventeenth century, an ironworks at Brougham near Penrith used high-grade Furness haematite brought by packhorse to Windermere, up the lake to Ambleside by boat, then by packhorses again via Shap (Spence 1991). Over short distances, and downhill, heavier loads were transported by sledge, as at the Honister slate quarries in the Lake District. Sledges were also used for transporting stone from Honister by a sled-gate known as Moses Trod, over the shoulder of Great Gable and down into Wasdale and so to the coast (Hindle 1984, p. 115). At a later date, carts were used on more carefully constructed road surfaces. The cobbled road descending steeply from the Wrengill quarries at the head of Longsleddale is particularly impressive (David & Brambles 1992). Where deposits were worked from large numbers of sites relatively close together, as with bell pits for coal, dense networks of tracks sometimes survive, as in the upper Goyt Valley in the Peak District (Barnatt & Smith 1998, p. 87). The exploitation of mining areas sometimes led to the upgrading of roads. In the later seventeenth century, the Hope family was given special permission by the Scottish Parliament to upgrade a cart road from their mines at Leadhills to the port of Leith (Smout 1972, p. 111). The Gargrave-Grassington road was improved in 1790s by Duke of Devonshire to provide better access to the lead mines on Grassington Moor and to allow coal to be brought in (White 1997, pp. 98-9).

The difficulty and expense of using packhorses meant that water transport was used where possible. Ore from Coniston was carried by boat down Coniston Water and then overland to the port of Greenodd. Slate from the Troutbeck valley was sent down Windermere to Newby Bridge (Tyson 1984). Quarried stone was an important cargo on some canals such as the Leeds-Liverpool and Lancaster-Kendal. Sea transport was the key factor allowing the expansion of slate quarrying at West Highland sites like Ballachulish, where harbour piers were formed by dumping quarry waste.

The development of horse-drawn tramways to bring ore out from mines was a feature of the late eighteenth and early nineteenth centuries. On steep slopes, inclined planes, with loaded wagons running downhill on a cable pulling empty ones back uphill, were used. Good examples can be seen at the Coniston copper mines and the Honister quarries. More extensive surface tramway systems developed in the early nineteenth century. The North Wales slate quarries needed efficient transport to move stone within the quarries and to export it. At Port Penrhyn a horse-drawn tramway linked the harbour to the quarries as early as 1801. The Ffestiniog Railway was built in the 1830s with wagons running downhill from the quarries under gravity and being hauled back uphill by horses. Later in the nineteenth century, railways opened up new areas for the extractive industries: the granite quarries at Shap for example, while the construction of branch lines, as in Weardale and Wensleydale, was often undertaken to serve existing mining areas and quarrying (Hallas 1986). Towards the end of the nineteenth century, light railways were built to serve more remote areas including upland mining communities. The Leadhills and Wanlockhead light railway, opened in 1902, boasted the highest railway summit in Britain at 457 metres.

ENVIRONMENTAL IMPACTS

The diversion of streams due to mining activity was a small-scale impact. More seriously, the storage of water in large reservoirs in upland catchments liable to flash floods sometimes created the danger of dams bursting, as happened at Greenside in 1927 when the village of Glenridding was inundated due to the bursting of an earth dam in Keppel Cove (Adams 1995, p. 131). Spoil from mines or from crushing and dressing, when left in valley bottoms, could alter the characteristics of streams and cause them to become braided. This can be seen in the Church Beck above Coniston. In the valley of the Great Rundale Beck, on the Cross Fell escarpment, waste material has completely choked the valley. When left on slopes, such material could sometimes become unstable, especially after heavy rain, as at Greenside where consolidation work has been undertaken in recent years.

Pollution was a widespread feature of extractive industries in the uplands, whether in the form of waste material or the impact of heavy metals on soils and vegetation. Pollution from mines and dumps could cause heavy metal residues to contaminate both streams and groundwater, affecting crops, livestock and people. The release of water due to hushing could also affect the lower parts of stream catchments. In 1759, the Murton Beck and the River Eden in Westmorland were polluted by hushing for lead ore among the steep valleys below Cross Fell (Curwen 1932, p. 82). The impact of heavy metal pollution can continue long after mining has ceased. The extinction of char in Ullswater has been blamed on pollution from the Greenside lead mines (Pearsall & Pennington 1983, p. 83). The exceptional floods of the autumn/winter of 2000–2001 caused land in the Vale of York to be contaminated with dangerously high levels of lead from mines 80 km/50 miles away in the Yorkshire Dales. Lead fumes from smelters shortened the lives of smelt-mill workers. By the nineteenth century, efforts were made to keep the fumes away from communities in valleys first by moving the smelters, as at Wanlockhead where the smelt mill near the village was replaced by one further away at Sowen Burn (Whyte & Whyte 1987, pp. 49-52). Or the fumes could be carried away by long flues with chimneys emerging on hilltops where the fumes could be dissipated by the wind, for example Langley chimney near Allendale. This had the additional advantage of providing a stronger draught for the reverberatory furnaces while significant amounts of lead were deposited on the inside walls of flues that were periodically scraped clean. One of the longest flues was at Grassington, over 1.8 km long with two condenser houses and two settling ponds for the scrapings. The effect of lead in the spoil or of lead fumes on vegetation in neighbourhood of smelt mills can sometimes be noted by the occurrence of bare, poisoned ground, sometimes producing miniature gullied badlands as at Wanlockhead.

MINING COMMUNITIES

Miners often lived in existing, predominantly agricultural, settlements; many small cottages in communities in the Pennine Dales or the South-West were probably once occupied by them. Even in the nineteenth century, quarrying was often a part-time activity by men whose principal occupation was in agriculture. This helps to explain the lack of quarry settlements or housing in valleys like Troutbeck or Longsleddale (David

Plate 10.V. The area of improved land around Leadhills, formerly cultivated intensively by the miners.

1987). In order to attract workers to remote mining communities employers sometimes had to provide housing. At Leadhills and Wanlockhead rows of cottages without a regular plan were constructed by the lead-mining companies (Whyte & Whyte 1987, p. 43) (Pl. 10.V). At Nenthead, near Alston, a planned settlement was laid out, complete with chapel and social facilities provided by the London Lead Company. At the remote lead mines at Strontian in the West Highlands the York Buildings Company, which leased the workings in the 1730s, created the community of New York for up to 500 workers (RCAHM 1980, pp. 243-5).

Accommodation was sometimes more primitive, even in the early twentieth century, such as the barracks built for workers at remote quarry sites such as Wrengill in Longsleddale (David 1987) or at Honister. Some mines also lodged on site in primitive bunkhouses or 'shops', often damp and cheerless, used from Monday to Saturday. But mostly miners lived in the valleys and walked to work; rows of cottages were built for them in villages like Grassington, Gunnerside and Keld. Some miners had smallholdings: the part-time, sometimes seasonal nature of employment in mining is still evident on Alston Moor in the dense pattern of enclosures formerly belonging to miner/smallholders. At Leadhills, miners were encouraged to grow as many potatoes and vegetables as they could. At one time 600 acres were improved but much of this was let go during the nineteenth century when communication with the outside world improved (Whyte & Whyte 1987, pp. 43-4) (Pl. 10.VIII).

CONCLUSION: MINING LANDSCAPES AND MINING HERITAGE

Mining and quarrying have transformed the landscapes of extensive areas of upland Britain, particularly in England and Wales, where hill and moorland areas are relatively small and lie close to substantial urban populations. A survey of the Yorkshire Dales carried out in 1993 by English Heritage indicated that some 400 sq km could be classed as Mining Affected Landscapes (White 1997, p. 89). In addition, more peripheral areas were classed as Mining Related Landscape on the basis of features such as higher than usual population density, and the existence of high-altitude smallholdings.

Despite the relative lack of disturbance, such landscapes have been modified by the processes of decay and deliberate dismantling. Concern over pollution by heavy metals has led to the removal of spoil while the danger posed by open shafts and levels and ruined buildings has led to some demolition. The colonisation of spoil heaps by rare plants has provided an ecological argument for preservation in some cases. The remains of upland mining and quarrying within national parks or on land owned by the National Trust are more likely to have been surveyed and consolidated than elsewhere. Yet, even in national parks, some authorities have been slow to undertake such work or to produce plans for future management. EU funding has helped in some cases, as in the recent restoration work at Myers Head lead mine near Hartsop in the Lake District. In other cases, mining and quarrying landscapes have been privately restored and developed into museums and heritage centres. Much research, however, has focused on a limited number of well-known sites. There is ample scope for work in less well-known but locally significant areas, examining in particular how mining and quarrying were integrated with the rest of the local economy and society.

Col. Plate VIII (see ch. 10). The Goldscope Mine, Newlands valley, near Keswick: a sixteenth-century copper mine (Photo. A. Winchester).

Col. Plate IX (see ch. 10). Early stope workings, probably from the seventeenth century, Levers Water, Coniston (Photo. I. Whyte).

Col. Plate X (see ch. 10). Wanlockhead: a company-financed mining community (Photo. I. Whyte).

Col. Plate XI (see ch. 13). Modern afforestation in the uplands, Galloway (Photo. I. Whyte).

North Snowdonia: an upland landscape under pressure

Mark Brayshay & Andrew Williams

ABSTRACT

The nature of landscape development in upland areas is discussed and a case made for many areas being affected by relatively brief phases of rapid change punctuating longer-term continuity. This model is discussed in relation to north Snowdonia from medieval to recent times. An area often described as a 'natural' landscape is shown to be a highly dynamic one in which the culture, activities and farming methods of the inhabitants have been crucial in fashioning and re-fashioning the appearance of the area.

KEYWORDS

Snowdonia, upland farming, rural settlement, quarrying, foot-and-mouth disease

INTRODUCTION

In August 1998, a newspaper article reporting the National Trust's bid to buy a large farm, and thereby 'save' a tract of Snowdonia in north Wales, began with a question:

> What price a natural masterpiece admired by millions, tramped and sweated upon each year by tens of thousands, dating from the mists of time, irreplaceable and immovable? (*The Times*, 8 August, 1998).[1]

This notion of an immutable and timeless landscape, wrought only by natural processes, offers a romantic but distorted image of the Snowdonia region. While the mountains themselves may not have been fashioned by the generations of men and women who have lived and worked upon their slopes, the fields, farms, rough grazing and tracks that cloak these majestic uplands bear the unmistakable signature of human hands. Snowdonia's mantle of man-made scenery defines its identity and enhances its elemental beauty but the creation of that scenery is the result of complex responses and adaptations made by each new generation as it sought to derive a livelihood from the resources that the landscape offers. In a recent paper, Charles Withers challenged the orthodox notion that Snowdonia's landscape had been fashioned by means of a stage-by-stage progressive evolution. He questioned the validity of a linear model of gradual forward advance in explaining landscape change, suggesting instead that there were 'moments of rapid change punctuating the continuity of the upland scene' (Withers 1996, p. 45). We argue here that new pressures and demands that were made upon the Snowdonia landscape by its occupants triggered such 'moments of rapid change'. Thus, the history of the Snowdonia landscape, and indeed upland landscapes in general, may perhaps best be understood as a set of responses through time to changing pressures.

While vestiges of the prehistoric and medieval landscape remain, the human geography of Snowdonia is largely a product of the last three or four centuries with a quickening in the pace of change in the last hundred years. It reflects decisions made by owners and occupiers, past and present, in response not only to the physical capability of the land for agriculture and primary extractive industry, but also to profound shifts in local economic, demographic and social circumstances. Until relatively recently, those who occupied the upland landscape derived their livelihood directly from it. The resource capacity of the landscape to supports its inhabitants was therefore critical. Expansion could occur only if new resources were exploited, or existing capacities were somehow stretched further. However, during the past fifty years or so, there has also been an unprecedented breakdown in the intimate and direct link between the locally available resources of the landscape and the livelihood of its occupants. Unlike their antecedents, few of those who now live in Snowdonia depend solely for their income on what the locality itself can provide (BBC 2001).

The aims of this chapter are to explore the pressures that have influenced the inhabitants of northern Snowdonia during the past three centuries and to examine the impacts that their responses to those pressures have had upon the landscape. Attention will focus on the agricultural landscapes of northern Snowdonia during the past century and an assessment will be made of the new pressures and threats that today confront this precious and treasured part of Wales. At the beginning of the twenty-first century, we are witnessing yet another key 'moment of change'. Although the results for the future appearance of the landscape and the way of life of its occupants are not yet clear, it seems likely that this particular moment of change may well prove to be the more far reaching than any that have occurred before.

Snowdonia covers 1,352 square km (840 square miles) and comprises a majestic landscape that stretches southwards from the Conwy River as far as Machynlleth, and eastwards to Bala (Fig. 11.1). The region includes several mountain ranges: Snowdon itself, Tryfan, the Glyderau, the Moelwynion, Aran and Arenig, and Cader Idris. Declared one of Britain's National Parks in 1951, some 26,000 people now reside within its boundaries but it attracts another six million as tourists each year. Snowdonia is also the heartland of the Welsh language but traditional mainstays of the local economy — mining and slate quarrying — have declined and hill farming is in crisis.

In this study attention will focus mainly on just two parishes or 'community areas' that encircle Snowdon's peak, namely Llanberis and Beddgelert, together occupying 13,207 ha (32,636 acres) (6.07 *per cent* of the National Park). Their combined population in 1991 was only 2,521: a total that had been virtually stationary over the preceding ten years, but was 42 *per cent* below that recorded just over a century earlier, in the peak census year of 1881. Indeed, in keeping with much of the Snowdonia massif, the average population density of the study area is now less than 0.5 persons per hectare (Fig. 11.2). Within Llanberis lies the great natural 'fortress' of land girdled by the five mountain peaks of Yr Wyddfa (Snowdon), Glyder Fawr, Y Garn, Elider Fawr and Moel Eilio. At its core lies Nant Peris and the dramatic Pass of Llanberis. Until 1967, this land was part of the vast Vaynol estate, and its recent landscape history may therefore be recovered in considerable detail by studying *inter alia* the surviving surveys and other records of the Vaynol properties (Parry 1970; Roberts 1973; Brayshay & Williams 1995; Withers 1996). Bordering land belonged to the Bulkeley family, Lord Penrhyn and the Marquis of Anglesey. In the decades after the Second World War, much of this estate land was sold piecemeal to its occupiers. However, the National Trust has also gradually acquired substantial tracts of land on the southern side of Snowdon in Beddgelert. The Trust now owns seven properties covering 2,801 hectares (6,922 acres) extending northwards from the Aberglaslyn Pass to include the entire south-eastern quadrant of Snowdon from its summit to the valley floor of the Afon Glaslyn (National Trust 2001a) (Fig. 11.3). The role of the National Trust, not only in re-shaping the large areas of Snowdonia that it now controls, but also in moulding attitudes towards the landscape as a whole will be considered.

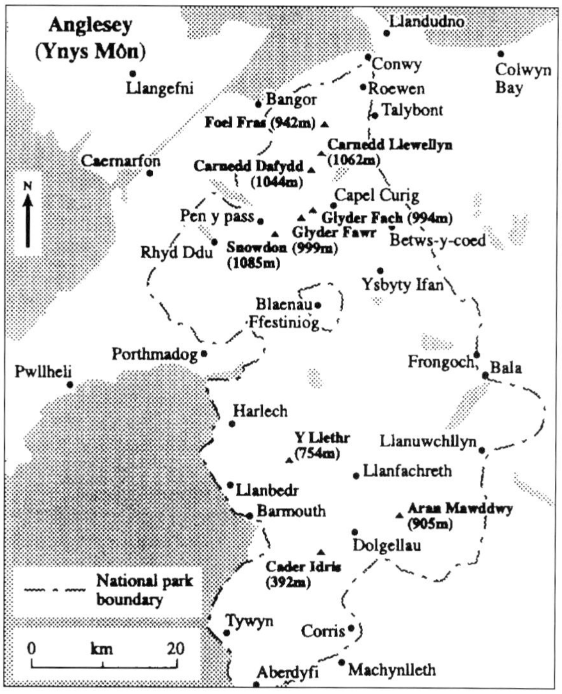

Fig. 11.1. The uplands of North Wales and the boundaries of the Snowdonia National Park.

THE CHALLENGE OF THE NATURAL ENVIRONMENT

As in all upland areas, Snowdonia's relief exerts a control on all aspects of the physical environment. Spectacular variations in altitude occur within short distances and steep slopes dominate the landscape. Great altitudinal ranges result in marked variations in rainfall, temperature, soils, vegetation and drainage conditions. In turn, these factors have influenced the pattern of settlement, communications and agricultural holdings. Average air temperatures in the Nant Peris and the Glaslyn Valley are 2°–5C° lower than in the coastal lowlands and the upland area growing season lasts less than 200 days. Above 325 metres (1,066 ft), it is even shorter (Elfyn Hughes 1973; Perkins 1978). Heavy rainfall, approaching 5,000 mm (197 inches) per annum, leaches soil nutrients and, compared with Anglesey, cloud cover reduces photosynthesis by up to 30 *per cent* (Elfyn Hughes 1973). High wind speeds damage the vegetation and accelerate evapo-transpiration. Thus, despite high rainfall totals, the Snowdonia sward is frequently affected by a shortage of water.

Northern Snowdonia comprises Cambrian and Ordovician rocks that have been subjected to considerable tectonic uplift and folding. Three geological zones may be identified: first, the Cambrian slates and grits; second, the Ordovician slates and shales; and third, the volcanic rocks, mainly rhyolites, that are also of Ordovician age (Williams 1927, 1930). The rhyolitic rocks are exceptionally resistant and

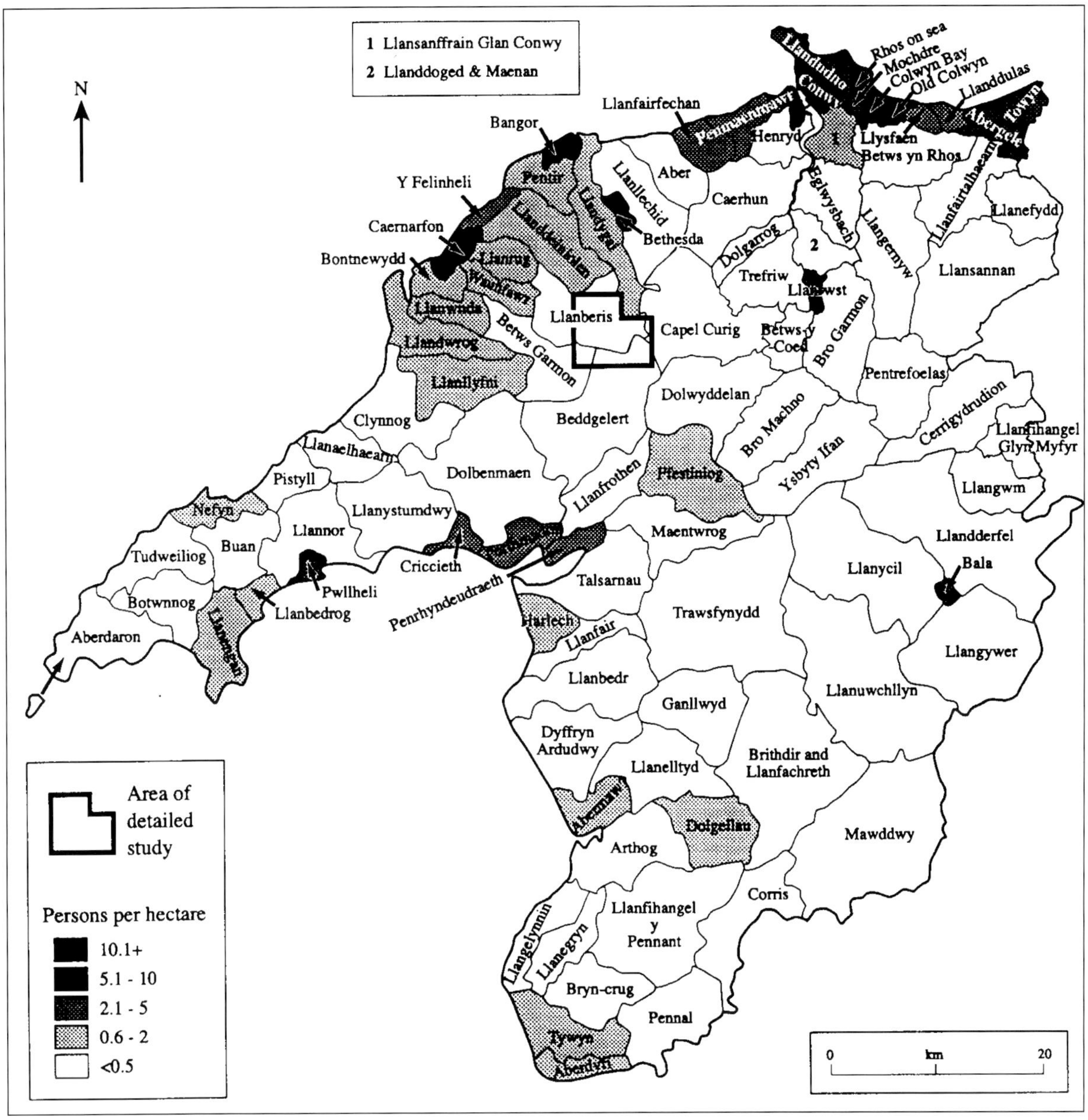

Fig. 11.2. Population density in the Community Areas of north-west Wales, 1991 and the specific area of study.

form the highest peaks, including Snowdon, while the Cambrian slates are exposed for example at Dinorwic, where they proved easy to quarry and were commercially exploited until the late 1960s, leaving extensive scars on the landscape (Lindsay 1974).

Glacial erosion and deposition have profoundly affected the landscape (Lewis 1949; Seddon 1957; Whittow & Ball 1970; Unwin 1973). While ice action was predominantly erosional, patches of depositional drift do occur. There are late-stage moraines across the mouth of many of the cwms and some glacial sediment was brought down the valleys by later fluvial action (Unwin 1975). Periglacial processes were also active, producing extensive scree slopes, particularly in some sections of the Llanberis Pass (Ball & Goodier 1970).

The striking variability of Snowdonia's soil reflects sharp changes in local climate and relief (Ball 1968; Ball *et al.* 1969). Brown earths, the most fertile soils, occupy the valley bottoms around Nant Peris and Nantgwynant. Large spreads of alluvium cover fluvioglacial boulders in the valley floors, while drift is encountered at the base of the valley sides. These silty loams are well structured and well drained, but generally shallow. Small pockets of brown earth associated with base-rich volcanic ash deposits occur at high altitudes, and were picked out by farming communities for exploitation and settlement in the past in what were otherwise highly marginal sites.

Snowdonia was more thickly wooded in the past than it is today. Although increased summer grazing and browsing, as well as coppicing and

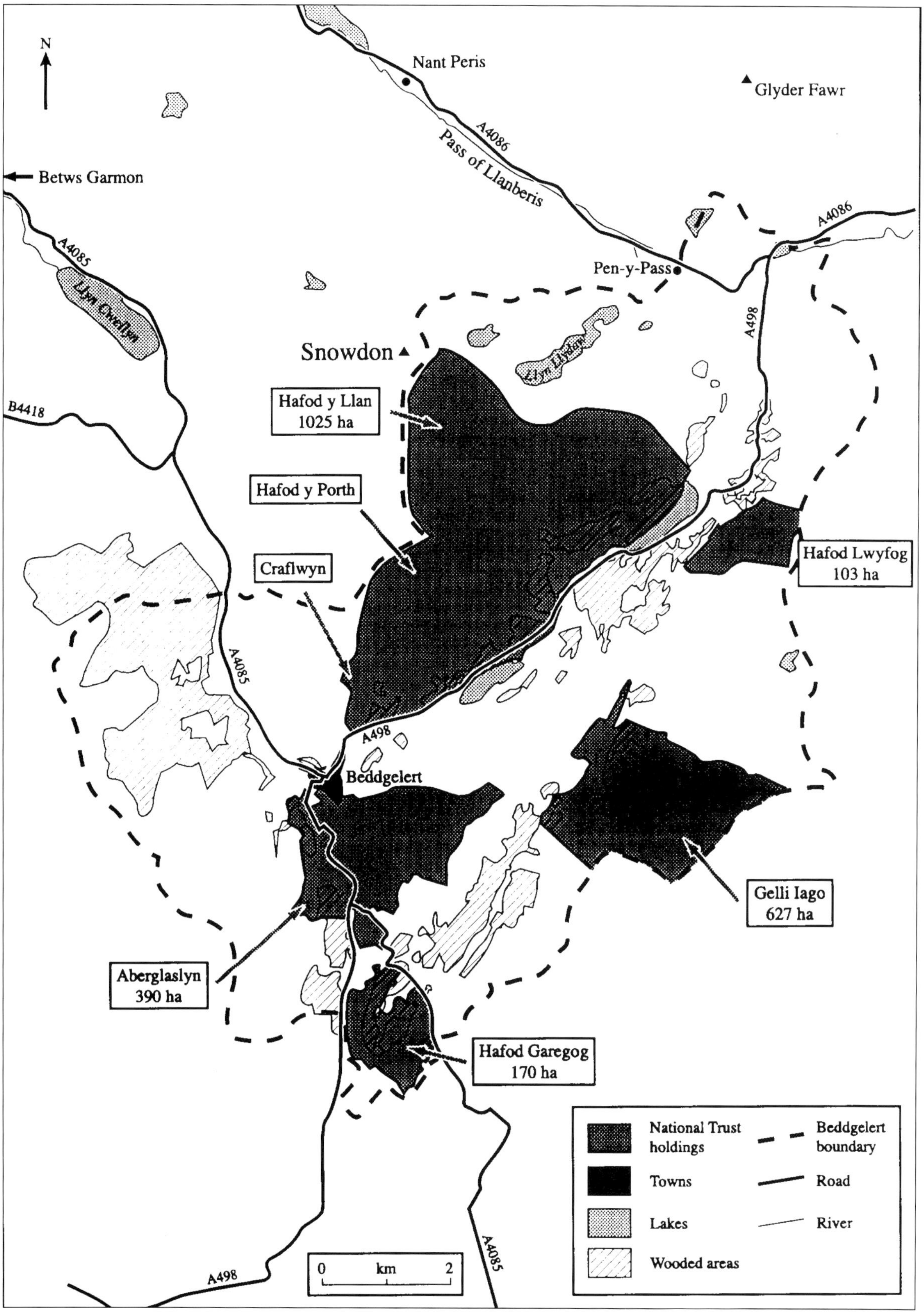

Fig. 11.3. National Trust property in Beddgelert, 2001.

felling timber for fuel and building, must have increased in the medieval period as the number of *hafodau* (summer shielings) multiplied, there was still a significant tree cover in the early 1700s. However, in the first half of the eighteenth century, some parts of Snowdonia were subjected to over-exploitation and stagnation. Timber was indiscriminately felled and not replaced (D. Thomas 1963; Aris 1977). Once deforested, the valley floors supported *Agrostis-Festuca* grassland, from which a hay crop could be taken (Perkins 1978). However, gleyed soils adjacent to the major rivers and valley lakes were prone to rush-infestation, especially by *Juncus effusus* and *Juncus squarrosus*, and were probably never capable of supporting a fodder crop (Dale 1973; National Trust 2001a). On the lower slopes immediately above the valley floor, bracken infestation is nowadays a considerable problem. Higher ratios of goats and cattle in the livestock population in the past helped to trample and suppress the bracken and these areas were therefore once capable of supporting *Agrostis-Festuca* grassland (Jones 1952; Roberts 1959). At very high altitudes, the natural sward always comprised mostly purple moor grass, or *Molinea caerula*. On the mountain summits, mat grasses (*Nardus stricta*) with some *Molinea caerula* dominated poor, nutrient-deficient grazing that offered only a very low livestock carrying capacity.

PERMANENT FARMS AND SETTLEMENTS IN THE MOUNTAIN LANDSCAPES

Considerable attention has been paid by previous authors to the character of the cultural landscape and human settlement of northern Snowdonia in the era before and after the conquest of Wales by Edward I in the thirteenth century (Jones Pierce 1940; Roberts 1949; Jones 1964; Roberts 1977; Beverley Smith 1966; Elfyn Hughes *et al.* 1979; Johnson 1981). Evidence of prehistoric high upland settlement survives at locations such as Cwdwythwch, but little is known for certain about the character of any associated farming (RCAHMW 1956–57). However, farms and settlements permanently occupied throughout the year do not appear to have existed in the mountains of Snowdonia in the early medieval period. The 1352 *Record of Caernarvon* mentions 'havotries', or summer-season farms located in the mountains; climatic deterioration by the fourteenth century probably made these sites too cold and exposed for year-round occupation (Ellis 1838; Parry 1978, 1985). In general, increasing summer wetness and declining temperatures were significant factors in reducing the potential for successful cropping in upland areas (Bell & Ogilvie 1978; Parry 1978; Campbell 1991). However, there is evidence that farmers from the lowlands customarily moved sheep, goats and cattle to graze the mountain pastures of northern Snowdonia in early May (Thomas 1968, 1978). This allowed the meadow grasses to grow in the fields of the *hendref* (lowland farm) and a hay crop to be taken to supply winter fodder when the livestock returned (Roberts 1959; Thomas 1968; Elfyn Hughes 1973; Davies 1979). This transhumance depended on plentiful land resources in both the lowlands and the uplands (Williams 1981). However, partible inheritance or *gavelkind* was common in medieval North Wales and was responsible after a time for rendering lowland holdings too small to support a family. To ease the pressure, mountain summer pastures often then became permanent farms, severed from their former lowland counterparts. While it is impossible to pinpoint exactly when such permanent mountain farms were formed in Snowdonia, a dozen well-established tenancies, arranged along the valley floor of the Afon Nant Peris and the Afon Arddu, are recorded in a Vaynol rent roll of 1696.[2]

EIGHTEENTH-CENTURY PRESSURES TO ESTABLISH MORE TENANCIES

A survey of the Vaynol Estate made in 1777 includes maps of every farm by then established.[3] Studies elsewhere indicate that enclosure was generally underway in North Wales by the mid-eighteenth century and the Vaynol survey shows that a patchwork of enclosed fields cloaked Snowdonia's valleys in the 1770s (Edwards 1963, Jones 1973; Chapman 1992). In the Pass of Llanberis and the valley of the Afon Arddu (occupied by twelve holdings in 1696), a total of twenty–four farms existed by 1777 (Fig. 11.4a).[4] In contrast to the medieval 'havotries', which avoided poorly-drained bottom land in Llyn Dwythwch and the Afon Nant Peris, each farm in the Pass of Llanberis and the Afon Arddu valley was allocated, by the later eighteenth century, a portion of enclosed 'in-bye' land on the floor of the valley,[5] in which hay crops or potatoes were cultivated in these fields (Kay 1794; Davies 1810; Williams 1941). In cases where a holding did not extend as far as the valley bottom, a separate area of *in-bye* land or *tir coch* (literally: brown soil) was assigned to it elsewhere, sometimes as much as 1.5–2.5 km (1–1.5 miles) from the main farm. Above their *in-bye* fields, the Vaynol maps show that each farm in the Pass of Llanberis had a portion of enclosed *ffriddoedd*, or holding land, on the lower slopes of the mountains.[6] Here, livestock grazed in early spring until the grasses started to grow in the unenclosed mountain 'sheepwalk' pastures above. Vacated *in-bye* meadows could then yield a hay crop for winter fodder. The unenclosed mountain grazing was shared in common by groups of farms, each being assigned a notional

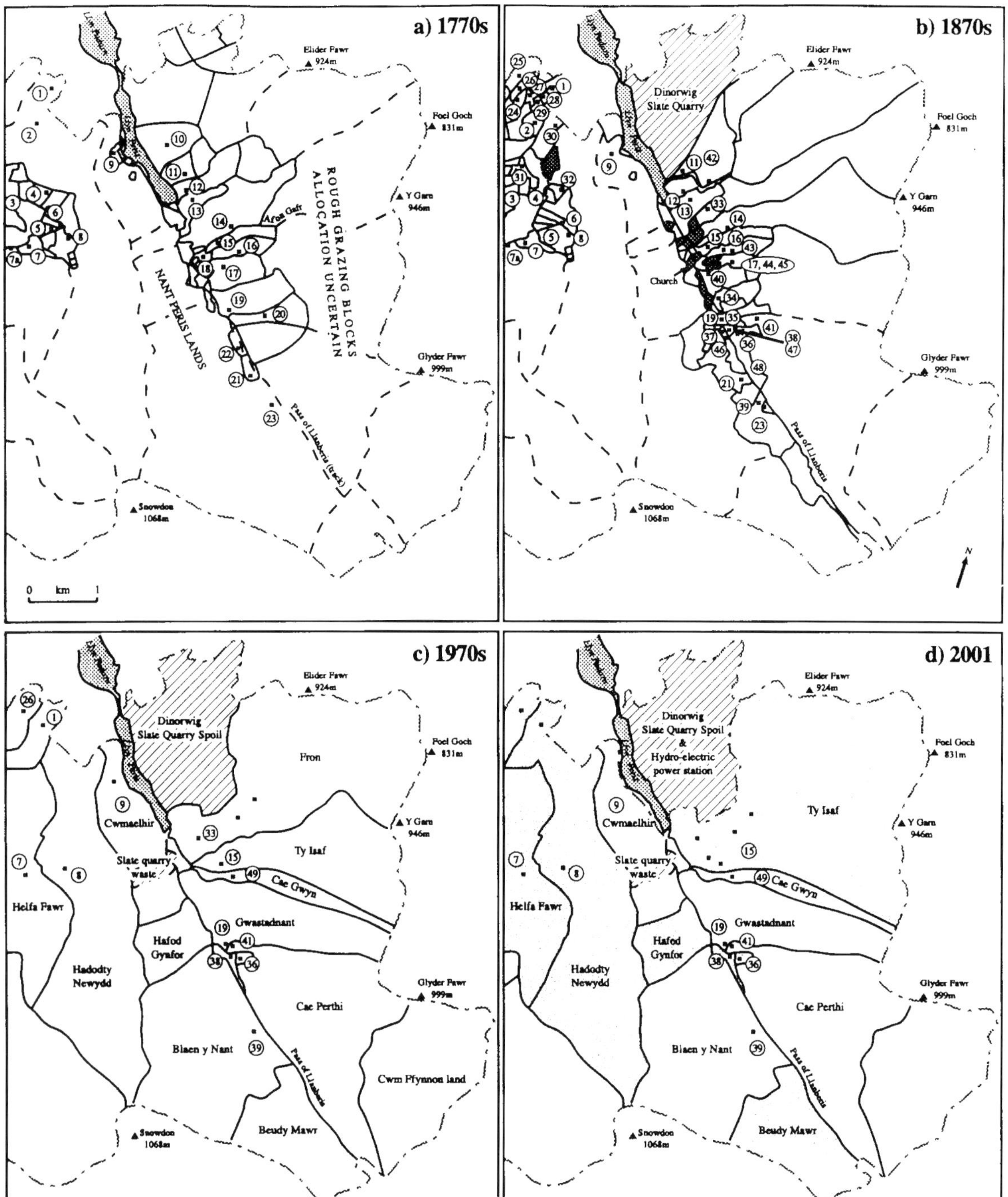

Farm tenancy boundaries · Buildings · Farms occupied and operated full-time, 2001
Boundaries of shared sheep-walk (grazing) · Small holdings with cottages/houses, 1870s · Grazing land / campsites (not full-time farm), 2001

1 Tyddyn Charles
2 Cae Esgob
3 Tynyraelgarth
4 Adwyraen
5 Nant ddu Bach
6 Nant ddu Fawr
7 Helfa Fawr
(7a Helfa Fain)
8 Hadodty Newydd
9 Cwm Aelhir
10 Pant y Ceubren
11 Garagwen
12 Pen y llyn
13 Llyn Bedw
14 Ceunant
15 Ty Isaf
16 Bryn Glas
17 Cwm y Wrach
18 Tyddyn y llan
19 Gwastadnant
20 Mur Mawr
21 Cwm Glas
22 Cwm Glas Bach
23 Ynys Ettws
24 Hafod
25 Llwyn Celyn
26 Halfod Lydau
27 Mur Mawr II
28 Tyn y Gadlas
29 Mur Mawr III
30 Pen y Ceunant
31 Cae Newydd
32 Bryn Coch
33 Fron
34 Gwastadnant II
35 Gwastadnant III
36 Hafod Gynfor
37 Bryn fforch
38 Beudy Mawr
39 Blaen y Nant
40 Tan y Dderwen
41 Cae Perthi
42 Garegwen II
43 Bryn Glas II
44 Cwm y Wrach II
45 Cwm y Wrach III
46 Bryn fforch II
47 Beudy Mawr II
48 Mur Mawr IV
49 Cae Gwyn

Fig. 11.4. The increase and decrease in farm units in the Pass of Llanberis since the 1770s
(a) Farms recorded in 1770s (based on MSS Vaynol 4055; MSS Vaynol 4057; MSS Vaynol 4063)
(b) Farms recorded in 1870s (based on MSS Vaynol 4108; MSS Vaynol 4195)
(c) Farms recorded in 1970s (authors' fieldwork)
(d) Farms recorded in 2001 (authors' fieldwork)

acreage of the 'sheepwalk' in proportion to their 'severally' held farms below (Rowlandson 1846; Dodd 1926–7; Roberts 1973; Thomas 1989). The crucial importance of these three management units (*in-bye* land, *ffriddoedd* and mountain sheepwalk) has been discussed elsewhere (Jones 1952; Elfyn Hughes 1973; Thomas 1978, 1992; Williams 1981; Brayshay & Williams 1995). In short, the amount of hay yielded by the *in-bye* land determined the total carrying capacity of each farm.

NINETEENTH-CENTURY POPULATION GROWTH PRESSURES AND THEIR IMPACT ON THE LANDSCAPE

Although owners of the Vaynol Estate encouraged their tenants to make improvements, scope to challenge the fundamental geographical controls was limited. Yet, despite its ruggedness, northern Snowdonia has always been a fragile landscape, easily damaged by over-exploitation. During the nineteenth century, largely in response to population pressure and the development of smallholdings for slate quarrymen, the number of farms established in some parts of northern Snowdonia sharply increased. Many possessed little or no *in-bye* land and were therefore obliged to cultivate late-season hay crops in the fields of the *ffriddoedd* in an effort to sustain livestock during the winter.

The population of Llanberis increased five-fold between 1801 and 1881 (Fig. 11.5). While some slate workers migrated from neighbouring parishes and lived in barracks at the quarry, considerable numbers were Llanberis-born. Extractive industries provided for a 'dual economy' whereby farming could be combined with mining and quarrying. The manuscript census enumerators' books, for 1841–1891, show that many households contained both farmers

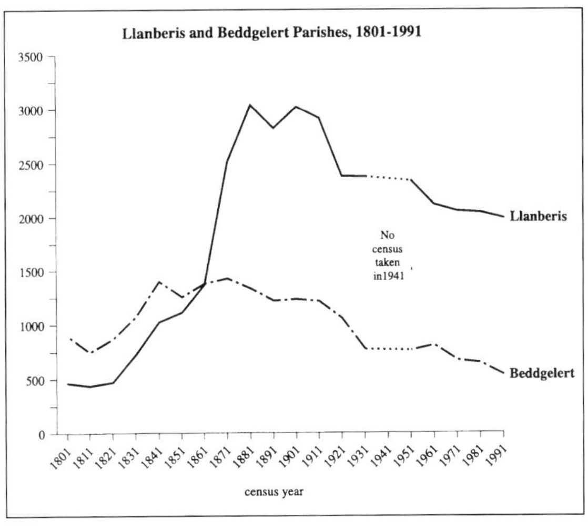

Fig. 11.5. Population change in Llanberis and Beddgelert, 1801–1991.

and quarrymen.[7] Moreover, in order to provide homes and added income as an encouragement to the industrial workforce, Vaynol created many new small holdings and permitted the building of industrial cottages on the land of existing agricultural tenancies in the Pass of Llanberis.[8] The number of farm units grew from twenty-four in 1777, to forty-seven by 1868 (Fig. 11.4b). In addition, by the late 1860s, there were another thirty-five dwellings in the Pass, mostly slate quarrymen's cottages.[9] Some were built adjacent to existing farmhouses; others were erected by the valley-floor road and provided with a small garden plot carved from precious in-bye fields. The ever-expanding spoil heaps of the slate quarries encroached remorselessly on the farmland at the north-western end of the Pass and some tenancies were simply buried under waste (Vaynol MS 2903).[10] Several other old-established farms were fragmented and had inadequate in-bye land and ffriddoedd in the key morphological units (Fig. 11.6). There can be little doubt that population pressure on the landscape was increasing.[11]

The Victorian census enumerators' books provide an extraordinary snapshot of the cultural landscape of this small portion of Snowdonia at a point when the population reached a peak and the landscape was intensively settled and its resources heavily exploited. This was a classic 'moment of rapid change'. The 1891 census shows that there were 385 people living on farmland in the study area. Of these, 303 resided on tenancies in the Pass of Llanberis. While the average household size was 4.7 persons, 35 *per cent* contained six or more people. Almost a third of the dwellings comprised four rooms or less, and several families of five or six people lived in two- or three-roomed cottages.[12] Thus, both the landscape and many of the houses were overcrowded. The vast majority of the people were either born in the parish or a near neighbour; there were scarcely any outsiders. Moreover, 92.4 *per cent* spoke only Welsh, 6.6 *per cent* were bilingual, and English speakers represented just 1 *per cent*. The census shows that a majority of household heads recorded slate quarrying as their occupation. In the 1871 census, 10 *per cent* had recorded their occupation as 'farmer'; by 1891, this had fallen to only 4.1 *per cent*.[13] Yet the Vaynol rent records show that two-thirds of these slate quarrymen household heads occupied a farm tenancy.[14] Moreover, even including the newly-created smallholdings, the average farm size was still 165 acres (67 ha).[15] The scale of farming activity in the area may well have declined somewhat because of Britain's agricultural depression that began in the 1870s, but the lure of a job in the slate industry would have been a more significant factor. In a few cases, younger sons were recorded as 'farm servants' or (very rarely)

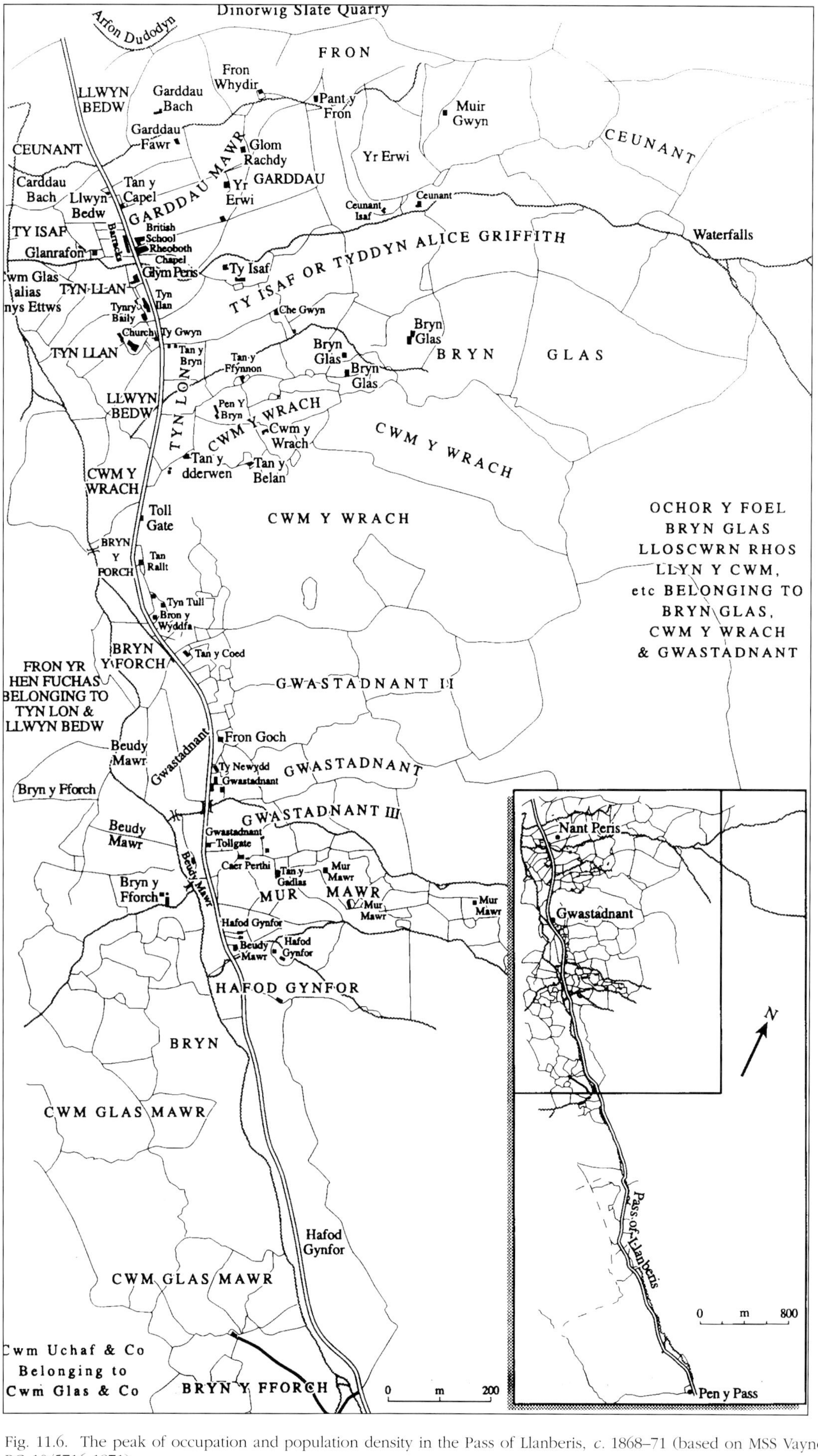

Fig. 11.6. The peak of occupation and population density in the Pass of Llanberis, *c.* 1868–71 (based on MSS Vaynol 4195; PRO RG 10/5716 1871).

as shepherds. Occasionally, a slate quarryman's widow headed the household and described herself as a farmer. Though diminished, farming thus continued as a secondary form of employment. By the late 1880s, most of the sheep farming work was left to the women and young boys, while the senior males were employed in the slate industry.[16] The flocks and herds were seen as a secondary source of income, and stocking rates were probably quite small — perhaps less than half a ewe to the acre. Thus, while the landscape was crowded, the sward was almost certainly not overgrazed in the manner of recent decades.

Making a living by combining small-scale stock rearing with work in the slate quarries cannot have been easy for the families crowded into this Snowdon valley at the end of the nineteenth century (Barnes 1970; Lindsay 1974). But, for the Vaynol Estate, the increase of population and dwellings on their lands meant a 47 *per cent* rise in their rent income. The new quarrymen's cottages yielded an average of £2 10*s* per annum, while the average rents charged in 1868 for agricultural land had been raised by 30 *per cent* since the last major re-evaluation made in 1823.[17]

In the later 1880s, foreign slate began to compete successfully for a share of the market and the quarry workforce in northern Snowdonia contracted sharply (Bassett & Davies 1977). The area's economy disintegrated and, together with the impact of a continuing and deepening countrywide depression in agriculture, tenant farmers could not pay their rent. Although the estate reduced some tenant debts, and waived others, decline was unavoidable. Out-migration ensued and, by the beginning of the twentieth century, the total population had begun to fall. The estate was no longer profitable. In 1914, land near Caernarfon, as well as in Pwllheli and Anglesey, was sold. By 1919, some 3,078 ha (7,607 acres) had been shed (Aris 1977). The 1921 census shows that the resident population of Llanberis had fallen by 22 *per cent.* Between the First and Second World Wars, the Vaynol properties were maintained in reasonably good order but made virtually no profit and, by the 1950s, the problems of dereliction of buildings, neglected drainage, vacant smallholdings and impoverished soils had accumulated (Richards 1961). A new agent was appointed in 1956 and, together with the owner, Sir Michael Duff, radical rationalisation was planned (Stuart 1961). In common with practices occurring elsewhere in Wales, the estate's farms were amalgamated to form economic units, rents were doubled, and new tenancy agreements were framed (Parry 1970). Government support in the form of hill sheep subsidies was introduced in order to increase agricultural production and safeguard the social structure of remote upland communities (Hill Farming Act 1946; Agriculture Act 1967). Even so, the prosperity of the Vaynol Estate continued to decline. In 1967, the remaining 8,732 ha (21,578 acres) of its holdings were sold (*The Times*, 14 July 1967).[18] Within two years, the Ministry of Agriculture had acquired the estate and the farms were thereafter re-sold individually, mostly to their tenants (Parry 1970). In 1973, Britain's entry into the European Common Market provided a further boost in the form of Common Agricultural Policy subsidies for Snowdonia livestock farming and yet another 'moment of change' had thus occurred.

THE RISE AND FALL OF THE SNOWDONIA SHEEP FARMING LANDSCAPE SINCE THE 1970S

The introduction in the 1970s of the Europe's 'Less Favoured Areas Directive' (Fennell 1975) had far-reaching ramifications. Its introduction coincided with substantial improvements in transport infrastructure and technology. Improvements in the UK motorway network linked North Wales to lowland winter pastures in the English midlands as well as to distant markets in Europe. Similarly, silage making reduced the hill farmers' dependence on the variable quality and quantity of their own grass for late and early season feed. However, it was the provision of generous headage payments for cattle and sheep that yielded the most dramatic effect (Hester 1996). The key to success was no longer the area of in-bye land required to over-winter stock but rather the area of land that could be exploited for grazing sheep in summer to qualify for the headage payments. Essentially, summer pasturing costs were minimal. The main investment needed to maintain much larger flocks was a four-wheel drive vehicle or quad bike. Hill farmers were thus able to secure high incomes by intensively 'ranching' their mountain pastures in summer and moving a large proportion of their livestock to lowland keep for the winter (*ibid.* 1996). As a result, sheep numbers escalated and the bigger farmers invested their growing surplus in land purchases. Amalgamations and rationalisations reduced the forty-seven holdings in the Pass of Llanberis and the Arddu of the 1880s to just thirteen by the later 1970s (Fig. 11.4c). For example, farms such as Ty Isaf, Ceunant, Fron and a portion of Garag Wen that had not been buried under Dinorwic slate waste were united as a single enterprise of 1,600 acres (648 ha) (Pl. 11.I).[19] The process has continued. In 2001, only ten holdings remained and just five of these were farmed full time (Fig. 11.4d). The area's self-contained economy and ecological balance was finally undermined completely as farmers bought or rented lowland farms where their livestock were sent for the winter. This meant that much larger flocks, no

Plate 11.I. Ty Isaf, Nant Peris, 2001. This farm comprises the land that also formerly belonged to several other separate holdings: Ceunant, Fron and those parts of Garagwen and Llyn Bedw not lost beneath the slate waste of the Dinorwic quarries. It is one of only five full-time farms that survive in the Pass of Llanberis.

longer dependent on the quantity of winter fodder produced on a confined acreage of in-bye land in the mountain valleys, could be grazed on Snowdonia's vast alpine pastures in summer. Increasingly profitable markets were found in southern Europe for the small Welsh lambs. Prospects for expansion seemed limitless. Huge numbers of animals were thus being reared on an industrial scale on some of the most unpromising and poorest land in the country. All these changes led on the one hand to a sharp decline in the total farming population, but on the other hand, to a significant rise in the standard of living of those few who remained. This was manifested in the appearance of the landscape itself as investments were made in new farm buildings, new or refurbished farmhouses, fencing, bracken spraying and fertiliser application (National Trust 2001a; HTV Wales 1995–6). The bright green, weed-free grass in the valley-floor fields bears witness to these profound shifts. As noted, quad bikes and silage (bought in from elsewhere) eased the task of shepherding and thus allowed more yearling ewes to remain on the mountain during the winter without losing condition, where they could be hefted before their first tupping and a second winter spent away from Snowdonia on lowland keep.

Although not easily perceived by visitors and tourists, the effects of all these major changes in the landscape have often been ecologically detrimental (Pl. 11.II). Unsustainably heavy grazing has replaced the sweeter (*Agrostis-Festuca*) sward with more of the mat grass-heath species (*Molinia-Nardus*). Remaining patches of natural woodland have been lost and the removal of taller vegetation on wetter sites has deterred some species of birds such as curlew and lapwing. Most of the remaining trees and scrubland have been removed. Bracken (*Pteridium aquilinum*) infestation has increased in the Llanberis Pass and, despite chemical spraying, it now dominates a large part of the valley floor and the fields of the lower slopes (Fig. 11.7). Soils have become seriously compacted in places, resulting in increased flooding and greater peak runoff rates (Sansom 1999).

The long-term prospects for the unsustainable system of hill sheep farming that has developed in Snowdonia since the Second World War, especially since Britain's entry into the European Common Market in 1973, have been

Plate 11.II. The Pass of Llanberis, 2001. A fragile landscape under pressure. Only ten farm holdings remain where once there were forty-seven and these now face severe pressures.

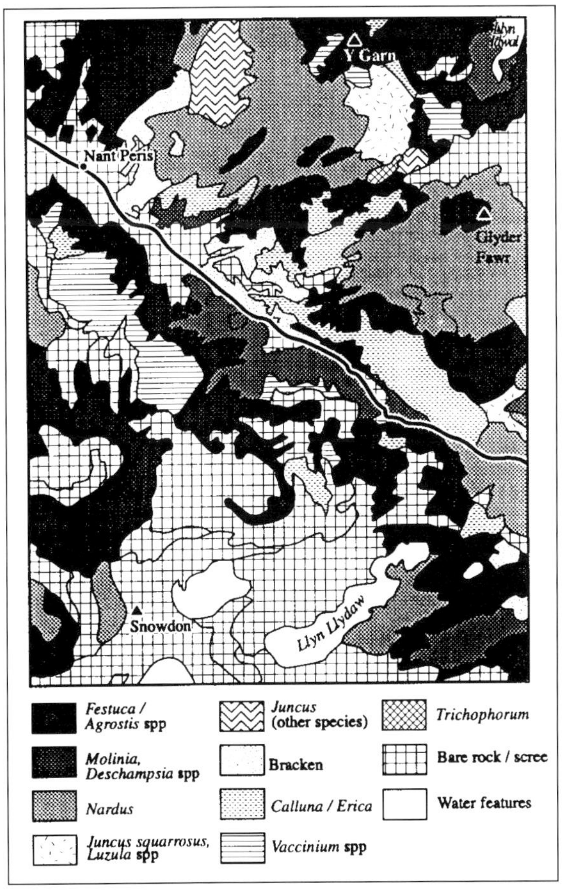

Fig. 11.7. Dominant vegetation species in the Pass of Llanberis, 2001 (based on a field survey by Environment Information Services, Martletwy, Narberth, Dyfed).

weakened by a series of crises. The high sterling exchange rate and the loss of foreign markets in Russia and elsewhere compounded problems. More recently, there has been a loss in consumer confidence due to bovine spongiform encephalopathy (BSE). But foremost amongst the crises that have struck North Wales must rank the impacts on northern Snowdonia of the 1986 Chernobyl nuclear accident, Britain's foot and mouth outbreak in 2001, and the withdrawal of hill sheep subsidies.

Heavy thunderstorms over north-west England and Wales on 2 May 1986 intercepted the main cloud of radioactive contamination from the Ukraine's Chernobyl nuclear reactor accident that had made a six-day 4,000 km (2,486 mile) journey across Western Europe. Radioactive materials rained down onto farmland, particularly in the Lake District and Snowdonia (Wynne 1991, 1996; Irwin & Wynne 1996). Indeed, the mountains of Snowdonia suffered one of Europe's highest levels of contamination by radioactive caesium with totals in the range of 500–1000 Bq/m2 being recorded (Fig. 11.8). Fifteen years later, Snowdonia's farms are still subject to testing and restrictions because the caesium has remained chemically mobile and is absorbed by each new growth of grass and thence taken up by the livestock (HTV Wales, 1995–6). Animals must be licensed before they can be sold and high readings still often occur

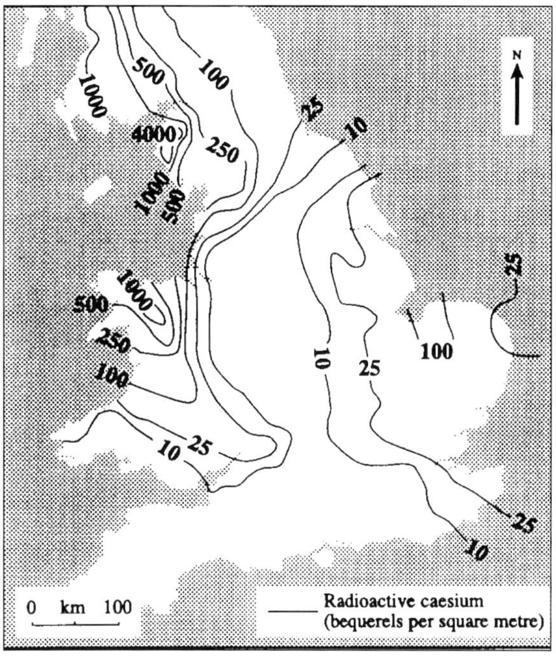

Fig. 11.8. Radioactive caesium contamination in vegetation, June–July 1986 (based on survey by the Institute for Terrestrial Ecology).

unexpectedly, causing a ban on movement until tests suggest a return to 'safe' levels (*The Times*, 1 March 1994).[20]

In February 2001, Snowdonia faced another threat when an outbreak of foot and mouth disease commenced in Britain (Fig. 11.9). Within days, a case of the disease was confirmed in Anglesey and a narrow northern fringe of the National Park fell within the 'infected area' designated by the Ministry (SNPA, 2 March 2001).[21] All movements of Snowdonia's livestock were banned and the restriction lasted for seven weeks (SNPA 20 April 2001; 7 May 2001). Although no cases of the disease were found in the mountains, the impacts of the outbreak were nonetheless savage. When livestock movements were banned, the flocks of many farmers were trapped on their winter lowland farms not only in Anglesey, but also as far away as the English midlands. Thousands were slaughtered as 'contiguous contacts' and others were killed on welfare grounds as the winter keep became exhausted. The consequences of the loss of hefted flocks, with their inbred knowledge of the mountains, have yet to be fully appreciated. Even when movement restrictions were eased, local livestock markets remained closed, prices were low and buyers had become scarce. Moreover, the vital and lucrative European exports market for small ('light') Welsh lambs remained closed.

Many of Snowdonia's hill farmers, whose average income had fallen from an annual average of £6,600 in 1997 to £5,600 in 1995 to only £2,700 by 1999, now face an uncertain future. In March 2000, the National Assembly for Wales developed a new scheme — *Tir Gofel* (literally, 'land care') — to encourage farmers to ensure that semi-natural communities of flora and fauna are protected in all the landscapes of the Principality. The scheme recognises that the exceptionally high numbers of sheep in Snowdonia have resulted in the loss of highly-valued wildlife habitats and caused a decline in many species. Thus, although *Tir Gofel* acknowledges the vital role of sheep grazing in maintaining the ecological diversity in the mountains, it is seeking mutually-agreed stocking plans, based on the realistic carrying capacity of the land. Smaller flocks of much higher quality Welsh lamb would, it is argued, command a price premium. In addition, operating costs such as feed, veterinary services and transport would be reduced. Compensation payments resulting from the 2001 Foot and Mouth outbreak may offer an opportunity for farmers to embrace *Tir Gofel*-style changes. While some may choose to re-stock at former high levels, new subsidy regulations ensure that headage payments will in future be made only if semi-natural vegetation communities are properly conserved. Access to subsidies at the former very high rates has thus been removed. Unable to contemplate the drastic changes that lie ahead, some of Snowdon's farmers are likely to leave farming (authors' interviews). Those aged over fifty have begun to consider retirement but they recognise the difficulties involved. Their assets mainly comprise the land

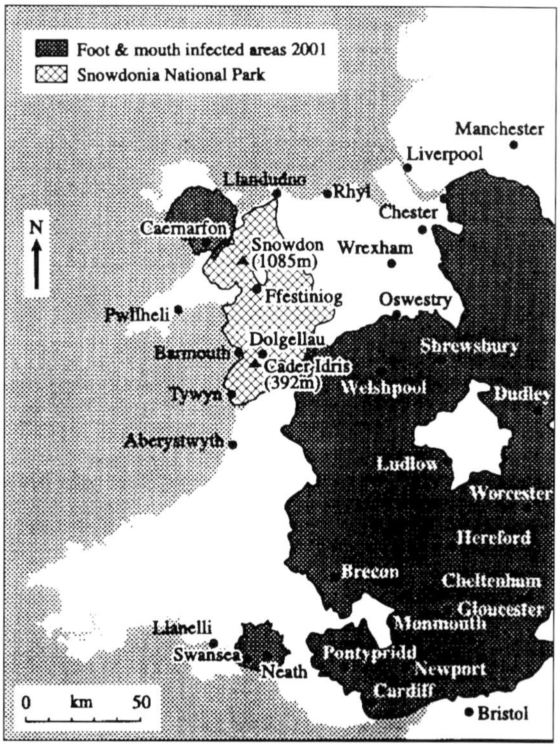

Fig. 11.9. Foot and Mouth 'infected areas' designated by the Ministry (MAFF), February–April 2001.

they own. But a part of its value formerly reflected the scale of the headage payments that it could attract. Now that subsidies have fallen, the land is worth much less and buyers will not readily be found.

While the introduction of agri-environmental schemes such as *Tir Gofel* and a reformed agricultural subsidies system for hill farming offer perhaps the only way of managing Snowdonia for the benefit of all the stakeholders, for the farmer the pain of change will be acute (*The Guardian* 2001).[22] They have been asked to exchange the dignity and financial security of rearing large flocks of (heavily subsidised) sheep, for the uncertainties of a biodiversity action plan. Moreover, although environmental payments are a form of direct subsidy, there is no guarantee that further re-negotiations will not cut them in future.

In recent years, organisations and agencies such as the Snowdonia National Park Authority, the National Trust and the Countryside Commission for Wales have sought to promote and encourage environmentally responsible land management and conservation (Morris & Young 1997; Burgon 1999; Johnson 2000). The National Trust owns seven farms in Beddgelert, the latest and largest being Hafod y Llan and Gelli Iago, purchased following a high profile public appeal in 1998 (*The Sunday Times, The Times* 1998;[23] National Trust 2001a). By its actions and its attitudes, the Trust is now significantly reducing stocking levels and focusing on the hardy native breeds: the Welsh Mountain Ewe and the Welsh Black cattle (Neale 1999). Land is being taken out of intensive agriculture altogether to allow areas of woodland and scrub to regenerate. In future, stock will be reintroduced to these wooded zones, but at low and sustainable levels (National Trust 2000b). In 2001, the Trust poured more that £400,000 per annum into its Beddgelert properties (National Trust 2001). In partnership with Snowdonia National Park, clear biodiversity targets have been identified and an action plan has been devised. At its centre are family-run livestock farm tenancies. However, the Trust is seeking to encourage a diverse farming system that blends livestock rearing with appropriate green tourism developments. Snowdonia Biodiversity Action Plans will in future cover all the Trust's tenanted properties. Large, wealthy organisations with no need to worry about profits can, of course, afford to be conservation-minded. For farmers running a business, such an approach may be much less easily adopted.

Fewer farmers will be needed to achieve the kind of sustainable upland management envisaged by government and organisations like the National Trust and the Snowdonia National Park Authority. There will also be an associated loss of agricultural advisers, fertiliser salesmen, hauliers, auctioneers and abattoir employees. Such changes in the local economy will undoubtedly weaken the capacity of the Welsh culture and language to survive in the mountains. The process of change is already underway: in 2001 only five full time farms survived in Llanberis Pass (Table 1). Another five clung on as part-time enterprises run by absentee owners who also provided camp-sites and holiday cottages on their land. Huge pressures for further radical adaptations are building; this is surely an upland area on the cusp of yet another 'moment of rapid change'. To return to the comment with which we opened the paper, it is perhaps worth saying that newspaper journalists are unlikely to examine landscapes with the same piercing gaze as an historian or a geographer. But to characterise Snowdonia's scenery as a 'natural masterpiece... dating from the mists of time' offers a grossly simplistic image of a tract of country where people, their culture and activities, and their farming methods have played so crucial a role in fashioning and re-fashioning its appearance. Snowdonia is a highly dynamic landscape, subject in the past to far-reaching alteration and likely now to undergo a further profound and rapid transformation.

TABLE 1. FARMS IN THE PASS OF LLANBERIS, SNOWDONIA

1770s	1870s	1970s	2001
1. Tyddyn Charles	24. Hafod	9. Cwm Aelhir	9. Cwm Aelhir □
2. Cae Esgob	25. Llwyn Celyn	33. Fron	19. Ty Isaf ■
3. Tynyraelgarth	26. Hafod Lydau	19. Ty Isaf	49. Cae Gwyn □
4. Adwyraen	27. Mur Mawr II	49. Cae Gwyn	19. Gwastadnant □
5. Nant Ddu bach	1. Tyddyn Charles	19. Gawstadnant	42. Cae Perthi □
6. Nant Ddu fawr	28. Tyn y Gadlas	42. Cae Perthi	36. Haford Gynfor ■
Cwm Brwynog:	29. Mur Mawr III	36. Hafod Gynfor	38. Beudy Mawr ■
7. Helfa fawr	30. Pen y Ceunant	38. Beudy Mawr	39. Blaen y Nant □
7a. Helfa fain			
8. Hadodty Newydd	2. Cae esgob	39. Blaen y Nant	7. Helfa fawr ■
9. Cwm Aelhir	31. Cae Newydd	8. Hadodty Newydd	8. Hadodty Newydd ■
10. Pant y Ceubren	4. Adwyraen	7. Helfa fawr	
11. Garag Wen	3. Tynyraelgarth	26. Hafod Lydau	
12. Pen y Llyn	32. Bryn Coch	1. Tyddyn Charles	
13. Ll[w]yn Bedw	5. Nant Ddu bach		
14. Ceunant	7a Helfa fain		■ full-time farm
15. Ty Isaf	7. Helfa fawr		□ part-time farm
16. Bryn Glas	8. Hadodty Newydd		
17. Cwm y Wrach	6. Nant Ddu fawr		
18. Tyddyn y Llan	9. Cwm Aelhir		
19. Gwastadnant	11. Garag Wen		
20. Mur Mawr	12. Pen y Llyn		
21. Cwm Glas	13. Llwyn Bedw		
22. Cwm Glas bach	33. Fron		
23. Ynys Ettws	14. Ceunant		
	15. Ty Isaf		
	16. Bryn Glas		
	17. Cwm y Wrach		
	10. Pant y Ceubren		
	34. Gwastadnant II		
	19. Gwastadnant		
	35. Gwastadnant III		
	36. Hafod Gynfor		
	22. Cwm Glas bach		
	37. Bryn fforch		
	38. Beudy Mawr		
	21. Cwm Glas		
	39. Blaen y Nant		
	40. Tan y Dderwen		
	23. Ynys Ettws		
	41. Cae Perthi		
	42. Garag Wen II		
	43. Bryn Glas II		
	44. Cwm y Wrach II		
	45. Cwm y Wrach III		
	46. Bryn fforch II		
	47. Beudy Mawr II		
	48. Mur Mawr IV		
Total = 24	Total = 47	Total = 13	Total = 10

Note: The numbers refer to Map (Fig. 11.4a–11.4d)

Sources: (GASC) MSS. Vaynol 4055. A Survey of the Vaynol Estate. Vol. I, 1777; MSS. Vaynol 4195. A Survey of the Vaynol Estate. Vol. III, 1869; MSS. Vaynol XSC 807. Sale Catalogue, 1967; Authors' fieldwork, 1980–2001

NOTES

1. *The Times*, 8 August 1998, Property Section, p. 16: 'Your own rocky mountain high'.
2. (Caern RO) (GASC) MSS. Vaynol 3643. A rentroll of the estate of Sir William Williams of Vaynol in the county of Caernarvon — Baronet deceased, 1696.
3. (GASC) MSS. Vaynol 4055. A Survey of the Vaynol Estate. Vol. I, 1777.
4. (GASC) MSS. Vaynol 3643; MSS. Vaynol 4057. Survey and Abstract of the Vaynol Leases in the Parish of Llanberis, 1778 and *c.* 1800.
5. (GASC) MSS. Vaynol 3751. Michaelmas Rental of the estates of Thomas Assheton Smith in Llanberis, 1799; MSS. Vaynol 4057. Survey and Abstract of the Vaynol Leases in the Parish of Llanberis, 1778 and *c.* 1800.
6. (GASC) MSS. Vaynol 4055; MSS. Vaynol 4202. Valuation of the Vaynol Estate *c.* 1832.
7. Census Enumerators Books, Public Record Office (PRO) HO 107/1393 1841; HO 107/2515 1851; RG 9/4330 1861; RG 10/5716 1871; RG 11/5566 1881; RG 12/4658 1891.
8. (GASC) MSS. Vaynol 4427. John Millington's Account Book, 12 November 1869.
9. (GASC) MSS. Vaynol 4108. Particulars for Valuation of Lands in the Parish of Llanberis; the property of George William Duff Assheton Smith, 1868.
10. (GASC) MSS. Vaynol 2903. Notebook of Vaynol Estate Agent: complaints and requests, 1871–4.
11. (GASC) MSS. Vaynol 4195. A Survey of the Vaynol Estate. Vol. III. 1869.
12. Census Enumerators Books, PRO, RG 12/4658 1891.
13. Census Enumerators Books, PRO, RG 10/5716 1871; RG 12/4658 1891.
14. (GASC) MSS. Vaynol 4427.
15. A useful comparison of farm sizes may be made using the rentals of 1832 and 1869: (GASC) MSS. Vaynol 4376. John Millington's Account with Thos. A. Smith, esq. For the Rents of his Estates in Caernavonshire and Anglesey for one year due Lady Day, 1832; (GASC) MSS. Vaynol 4427.
16. Census Enumerators Books, PRO, RG 12/4658 1891.
17. (GASC) MSS. Vaynol 4063. Survey and Valuation by Mr Walter Jones, 1810–11; MSS. Vaynol 4066. Valuation by Mr Evans, 1823; (GASC) MSS. Vaynol 4067. A survey of the Vaynol Estate. Vol. I. 1832; MSS. Vaynol 4376.
18. (GASC) MSS. Vaynol XSC 807. Sale Catalogue, 1967; *The Times*, 14 July 1967, p. 3: 'Snowdon is sold privately'; The Times, 21 July 1967, p. 8: 'The Commons: new owners on Snowdon'.
19. The extent of these four holdings is shown in the maps contained in (GASC) MSS. Vaynol 4195.
20. *The Times*, 1 March 1994, p. 22: 'Hill farmer is still paying the price of Chenobyl'.
21. SNPA: Snowdonia National Park Authority Press Releases: 26 Feb 2001, 2 March 2001, 20 April 2001; 7 May 2001.
22. *The Guardian*, 20 April 2001, p. 10: 'Hill farmers need to be land stewards'.
23. *The Sunday Times*, 5 July 1998, Property Section. p. 16: 'Snowdon goes up for sale'; *The Times*, 5 August 1998, p. 9: 'National Trust fights foreign Snowdon bid'; *The Times*, 6 August 1998, p. 8: 'Trust appeals for £3m after winning fight for Snowdon'; *The Times*, 8 August 1998, Property Section, p. 16: 'Your own rocky mountain high'.

ABBREVIATIONS

Caern RO	Caernarfon Record Office
GASC	Gwynedd Archives Service
PRO	Public Record Office

Gendering an upland landscape: masculinity and place identity in the Peak District, 1880s–1920s

Melanie Tebbutt

ABSTRACT

This chapter argues that landscapes are more than static physical locations; they are also formed in the imagination, mediated by art and literature and informed by popular culture affected by social, cultural and ideological differences. These insights are developed in the context of the landscapes of the Peak District between the 1880s and the 1920s. Emphasis is laid on how certain kinds of masculine values became identified with particular kinds of landscape in this area, especially the Dark Peak and particularly during and following the First World War.

KEYWORDS

Peak district, landscape imagery, outdoor recreation, gendered landscapes, symbolic landscapes

On the moors, alone, my tracks I make.
Nought 'twixt blue skies, the rolling clouds, and me,
Suns kiss; winds waft my cheeks;
frosts urge me onward;
Rains pat my face; mists enshroud me;
I sit, I lie, I think; look upward to the heavens.
I sleep, I dream; and heaven is
with me in my dreaming.
Man free — man happy — child of the moor and hill
Lover of the valley — Nature's bridegroom — when?
The 'Lonely Land' charms, compels me. —
Yes. I come!
When my heart no longer bids;
When my limbs refuse to take me;
Then, bear me to the sombre moors,
the everlasting hills
There let me sleep and rest (G. H. B. Ward).[1]

As this poetic evocation of the Derbyshire moors suggests, regional landscapes are more than static, physical locations; they also formed in the imagination, mediated by art and literature and informed by popular culture, their meanings continually infiltrated and transformed by social, cultural and ideological influences. How such landscape imagery contributes to notions of national identity has become a familiar theme (Cosgrove & Daniels 1993; Daniels 1988). How these understandings might be inflected by gender was until recently much less appreciated, although feminist geographers have, since the late 1980s, encouraged new ways of thinking about landscape representation, place identity and gender (Ford 1991; Nash 1993; Rose 1993; Morris 1996). The aim of this chapter is to develop such insights in relation to parts of the Peak District, focusing on the period between the 1880s and the 1920s when certain kinds of masculine values became identified with particular kinds of landscape.

The Peak District is strongly identified with Derbyshire although it spreads into parts of Staffordshire, Cheshire, Yorkshire and the old county of Lancashire. The region is split into two distinct geological divisions that have often been defined in terms of gendered polarities. To the south are the soft and 'scenic' limestone hills and dales of the White Peak and upper Derwent Valley, which are also home to important estates and centres of landed culture, notably Chatsworth. To the north are the bleak and largely treeless gritstone vistas of the Dark Peak', an altogether different terrain of rough grass, heather and peat bogs whose northernmost valleys were once smudged with industrial settlements more redolent of the Lancashire cotton districts than rural Derbyshire (Garfield, n.d., p. 2; Redfern 1965, p. 132). The Dark Peak is this chapter's main focus, particularly the northern moors around Kinder Scout, a high, largely uninhabited area which rises to 2,088 ft (636 metres). These uplands have acquired a powerful reputation as a 'wild and savage' country and together with the Howden Moors, Bleaklow and Black Hill 'form one of the last real wildernesses in England' (Hurt 1988, p. 7). Unpredictable weather and difficult ground conditions have made this a challenging yet accessible walking area since the end of the nineteenth century, the iconic potency of such apparent remoteness enhanced by its very proximity to the large urban centres such as Sheffield, Stockport and Manchester which cluster around it. Baker's Guide to the *Moors, Crags and Caves of the High Peak and Neighbourhood* (1903) unhesitatingly placed the

Peak 'right in the centre of England ... at the threshold of the world's most populous cluster of manufacturing towns ... a broad area of wild country, as lone and untamed as any south of Cheviot' (Baker 1903, p. 9). At the edges of the urban world, this is a border area where northern and southern England meet, a place of imagined frontiers, both personal and physical.

THE PEAKLAND LANDSCAPE

The Peak District has been recognised as a national 'heritage' landscape since the 1880s, when its symbolic significance was placed within broader ideas of the rural as well-spring of English national moral character. Urban life in the late nineteenth century was associated with environmental pollution, moral contamination and materialism; it was unhealthy, diseased and racially 'diluted' by immigrants, the degenerate poor and sexually promiscuous. City and upland landscapes juxtaposed ideas of sexual excess and puritanism. The 'virgin', 'barren' contours of the uplands offered purer, simpler, unchanging values, a refuge from claustrophobic domesticity, places of adventure and endurance where the male body could be controlled and tested in a character-building battle between self and the physical world.

Narratives of the Peakland landscape were also shaped within a wider framework of northernness and southernness which combined older regional traditions with more recent manufacturing ones and set the independence, individualism and physicality of the upland environment against the 'softer', domesticated landscapes of the south. Independence, stoicism, self-reliance, strength and perseverance were key elements in northern ideas of northern England, which presented northerners as hardier and less deferential than their southern equivalents. Such notions long pre-dated industrialisation and were based in part on the strength of pastoral traditions in the rural north, which encouraged greater independence, individuality and reliance on the family group than was common in the village communities of more southern districts. They also reflected northern discomfort at political power that favoured the landowning, privileged classes of southern England. With industrialisation, these survivalist ideas of hard, physical labour merged with new stereotypes as northernness was transformed into an occupational identity associated with manufacturing and urbanisation. The predominant northern stereotype of the male, working-class worker became a symbol of manliness in a range of literary works which often contrasted the 'hard' values of northern industry with the softer 'feminised', more domestic qualities of 'civilised' southern England (Jewell 1994, pp. 208, 212). Mid-Victorian dialect literature in Lancashire and Yorkshire emphasised southern effeteness and the decadence and immiseration of London life. Southern representations of the north, on the other hand, more often drew on ideas of uncivilised 'otherness', which were invigorated from the end of the nineteenth century by the north's economic decline (Samuel 1998, p. 56; Joyce 1991, p. 62; Shields 1991, p. 213).

The Peak, landlocked, and located midway between the north and south of England, occupied a particular place within these regional narratives, which also drew on distinctive political mythologies such as Whiggish notions of the Freeborn Englishman's recurring struggles for rights and liberties. Remote upland areas were commonly associated with radicalism and freethinking and dissent (as well as poaching) had long flourished in the 'high heath lands' of the Derbyshire and Yorkshire moors (Marshall 1986, p. 9; SCR 1925–6, pp. 59-79, 81-5). Early Methodists had met there while the mass political platform of the early nineteenth century was invigorated by the freedom of moorland meetings far away from the legal restraints and interference of urban communities (Belchem & Epstein 1997, pp. 183-4). Important political (and religious) territory since the early days of radical activity, they remained significant symbolic spaces in the northern imagination. Even after politics changed to more formal, structured, less public forms, unregulated moorland areas retained such associations with freedom, as other mythologies were layered upon these localised associations. Northern writers towards the end of the nineteenth century often represented the Peak as the manly 'heart' of the nation, England's rugged interior to which the population traditionally fled in times of danger (Hill 1980, p. 127). John Leyland typically drew on the region's traditional untamed aspect when he wrote in 1891 of how 'The fastness of the Peak doubtless afforded shelter, during the Roman occupation, to turbulent Britons, whom the strong forts and frequent garrisons hereabouts were intended to overawe and hold in check', and Cox's history of the county in 1903 perpetuated a similar survivalist message (Cox 1903, p. 30; Moncrieff 1908, p. 7).

Such views reflected contemporary constructions of national character which divided Britain geographically between a much invaded but mixed and dynamic Lowland south and east and a Highland north and west, isolated, pure, and distinctively Celtic (Gruffudd *et al.* 2000). These ideas were influentially shaped by Sir Cyril Fox in his book, *The Personality of Britain* (1932), but the division also had a peculiarly English inflection (Fox 1943). *The Victoria County History of Derbyshire*, for example, placed the county's own lowland and upland identities within a broader context of England's upland and lowland areas. The civilised southern lowlands were a soft, effete place, whose feminisation was implied in the ease with which it had so often succumbed to conquest while the harsh, rude qualities of early northern life were infused with resentment and defiance at Roman military occupation. The 'wild hill-men' of England's 'northern counties' shared a common warlike, independent spirit. 'Even when conquered, these uplands remained imperfectly subdued. Wales, it would seem, lay quiet, but the hills of Derbyshire and Lancashire and Yorkshire were the scenes of fighting on many occasions during the second century' (*VCH Derbyshire I* 1905, p. 192). Such characterisations were re-invigorated by the First World War and repeated during the interwar years when the 'salt-of-the earth', 'simple' qualities of these men at the heart of England's central county came to exemplify the honest essence of the national character, the indomitable spirit of the Peak's 'turbulent forefathers' who 'did not fight against the invader for nothing' (Du Garde Peach 1934, p. 9).

The Peak District's upland landscape shared characteristics with 'mountainous' terrain in other parts of Britain, particularly as far as being a refuge and fortress against the invader were concerned. The Welsh mountains became with industrialisation '*Gwlad y Bryniau* (Mountain Land)', a 'fastness or fortress for the nation' where Welshmen were as 'sturdy tough, free as mountain air' (Yorkshire people's 'hardiness and love of liberty' was often attributed to the same cause: Dellheim 1986, p. 220). However, the Welsh mountains also had other cultural meanings as the heartland of Welsh language and culture. In the eyes of English commentators, their remoteness and mystery were responsible for a poetic, emotional weakness (gendered as feminine) which qualified the masculinity of the more militaristic fortress metaphor (Morgan 1983, p. 89). In 1932, for example, H. V. Morton alluded to the racialised, feminised pessimism of Wales in describing how the Llanberis Pass gathered into it 'all the loneliness, all the sadness, all the brooding melancholy which are at the heart of all Celtic countries. It might be in Ireland. It might be in Scotland: it could never be in England' (Morton 1932, p. 121). It could, of course, quite easily have been in England. Mrs Humphrey Ward, who celebrated Kinder Scout in *David Grieve*, described the 'ebon black' crevasses which ripped the landscape and made 'the crossing of the Peak in the dark or in mist a matter of danger sometimes even for the native ... a region which has no features and no landmarks, where the earth lays snares for you, and the mists betray you, and where, even in bright sunshine, there reigns an eternal and indescribable melancholy' (Moncrieff 1908, p. 23). Yet if such writers frequently emphasised the harsh, elemental, somewhat sombre character of the Dark Peak, its place within the national 'character' was rarely feminised in the way of the Llanberis Pass. Morton's own remarks are usefully compared with his earlier descriptions of the Dark Peak where a similarly dour terrain is presented as an invigorating, masculinised environment quite capable of transforming even women ramblers. Tramping the wet Peakland moors with a 'pale Amazon' who walked like a man, he was at pains to describe the unfamiliarly bracing character of their conversation as they talked 'all the time like a couple of men' (Morton 1928, pp. 167-8).

For a large part of the nineteenth century, the Dark Peak's wild, austere scenery lurked largely forgotten in the shadow of the White Peak's more 'picturesque' landscape. It was thought best to gaze upon Kinder from a distance, a romantic viewpoint that rendered its terrain misleadingly mountainous (Moir 1964, p. 141). Those who ventured nearer, as did Pilkington in 1789, found these moorlands 'unpleasant and disgustful to the imagination', a description that is repeated in subsequent guide books such as Britton and Brayley's *Topographical and Historical Description of Derbyshire*, where the 'bleak barren heights' and 'long extended moors', of the Peak uplands were 'dreary' areas with often not a 'single house or tree to be seen, to divert the eye of the traveller, or relieve the weariness that arises from the contemplation of sterility and nakedness' (Firth 1905, p. 12; Britton & Brayley 1810, p. 293). Preferences for the pastoral lyricism of the White Peak's dales and valleys reflected the growth of 'picturesque tastes of landscape appreciation' between 1740 and 1860 and were further encouraged from the mid-1820s by fictional accounts such as Sir Walter Scott's romance of the Peak, *Peveril*, and the publication of illustrated guide books such as those by Edward Rhodes and Sir Francis Chantrey (Hall 1863, pp. lii, 3, 201; Cox 1903, pp. 3-4, Glover 1830, p. iii). Such influences framed the countryside within a safe, gentle and frequently nostalgic convention of the picturesque which as Ann Bermingham suggests could be 'widely *consumed*, and with all the more enthusiasm in that the landscape it celebrated was beginning to vanish' (Bermingham 1986 p.85). In the Peak District's case, consumption was aided by the arrival of the railways that from the 1860s carried increasing numbers of day trippers attracted by the romanticised images also popularised by professional and amateur photography Baddeley 1908, p. xi; Firth 1905, p. 13). However, growth of the outdoors movement from the same period encouraged interest in rather different kinds of Peakland landscape, as from the 1870s and 1880s stations in towns and villages at the edge of the Dark Peak such as Hayfield, Hadfield, Glossop and Broadbottom brought the once distant reaches of Kinder, Charlesworth Coombs, Peaknaze and Snake Moors within easy reach of Manchester and Stockport. Rambling became a 'favourite pastime of young working men' in the 1880s and by the end of the nineteenth century the region had become a cheap and easy destination for both walkers and mountaineers (although climbing, developed rather later here than in the Welsh and Scottish mountains and the Lake District) (Pimlott 1947, pp. 166, 167; Byne & Sutton 1966, p. 65, Mais 1936, p. 88; Liniado 1996, p. 14).

The outdoors movement helped popularise wild, elemental, upland landscapes which were very different from the cosy, feminised, domesticated southern downland of a romanticised, 'essential England'. These cultivated southern landscapes of half-timbered houses, village greens and hedgerows, epitomised by the 'medieval' architecture of the Cotswolds (and parts of the southern White Peak), were reminders of a quieter, gentler time before industrialisation whose once reassuring security was becoming much less easy by the end of the nineteenth century (Howkins 1986, pp. 62-3). Crowds of 'fatuous trippers' and commercialisation increasingly tarnished the appeal of the White Peak's 'picturesque' valleys and villages, threatening to 'ravage' and 'despoil' them. Tourist consumption of popular 'honey-spots' in the scenic limestone dales of the White Peak was likened to the advance of a decadent and more effete civilisation that challenged the masculinity of the English 'national character' by substituting strength, vigour and 'manly virtues' with a frivolous, feminine materialism. Opponents of the Dore and Chinley Railway line, which opened up Edale and the 'wild' eastern moorlands to Sheffield, objected that it would carry 'a noisy and obnoxious civilization into the virgin hills and unsmirched valleys of 'undiscovered Derbyshire', and the line's completion in 1894 saw 'armies' of pedestrians seeking 'new routes across the wild peat-mosses', trying to find the isolation no longer possible on the lower slopes (Baddeley 1908, pp. xi, xii; Firth 1905, p. 13; *SCR* 1935–1936, p. 146). Their arrival was symptomatic of broader changes in aesthetic taste. Writers in the early 1900s described a growing desire for the peace, wilderness and sense of adventure no longer available in the 'tamed' and crowded valleys, and many were said to prefer the 'elemental grandeur of the barren moors and gritstone edges to the exquisite beauty of the limestone dales' where the 'primitive virtues of rustic seclusion' were 'spoilt by tourists' (Baddeley 1908, p. xi; Firth 1905, p. 13). In 1908, A. R. Hope Moncrieff writing of Kinder Scout could observe how, 'The early Peak guides pass by with lack-lustre indifference, if not with a shudder, those open moors that are the delight of our close-packed generation' (Moncrieff 1908, p. 21). 'Unspoilt', 'authentic', untouched by contemporary life, they were an 'unexplored region whose romance becomes religion — where the austere heights stand out lonely and lovely as if they belonged to a new-made world where man is unknown'. The stern, undefiled purity of the high peat uplands had none of the 'effeminate' distractions of the White Peak's prettier hills and valleys. Unlike the snapshot views encouraged by the train, motor car or even bicycle, their ancient, timeless 'purity' required effort, energy and resourcefulness which contrasted with the 'feminised' passivity of the White Peak's valleys where tourist attractions were often described in terms of 'desecration'. A difficult photographic subject, their lack of conventionally picturesque views encouraged an austere, even puritanical emphasis also apparent in the distinction which some writers made between the worthy rambler and less 'deserving', fun-loving day tripper (Morris 1914, p. 10).

> The young man and the lover of loneliness will always be lured to Kinder but the average person will be content with the Edges and say that the thousand peat trenches are more 'experience' than pleasure (Anon. 1946, p. 188),

observed the much re-printed book, *Across the Derbyshire Moors,* 'the first popular book of rambles round Sheffield' which was first published in 1904 (SCR 1935–6, p. 145). Thirty years later, a letter in the *Sheffield Clarion Ramblers* handbook observed how the '"tripper" and "litter scatterer" would not walk twice' over the 'trenches ... mossy places and many thousand tumps of cotton grass' which characterised the 'wild moorland' of north Derbyshire and south Yorkshire (*SCR* 1935–6, p. 21).

Kinder's symbolic importance was, of course, reinforced by its transformation into a protected space for gamebirds and sportsmen after the agricultural depression of the 1870s, when growing accessibility to urban walkers and climbers made local landowners much fiercer about protecting their property rights than was the case with similar areas elsewhere (Marsh 1982, p. 4; Moncrieff 1908, p. ix; Holt 1987, p. 62). The first legal walkway over Kinder, from Hayfield to the Snake, was opened in 1897 (after twenty-one years of 'agitation') and the next three decades saw it become 'the most popular ramble in the Peak District', despite the prominence of warning notices and gamekeepers (*SCR* 1927–8, p. 153). The martial associations of grouse shooters' 'miniature castles' and fortresses perhaps even added a certain thrill to such walks, heightened by the unpredictability of Kinder's weather which famously claimed several fatalities in the early 1920s (Moncrieff 1908, pp. 25, 31; Morris 1914, p. 10; *SCR* 1925–6, p. 101). Its upper moorlands, neglected and little inhabited, encouraged a spirit of exploration and walkers there often experienced a sense of entering into uncharted territory, the tops 'wind-swept, unlovely, plateau-like and bare', some of its names noted on maps but many unrecorded and most needing to be 'investigated and explained' (Taylor 1994; *SCR* 1925–6, p. 61).

A FRONTIER REGION

Representations of the Dark Peak were increasingly influenced by the kind of healthy, physical activities which came to define masculinity in the late nineteenth century, since the search for (and contestation of) Derbyshire's 'loneliest wildest places' coincided with a growing interest in testing character against the environment under the influence of Social Darwinism and a martial new imperialism (Baker 1903, p. 9). The military values of courage, a cool head, resolution, self-control, restraint and character privileged particular kinds of sporting activity such as mountaineering which pitted the individual against nature in a character building battle with self and the physical world. The Dark Peak's gritstone edges and peatland bogs offered climbers and fell walkers similar challenges of 'stoicism, hardiness and endurance' which were central to late nineteenth-century ideals of manliness, and although this landscape was the subject of different discourses, a particularly significant one during this period was its celebration as a masculine frontier (Mangan & Walvin 1987, pp. 1-5; Connell 1995, pp. 185, 194). This conceptualisation is very apparent in the writing of G. H. B. Ward, first secretary of the Sheffield Labour Representation Committee (1903–1911), who became a powerful force in the Sheffield rambling movement, having founded the Sheffield Clarion Ramblers in 1900 as probably the first Sunday walking club in the area. He was later described as having walked around repeating 'pioneers, oh pioneers' during the first ramble, a phrase which not only resonated with a sense of the historic moment but also encapsulated the feelings of adventure and exploration which were so closely entwined with ideas of the Dark Peak at this time (*SCR* 1958-9, p. 7). Ward delighted in going 'off the beaten track' to seek out the Peak District's wildest places and became quite an expert in its folklore, local history and geography, campaigning too about the lack of public access to the moorlands and fells, which were increasingly constructed as an asylum from the confines of urban, industrialised Britain (Morton 1928, pp. 167–8). Much of this material was published in his annual pocket-sized rambling handbooks that were much prized by several generations of ramblers. (Many older walkers still have well thumbed original copies in their possession.)

H. V. Morton considered this 'roof of the north' in Derbyshire a 'safety-valve' for the 'healthy youth' of Manchester and Sheffield and Ward was supposedly inspired by the desire to offer young men an alternative to standing at the street corners on Sunday morning waiting for the pubs to open (*SCR* 1959–60, pp. 5-6). The 'imaginative geographies' of the Dark Peak which invoked a language of purification against the disease ridden temptations of the city are very apparent in Ward's own works. 'The man of the hills' had a characteristic 'posture and stride':

> There's no slouch about it and no street-corner boy, masturbator, or syphilitic, could obtain it, for he would be 'laid up' in half a day's attempt to crawl where we run ... (*SCR* 1925–6, p. 101; *SCR* 1916-17, pp. 24, 35).

He believed hearty, healthy walking in the high moorlands would create a new breed of men, and his writings between the mid 1900s and the 1930s were infused with ideas of 'supermen, manliness and the British race' (*SCR* 1916–17, p. 47, Sissons 1992, p. 88). Kinder in particular was a harsh, testing place where man could compete against both the elements and himself, prolonging life, conserving virility helping to create 'clean-limbed and clean-hearted manhood who are fit to wed and continue our British race' (*SCR* 1925–6, p. 101). However, another important motif in the handbooks was that of the vagabond, carefree wanderer and king of the open road who sloughed off the responsibilities of daily life and the cosy, feminised domesticity that supposedly sustained women's emotional needs. Ward's views reflected a strong sense of the married man's entitlement to free time and independent leisure. His wife naturally packed up for him, seeing that the main result of him attempting to slice a loaf of bread was a 'cut on his left thumb'. A lion on the moors, Ward was meek as a lamb at home where his wife chivvied him like a child not to forget anything before he left for his walks. In both places Ward happily remained as irresponsible as a lad, his own association of the domestic with infantilisation suggesting the significance of Kinder's somewhat masochistic environment as a masculinised space of freedom, movement and challenge (*SCR* 1916–17, pp. 53-4). Women were welcome enough on most walks but only 'men and brothers' were considered robust enough for more strenuous ones, those which took place in harsh weather or male only overnight walks known as Revellers' Rambles (*SCR* 1921–2, p. 21; *SCR* 1923–4, p. 22).

Rambling in such open, wild countryside helped build up not only a physically confident but a spiritually strong masculinity, for the moorlands held more than just physical appeal and the founders of the *Sheffield Clarion Ramblers* were romantics as well as fitness enthusiasts. Several early members were poets, including Ward, Bert Driver and Bill Whitney. Membership cards and subsequent handbooks were laced with verses by Wordsworth, Pope, Keats, Clare and lesser-known poets and writers. Ward's own verse on moorlands quoted at the beginning of this chapter came at the end of a piece entitled, 'The Unknown', a paien to 35 square miles (91 sq km) of northern Derbyshire which included Kinder and Bleaklow, 'trackless, lone, and silent, untrodden save by a few solitary keeps and upland shepherds'. Persistent references to streams and waterfalls suggested physical cleansing, spiritual refreshment and sexual catharsis in the 'virgin' purity of the upper moorlands'. Unlike the tourism of the lower slopes, 'prostituted' to mass culture and modernity, this unsullied landscape allowed more assertive models of female behaviour epitomised by the 'New Woman' to be left far behind, 'Some day they'll come along the Rough Revellers' way, but not until the new woman bravely puts the breeches on' (*SCR* 1917–18, p. 31).

Unconfined moorland was deemed particularly suited to male sensibility, an exquisite mix of the physical and spiritual, aestheticism and individualism jostling with ideas of physical endurance, sport and comradeship. Sissons refers to a Whitmanesque 'combination of fresh air, exercise, sunshine, nudity and male comradeship' and there is an undeniable homoerotic element in some of the handbooks' writings (Sissons 1992, p. 8). At their heart was an intense, emotional engagement with the moorland landscape as a 'soul renewing' place where man could meet his maker.

> The heights will, more and more, and for ever be a magnet for the virile youth and man, and the temple not made with hands be our place of worship. There we are rejuvenated. Upon them we cast our carking cares and are enabled to carry our roguish, laughing, care free boyhood into middle life (*SCR* 1925–6, pp. 92, 101).

The Dark Peak, hardly a nurturing environment, was not a place for metaphors of Nature as Mother. More common was Nature as Virgin, strikingly expressed in the frontispiece of early Clarion handbooks whose lyrical engraving of two young women playing music and reading beneath a moorland tree was accompanied with the a verse: 'The rambler's gone a-courting, Miss Nature is his lady-love' (*SCR* 1908). However, this pictoral lyricism was relatively short-lived, and other imagery became more prominent once photographs took over from line drawings in the 1912–13 edition (Massey 1994, p. 10). This iconography had a strong individualistic strain, particularly in the 1920s, and often depicted a solitary male rambler, sitting on or near a crag or standing stones against a backdrop of apparently endless moors. Such panoramic vistas of a lone male standing on a high place ('monarch' of all he surveyed) were common to male mountaineering stories and European romanticism and also encapsulated a particular walking mentality (Myers 2000, p. 25, Carter 2001, p. 30).

> individually, we are self-reliant Anarchists, although we know nothing of the meaning of the word. No practised rambler will be placed in leading strings and, in ordinary circumstances, we will go our own way, and, if alone, take the greater risk (*SCR* 1925–6, p. 102).

The heroic associations of this 'great outdoors' as a place of men defined against a nurturant concept of indoors, female home life were nuanced in new ways after 1918 as the losses of the war years intensified the symbolic significance of open land which remained closed to walkers. (An admonition to younger walkers of the perils of upland rambling, in the mid-1920s, included the reminder to 'stick together in your party, and do not forget that a mother, wife or sister stays at home, and, thinking of her boy or man, suffers the suspense, and *waits for the news*' *SCR* 1925–6, p. 102). Keith Grieves makes clear how memories of such 'pre-war landscapes were re-invented' after the First World War in discussing the views of C. E. Montague, chief leader writer of the *Manchester Guardian*, and C. P. Scott's son-in-law. Montague was both a keen Lakeland walker and ex-soldier who had volunteered for military service (despite being 47 and having seven children). His love of the Lake District, like Ward's of the Peak, was a similar synthesis of emotion and belief in its capacity to test manly character (Grieves 1995, pp. 95-6). Drawing on the kind of imagery described earlier, Montague regarded 'upland areas in general and the Lake District in particular as a great "delousing station"', and he responded particularly to the 'practical utility and emotional appeal' of the schemes of remembrance for Lakeland volunteers who had died during the war, such the National Trust's acquisition of Scafell Pike in 1919 or the purchase, in 1923, of 3,000 central Lake District acres in memory of the dead of the Fell and Rock Climbing Club. Montague's leaders supporting the Access to Mountains Bill in 1924 'reminded post-war hill-walkers and other readers that the transition to peacetime society was incomplete' because the purposes of the British war effort had not yet been fulfilled, and the *Sheffield Clarion Ramblers* handbooks offered similar reminders that Kinderscout and Bleaklow were the 'only English mountains still closed to the non-trespasser' (Grieves 1995, p. 94).

> Surely it is time that these old common lands were made a common preserve for the middle class and enlightened workmen to walk over. This is not 'the land fit for heroes' which I fought for (*SCR* 1921–2, p. 102).

> In the teens and twenties of years ago the early modern rambler, whether Clarionite, Rucksacker, or non-clubber, went cautiously over and was only surprised when he saw another human form. But the man who fought for liberty in the war and received his early training in the Boy Scout or Boys' Brigade does not see the reason for this cautious and circumspect walking (*SCR* 1923–4, p. 132; King 1998, p. 198).

The issue of access, more complex than purely a question of rights and liberties, was also connected to a sense of loss and bereavement of which the very contours of the peat uplands were a reminder. Ward's writings are suggestive of how landscape might mediate anxiety and emotion in times of both peace and war, although the human losses of military action are remarkably understated in the wartime handbooks that are notably lacking larger expressions of loss or grief. (This perhaps owed something to Ward's own war work: he served in the Ministry of Munitions in London (*SCR* 1919–20, p. 122.) Walking was an antidote to depression, frustration, emotional lethargy and exhaustion and the middle years of the war saw Ward and a friend spending a long week-end out on the moors precisely 'to escape for a few hours the environment of factories and war editions … as far away from the habitations of men as we could conveniently get' (*SCR* 1916–17, pp. 53-5). There are hints of how Kinder's commonly described peat 'trenches' gradually acquired a deeper resonance as hostilities progressed. The 1915–16 handbook contained a photograph of two men standing in one of Kinder's deep ruts which was accompanied by the caption, 'Not in Belgium — but a trench on Kinder Scout', its apparently shell-pocked peat bogs a potent reminder of how the battles in foreign fields were also a struggle for the national soil. (The handbook was prefaced with the reminder that it was 'patriotic to walk and keep well' (*SCR* 1915–16.)

The photo's caption illustrates the ease with which the war was layered upon earlier understandings of Kinder, whose punishing weather and often sodden landscape gave walkers both a feeling of kinship with those at the front and a sense of building up the physical and emotional strength necessary for victory. Indeed, during the course of a long moorland walk described in the 1917–18 handbook, Ward and his fellow ramblers stopped to make 'a toast to the boys that's away' who had 'found manhood and mastery of many things besides hills and moors from their acquaintance with the Clarion Revellers' Day'.

> The Ramblers' Book is in the soldier's wallet now, and they'll be thinking while we fortunate 'Munitioneers' play. The thoughts cross overseas from muddy roads and shell-sunk holes to Cut gate's snow-filled trench, and we hear them say 'Would that I were there to-day.' We think of the icy Heaven we are in, and our toast takes them from the Hell they know (*SCR* 1917–18, p. 30).

Short, unadorned obituaries marked the deaths of former walkers, similarly simple references recording those who had become war casualties. The depth of emotion in these losses may only be inferred from one of Ward's poem printed next to the obituary of John Bingley, 'a bonny, well-built rambler … and a sturdy Reveller on the roughest moors', who died on the 25th April 1918 (*SCR* 1919–20, pp. 116-17). 'Land of Moor and Heather. Derbyshire' (sung to the tune of 'Land of Hope and Glory'), was written in memory of all the Sheffield Clarion Ramblers who had lost their lives:

> To the sacred determination that the Freedom for which, on foreign soil, they fought and fell shall bring the Freedom of the Hills and Moorlands for the feet of health-seeking men and women (*SCR* 1900–61, pp. 5-6).

If its rousing chorus to 'Derbyshire the Free' drew on the long established narratives referred to earlier, its sentiments also suggested how their deaths were indissolubly linked to a landscape whose contours were so similar to the Belgian battlegrounds.

> Land of Moor and Heather, Derbyshire the Free
> How shall we adore thee, who roam over thee?
> Wider still and wider shall our paths be set:
> Men who make thee Freeland, make thee mightier yet!

The carnage of technological warfare helped intensify the emotional significance of nature and landscapes such as this where the absence of human intervention further memorialised the spirits of the dead for a pre-war generation of walkers. Walking through Kinder's peat trenches not only reinforced a sense of connection with those who were experiencing the much worse horrors of war but helped sanctify an already hallowed soil by infusing it with the memories of lost friends and walking companions. As later editions of the handbook reminded readers, many former walkers had taken copies of Clarion Rambler booklets as 'pocket companions' in the trenches, and Ward's post-war disapproval of the less serious attitudes he discerned among younger ramblers may have owed something to this rather different emotional engagement with the high moorlands (*SCR* 1924–5, p. 98). Even in the 1950s, Crichton Porteous was still using trench analogies to highlight the Dark Peak's significance to a particular notion of Englishness:

> To live among these hills one must be more like the men of line regiments who crouched and swore and somehow grinned in Somme mud and came out with not much glory but very mucky. These Derbyshire hills are of the sort that demand a quiet endurance, a kind of greyness of life, and to find a Derbyshire man with a kilt and sporran and the Cock-of-the-North air of a Highlander would be strange. There is a normality here which is akin with the core of life; well, which is life as most of us know it. Not romance; everydayness (Porteous 1950).

The Celtic references again suggest the Dark Peak's place both within the iconography of northern England and within a wider sense of national identity. A populist discourse had developed in which the landscape epitomised democratic everydayness rather than the 'élitism' of the sublime. The peat uplands were a place of private vision and imagination where those of the mass could recover a sense of self and individuality, a blank canvass, 'boundless, featureless, homogeneous space' which was most strikingly apparent on Kinder's plateau, 'roof of the world' (Myers 2000, p. 31). Here, the understated and mundane had heroic, transformative capacities; silence, purity and simplicity elided with a familiar emphasis of post-war, commemorative symbolism as testimony to the basic decency of the ordinary worker and the 'common' people (King 1998, pp. 175-9). This metaphorical frontier tested more than physical prowess; it was also a place of emotional release and catharsis whose significance was enhanced in the charged climate of the immediate post-war years when remembrance of the war dead, marked by the shadow of foreign trenches, was inscribed into the very earth of Kinder's deep crevasses. Such associations were a powerful motif in the masculinist discourses of the 'male wage slave' that surrounded the interwar access movement.

Ward's writings are a window into the imaginative geographies of the Peak, the changing perspectives of his individual view framed by larger ideas of nature, nation, gender and class. Dominant discourses of romanticism, aesthetics and history infused his views of these uplands as a place for mind and body, of spiritual and physical desire, where Nature as Woman could possess and be possessed. Yet his works also reveal a more complex and changing relationship with the landscape whose subtleties (of time and age) deserve greater attention than is possible here. How such landscapes might be read in other ways is suggested by the rather different inflections of Nan Shepherd's feminised engagement with another upland terrain, that of the Cairngorms in her book *The Living Mountain,* although what was common to both writers were similar needs for 'an "elsewhere" that exists beyond the constraints of daily life, yet is still part of daily life' (Shepherd 1977, p. 34). This phrase resonates with the ambivalences and tensions of the period. Ward's engagement with the Peakland landscape was a Sheffield-based one, an important reminder that the masculinist space he constructed in his attempted flight from domesticity and the city formed part of a 'wilderness' more bounded than any other upland area in Britain. The Peak uplands were a place for fantasies and dreams; they were a play area, the Sheffield resident's back yard where despite Ward's heroic ideals and manly emphasis, a sense of place was also combined with a strong sense of home.

ACKNOWLEDGEMENTS

I would like to thank staff in Derbyshire Local Studies Library, Matlock and in Sheffield Local Studies Library (particularly Mike Spick) for their help in researching this chapter. I am especially grateful to David Sissons of Sheffield Library and Information Services for so generously sharing his research into the life G. H. B Ward, to Keith Grieves for his helpful references and to Roy Bullen for his insights into Ward and the Sheffield rambling movement.

NOTES

1. Quoted in the *Sheffield Clarion Ramblers* (hereafter, SCR), *Membership Card*, 1907.
2. The terms Peak District, Peak and High Peak (an administrative district of north Derbyshire) were frequently interchangeable in tourist literature of the period.
3. The last edition was in 1963–4. They were already collectors' items by the late 1950s.
4. *SCR* 1900–1961, 60th Anniversary edition, pp. 5-6.
5. *SCR* Membership card 1907, pp. 11-12.

A kind of national property?

Guy M. Robinson

ABSTRACT

The chapter reviews the ways in which upland landscapes in Britain have become seen as the embodiment of natural heritage and a focus for both traditional and new forms of recreation, starting with the work of Romantic writers in the early nineteenth century. The origins of concerns over upland landscapes and their conservation are examined and the movement for the establishment of national parks considered, leading to a discussion of modern management issues within upland national parks and Areas of Outstanding Natural Beauty. The need for sensitive management strategies in order to cope with the multiplicity of ideas regarding what functions our upland areas should fulfil is paramount.

KEYWORDS

National parks, Areas of Outstanding Natural Beauty, recreation, Environmentally Sensitive Areas, upland conservation

INTRODUCTION

In H. L. Edlin's *The Changing Wildlife of Britain* (1952) there is a significant reference to the country's flora and fauna as 'a heritage of the people as a whole'. In part, this notion can be seen as a reflection of the changing attitude to the countryside, and to the uplands in particular, in the early post-war years when public interest in nature study and endeavours to preserve and enhance nature were making strong headway through new legislation. The latter took several forms, but included ambitious plans for advancing the interests of farming and forestry, improving the appearance and recreational potential of the countryside, conserving wildlife and providing protection from urban sprawl through a national system of planning controls. However, Edlin's comment also reflects a long-held view by certain sections of society regarding the rural landscapes of Britain as 'belonging' to them, and especially those landscapes associated with upland environments.

In the 1940s and 1950s, government policies on several fronts were aimed at tackling a series of problems in rural Britain that had been apparent in the inter-war years. However, the initiatives that gave rise to concrete legislation often had long periods of gestation, as attitudes to the countryside, both amongst the general public and in government circles, changed and crystallised. Indeed, it was the nature of the gradual evolution of ideas on conservation, and the most appropriate forms for rural development, that contributed to a fragmentation of rural management initiatives, ultimately bringing conflicts between the interests of farming, forestry, recreation, mineral extraction and conservation. In the last half century, these conflicts have increasingly reflected the public desire to see the countryside as more than just an arena of production, but also as a playground required to provide appropriate scenery, wildlife and livelihoods commensurate with the tastes of the urban-dwelling majority.

Today, the revenue generated from tourism in rural areas surpasses that accruing from farming. This symbolises a crucial change in the prime role of the countryside: from a site of production to one of consumption (Robinson 1999). This transformation has been part of growing pressure upon the countryside to fulfil multiple roles, thereby adding to the complexity of rural planning and land management. In particular, the growth in private ownership of cars and improvements in transport links between urban and rural areas have helped to direct a substantial proportion of leisure activity towards the countryside, with urban residents especially attracted by the aesthetic qualities of the uplands. This is evidenced in the growing popularity of visits to the national parks in England and Wales (all but one of those designated in the 1950s being in the uplands), with 76 million recreational visits recorded to the national parks and the national forest parks in a survey in 1994 (English Nature 2001a). It is this desire to experience upland environments and to pursue both traditional and new types of recreation in these areas that forms the subject matter of this chapter. In essence, it is a consideration of why and how the uplands of Britain have become the embodiment of the general public's natural heritage, to be visited and enjoyed repeatedly.

APPRECIATING THE UPLANDS

It is the physical fabric of the uplands and their history of human occupation that together have produced environments that have attracted public admiration and engendered certain romantic attitudes towards their maintenance. In particular, these attitudes have been strongly influenced by literary accounts of the character of the uplands, and especially the work of early nineteenth-century writers and poets known collectively as the Romantics (J. Wordsworth *et al.* 1987). These included Wordsworth, Keats, Shelley and Coleridge, who emphasised the aesthetic qualities of the uplands and rural Britain. In some of this writing, and in that later the same century, there was also a recognition not only of how human impact had created and maintained many of the valued wildlife communities, such as the heather moorlands and limestone grasslands, but also of the destructive qualities of that impact, as in the removal of woodlands and wetlands. The wider public appreciation of the ecological heritage of the uplands also had small beginnings in the nineteenth century before evolving into a powerful movement for conservation that has embraced various components of activity in the last 150 years.

Amongst the Romanticists, William Wordsworth's poetry and writing about the Lake District was particularly influential. For example, his *Guide to the Lakes* (Wordsworth, 1810) has been described as 'an exemplar of romantic ecology' (Bate 1991, p. 95). He also introduced the idea of the Lake District as 'a sort of national property' to be treasured by the nation (Whyte 2000b). His poetry and prose on the Lake District, portraying the intimate and intricate linkages between the human inhabitants and nature, have been regarded as the quintessential Romanticist view of the world, or an idealisation of nature, countryside and folk society. Wordsworth's contribution may be seen as part of a longer tradition of writing stretching back to classical times in that it was an arcadian notion that romanticised nature. It contained ideas and attitudes that were adopted by several other influential people later in the nineteenth century, including William Blake, Thomas Carlyle, John Ruskin and William Morris (Wiley 1998). Collectively these provided a view of the countryside that was initially conveyed to the élite in society in the form of a consistent message to value the countryside for its aesthetic qualities and the 'honest toil' of its inhabitants. This can be seen clearly in Wordsworth's *Prelude* (1799–1805), with its ecological vision of the rural community of Grasmere (J. Wordsworth *et al.* 1979). But, as Pepper argues, 'this was no neo-classical pastoral Arcadia. It was a harsh and hard work paradise. Wordsworth aggrandised common people and wrote them into history' (Pepper 1996, p. 196). Thus, the beauty of the upland landscape and the presence of the hard-working human inhabitants were both seen as essential elements in the character of the Lake District.

Wordsworth's writings about the Lake District contained a preservationist ethic, but with a strong degree of élitism, as typified in 1844 by his opposition to the proposed Kendal to Windermere railway. His attitude was that the railway would introduce people who might contribute to the destruction of the Lakeland environment. Moreover, the intruders might not be people who would be able to perceive and enjoy the environment in the way that 'cultivated' people would. Nearly forty years later similar sentiments prompted the formation of the Lake District Defence Society following unsuccessful attempts to prevent Manchester Corporation from turning Lake Thirlmere into a reservoir. Leading members of the Society were John Ruskin, William Morris and Thomas Carlyle. It was the forerunner to the National Trust for Places of Historic Interest or Natural Beauty, established in 1895, although an older preservationist organisation was the Commons, Open Spaces and Footpaths Preservation Society (COSFPS), initially closely associated with an élitist reaction against the influx of tourists to beautiful scenery. COSFPS was formed in the mid-1860s to contest the enclosure of the remaining common lands for agriculture.

The irony was that the general public's growing awareness of the beauty of the uplands, and the associated desire to see these fine landscapes, was inculcated by the writings of those who would have preferred to keep tourists away from such environments. Moreover, it was reaction to the upper classes' hunting and shooting pursuits in the countryside that provided the stimulus for the formation of wildlife and rural protection agencies in the late Victorian period, notably the Royal Society for the Protection of Birds (RSPB), founded in 1899, and the National Trust, which was formed as a body that could hold land in perpetuity, with its central aim as the preservation of the natural aspect of the countryside and its animal and plant life (Fedden 1974). However, although its early acquisitions included nature reserves in East Anglia, it became more concerned with landscape, ancient monuments and buildings than wildlife (Nicholls, 1998). Hence, the more extensive initiatives promoting conservation in the early twentieth century came from other sources, such as advocates of national parks and the Society for the Promotion of Nature Reserves, formed in 1912 to help the National Trust to create nature reserves.

ESTABLISHING THE NATIONAL PARKS AND AREAS OF OUTSTANDING NATURAL BEAUTY

The growing popularity of naturalist and field societies in the Victorian period reflects one effect on the wider populace of the images of nature and countryside in art, poetry and literature, whilst also demonstrating the growing availability of leisure time and the means to reach rural and upland scenery via the rail network. In many ways the national parks, created in the 1950s, are a more recent consequence of these two intersecting forces, though the huge popularity of the parks as sites for mass recreation was not envisaged by their initial proponents.

National parks were initiated in North America as a response to calls for the preservation of forest and 'wilderness', initiated by J. J. Audubon, Henry David Thoreau and John Muir amongst others. With no pristine wilderness to preserve in the United Kingdom, the preservationist sentiment was transferred to a desire to protect the countryside from 'threats' posed by industrialisation, urban sprawl and afforestation. This was part of the romantic reading of the landscape, with a strong degree of cultural élitism which was also embodied in the Council for the Preservation (now Protection) of Rural England (CPRE), formed in 1926 (with subsequent Scottish and Welsh equivalents) (Sheail 1981). The CPRE joined other groups in pressing for the creation of national parks, but its approach can be contrasted with a more scientific and managerial attitude to wildlife and landscape conservation associated with the growth of ecological research during the inter-war period.

The CPRE's first two key actions were, first, the drafting of a Rural Amenities Bill, which eventually became the Town and Country Planning Act of 1932, empowering local authorities to devise and implement planning schemes wherever warranted by building development (Sheail 1981, pp. 71-9). And, second, it persuaded the Prime Minister, Ramsay MacDonald, to appoint a National Parks Committee to investigate the need for one or more parks for the preservation of the natural character, including flora and fauna. This Committee advocated a series of parks and also suggested that the most effective way of selecting and managing them would be through national parks authorities, one for England and Wales, and another for Scotland. Unfortunately, the economic crisis of the time led to these ideas only taking hold in the form of voluntary pressure groups such as the Friends of the Lake District and a standing Committee on National Parks (under the aegis of the CPRE). However, the latter was influential, especially through its drafting secretary, John Dower, who in 1938 published a pamphlet, 'The case for the national parks in Great Britain', following an earlier one entitled 'National Parks — an appeal' (Sheail 1995a). Both of these contained detailed proposals for how national parks in the UK should be managed and designed.

An additional element in the growing pressure for national parks to be established in the UK during the 1920s and 1930s was the demand from sections of the urban populace to be allowed greater access to rural land for leisure and recreation. This was embodied in the mass trespass on Kinder Scout in the Peak District in 1932, followed by the foundation of the Ramblers Association in 1935. The argument for greater public access to the countryside was pursued during the Second World War when COSFPS began lobbying government ministers on the need to include greater facilities for outdoor recreation in plans for post-war reconstruction. This group especially stressed the need to preserve commons, footpaths and bridleways. The issue of access was taken up by the wartime Chancellor of the Exchequer, Hugh Dalton, who was an activist in the Ramblers Association and who had a commitment to working people having access to the countryside, through the creation of national parks and a system of long-distance footpaths.

This commitment was embodied in the 1949 National Parks and Access to the Countryside Act (NPACA), which established the means for designating national parks, and confirmed 140,000 miles (87,500 km) of footpaths as public rights of way. However, there was no granting of a right for people to roam freely across privately owned moorland, mountain, heath, downland, cliffs and foreshore in the parks. It took another half century for further legislation to be introduced to extend these rights, though with farmland still remaining out of bounds.

The support for the national parks concept in the 1942 Scott Report provided further impetus towards realisation of Dower's proposals, as did his appointment to produce a report on national planning and the use of land (Sheail 1995b). In 1945 he was part of a new National Parks Committee appointed by the Minister of Town and Country Planning, and both his role and his earlier reports seem to have been highly influential. As someone raised in Northumberland and the Yorkshire Dales, Dower echoed sentiments about upland Britain that had what Shoard (1982) refers to as 'a strong romantic legacy', which linked the conservationist movements involved in the national parks cause. As clearly stated by another of these champions of the uplands, Vaughan Cornish, the uplands possessed a series of qualities that appealed to the Romantics, such as wildness, naturalness, freedom through the opportunity afforded to wander at will, solitude, individuality and simplicity (Goudie 1972).

> The openness and grand vistas, in which the sky dominates, facilitate communion with the Creator, providing almost a religious experience (Pepper 1996, p. 226).

Hence, within the wartime lobby for the creation of national parks, there was strong pressure for the parks to be located in the uplands where they would embrace particular types of upland and mountain scenery.

The Dower report on 'National Parks in England and Wales', the Hobhouse Report on 'Footpaths and Access to the Countryside', and the Huxley Report on 'The Conservation of Nature in England and Wales', were all published in 1947 and contributed directly to the passing of the 1949 NPACA. However, whilst the Act was widely welcomed amongst the scientific community because of its concerns with wildlife conservation (including the creation of the Nature Conservancy and designation of 2,600 Sites of Special Scientific Interest — SSSIs), it was felt to have fallen well short of the expectations of the national parks and access lobbies (Hill 1980; Sculthorpe 1993). In large part, this was because farming and forestry in the newly designated national parks were to be exempted from development control, as they were elsewhere under the statutes of the 1947 Town and Country Planning Act. Indeed, more controls over some farm buildings in national parks were not instated until 1986. Moreover, in Scotland, where arguably the potential for national parks was greatest, there was no firm commitment to designating parks. The Ramsay Committee, Scotland's counterpart to Dower, Hobhouse and Huxley, proposed five areas as national parks, but these only became National Park Direction Areas, within which proposals for development were to be notified to the Secretary of State for

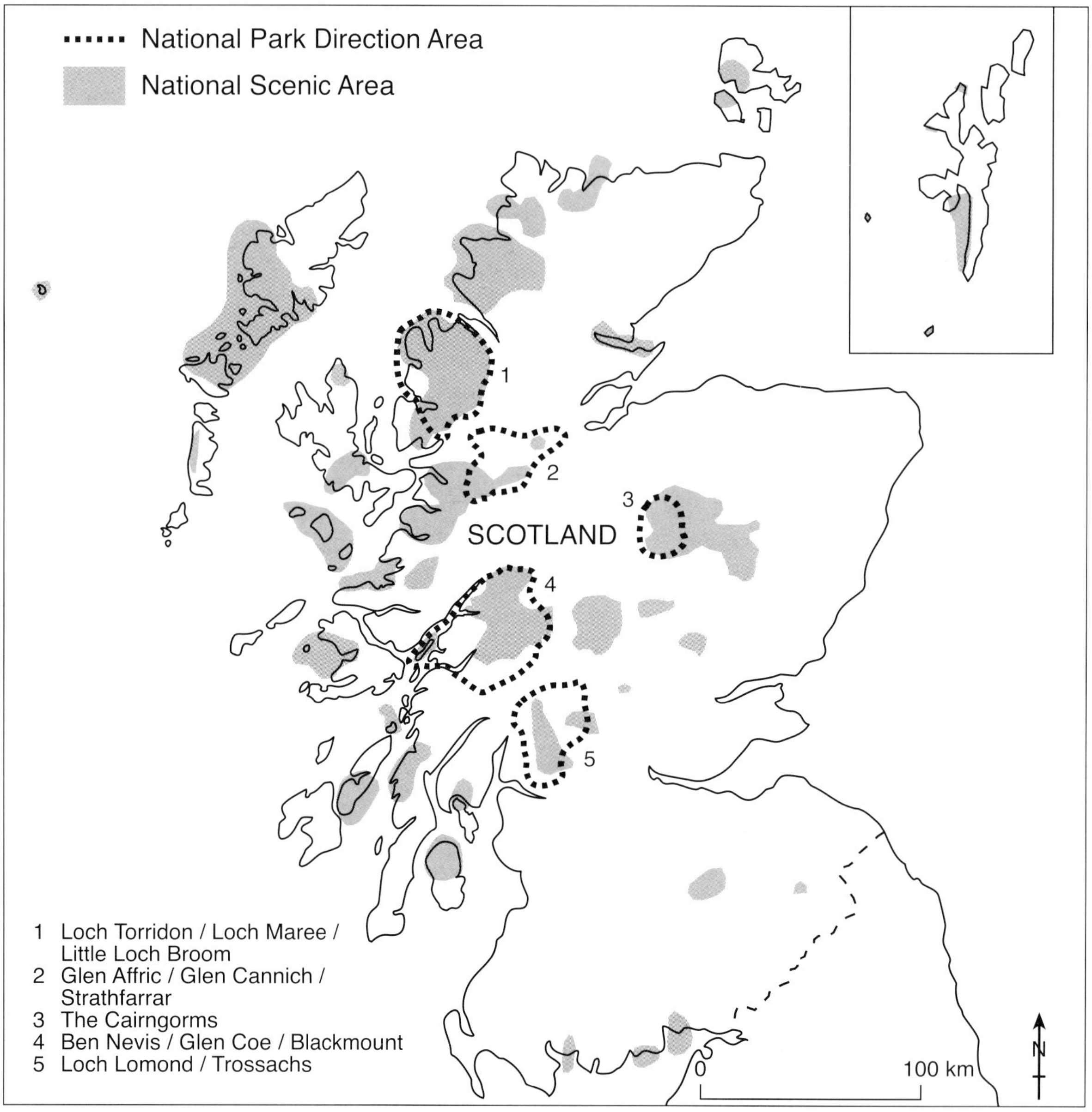

Fig. 13.1. Scotland's National Park Direction Areas and Scenic Areas

Scotland (Fig. 13.1). In Scotland, it was felt that the pressure of population on the countryside was much less than in England and Wales, and so the need for extra protection, via creation of national parks, was felt to be unnecessary (Selman 1988). A cogent factor in the decision may also have been the power of the large landowners, who owned vast tracts of the Highlands and who were not prepared to countenance the imposition of greater controls on their activities that may have accompanied park designation.

In the NPACA no lowland national parks were created, but, of land over 240 metres in England and Wales (the area currently defined as 'upland' by the Countryside Agency), nearly 70 *per cent* was designated as either national parks (Fig. 13.2) or Areas of Outstanding Natural Beauty (AONBs) (Fig. 13.3). However, other considerations in their designation meant that the powers of the new National Parks Commission (NPC) were significantly less than had been envisaged originally by Dower. This reflected the government's dilemma as to

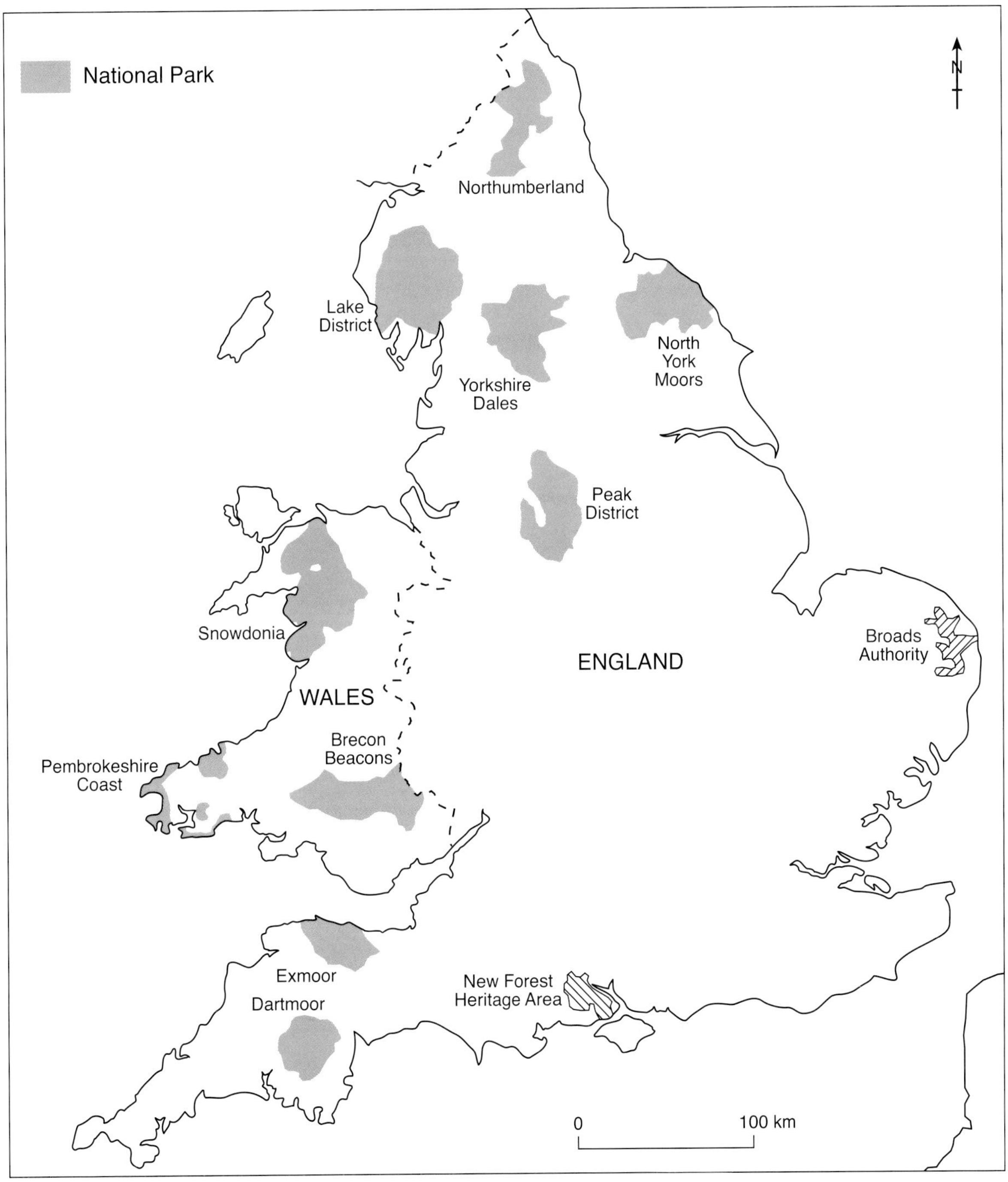

Fig. 13.2. National Parks in England and Wales

whether it was 'worth risking the disruption of the entire framework of town and country planning for the sake of the better preservation of the most outstanding parts of rural Britain' (Sheail 1998, p. 16). The dilemma was resolved in the NPACA by granting powers for the NPC to designate national parks subject to ministerial direction, but with powers only to advise the respective local authorities, in whose hands the planning powers effectively remained. Hence, the management of the national parks in the UK fell far short of the fundamental criteria that were to be recognised later as the basic standard for national parks by the International Union for the Conservation of Nature (IUCN) (IUCN 1969). In effect, it was the powers granted to local authorities under the 1947 Town and Country Planning Act that were held to be of paramount importance, and hence powers allocated to the NPC were limited.

The NPC was given five specific functions: to have an overall duty for preservation and enhancement of natural beauty throughout the country, although especially in relation to national parks and AONBs; to encourage the provision of facilities for the enjoyment of

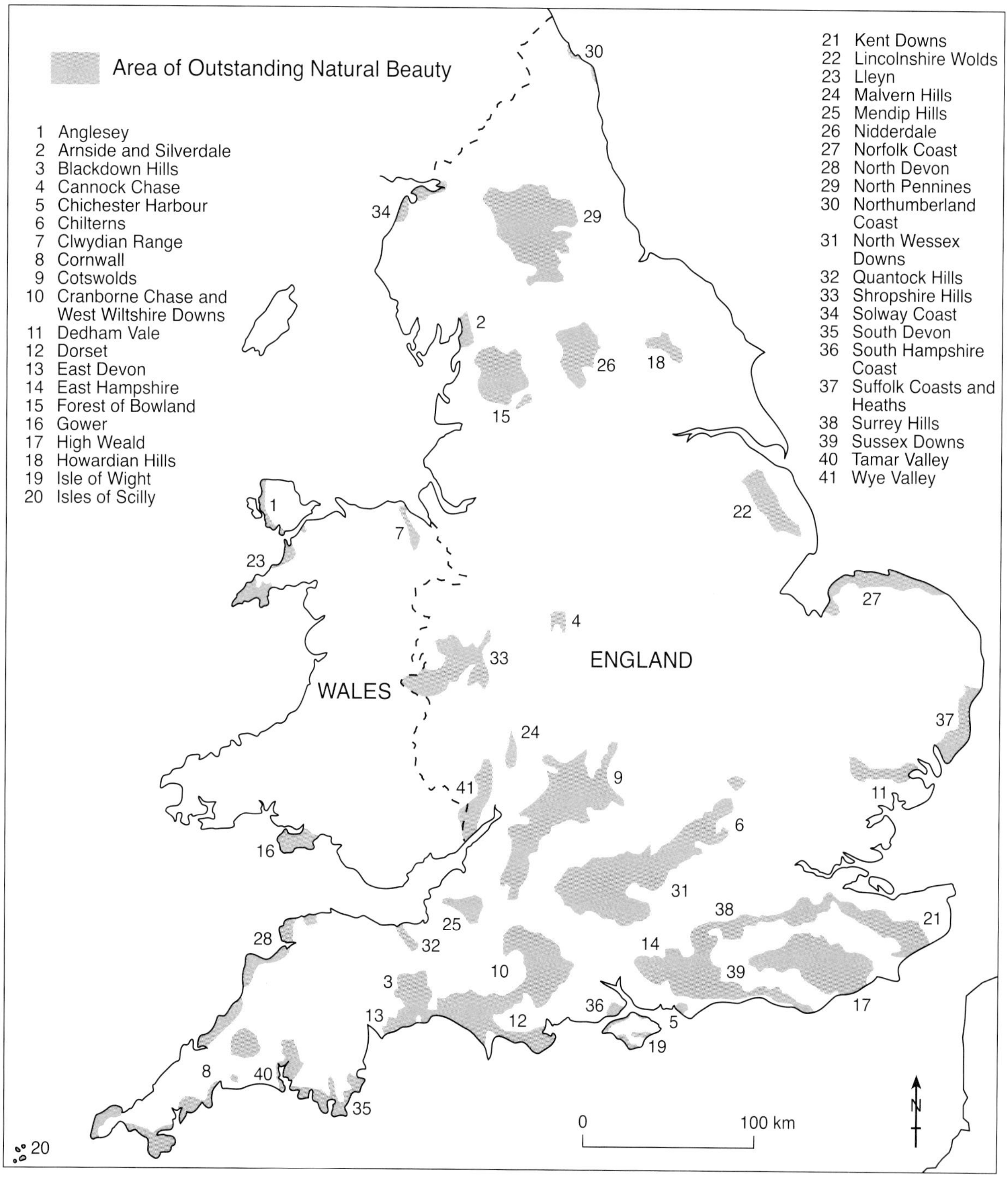

Fig. 13.3. Areas of Outstanding Natural Beauty (AONBs)

national parks; to designate national parks; to designate AONBs; and to give advice and assistance to local authorities.

Under the 1949 Act, any land in the newly-designated national parks could be acquired by agreement or compulsory purchase orders to give the public access to it for outdoor recreation. Indeed, special attention was given to public access, as recommended in Dower's report. For example, provision was to be made for the creation of special long-distance routes for walkers, cyclists and horse-riders. Where necessary existing rights-of-way could be added to through compulsory purchase. Powers for securing access and determining where it was required were placed in the hands of county councils who could negotiate access agreements with landowners or issue access orders, with landowners receiving compensation. In practice, though, the county councils did not have funds for compensation or land purchase, and large areas were exempted from access orders (though not from access agreements), including agricultural land (other than rough grazing), parks, gardens, golf courses and nature reserves. This list symbolises some of the conflicts between public access, conservation and economic activity, which have been present in the national parks throughout their existence, and exacerbated by the fact that three-quarters of the land in national parks is privately owned (McEwen, 1987). Indeed, since the first creation of national parks, only 1.6 *per cent* of land therein has been acquired by the parks' authorities.

The attraction of the uplands as the setting for various forms of recreation can be seen in the growing pressures through rising visitor numbers on both the parks and the AONBs. The latter had been first mooted in the Dower Report, which had identified 'other amenity areas' not suitable for designation as national parks due to their more limited size and lack of 'wilderness'. However, they were deemed to require some additional degree of development control beyond that afforded in other rural areas because of the need to cater for the demands of recreationists, especially in south-west England. When designated by the NPC, the AONBs were allocated a planning framework similar to that operating in the national parks. Thus the local authorities in the AONBs had similar powers to their national park counterparts to preserve and enhance local beauty, and with an obligation to consult the NPC when preparing development plans, though limited grant aid powers were given for landscape improvement, provision of public access to open country and warden services (Anderson 1990).

In total, thirty-five AONBs were designated, covering around 17,000 sq km, though half were located in lowland England (Fig. 13.3). Reviews of the AONBs conducted in the 1980s concluded that protection and enhancement had often been limited by inadequate resources and the lack of clear strategies for planning and management (Countryside Commission 1980, 1983). This led to the introduction of new policies seeking to improve co-ordination between local authorities, landowners and land managers. However, statutory management plans for AONBs were not forthcoming and hence concerns remain over their planning. Key problems are: the lack of explicit criteria for their designation, so that their boundaries do not mark distinct variations in landscape quality; insufficient controls over building development, and lack of complementarity over policies for nature conservation and landscape conservation in the absence of detailed management plans (Cooper *et al.* 1989; Preece 1981; Sellgren 1986, 1988).

PROBLEMS OF UPLAND MANAGEMENT

The 1949 NPACA established the first ten national parks in England and Wales, covering an area of 1.2 million hectares, all except the Pembrokeshire Coast being clearly within widely accepted definitions of the uplands (Table 1). The Act gave the NPC two main statutory duties that were often in conflict: preserving and enhancing the natural beauty of the countryside versus promotion of the enjoyment of the parks by the public. The conservation ideals have increasingly been compromised both by the need to cater for recreationists and by the presence in the parks of economic activities. Not only has there been too little opportunity to influence the activities of many landowners in the manner that certain conservation groups would have wished, but also government needs for forestry, mining and the military were often decisive in determining policy.

National Parks Authorities were created for each park, but their powers were relatively limited, mirroring those of local planning authorities, and focusing on the control of development. Yet, there have been several *causes celèbres* related to activities in the national parks that have been dictated by central government interests rather than local and conservationist concerns. These have included mineral extraction in the Yorkshire Dales, military training in Dartmoor, and a nuclear power plant in Snowdonia. Moreover, despite the stringent planning controls on building development, these have not extended to farming and forestry in the parks. As a result, there have been substantial land-use changes in the national parks and in the uplands in general. Two particular land-use problems are highlighted here because of the widespread interest they have attracted: the loss of moorland and afforestation.

TABLE 1 NATIONAL PARKS IN ENGLAND AND WALES DESIGNATED IN THE 1950S

Park	*Area designated (sq km)*	*Date of confirmation*	*Current population*
Peak District	1404	1951	37,400
Lake District	2243	1951	40,000
Snowdonia	2171	1951	2,171
Dartmoor	945	1951	29,100
Pembrokeshire Coast	583	1952	23,000
North York Moors	1432	1952	27,000
Yorkshire Dales	1761	1954	18,600
Exmoor	686	1954	10,000
Northumberland	1031	1956	2,200
Brecon Beacons	1344	1957	32,200

THE LOSS OF MOORLAND AND MANAGEMENT AGREEMENTS

One of the main landscape types in the uplands is moorlands. Although these rarely represent species of climax vegetation, their present characteristics have evolved over many centuries and their retention is felt to be highly desirable by many conservation groups. Yet, even within the national parks, there have been notable declines in the amount of open moorland and bordering woodland. Throughout the 1980s and 1990s, the loss of moorland averaged 5,000 hectares per annum, largely because of grants available for farmers to convert it into improved pasture, the creation of forestry plantations and the expansion of reservoir and recreation areas (*e.g.* Jones & Essex 1999) (colour Pl. XI). In the 1970s and 1980s, the loss of moorland was partly associated with the policies of the Forestry Commission. Of the Commission's 1.16 million hectares of land in 1990, 20 *per cent* were in the national parks, and this land was subject to the Commission's widespread policy of planting coniferous trees at the expense of both moorland and native deciduous woodland.

Around 15 *per cent* of the moorland area in Exmoor was lost between 1957 and 1966, causing a local outcry and attracting widespread interest. Similar losses were a cause of concern throughout the parks system, and gave rise to the Porchester Report in 1977. This acknowledged that over 15,000 hectares of moorland had been lost in the parks in the thirty years following their designation (Curtis 1983). Following the Report's publication, park authorities produced maps of moorland with 'high amenity value' to be used in conjunction with management agreements based on a voluntary notification system in which farmers notified the authorities of proposed alterations they intended to make to the moorland. Under such agreements, farmers receive compensation for profits lost by retaining moorland as rough grazing.

These agreements were copied in the Wildlife and Countryside Act of 1981, under which farmers within the national parks who are seeking government grant aid for agricultural changes must notify their park authority. If the authority feels that the proposed changes are not in the best interests of conservation, it may attempt to reach an agreement with the farmer, paying compensation for loss of income derived from the proposed change. The cost of such agreements has restricted the amount of intervention by the authorities. Nevertheless, the concept of payments to farmers for not 'damaging' the environment has been extended in various ways via schemes introducing grants for enhancement of the landscape. Several of these have concentrated their activities on upland areas. Forerunners to these schemes were the Upland Management Experiments (UMEX) in the Lake District and Snowdonia, first introduced in 1969, aimed at encouraging farmers to improve both the landscape and recreational facilities.

The notion of paying farmers to engage in environmentally friendly farming practices has been extended substantially in the last two decades, both in area-based policies and in schemes open to farmers throughout the country. Such schemes now account for around 2.5 *per cent* of the total agricultural budget of the European Union. In the case of the Environmentally Sensitive Areas (ESAs) scheme, introduced in the 1986 Agriculture Act, the majority of the forty-four designated areas were in upland Britain (Fig. 13.4), being areas where it was deemed particularly desirable to protect natural beauty, flora or fauna, or historical or archaeological features. These also offered scope for this objective to be assisted by the maintenance or adoption of particular agricultural methods (Robinson 1994b). In the

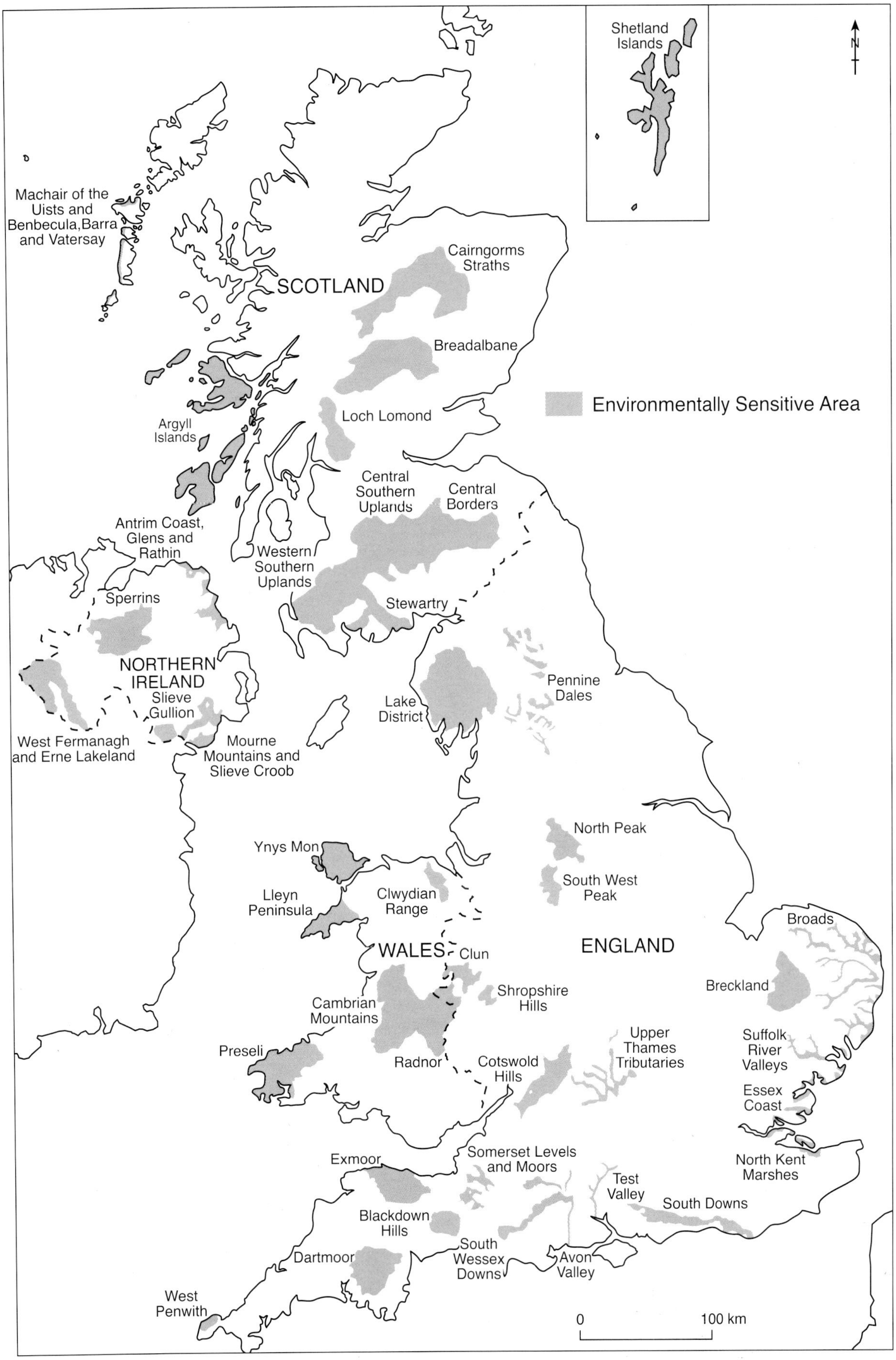

Fig. 13.4. Environmentally Sensitive Areas

ESAs, participation in the scheme is voluntary, and in most cases farmers do not have to enter all of their land into an agreement (though Clun, Exmoor and Lake District are notable exceptions). Hence, the impact upon the environment and landscape may have been somewhat restricted.

By the end of 1995, in the twenty-two English ESAs, 43 *per cent* of eligible landowners had entered 42 *per cent* of their land into management agreements. In Scotland at this time, 910 farmers had registered 28.1 *per cent* of their eligible area in ESA agreements (Egdell & Badger 1996, p. 32). However, there was variation between the ESAs, with a broad contrast between those in upland and lowland areas. Many of the schemes in the lowlands had less than 50 *per cent* of the farmland in the designated areas entered into agreements. Despite the lower figures for the Scottish ESAs as a whole, some of those designated first had high participation rates and higher proportions of whole farms entered. For example, in the Breadalbane ESA in Tayside, in the mid-1990s, three-quarters of farmers were participating and around 80 *per cent* of the agricultural land was covered by management agreements (Robinson 1994b). Farmers with conservation-oriented attitudes and a desire to pursue a 'traditional' approach to farming appear to be important factors in determining whether farmers will enter into management agreements (Battershill & Gilg 1996, 1997; Morris & Potter 1995; Wilson 1996).

Higher take-up rates and entry of land to some of the ESA schemes in Scotland and other parts of upland Britain are also related to the different role played by ESAs in the uplands in general. This role is not only one of attempting to act as a curb to destructive practices in areas of agricultural intensification, but as maintainers of traditional farming landscapes, often in locations where there is little economic alternative to land-based activity (Gaskell & Tanner 1991). So in the uplands the focus has been upon encouraging farmers to undertake tasks that they had perhaps been neglecting because of the high costs of labour involved, such as rebuilding stone walls, replanting woodland, and active conservation tasks such as the protection of rough grazing, protection of unimproved, unenclosed land in valleys, and general restraint from overstocking. The rates of uptake in the uplands suggest that farmers have been willing to accept payments for undertaking tasks that they wanted to implement on their farm but had not done so through lack of money. The receipt of the requisite money has led to more labour being hired to carry out various conservation tasks and, in some cases, has added to overall farm incomes (Froud 1994).

Assessments of the conservation value of ESAs have varied considerably. Some have claimed that farmers are being paid to do what they would do in any case, and therefore the ESA management agreements are having little impact on the environment (Colman 1994). Others have stressed particular conservation and economic benefits arising from the scheme (Evans & Morris 1997; Garrod *et al.* 1994; Garrod & Willis 1995), including increased incomes per unit area (Froud 1994). Similar conflicting opinions over impacts have been expressed with regard to the non-area-based Countryside Stewardship Scheme, which by the end of 1998 had 143,055 hectares enrolled in 8,614 management agreements (an average of 16.61 hectares per agreement), the majority being in the uplands. In this scheme agreements focusing on field boundaries, waterside land and old meadows and pasture have been most popular (Simpson & Robinson 2001). These measures, and those undertaken in the ESAs, have become part of the notion that, in order to enable the uplands to function as 'a kind of national property', the landscape has to be maintained in a particular way by those living and working within it.

AFFORESTATION

Created in 1919, the Forestry Commission (FC), a government body with state funding, embarked on a concerted policy of upland afforestation post-1945, fulfilling the intentions stated in the 1943 White Paper on Post-War Forest Policy to produce a strategic timber reserve and reduce timber imports. Much of this increased production came from upland farmland acquired by the FC at times of economic difficulty for hill farmers, as in the late 1960s. Large areas of the Southern Uplands and parts of the Scottish Highlands were acquired and planted with conifers: at a rate of 14,000 hectares per annum throughout the 1970s. In the 1980s, following the Forestry Act of 1981 which empowered the FC to dispose of plantations to the private sector, it was private landowners who came to dominate the afforestation programme (Mather 1988), but often with a similar focus on planting dense stands of mono-species conifers. As a result a new upland landscape was created in many areas, with non-native trees replacing open moor. The loss of amenity value was keenly felt in some quarters before reforms to the FC brought about planting policies that embraced diversity of species and less emphasis upon commercial timber production.

It was not until 1957, following a review of forestry by the Zuckermann Committee, that the FC was put under a duty to pay 'due regard [to] the effect of forestry on wildlife and on the beauty of the countryside' (FC 1957, p. 9). However, the active promotion of the

Commission's forests as locations for recreation did not occur to a significant degree until the 1970s when there was also more concern for the relationship between forestry practice and landscape appearance (Tsouvalis 2000, pp. 126-7). Yet, under the 1924 Forestry Act, the FC had been empowered to create by-laws in relation to access and had established forest parks, beginning with Argyllshire (14,000 ha) in 1936, followed by the Forest of Dean (9,200 ha) in 1939 and Snowdonia (8,200 ha) in 1940. In effect, these first forest parks were largely areas of land belonging to the FC that were unsuitable for planting commercial stands of timber.

Other forest parks were designated from 1950 onwards as part of the expansion of the FC's land holding, and by the 1990s there were seventeen, covering 300,000 hectares. Gradually, more thought was given as to how a combination of recreational needs, conservation and timber management could be balanced, not just in the parks but throughout the FC's estates, and hence the notion of multi-purpose forestry gained greater currency (Pringle 1994). The reality, though, was that the needs of recreationists came a long way behind other concerns until the 1960s when there was government pressure for the recreational component of forests to receive closer attention. This prompted the FC's first comprehensive recreation policy involving Regional Recreation Plans (FC 1971). These incorporated greater right of public access on foot, provision of facilities such as small car parks and information centres, and charges levied where feasible. Forest roads were only to be used where they gave access to car parks and sites for camping and caravanning and picnicking. Opportunities for fishing were extended and some forest drives were operated as toll roads. Stress was placed upon interpretation facilities, souvenirs, aesthetics and commercialisation of recreation as 'forests gradually became part of a commercialised tourist industry that catered for a markedly different type of forest user from the rambler of the early part of the century: namely, the forest consumer' (Tsouvalis 2000, p. 145). Mather (1991) recognises this as part of the dawn of a post-industrial phase in British forestry in which priority afforded to wood production has been reduced or removed, and recreation and environmental conservation have attained at least equal importance. Moreover, not only have significant amounts of FC land been sold to the private sector, but within both the public and private spheres of forestry management, activities are increasingly circumscribed by public or social influences that have promoted forest-based recreation.

RETAINING THE UPLANDS AS THE NATION'S NATIONAL PROPERTY

In 1967, the Countryside Act put into place reforms that created the Countryside Commission (CC). Similar legislation created a Scottish counterpart (Sheail 2000). The CC subsumed the NPC and assumed the task of encouraging the provision or improvement of facilities for the enjoyment of the countryside generally. Although strongly influenced by the growth of recreational activity in the uplands, and the national parks in particular, the Act recognised the growth of recreational activity throughout the countryside as a whole. The legislation followed closely upon the release of a paper published by the Civic Trust, in which Michael Dower (1965) referred to the growth of leisure as the 'fourth wave', a challenge comparable with industrialisation, the railways, and suburbanisation. He argued that the 'wave' might have major impacts upon attractive upland locations, but it would also be evident in the countryside around major urban centres, and so the new agencies' remits were for all the countryside and not only national parks and the AONBs.

The magnitude of the 'fourth wave' has placed immense pressure on the national parks and other parts of the uplands where the numbers of recreationists and tourists have grown steadily, especially in those uplands most readily accessible to large numbers of urban residents via the motorway network. Although the two CCs have introduced initiatives to provide more recreational facilities in the lowlands, the overwhelming evidence is that the general public, more than ever before, wishes to see at first hand the 'nation's national property': the uplands. In so doing, the general wish is to see upland landscapes that represent the essential combination of physical and human qualities portrayed by the Romanticists. Hence planning and management policies adopted in national parks, ESAs and AONBs have strong preservationist and conservationist qualities designed to mitigate the worst excesses of modern farming, forestry and the encroachment of urban development. Indeed, there are prospects of new conservation measures.

Of the latter, perhaps the best current illustration is the establishment of national parks in Scotland. Arguments over whether Scotland should have national parks have surfaced periodically, but came to a head in the 1990s, partly reflecting the growing pressures in two particular areas: around Loch Lomond and in the Cairngorms (CCS 1990; Dickinson 1991). With its southern shores only 20 km from the outskirts of

Glasgow, Loch Lomond has been the premier destination for day recreationists from throughout central Scotland, with two million visits annually recorded in a survey in the mid-1990s (Dickinson 2000). With a separate Parliament for Scotland established in 1999, the case for Scottish national parks was supported in the new Assembly, and the Loch Lomond and Trossachs National Park was officially designated in 2002, extending the protection of the Loch and its shoreline that was previously afforded by the creation of the Loch Lomond National Nature Reserve. Proposals for a Cairngorms National Park covering 4,500 sq km are now under consideration, which, if accepted, would make this the biggest national park in Britain, almost double the size of the Lake District. Again, much of the debate has concerned the relationship between the responsibilities to be allocated to the national park authority and the local authorities, with the initial proposal giving the latter key rights over development control. This threatens to re-create the same battleground between the park board and local authorities that has occurred in the English and Welsh national parks.

The changes occurring throughout the uplands continue to cause concerns over the best means of retaining their special character, especially given the growing evidence of damage to key environmental sites. For example, Table 2 shows that the relative lack of protection afforded the SSSIs has resulted in significant amounts of destruction and degradation. In part, this reflects the lack of development of appropriate solutions, notwithstanding the initiation of the various management agreements discussed above. It was felt in some circles that, when the CC was created as an advisory body to the Department of the Environment, its powers would be insufficient to bring about a more integrated approach to rural planning that would be so vital to obtaining a balance between the competing interests in the uplands (Shoard 1987). This desire for integrated management has still not been adequately realised in 'the current administrative spider's web that provides the framework for countryside management in Britain' (Robinson 1994a, p. 325).

Despite various items of legislation introduced in the last two decades, many feel they have been insufficient to curb exploitative development of rural resources in the uplands (Curry & Owen 1996), and hence there are continued calls for stronger controls. For example, the RSPB (2001) has recently urged that 16,200 hectares be taken out of food production as part of a vigorous programme of habitat re-creation. This would include 10,120 hectares of upland deemed to have been adversely affected by industrial farming activities. In addition to protecting wildlife, the RSPB wish to see more opportunities for recreation, for example by returning much of the grazing land in the Lake District to its natural habitat of woodland, heather and gorse. There are also growing pressures for the independent park authorities to be granted more powers to protect moorland and rough pasture, in addition to controlling development of farm buildings, currently exempt from planning laws.

The presence of towns and villages within the national parks continues to prove problematic in terms of balancing the demands of their inhabitants for adequate provision of economic opportunities and services versus conservation

TABLE 2. UPLAND HABITATS IN SITES OF SPECIAL SCIENTIFIC INTEREST (SSSIS) IN ENGLAND

Habitat	*Number of SSSIs*	*% of SSSI area in unfavourable condition*	*Total area (ha)*	*Area in SSSIs (ha)*
Upland oak woods	217	32	100,000	na
Upland ash woods	236	39	67,000	na
All upland woodland	453	71	167,000	15,800
Upland heathland	87	72	270,000	179,000
Upland calcareous grassland	39	67	10,000	7,500
Upland hay meadow	75	16	<1,000	770
Blanket bog	51	60	215,000	100,000
Standing waters	39	50	na	4,100
Limestone pavement	30	36	2,340	1,396
Montane habitats	33	64	na	26,000

Source: English Nature 2001a

interests. The growth of tourism has added greatly to the economic well-being of the parks' inhabitants, but it has brought serious problems of congestion, overcrowding, damage to popular sites and conflicts over the growth of second home ownership. The latter has brought periodic protests from local residents, especially over the impacts upon property prices, effectively pricing young locals out of the market. Controls on second-home ownership have been instituted at various times in both the Lake District and the Peak District, though such restrictions have proved both difficult to operate and open to legal challenge (Clark 1982). Recently, more concerted action to control second home ownership is promised by all the national parks, following plans proposed by Exmoor National Park Authority (where 13 *per cent* of the housing stock are second homes) that would restrict purchasers of newly-built homes to people who have lived there for ten years or who have a job in the area. Purchasers of existing property would have to obtain planning permission if they intended to use it for less than six months per annum. Meanwhile, the Welsh Assembly is considering legislation proposing to increase council tax for second home-owners as a means of controlling this particular aspect of tourism.

There is an extremely fine balance to be attained between maintaining certain types of human activity and land management in the uplands that will allow natural biological and ecological systems to flourish. For example, indications of the likely impacts upon wildlife through the removal or reduction in sheep grazing have been gained recently in areas affected by foot and mouth disease. Rare plants such as the marsh saxifrage, hairy stonecrop and alpine forget-me-not have blossomed and set seed for the first time in areas affected by the disease when sheep have been removed from grazing land. Cottongrass, an important food source for the black grouse, and heather have also thrived as a result of the removal of sheep. In areas such as the Moor House and Upper Teesdale national nature reserve and around Skiddaw in the Cumbrian fells, where 60 *per cent* of sheep on common land have been slaughtered, there are prospects for a flush of oakwood and juniper regeneration (English Nature 2001b). Nevertheless, the delicate balance between wildlife, landscape appearance and human activity is also demonstrated by the continued need for grazing and other management, such as bracken cutting, in order to retain the presence of certain species, *e.g.* the high brown fritillary butterfly whose continuing presence in the Malvern Hills will be threatened if traditional management practices are not maintained. In endeavouring to maintain 'balance' some imaginative schemes have been adopted, as in the North York Moors National Park where former moorland, now converted largely to enclosed arable land, is being developed into broadleaved parkland landscape open for public access, and combined with areas of heath or common land. The nature of the landscape is being modified by management agreements and direct purchase of land by the park authority (Statham 1993).

CONCLUSIONS

The various issues of upland management discussed above are all tied in different but interlinked ways to the notion of the uplands as a kind of national property. Wordsworth's idea of the Lake District as a region that was more than just a collection of mountains, lakes, forests and hill farms but 'belonged' to the nation, has been translated into a broader conception of uplands as the setting for myriad forms of regulation and protection. Regulation has increasingly had to provide for the needs of recreationists who wish to indulge in more than just passive enjoyment of the most attractive upland scenery. The huge rise in the number of visitors to these attractive areas has been accompanied by new forms of recreational and other activity that have added to management difficulties and to the conflicts between different types of activities and land uses. The delicate balance between maintenance of scenery, wildlife habitats, access for people and vehicles and accommodating residents' needs has meant that the uplands have been at the forefront of planning activity. They look set to remain so, with a new chapter in planning to be opened with the creation of national parks in Scotland. Once again the notion of the uplands as national property will be reinforced, but accompanied by the need for ever more imaginative management if the multiplicity of ideas regarding what functions that national property should fulfil are to be reconciled.

Bibliography and Abbreviations

Acts of Parliament of Scotland, 9 vols, 1814–75 (Edinburgh).

Adams, I. H. (ed.), 1979. *Papers on Peter May Land Surveyor 1749–1793*, Scott Hist Soc, 4th ser, vol. 15 (Edinburgh).

Adams, J., 1995. *Mines of the Lake District Fells* (Clapham).

Aitchison, J. W., 1990. 'The commons and wastes of England and Wales 1958–1989', *Area*, 22 (3), pp. 272-7.

Aitchison, J. W., & Hughes, E. J., 1982. 'The common land registers of England and Wales: a problematic data source', *Area*, 14 (2), pp. 151-6.

Aitchison, J. W., & Hughes, E. J., 1988. 'The common lands of Wales', *Trans Inst Br Geogr*, new ser, 13, pp. 96-108.

Allen, R. C., 1992. *Enclosure and the Yeoman* (Oxford).

Altenburg, K., 1999. 'Space and community on medieval Dartmoor and Bodmin Moor: interim report', *Medieval Settlement Res Group, Ann Rep*, 14, pp. 26-8.

Anderson, M. L., 1967. *A History of Scottish Forestry* (Edinburgh).

Anderson, M., 1990. 'Areas of Outstanding Natural Beauty and the 1949 National Parks Act', *Town Planning Rev*, 61, pp. 311-40.

Anderson, P., & Shimwell, D., 1981. *Wild Flowers and other Plants of the Peak District* (Ashbourne).

Andrews, M., 1989. *The Search for the Picturesque* (Aldershot).

Anglo-Saxon Chronicle, The, trans. & ed. ed. M. Swanton, 1996 (London).

Anon., 1896. 'A description of ye Clee, ye lordships, commoners and strakers adjoyn'd, made about 1612, 10 Jac.', *Trans Shropshire Archaeol & Nat Hist Soc*, 2nd ser, 8, pp. 195-8.

Anon., 1946. *Across the Derbyshire Moors: rambles near Sheffield*, 23rd edn (Sheffield).

Ardron, P. A., 1999a. 'Peat cutting in upland Britain with special reference to the Peak District — its impact on landscape, archaeology and ecology', unpubl Univ Sheffield Ph.D. thesis.

Ardron, P. A, 1999b. 'The impact of peat cutting on fauna and flora', *Landscape Archael & Ecol*, 4, pp. 10-27.

Ardron, P. A., Rotherham, I. D., & Gilbert, O. L., 1996a. 'The influence of peat-cutting on upland landscapes: case studies from the South Pennines', in 'Landscape-Perception, Recognition and Management: reconciling the impossible? Abs Proc Landscape Conservation Forum Conf, 2–4 April 1996, Sheffield', *Landscape Archaeol & Ecol*, 2, p. 54-64.

Ardron, P. A., Rotherham, I. D., & Gilbert, O. L., 1996b. 'Peat-cutting and upland landscapes: case studies from the South Pennines', in 'Landscape-Perception, Recognition and Management: reconciling the impossible? Proc Landscape Conservation Forum Conf, 2–4 April 1996, Sheffield', *Landscape Archaeol & Ecol*, 3, pp. 65-9.

Ardron, P. A., Gilbert, O. L., & Rotherham, I. D., 1998. 'Factors determining contemporary upland landscapes: a re-evaluation of the importance of peat-cutting and associated drainage, and the implications for mire restoration and remediation', in *Blanket Mire Degradation: causes, consequences and challenges*, ed. J. H. Tallis, R. Meade & P. D. Hume (Aberdeen), pp. 38-41.

Ardron, P. A., Rotherham, I. D., & Gilbert, O. L., 1999. 'An evaluation of the South Pennines peatlands with reference to the impact of peat cutting', *Peak District J Nat Hist & Archaeol*, 1, pp. 67-75.

Aris, M., 1977. 'The Vaynol estate', in *Atlas of Caernvonshire*, ed. T. M. Bassett & B. L. Davies (Caernarfon), pp. 135-9.

Armstrong H. M., & Milne, J. A., 1995. 'The effects of grazing on vegetation species composition', in *Heaths and Moorland*, ed. Thompson, Hester & Usher, pp. 162-73.

Ashmore, O., 1982. *The Industrial Archaeology of North-West England* (Manchester).

Atherden, M. A., 1976. 'Late Quaternary vegetational history of the North York Moors III. Fen Bogs', *J Biogeogr*, 3, pp. 115-24.

Atherden, M. A., 1979. 'Late Quaternary vegetational history of the North York Moors VII. Pollen diagrams from the eastern-central area', *J Biogeogr*, 6, pp. 63-83.

Atherden, M. A., 1985. 'Land use change and the status of grasslands on the North York Moors', in *Biogeogr Monogr* 2, ed. R. T. Smith (Leeds), pp. 75-83.

Atherden, M. A., 1992. *Upland Britain: a natural history* (Manchester).

Atherden, M. A., 1999. 'The vegetation history of Yorkshire: a bog-trotter's guide to God's own county', *The Naturalist*, 124, pp. 137-56.

Atherden, M. A., & Butlin, R. A. (eds), 1998. *Woodland in the Landscape: past and future perspectives* (York).

Austin, D., Gerrard, G. A. M., & Greeves, T. A. P., 1989. 'Tin and agriculture in the middle ages and beyond: landscape archaeology in St Neot parish, Cornwall', *Cornish Archaeol*, 28, pp. 5-251.

Baddeley M. J. B., 1908. *The Peak District*, 9th edn (London).

Badenoch, C., 1997. 'Woodland origin and the loss of native woodland in the Tweed valley', *Scott For*, 51, pp. 15-20.

Baker E. A., 1903. *Moors, Crags and Caves of the High Peak and Neighbourhood* (Manchester).

Ball, D. F., 1968. 'Soils of Wales: the distribution of major soil groups', *Trans VIIIth Congress on Soil Science* (Bucharest), 5, pp. 69-79.

Ball, D. F., & Goodier, R., 1970. 'Morphology and distribution of features resulting from frost action in Snowdonia', *Field Stud*, 3, pp. 193-218.

Ball, D. F., Mew, G., & Macphee, W. S. G., 1969. 'Soils of Snowdon', *Field Stud*, 2, pp. 69-107.

Banks, R. W., 1880. 'The grange of Cwmtoyddwr', *Archaeol Cambrensis*, 1, pp. 30-50.

Barber, K. E., 1981. *Peat Stratigraphy and Climate Change — a palaeoecological test of the theory of cyclic peat bog regeneration* (Rotterdam).

Barber, K. E., Chambers, F. M., Maddy, D., Stoneman, R., & Brew, J. S., 1994. 'A sensitive high-resolution record of late Holocene climatic change from a raised bog in northern England', *The Holocene*, 4, pp. 198-205.

Barber, K., Dumayne-Peaty, L., Hughes, P., Mauquoy, D., & Scaife, R., 1998. 'Replicability and variability of the recent macrofossil and proxy-climate record from raised bogs: field stratigraphy and macrofossil data from Bolton Fell Moss and Walton Moss, Cumbria, England', *J Quaternary Sci*, 13, pp. 515-28.

Barber, K. E., Maddy, D., Rose, N., Stevenson, A. C., Stoneman, R., & Thompson, R., 2000. 'Replicated proxy-climate signals over the last 2000 years from two distant UK peat bogs: new evidence for regional palaeoclimate teleconnections', *Quaternary Sci Rev*, 19, pp. 481-7.

Barnatt, J., & Smith, K., 1998. *Book of The Peak District: landscapes through time* (London).

Barnes, F. A., 1970. 'Settlement and landscape changes in a Caernarvonshire slate-quarrying parish', in *Geographical Essays in Honour of K. C. Edwards*, ed. R. H. Osborne, F. A. Barnes, & J. C. Doornkamp (Nottingham), pp. 119-30.

Bassett, T. M., & Davies, B. L. (eds), 1977. *Atlas of Caernavonshire* (Caernarfon).

Bate, J., 1991. *Romantic Ecology: Wordsworth and the environmental tradition* (London).

Battershill, M. R. J., & Gilg, A. W., 1996. 'Traditional farming and agro-environment policy in Southwest England: back to the future?' *Geoforum*, 27, pp. 133-47.

Battershill, M. R. J., & Gilg, A. W., 1997. 'Socio-economic constraints and environmentally-friendly farming in the south-west of England', *J Rural Stud*, 7, pp. 91-7.

BBC, 2001. British Broadcasting Corporation, Radio 4, *Seat of Eagles*: programmes marking fiftieth anniversary of Snowdonia National Park, 12 & 19 January 2001.

Bede, *A History of the English Church and People*, trans.L Sherley-Price, revised R. E. Latham, 1968 (Harmondsworth).

Belchem J., & Epstein J., 1997. 'The nineteenth-century gentleman leader revisited', *Social Hist*, 22 (2), pp. 183-4.

Bell, W. T., & Ogilvie, A. E. J., 1978. 'Weather compilations as a source of data for the reconstruction of European climatic change during the medieval period', *Clim Change*, 1, pp. 331-48.

Beresford, M. W., 1964. 'Dispersed and grouped settlement in medieval Cornwall', *Agric Hist Rev*, 12, pp. 13-27.

Berkes, F. (ed.), 1989. *Common Property Resources: ecology and community-based sustainable development* (London).

Bermingham, A., 1986. *Landscape and Ideology: the English rustic tradition*, 1740–1860 (Berkeley).

Berry, A. Q., Gale, F., Daniels, J. L., & Allmark, W. (eds), 1996. *Fenn's and Whixall Mosses* (Mold).

Beverley Smith, J., 1966. 'Crown and community in the principality of North Wales in the reign of Henry Tudor', *Welsh Hist Rev*, 3, pp. 145-71.

Bick, D., 1991. *The Old Metal Mines of Mid-Wales. Part 6: A Miscellany* (Newent, Glos.).

Bick, D., & Davies, P. W., 1994. *Lewis Morris and the Cardiganshire mines* (Aberystwyth).

Bil, A., 1990. *The Shieling 1600–1840: the case of the central Scottish Highlands* (Edinburgh).

Bingham, R. K., 1987. *The Chronicles of Milnthorpe* (Milnthorpe).

Birtles, S., 1998. 'The impact of commons registration: a Norfolk study', *Landscape Hist*, 20, pp. 83-97.

Black, J. L., 1983. 'Growth and development of lambs', in *Sheep Production*, ed. Haresign, pp. 21-58.

Blackford, J. J., & Chambers, F. M., 1993. 'Determining the degree of peat decomposition for peat-based palaeoclimate studies', *Int Peat J*, 5, pp. 7-24.

Blackford, J. J., & Chambers, F. M., 1999. 'Harold's Bog, East Bilsdale Moor', in *The Quaternary of North-East England*, ed. D. R. Bridgland, B. P. Horton & J. B. Innes (London), pp. 91-8.

Booth, J. (ed.), 1889. *Halmota Prioratus Dunelmensis*, Surtees Soc 82 (Durham).

Bowden, M., 2000. *Furness Iron* (London).

Bowrie R. (ed.), 1855. *Black Book of Taymouth*, Maitland Club (Edinburgh).

BPP, 1884. *Report of the Commission of Inquiry into the Condition of the Crofters and Cottars*, Br Parliamentary Pap 1884, 32–39 (London).

Brayshay, M., & Williams, A., 1995. 'A rough and cold country: farming and landscape changes in northern Snowdonia since *c.* 1600', in *Ecological Relations in Historical Times*, ed. R. A. Butlin & N. Roberts (Oxford), pp. 122-45.

Briggs, A., 1994. *A Social History of England*, new edn (London).

Britton, J., & Brayley E. W., 1810. *A Topographical and Historical Description of Derbyshire* (London).

Burgon, J., 1999. 'The National Trust's part in conserving rich and diverse landscapes', *Europa Nostra*, issue 1.

Butzer, K. W., 1982. *Archaeology as Human Ecology* (Cambridge).

Byne, E. & Sutton G., 1966. *High Peak: the story of walking and climbing in the Peak District* (London).

Cal. Inq. Misc Calendar of Inquisitions Miscellaneous, 7 vols, 1916–69 (London).

Cal. IPM Series II. Calendar of Inquisitions Post Mortem Second Series [Hen. VII], 3 vols, 1898–1956 (London).

Cal. IPM. Calendar of Inquisitions Post Mortem and other analogous documents, 20 vols [Hen. III to Hen. V], 1904–1995 (London).

Cal. Pat. Ed. I. Calendar of Patent Rolls, Edward I, 4 vols, 1893–1901 (London)..

Campbell, B. M. S., 1991. *Before the Black Death: studies in the 'crisis' of the early fourteenth century* (Manchester).

Campbell, C. K., Tipping, R., & Cowley, D., 2002. 'Continuity and stability in past upland land uses in the western Cheviot Hills, southern Scotland', *Landscape Hist*, 24, pp. 111-20.

Carr, R., 1981. 'Country sports', in *The Victorian Countryside*, ed. G. E. Mingay (London).

Carter, G., 2001. ' "Domestic geography" and the politics of Scottish landscape in Nan Shepherd's *The Living Mountain*', *Gender, Place & Culture*, 8(1), pp. 25-36.

Carter, S., Tipping, R., Davidson, D., Long, D., & Tyler, A., 1997. 'A multi-proxy approach to the function of post-medieval ridge-and-furrow cultivation in upland northern Britain', *The Holocene*, 7, pp. 447-56.

CCS. Countryside Commission for Scotland, 1990. *The Mountain Areas of Scotland: conservation and management* (Perth).

Chapman, J., 1961. 'Changing agriculture and the moorland edge in the North York Moors, 1750 to 1960', unpubl Univ London M.A. thesis.

Chapman, J., 1972. 'Agriculture and the "waste" in Monmouthshire from 1750 to the present day', unpubl Univ London Ph.D. thesis.

Chapman, J., 1976. 'Parliamentary enclosure in the uplands: the case of the North York Moors', *Agric Hist Rev*, 24, pp. 1-17.

Chapman, J., 1987. 'The extent and nature of Parliamentary enclosure', *Agric Hist Rev*, 35, pp. 25-35.

Chapman, J., 1991a. 'Confidence limits and enclosure estimates: some comments', *Agric Hist Rev*, 39, pp. 48-51.

Chapman, J., 1991b. 'The later parliamentary enclosures of Wales', *Agric Hist Rev*, 39, pp. 116-25.

Chapman, J., 1992. *A Guide to Parliamentary Enclosures in Wales* (Cardiff).

Chapman, J., & Harris, T. M., 1982. 'The accuracy of enclosure estimates: some evidence from northern England', *J Historical Geogr*, 8, pp. 261-4.

Chapman, J., & Seeliger, S., 2001. *Enclosure, Environment and Landscape in Southern England* (Stroud).

Charman, D. J., Hendon, D., & Packman, S., 1999. 'Multiproxy surface wetness records from replicate cores on an ombrotrophic mire: implications for Holocene palaeoclimate records', *J Quaternary Sci*, 14, pp. 451-64.

Chiverrell, R. C., 1998. 'Moorland vegetation history and climate change on the North York Moors during the last 2000 years', unpubl Univ Leeds Ph.D. thesis.

Chiverrell, R. C., 2001. 'A proxy record of late Holocene climate change for May Moss, north-east England', *J Quaternary Sci*, 16, pp. 9-29.

Chiverrell, R. C., & Atherden, M. A., 1999. 'Climate change and human impact — evidence from peat stratigraphy at sites in the eastern North York Moors', in *The Quaternary of North-East England*, ed. D. R. Bridgland, B. P. Horton & J. B. Innes (London), pp. 113-30.

Claris, P., & Quartermaine, J., 1989. 'The Neolithic quarry and axe factory sites of Great Langdale and Scafell Pike: a new field survey', *Proc Prehist Soc*, 55, pp.1-25.

Clark, G., 1982. 'Housing policy in the Lake District', *Tran Inst Br Geogr*, new ser, 7, pp. 59-10.

Clark, J. G. D., 1954. *Excavations at Star Carr* (Cambridge).

Clarke, E., 1971. *The Valley* (London).

Clay, C. T. (ed.), 1949. *Early Yorkshire Charters Vol. VIII: the honour of Warenne*, Yorkshire Archaeol Soc Rec Ser, extra ser, 6 (Leeds).

Cleasby, I., 1994. 'Limekilns and limeburning in Sedbergh, Garsdale and Dent', *Sedbergh Hist*, 3 (3), pp. 2-9.

Clements, L., 1992. 'The statutory protection of hedgerows', *Ecos*, 13, pp. 34-9.

Clymo, R. S., Oldfield, F., Appleby, P. G., Pearson, G. W., Ratnesar, P., & Richardson, N., 1990. 'The record of atmospheric deposition on a rainwater-dependent peatland', *Phil Trans R Soc London*, B327, pp. 331-8.

Cohen, J. S., & Weitzman, M. L., 1975. 'Enclosures and depopulation: a Marxian analysis' in *European Peasants and their Markets*, ed. W. N. Parker & E. L. Jones (Princeton), pp. 161-76.

Collingwood, W. G., 1912. *Elizabethan Keswick*, Cumberland & Westmorland Antiq & Archaeol Soc Tract Ser 8 (Kendal).

Colman, D., 1994. 'Comparative evaluation of environmental policies', in *Incentives for Countryside Management: the case of environmentally sensitive areas*, ed. M. Whitby (Wallingford), pp. 219-52.

Connell, R. W., 1995. *Masculinities* (London).

Conway Davies, J., 1944. 'Montgomeryshire manorial records in the National Library of Wales from 1536 onwards', *Montgomeryshire Collect*, 48, pp. 53-85.

Cooper, A., Murray, R., & Warnock, S., 1989. 'Agriculture and environment in the Mourne AONB', *Applied Geogr*, 9, pp. 35-56.

Cornwall County Council, 1996. *Cornwall Landscape Assessment*, 1994 (Truro).

Cosgrove, D., & Daniels, S. (eds.), 1993. *The Iconography of Landscape* (Cambridge).

Counsell, D., 1988–9. 'Medieval forests in north-east Yorkshire', *Ryedale Hist*, No. 14, pp. 9-17.

Countryside Commission, 1980. *Areas of Outstanding Natural Beauty: response to the Countryside Commission's Discussion paper* (Cheltenham).

Countryside Commission, 1983. *Areas of Outstanding Natural Beauty. Policy statement* (Cheltenham).

Courtney, P., 1991. 'A native-Welsh mediaeval settlement: excavations at Beili Bedw, St Harmon, Powys', *Bull Board Celtic Stud*, 38, pp. 233-55.

Cowell, R., & Innes, J., 1994. *The Wetlands of Merseyside* (Lancaster).

Cox, C. J., 1903. *Derbyshire* (London).

Crossley, J. C., 1955. 'On the rural landscape of Middle Wharfedale', unpubl Univ Sheffield M.A. thesis.

Curia Regis Curia Regis Rolls, 16 vols, London, 1923–79.

Curley, M. J., 1982. 'A new edition of John of Cornwall's *Prophetia Merlini*', *Speculum*, 57.2, pp. 217-49.

Curry, N.. & Owen, S. (eds), 1996. *Changing Policy in Rural Britain: planning, administration, agriculture and the environment* (Cheltenham).

Curtis, L. F., 1975. 'Landscape periodicity and soil development', in *Processes in Physical and Human Geography*, ed. R. Peel, M. Chisholm & P. Haggett (London), pp. 247-65.

Curtis, L., 1983. 'Reflections on management agreements for conservation of Exmoor moorland', *J Agric Econ*, 34, pp. 397-406.

Curwen, J. F., 1932. *The Later Records Relating to North Westmorland or the Barony of Appleby*, Cumberland & Westmorland Antiq & Archaeol Soc Rec Ser 8 (Kendal).

Dale, J., 1973. 'Sheep grazing experiments in Snowdonia', *Nature in Wales*, 13(4), pp. 229-34.

Daniels, S., 1988. *Fields of Vision: landscape imagery and national identity in England and the United States* (Princeton).

Darby, H. C., 1977. *Domesday England* (Cambridge).

Darvill, T., 1986. *The Archaeology of the Uplands: a rapid assessment of archaeological practice and knowledge* (London).

David, R., 1984. 'The slate quarrying industry of south Westmorland' unpubl Univ Liverpool Dipl in Local History diss.

David, R., 1987. 'The slate quarrying industry in Westmorland. Part 1. The valleys of Troutbeck, Kentmere and Longsleddale', *Trans Cumberland & Westmorland Antiq & Archaeol Soc*, 87, pp. 215-35.

David, R. G. & Brambles, G. W., 1992. 'The slate quarrying industry in Westmorland Part II. A field survey of selected sites in Troutbeck and Longsleddale', *Trans Cumberland & Westmorland Antiq & Archaeol Soc*, 92, pp. 213-27.

Davies, E., 1905. *A General History of the County of Radnor compiled from the manuscript of the late Reverend Jonathan Williams* (Brecon).

Davies, E., 1979. '*Hendre* and *hafod* in Caernarvonshire', *Trans Caernarvonshire Hist Soc*, 40, pp. 17-46.

Davies, E., 1980. '*Hafod, hafoty,* and *lluest*: their distribution, features and purpose', *Ceredigion*, 9.1, pp. 1-41.

Davies, E., 1984–85. '*Hafod* and *lluest*', *Folk Life*, 23, pp. 76-96.

Davies, L., 1920. *Radnorshire* (Cambridge).

Davies, R. R., 1978. *Lordship and Society in the March of Wales, 1282–1400* (Oxford).

Davies, T. P., 1948. 'Extracts from the records of some Radnorshire manorial courts', *Trans Radnor Soc*, 18, pp. 72-5.

Davies, T. P., 1949. 'Extracts from the records of some Radnorshire manorial courts', *Trans Radnor Soc*, 19, pp. 71-7.

Davies, W., 1810. *A General View of the Agriculture and Domestic Economy of North Wales* (London).

Davies, W., 1813. *A General View of the Agriculture of North Wales* (London).

Davies, W., 1815. *General View of the Agriculture and Domestic Economy of South Wales* (London).

De Vries, J., 1974. *The Dutch Rural Economy in the Golden Age, 1500–1700* (New Haven & London).

Defoe, D., 1971. *A Tour through the Whole Island of Great Britain*, ed. P. Rogers (Harmondsworth).

DEFRA, 2002. Department for Environment, Food and Rural Affairs: 'Common Land, Town and Village Greens', at www.defra.gov.uk/wildlife-countryside/issues/commons/index.htm

Dellheim, C. 1986. 'Imagining England: Victorian views of the north', *Northern Hist*, 22, pp. 216-30.

Dennis, R., 1999. 'The importance of extensive livestock grazing for woodland biodiversity: traditional cattle in the Scottish Highlands', in *Managing farmland of High Nature Conservation Value: policies, processes and practices*, ed. M. W. Pienkowski & D. G. L. Jones, European Forum on Nature Conservation & Pastoralism (Islay), pp. 26-41.

DETR, 2000. *Greater Protection and Better Management of Common Land*, Department of Environment, Transport and the Regions consultation document (London).

Dickinson, G., 1991. 'National parks — Scottish needs and Spanish experience', *Scott Geogr Mag*, 107, pp. 124-9.

Dickinson, G., 2000. 'The use of the Loch Lomond area for recreation', *Scott Geogr Mag*, 116, pp. 231-44.

Dickson, J. H., 1973. *Bryophytes of the Pleistocene* (Cambridge).

Dilley, R. S., 1972. 'Common Land in Cumberland, 1500–1850', unpubl Univ Cambridge M.Phil. thesis.

Dodd, A. H., 1926–27. 'The enclosure movement in North Wales', *Bull Board of Celtic Studies*, 3(3), pp. 78-97.

Dodgshon, R. A., 1976. 'The economics of sheep farming in the Southern Uplands during the Age of Improvement, 1750–1833', *Econ Hist Rev*, 29, pp. 551-69.

Dodgshon, R. A., 1981. *Land and Society in Early Scotland* (Oxford).

Dodgshon R. A., 1998a. 'Livestock production in the Scottish Highlands before and after the clearances', *Rural Hist*, 9, pp. 19-42.

Dodgshon, R. A., 1998b. *From Chiefs to Landlords: social and economic change in the Western Highlands and Islands c. 1493–1820* (Edinburgh).

Donald, M. B., 1955. *Elizabethan Copper* (London).

Done, A. B., 1999. 'The impact of grouse shooting on the development of the cultural landscape of the Yorkshire Dales', unpubl Univ Leeds M.A. thesis.

Dower, M., 1965. *The Fourth Wave: the challenge of leisure* (London).

Drayton, R., 2000. *Nature's Government: science, imperial Britain and the 'improvement' of the world* (Yale).

Drury, J. L., 1978. 'Durham Palatinate forest law and administration, specially in Weardale up to 1440', *Archaeol Aeliana*, 5th ser, 6, pp. 87-105.

Du Garde Peach, L., 1934. *Come to Derbyshire Guide* (Derby).

Dumayne, L., Stoneman, R., Barber, K., & Harkness, D., 1995. 'Problems associated with correlating calibrated radiocarbon-dated pollen diagrams with historical events', *The Holocene*, 5, pp. 118-23.

Dumayne-Peaty, L., & Barber, K., 1998. 'Late Holocene vegetational history, human impact and pollen representativity variations in northern Cumbria, England', *J Quaternary Sci*, 13, pp. 147-64

Dumayne-Peaty, L., 1999. 'Late Holocene human impact on the vegetation of southeastern Scotland: a pollen diagram from Dogden Moss, Berwickshire', *Rev Palaeobot & Palynol*, 105, pp. 121-41.

Edlin, H. L., 1952. *The Changing Wildlife of Britain* (London).

Edwards, J. W., 1963. 'Enclosure and Agricultural Improvement in the Vale of Clwyd', unpubl Univ London M.A. thesis.

Egdell, J., & Badger, R., 1996. 'A "new political economy" perspective on Scottish agri-environmental policy', *Scott Agric Econ Rev*, 9, pp. 21-33.

Elfyn Hughes, R., 1973. 'Studies in sheep population and environment in the mountains of North West Wales', *J Appl Ecol*, 10, pp. 107-12.

Elfyn Hughes, R., Williams, J., & Smith, M., 1979. 'Quantitative analyses of the 13th/14th century landholding systems of North West Wales', *Agro-Ecosyst*, 5, pp. 191-211.

Elgee, F., 1912. *The Moorlands of North Eastern Yorkshire* (London).

Elliott, G., 1956. 'Some Aspects of the Changing Agricultural Landscape in Cumberland', unpubl Univ Liverpool M.A. thesis.

Ellis, H., (ed.), 1838. *The Record of Caernarvon* (London).

Emery, F. V., 1967. 'The farming regions of Wales', in *The Agrarian History of England and Wales, Vol. IV, 1500–1640*, ed. J. Thirsk (Cambridge), pp. 113-60.

English, B., 1996. *Yorkshire Hundred and Quo Warranto Rolls*, Yorkshire Archaeol Soc Rec Ser 151.

English Nature, 2001a. *State of Nature — the upland challenge* (Peterborough).

English Nature, 2001b. 'Interim assessment of the effects of the Foot and Mouth Disease outbreak on England's biodiversity', *Engl Nat Res Rep*, no. 430.

Evans, A. T., & Moore, P. D., 1985. 'Surface pollen studies of *Calluna vulgaris* (L.) Hull and their relevance to the interpretation of bog and moorland pollen diagrams', *Circaea* 3, pp. 173-8.

Evans, D. G., 1983–4. 'The Hope Enclosure Act of 1791', *Flintshire Hist Soc J*, 31, pp. 161-86.

Evans, E., 1949. 'Arwystli and Cyfeiliog in the sixteenth century', *Montgomeryshire Collect*, 51, pp. 23-37.

Evans, E., 1949–50. 'The manor of Uwchmynydd, Radnorshire,in 1618', *Natl Libr Wales J*, 6, pp. 385-90.

Evans, N. J., & Morris, C., 1997. 'Towards a geography of agri-environmental policies in England and Wales', *Geoforum*, 28, pp. 189-204.

Evelyn, J., 1729. *Silva* (London).

Everitt, A., 2000. 'Common land', in *The English Rural Landscape*, ed. Thirsk, pp. 210-35.

Eversley, Lord (George Shaw-Lefevre), 1910. *Commons, Forests and Footpaths: the story of the battle during the last forty-five years for public rights over the commons, forests and footpaths of England and Wales* (London).

Eyre, S. R., 1957. 'The upward limit of enclosure on the East Moor of North Derbyshire', *Trans Inst Brit Geogr*, 23, pp. 61-74.

Farrer, W., 1902. *The Lancashire Pipe Rolls ... and early Lancashire Charters* (Liverpool).

Farrer, W., 1903–15. *Lancashire Inquests, Extents and Feudal Aids*, 3 vols, Rec Soc Lancashire & Cheshire 48, 54, 70.

Farrer, W., 1923–4. *Records Relating to the Barony of Kendale*, 2 vols, Cumberland & Westmorland Antiq & Archaeol Rec Ser IV and V (Kendal).

Fedden, R., 1974. *The National Trust: past and present* (London).

Feehen, J., & O'Donovan, G., 1996. *The Bogs of Ireland: an introduction to the natural, cultural and industrial heritage of Irish peatlands* (Dublin).

Fennell, R., 1975. 'United Kingdom structural policy and guidance section of FEOGA', *J Agric Econ*, 23 (3), pp. 346-8.

Fenton, A. (ed.), 1986. *The Shape of the Past 2. Essays in Scottish ethnology* (Edinburgh).

Fernandez, J.W., 1987. 'The call to the commons: decline and recommitment in Asturias, Spain', in *The Question of the Commons: the culture and ecology of communal resources*, ed. B. J. McCay & J. M. Acheson (Tuscon).

Fieldhouse, R., & Jennings, B., 1978. *A History of Richmond & Swaledale* (Chichester).

Finberg, H. P. R., 1969. *Tavistock Abbey: a study in the social and economic history of Devon*, 2nd edn (Newton Abbot).

Firth, J. B., 1905. *Highways and Byways in Derbyshire* (London).

Fitter, A., & Smith, C. (eds), 1979. *A Wood in Ascam — a study in wetland conservation* (York).

Flatres, P., 1957. *Geographie rurale de quatre contrees Celtiques: Irlande, Galles, Cornwall and Man* (Rennes).

Fleming A., 1996. 'Early roads to the Swaledale lead mines', *Yorkshire Archaeol J*, 68, pp. 89-100.

Fleming, A., 1997. 'Towards a history of wood pasture in Swaledale (North Yorkshire)', *Landscape Hist*, 19, pp. 57-73.

Fleming, A., 1998a. 'Wood pasture and the woodland economy in medieval Swaledale', in *Woodland in the Landscape*, ed. Atherden & Butlin, pp. 26-42.

Fleming, A., 1998b. *Swaledale: valley of the wild river* (Edinburgh).

Flenley, R., 1916. *A Calendar of the Register of the Council in the Marches of Wales [1535] 1569–1591* (London).

Ford, S., 1991. 'Landscape revisited: a feminist reappraisal', in *New Words, New Worlds: reconceptualising social and cultural geography*, ed. C. Philo, (Lampeter), pp. 151-5.

Forestry Commission, 1957. *Annual Report* (London).

Forestry Commission, 1971. *Annual Report* (London).

Fox, A., 1939. 'Early Welsh homesteads on Gelligaer Common, Glamorgan', *Archaeol Cambrensis*, 94, pp. 163-99.

Fox, C., & Fox, A., 1934. 'Forts and farms on Margam Mountain, Glamorgan', *Antiq*, 8, pp. 395-413.

Fox, C. F, 1943. *The Personality of Britain, its influence on inhabitant and invader in prehistoric and early historic times*, 4th edn (Cardiff).

Fox, H. S. A., 1971. 'A Geographical Study of the Field Systems of Devon and Cornwall', unpubl Univ Cambridge Ph.D. thesis.

Fox, H. S. A., 1994. 'Medieval Dartmoor as seen through its account rolls', in *The Archaeology of Dartmoor: perspectives from the 1990s*, ed. D. Griffiths, Proc Devon Archaeol Soc 52, pp. 149-71.

French, C. N., & Moore, P. D., 1986. 'Deforestation, *Cannabis* cultivation and schwingmoor formation at Cors Llyn (Llyn Mire), Central Wales', *New Phytol*, 102, pp. 469-82.

Froud, J., 1994. 'The impact of ESAs on lowland farming', *Land Use Policy*, 11, pp. 107-18.

Gadsden, G. D., 1988. *The Law of Commons* (London).

Gailey, A., & Fenton, A., 1970. *The Spade in Northern & Atlantic Europe* (Belfast).

Garfield G., (undated). *Derbyshire Sketchbook: New Mills* (photocopied typescript, New Mills Library).

Garnett, F. W., 1912. *Westmorland Agriculture, 1800–1900* (Kendal).

Garrod, G., & Willis, K., 1995. 'Valuing the benefits of the South Downs Environ-mentally Sensitive Area', *J Agric Econ*, 46, pp. 160-73.

Garrod, G., Willis, K., & Saunders, C., 1994. 'The benefits and costs of the Somerset Levels and Moors ESA', *J Rural Stud*, 10, pp. 131-45.

Gaskell, P. T., & Tanner, M. F., 1991. 'Agricultural change and Environmentally Sensitive Areas', *Geoforum*, 22, pp. 81-90.

Gelling, M., 2001. *The Place-Names of Shropshire, Part III*, Engl Place-Names Soc Vol. 76 (Nottingham).

Gerrard A., 2000. *The Early British Tin Industry* (Stroud).

Gibson A. J. S., & Smout, T. C., 1995. *Prices, Food and Wages in Scotland, 1550–1780* (Cambridge).

Gibson, A. J. S., 1988. 'The size and weight of cattle and sheep in early modern Scotland', *Agric Hist Rev*, 36, pp. 162-71.

Gilbert, J. M., 1979. *Hunting and Hunting Reserves in Medieval Scotland* (Edinburgh).

Gill, C. (ed.), 1971. *Dartmoor: a new study* (Newton Abbot).

Gimingham, C. H., 1972. *Ecology of Heathland* (London).

Gimingham, C. H., 1995. 'Heaths and Moorlands: an overview of ecological change', in *Heaths and Moorland* ed. Thompson, Hester & Usher, pp. 9-19.

Gledhill, T., 1998. 'Medieval woodland in North Yorkshire', in *Woodland in the Landscape*, ed. Atherden & Butlin, pp. 103-19.

Glover S., 1830. *The Peak Guide, containing the topographical, statistical and general history of Buxton, Chatsworth, Edensor, Castleton, Bakewell, Haddon, Matlock, and Cromford* (Derby).

Godwin, H., 1978. *Fenland: its ancient past and uncertain future* (Cambridge).

Gonner, E. C. K., 1912. *Common Land and Inclosure* (London).

Goudie, A. S., 1972. 'Vaughan Cornish: geographer, with a bibliography of his published works', *Trans Inst Br Geogr*, 55, pp. 1-16.

Gowland, T. S., 1938. 'The honour of Kirkby Malzeard and the chase of Nidderdale', *Yorkshire Archaeol J*, 33, pp. 349-96.

Greeves, T. A. P., 1981a. 'The archaeological potential of the Devon tin industry', in *Medieval Industry*, ed. D. W. Crossley, Counc Br Archaeol Res Rep 40 (London), pp. 85-95.

Greeves, T. A. P., 1981b. 'The Devon tin industry 1450–1750: an archaeological and historical survey', unpubl Univ Exeter Ph.D. thesis.

Grieves K., 1995. 'C. E. Montague, Manchester and the Remembrance of War, 1918–25', *Bull John Rylands Univ Libr Manchester*, 77(2), pp. 95-6.

Griffiths, M., 1989. 'The emergence of the modern settlement pattern, 1450–1700', in *Settlement and Society in Wales*, ed. D. H. Owen (Cardiff), pp. 225-48.

Griffiths, W. A., 1949. 'Some notes on the earlier records of the manor of Deytheur', *Montgomeryshire Collect*, 51, pp. 41-53.

Grove, J., 1988. *The Little Ice Age* (London).

Gruffudd, P., Herbert D. T., & Piccini, A., 2000. 'In search of Wales: travel writing and narratives of difference, 1918–50', *J Hist Geogr*, 26 (4), pp. 589-604.

Hall, D., Wells, C. E., & Huckerby, E., 1995. *The Wetlands of Greater Manchester* (Lancaster).

Hall, G. W., 1993. *Metal Mines of Southern Wales* (Kington, Herefordshire).

Hall, S. T., 1863. *Days in Derbyshire* (London).

Hallas, C., 1986. 'The social and economic impact of a rural railway. The Wensleydale Line', *Agric Hist Rev*, 34, pp. 29-44.

Halsbury, 1991a. *Halsbury's Laws of England*, Vol. 6, 4th edn (London).

Halsbury, 1991b. *Halsbury's Statutes of England and Wales*, Vol. 7, 4th edn (London).

Hamilton-Jenkins, A. K., 1932. *Cornwall and its People* (London).

Hammond, J. L., & Hammond, B., 1911. *The Village Labourer* (London).

Handley, J. E., 1953. *Scottish Farming in the Eighteenth Century* (London).

Hardin, G., 1968. 'The Tragedy of the Commons', *Science*, 162 (13 Dec. 1968), pp. 1243-8. (Repr in *Managing the Commons*, ed. G. Hardin & J. Baden (San Francisco, 1977), pp. 16-30.

Haresign W. (ed.), 1983. *Sheep Production* (London).

Harris, B., & Ryan, G., 1967. *An Outline of the Law Relating to Common Land* (London).

Harrison, B. J. D., & Roberts, B. K., 1989. 'The medieval landscape', in *The North York Moors*, ed. Spratt & Harrison (Newton Abbot), pp. 72-112.

Hartley, M., & Ingilby, J., 1968. *Life and Tradition in the Yorkshire Dales* (London).

Hartley, M., & Ingilby, J., 1972. *Life and Tradition in the Moorlands of North-East Yorkshire* (Otley).

Hartley, M., & Ingilby, J., 1982. *A Dales Heritage* (Clapham).

Hatcher, J., 1970. *Rural Economy and Society in the Duchy of Cornwall 1300–1500* (Cambridge).

Henderson, C., 1935. *Essays in Cornish History* (Oxford).

Herring, P. C., & Giles, C., forthcoming. 'Agriculture', in Herring *et al.* forthcoming.

Herring, P. C., & Smith, J. R., 1991. *The Archaeology of the St Austell China-Clay Area* (Truro).

Herring, P. C., & Thomas, S. N. H., 1988. *The Archaeology of Kit Hill* (Truro).

Herring, P. C., 1986. 'An exercise in landscape history. Pre-Norman and medieval Brown Willy and Bodmin Moor, Cornwall', unpubl Univ Sheffield M.Phil. thesis.

Herring, P. C., 1996. 'Transhumance in medieval Cornwall', in *Seasonal Settlement*, ed. H. S. A. Fox (Leicester), pp. 35-44.

Herring, P. C., 1998. *Cornwall's Historic Landscape: presenting a method of historic landscape characterisation* (Truro).

Herring, P. C., 1999a. 'Farming and transhumance in Cornwall at the turn of the first millennium AD, part 1', *J Cornwall Assoc Local Hist*, Spring 1999, pp. 3-8.

Herring, P. C., 1999b. 'Farming and transhumance in Cornwall at the turn of the first millennium AD, part 2', *J Cornwall Assoc Local Hist*, Autumn 1999, pp. 19-25.

Herring, P. C., forthcoming. 'Turf', in Herring *et al.* forthcoming.

Herring, P. C., Sharpe, A., Smith, J. R., & Giles, C., forthcoming. *Bodmin Moor. An archaeological survey, Volume 2: The Post-medieval and Industrial Landscape* (Engl Heritage & Cornwall Archaeol Unit, London).

Hester, A. J., 1996. *Overgrazing in Upland Habitats: a literature review*, Rep for the Countryside Counc Wales, Macauley Research & Consultancy, Craigiebuckler (Aberdeen).

Hey, D., 1991. *The Fiery Blades of Hallamshire: Sheffield and its neighbourhood 1660–1740* (Leicester).

Hey, D., 2000. 'Moorlands', in *The English Rural Landscape*, ed. Thirsk, pp. 188-209.

Higham, M. C., 1994. 'The boundary of Burton-in-Lonsdale Chase', *Yorkshire Archaeol J*, 66, pp. 91-105.

Hill, H., 1980. *Freedom to Roam: the struggle for access to Britain's moors and mountains* (Ashbourne).

Hill, O., 1877. *Our Common Land (and other short essays)* (London).

Hindle, B. P., 1984. *Roads and Trackways of the Lake District* (Ashbourne).

Hobbs, J. R., 1984. 'Length of burning rotation and community composition in high-level *Calluna-Eriophorum* bog in N. England', *Vegetatio*, 57, pp. 129-36.

Hobbs, J. R., Mallik, A. U., & Gimingham, C. H., 1984. 'Studies on fire in Scottish heathland communities. III. Vital attributes of the species', *J Ecol*, 72, pp. 963-76.

Hodgkinson, D., Huckerby, E., Middleton, R., & Wells, C. E., 2000. *The Lowland Wetlands of Cumbria* (Lancaster).

Hodgson, J., 1828. *A History of Northumberland* (Newcastle).

Holland, E., 1986. *Coniston Copper* (Milnthorpe).

Holt, A., 1987. 'Hikers and ramblers: surviving a thirties' fashion', in *Int J Hist Sport*, 4(1), pp 56-77.

Hooke, D., 1989. 'Pre-Conquest woodland: its distribution and usage', *Agric Hist Rev*, 37, pp. 113-29.

Hoskins, W. G., 1955. *The Making of the English Landscape* (London).

Hoskins, W.G., & Stamp, L.D., 1963. *The Common Lands of England and Wales* (London).

House of Commons Sessional Papers of the Eighteenth Century, Reports & Papers 1799–1800, Vol. 130.

House of Commons, 1844. Select Committee on Commons' Inclosure, Reports, Committees, vol. 5.

House of Lords, 2001. House of Lords judgements, Bettison and Others v. Langton and Others, 17 May 2001, UKHL 24 at http://www.parliament.the-stationery-office.co.uk

Howell, D. W., 2000. *The Rural Poor in Eighteenth-Century Wales* (Cardiff).

Howkins A., 1986. 'The discovery of rural England', in *Englishness, Politics and Culture, 1880–1920*, ed. R. Colls & P. Dodd (London), pp. 62-88.

Howkins, C., 1999. 'Human exploitation of southern, lowland heath', *Landscape Archaeol & Ecol*, 4, pp. 85-93.
Howlett, J., 1781. *Enclosure and Population* (London, repr 1973).
Howse, W. H., 1944. 'Court rolls of the manor of Norton', *Trans Radnor Soc*, 14, pp. 43-51.
Howse, W. H., 1949. *Radnorshire* (Hereford).
Howse, W. H., 1955. 'Encroachments on the king's waste in Cantref Maelienydd in 1734', *Trans Radnor Soc*, 25, pp. 27-33.
Hoyle, R. W., 1995. 'Thomas first Lord Wharton's parks at Ravenstonedale and Wharton', *Trans Cumberland & Westmorland Antiq & Archaeol Soc*, new ser, 95, pp. 111-18.
HTV Wales, 1995–96. 'Snowdon Shepherd', video programme produced and directed by Myrfyn Jones (Fideo Sain, Llandwrog).
Hudson, P. J., 1998. *Coal Mining in Lunesdale* (Settle).
Hughes, J., & Huntley, B., 1988. 'Upland hay meadows in Britain — their vegetation, management and future', in *The Cultural Landscape — Past, Present and Future*, ed. H. H. Birks, H. J. B. Birks, P. E. Kaland & D. Moe (Cambridge), pp. 91-110.
Humphries, A., 2000. 'Ancient lands cast long shadows: common land in the North West', *Reg Bull* (Lancaster Univ Centre for North West Reg Stud), new ser, 14, pp. 45-8.
Humphries, C. J., & Shaughnessy, E., 1987. *Gorse* (Aylesbury).
Hunt, R., 1881. *Popular Romances of the West of England* (London) [first publ 1865].
Hunter, J., 1869. *Hallamshire: the history and topography of the parish of Sheffield*, new ed with add by A. Gatty (London).
Hunter, R. F., 1962. 'Hill sheep and their pasture: a study of sheep-grazing in south-east Scotland', *J Ecol*, 30, pp. 651-80.
Hurt C., 1988. *On Foot in the Peak District: 40 circular walks in Europe's most popular National Park* (Newton Abbot).
Innes, C., 1854. *Origines Parochiales Scotiae* (Edinburgh).
Innes, J. L., 1983. 'Land use changes in the Scottish Highlands during the nineteenth century: the role of pasture degeneration', *Scott Geogr Mag*, 99, pp. 141-9.
Irwin, A., & Wynne, B. (eds), 1996. *Understanding Science? The public reconstruction of science and technology* (Cambridge).
IUCN, 1969. International Union for Conservation of Nature and Natural Resources, *Red Data Book*, 2 vols (Morges, Switzerland).
Jackson, S. T., 1994. 'Pollen and spores in Quaternary lake sediments as sensors of vegetation composition: theoretical models and empirical evidence', in *Sedimentation of Organic Particles*, ed. A. Traverse (Cambridge), pp. 253-86.
Jacobson, G. J., & Bradshaw, R. H. W., 1981. 'The selection of sites for paleoevegetational studies', *Quaternary Res*, 16, pp. 80-96.
Jeffrey, A., 1855. *The History and Antiquities of Roxburghshire* (Jedburgh).
Jenkins, G. (ed.), 1969. *Studies in Folk Life: essays in honour of Iorwerth C. Peate* (London).
Jenkins, J. G., 1965. *Traditional Country Craftsmen* (London).
Jennings, B. (ed.), 1967. *A History of Nidderdale* (Huddersfield).
Jennings, B. (ed.), 1992. *Pennine Valley: a history of upper Calderdale* (Otley).
Jewell, H. M., 1994. *The North-South Divide: the origins of northern consciousness in England* (Manchester).
Johnson, A., 2000. 'Breaking new ground', *Natl Trust Mag*, 89, pp. 61-4.
Johnson, N., & Rose, P., 1994. *Bodmin Moor: an archaeological survey, Volume 1, The Human Landscape to c1800* (London).
Johnson, N., 1981. 'The location of settlement in pre-Medieval Caernarvonshire', *Bull Board Celtic Stud*, 29, pp. 381-417.
Jones Pierce, T., 1940. 'Notes on the history of Caernarvonshire in the reign of Elizabeth', *Trans Caernarvonshire Hist Soc*, 2, pp. 39-57.
Jones, D., & Essex, S., 1999. 'Land use change in the British uplands: a case study of Bodmin Moor, Cornwall', *Geogr*, 84, pp. 11-24.
Jones, E. G. (ed.), 1952. *A Description of Caernarvonshire (1809–1811) by Edmund Hyde Hall, ed from the original MS in the Libr Univ Coll of North Wales* (Caernarvon).
Jones, G. R. J., 1964. 'The distribution of bond settlements in north-west Wales', *Welsh Hist Rev*, 2(1), pp. 19-36.
Jones, G. R. J., 1973. 'Field systems of North Wales', in *Field Systems in the British Isles*, ed. A. R. H. Baker & R. A. Butlin (Cambridge), pp. 430-79.
Jones, I. E., 1973. 'The Swydd Neithon enclosure and the development of Llandrindod Wells', *Trans Radnor Soc*, 43, pp. 24-33.
Joyce P., 1991. *Visions of the People* (Cambridge).
Kain, R. J. P., Chapman, J., & Oliver, R., 2004. *Enclosure Maps* (Cambridge).
Kay, G., 1794. *General View of the Agriculture of North Wales with Observations on the Means of its Improvement* (Edinburgh).
Kendall, H. P., 1926. 'The forest of Sowerbyshire', *Papers, Reports etc. read before the Halifax Antiquarian Society, 1926*, pp. 85-107.
King, A., 1998. *Memorial of the Great War in Britain: the symbolism and politics of remembrance* (Oxford).
King, J., 1960. 'Observations on the seedling establishment and growth of Nardus stricta in burned Callunetum', *J Ecol*, 48, pp. 667-77.
Kirkpatrick, A. H., & Macdonald, A. J., 2001. 'The impact of traditional peat cutting on Shetland's blanket bogs', *J Pract Ecol & Conserv*, 4 (2), pp. 3-21.
Lamb, H. H., 1977. *Climate, Present, Past and Future* (London).
Lambert, J. M., Jennings, J. N., Smith, C. T., Green, C., & Hutchinson, J. N., 1961. *The Making of the Broads: a reconsideration of their origin in the light of new evidence* (London).
Lancaster, W. T., 1915. *Abstracts of the Charters … in the Chartulary of the Cistercian Abbey of Fountains* (Leeds).
Latham P. R., 1883. 'Deterioration of mountain pastures and suggestions for their improvement', *Trans Highland & Agric Soc*, 4th ser, 15, pp. 111-30.
Leah, M. D., Wells, C. E., Huckerby, E., & Appleby, C., 1997. *The Wetlands of Cheshire* (Lancaster).
Leah, M. D., Wells, C. E., Huckerby, E., Stamper, P., & Welch, C., 1998. *The Wetlands of Shropshire and Staffordshire* (Lancaster).
Leland, J., 1891. *The Itinerary of John Leland in or about the years 1535–43* (London)
Lewis, E. A., & Conway Davies, J., 1954. *Records of the Courts of Augmentations relating to Wales and Monmouthshire* (Cardiff).
Lewis, E. A., 1941–2. 'Leet proceedings of the manor of Arwystli Uwchcoed at the National library of Wales, 1784–1800', *Montgomery Collect*, 47, pp. 183-207.
Lewis, E. A., 1944. 'Leet proceedings of the manor of Arwystli Uwchcoed in the National Library of Wales, 1802-1819', *Montgomeryshire Collect*, 48, pp. 11-29.
Lewis, W. V., 1949. 'Glacial movements by rotational slipping', *Geografiska Annaler*, 31, pp. 146-58.
Lhuyd, E., 1909. *Parochialia; being a summary of answers to parochial queries etc Vol I*, ed. R. H. Morris (London).
Liddell, W. H., 1966. 'The private forests of south-west Cumberland', *Trans Cumberland & Westmorland Antiq & Archaeol Soc*, new ser, 66, pp. 106-30.
Lindsay, J., 1974. *A History of the North Wales Slate Industry* (Newton Abbot).
Lindsay, J. M., 1975. 'Charcoal iron smelting and its fuel supply: the example of Lorn furnace, Argyllshire, 1753–1876', *J Hist Geog*, 1, pp. 283-98.
Liniado, M., 1996. *Car Culture and Countryside Change* (Cirencester).
Linnard, W., 2000. *Welsh Woods and Forests: a history* (Llandysul).

Lloyd, J. E., 1911. *A History of Wales* (London).

Locock, M., forthcoming. 'Deserted rural settlements in south-east Wales', in *Deserted Rural Settlements in Wales* (forthcoming Counc Br Achaeol Res Rep).

Lythe, S. G. E., 1960. *The Economy of Scotland in its European Setting, 1550–1625* (Edinburgh).

Mabey, R., 1993. *The Common Ground: the history, evolution and future of Britian's countryside* (London).

Macdonald, J., 1880. 'On the agriculture of the county of Sutherland', *Trans Highland & Agric Soc*, 4th ser, 12, pp. 1-90.

Macdonald, W., 1872. 'On the agriculture of the county of Inverness-shire', *Trans Highland & Agric Soc*, 4th ser, 4, pp. 1-65.

Mack, J. L., 1924. *The Border Line* (Edinburgh).

Maclean, Sir J., 1873–6. *Parochial and Family History of the Deanery of Trigg Minor, Cornwall*, 2 vols (Bodmin).

Maclean, Sir J., 1886. 'An ancient Cornish deed in English', *J R Inst Cornwall*, 9, pp. 27-36.

MAFF, 1970. Ministry of Agriculture, Fisheries and Food, *Annual Digest of Welsh Agricultural Statistics* (London).

Mais, S. P. B., 1936. *This Unknown Island* (London).

Mangan, J. A., & Walvin, J., 1987. *Manliness and Morality: middle class masculinity in Britain and America, 1800–1940* (Manchester).

Manwood, J. 1615. *A Treatise ... of the Lawes of the Forrest* (London).

Margules, C. R., 1984. 'Vegetation inventory and conservation evaluation: a case study from the North York Moors, England', *Appl Geogr*, 4, pp. 293-307.

Marsh, J., 1982. *Back to the Land: the pastoral impulse in England, from 1880 to 1914* (London).

Marshall, J. D., 1986. 'Why study regions (2): some historical considerations', *J Reg & Local Stud*, 6 (1), pp. 1-12.

Marshall, W., 1788. *The Rural Economy of the County of Yorkshire* (London).

Marshall, W., 1794. *General View of the Agriculture of the Central Highlands* (London).

Martin, M., 1982. *A Description of the Western Islands of Scotland*, based on 2nd edn, 1711 (Edinburgh).

Massey, D., 1994. *Space, Place and Gender* (Cambridge).

Mather, A. S., 1988. 'New private forests in Scotland: characteristics and contrasts', *Area*, 20, pp. 135-43.

Mather, A. S., 1991. 'Pressures on British forest policy: prologue to the post-industrial forest?', *Area*, 23, pp. 245-53.

Matthews, J. R., 1955. *The Origin and Distribution of the British Flora* (London).

Mauquoy, D., & Barber, K., 1999. 'A replicated 3000 yr proxy-climate record from Coom Rigg Moss and Felecia Moss, the Border Mires, northern England', *J Quaternary Sci*, 14, pp. 263-276.

Maxwell, T. J., 1983. 'Factors affecting the growth and utilization of sown grasslands for sheep production', in *Sheep Production*, ed. Haresign, pp. 187-205.

McArthur, M. M., 1936. *Survey of Lochtayside 1769*, Scottish Hist Soc, 3rd ser, 27 (Edinburgh).

McCay, B. J., & Acheson, J. M. (eds), 1987. *The Question of the Commons: the culture and ecology of communal resources* (Tucson).

McDermot, E. T., 1973. *The History of the Forest of Exmoor* (Newton Abbot).

McDonnell, J., 1989. 'After the middle ages: agriculture and settlement', in *The North York Moors*, ed. Spratt & Harrison (Newton Abbot), pp. 113-40.

McEwen, A., & McEwen, M., 1987. *Greenprints for the Countryside? The story of Britain's national parks* (London).

McKay, M. M. (ed.), 1980. *The Rev. Dr. John Walker's Report on the Hebrides of 1764 and 1771* (Edinburgh).

McNeill, G. P. (ed.), 1897. *Exchequer Rolls of Scotland, Vol. XVII, AD 1537–1542* (Edinburgh).

McNeill, J., 2000. *Something New Under The Sun: an environmental history of the twentieth century* (London).

McNulty, J. (ed.), 1933. *The Chartulary of the Cistercian Abbey of St Mary of Salley in Craven*, Yorkshire Archaeol Soc Rec Ser 87.

McVean, D. N., & Ratcliffe, D. A., 1962. *Plant Communities of the Scottish Highlands* (London).

Megaw, J. V. S., & Simpson D. D. A., 1979. *Introduction to British Prehistory* (Leicester).

Menuge, N. J., 1997. *Climate Change on the North York Moors*, PLACE Occas Pap No. 1 (York).

Mercer, R., & Tipping, R., 1994. 'The prehistory of soil erosion in the northern and eastern Cheviot Hills, Anglo-Scottish Borders', in *The History of Soils and Field Systems*, ed. S. Foster & T. C. Smout (Aberdeen), pp. 1-24.

Middleton, R., Wells, C. E. & Huckerby, E., 1995. *The Wetlands of North Lancashire* (Lancaster).

Miller, R., 1967. 'Land use by summer shielings', *Scott Stud*, 11, pp. 193-221.

Millman, R. N., 1975. *The Making of the Scottish Landscape* (London).

Moffat, A., 1985. *Kelsae — A History of Moffat from Earliest Times* (Edinburgh).

Moir, E., 1964. *The Discovery of Britain: English tourists, 1540–1840* (London).

Moncrieff, A. R. H., 1908. *The Peak Country* (London).

Morgan, P., 1983. 'From a death to a view: the hunt for the Welsh past in the Romantic period', in *The Invention of Tradition*, ed. E. Hobsbawm & T. Ranger (Cambridge), pp. 43-100.

Morgan, P., 2001. 'Engine of Empire, *c*.1750–1898', in *The Tempus History of Wales, 25,000 B.C–A.D. 2000*, ed. P. Morgan (Stroud).

Morris, C., & Potter, C., 1995. 'Recruiting the new conservationists: farmers' adoption of agri-environmental schemes in the UK', *J Rural Stud*, 11, pp. 51-63.

Morris, C., & Young, C., 1997. 'Towards environmentally friendly farming? An evaluation of the Countryside Stewardship Scheme', *Geogr*, 82(4), pp. 305-16.

Morris, J. E., 1914. *Beautiful Britain: the Peak country* (London).

Morris, M. S., 1996. ' "Tha'lt be like blush-rose when tha' grows up my little lass": English cultural and gendered identity in *The Secret Garden', Environ & Plann D: Society & Space*, 14, pp. 59-78.

Morton, H. V., 1928. *The Call of England* (London).

Morton, H. V., 1932. *In Search of Wales* (London).

Muir, J. W., 1956. *The Soils of the Country round Jedburgh & Morebattle* (Edinburgh).

Muir, R., 1997. *The Yorkshire Countryside: a landscape history* (Edinburgh).

Munro, R. W. (ed.), 1961. *Monro's Western Isles of Scotland* (Edinburgh).

Myers, G. A., 2000. 'Colonial geography and masculinity in Eric Dutton's Kenya Mountain', *Gender, Place & Culture*, 9(1), pp. 23-38.

Nash, C., 1993. 'Remapping and renaming: new cartographies of identity, gender and landscape in Ireland', *Feminist Rev*, 44, pp. 39-57.

National Assembly for Wales, 2000. *Tir Gofel (Land Care) Agri-environment scheme for Wales, Countryside Counc for Wales* (Bangor).

National Trust, 2000a. 'Response by the National Trust, April 2000', to DETR Consultation Document: 'Greater Protection and Better Management of Common Land in England and Wales', at www.nationaltrust.org.uk

National Trust, 2000b. 'Agriculture — 2000 and Beyond: an agricultural policy for the National Trust', at www.nationaltrust.org.uk/environment/html/land_use/papers/agpol02_01.htm

National Trust, 2001a. *A Vision for the Lake District after Foot and Mouth* (London).

National Trust, 2001b. 'The National Trust in the Beddgelert Community: a strategy plan', unpubl rep (Natl Trust Off, Beddgelert).

NCH *A History of Northumberland*, 15 vols, Newcastle upon Tyne: Andrew Reid for Northumberland County Hist Comm, 1893–1940.

Neale, R., 1999. 'Snowdon — one year on', *Natl Trust Mag*, Views Section, p. 31.

Neeson, J. M., 1993. *Commoners: common right, enclosure and social change in England, 1700–1820* (Cambridge).

Newman, R., Cranstone, D., & Howard-Davis, C, 2001. *The Historical Archaeology of Britain, c.1540–1900* (Stroud).

Nicholls, P., 1998. 'The National Trust: a spatial audit of conservation', *Geogr*, 83, pp. 377-82.

Noble, M. E., 1901. *A History of the Parish of Bampton* (Kendal).

North York Moors National Park, 1991. *Moorland Management Programme, 1985–1990* (Helmsley).

Nowakowski, J. A., & Herring, P. C., 1985. 'The beehive huts on Bodmin Moor', *Cornish Archaeol*, 24, pp. 185-96.

NSAThe New Statistical Account of Scotland, 15 vols (Edinburgh, 1845).

Oldfield, F. A., 1959. 'The pollen morphology of some of the West European Ericales', *Pollen et Spores*, 1, pp. 19-48.

Oldfield, F. A., 1969. 'Pollen analysis and the history of land use', *Advancement in Sci*, 125, pp. 298-311.

Oldfield, F., Crooks, P. R. J., Gedye, S. J., Jones, R., Plater, A. J., Richardson, N., Nijampurkar, V. N., Renberg, I., & Rose, N. J, 1994. 'Geochronology of the last millennium', in *Palaeoclimate of the Last Glacial/Interglacial Cycle*, ed. B. M. Funnell & R. L. F. Kay (Swindon), pp. 77-80.

OSA The Old Statistical Account of Scotland: The Statistical Account of Scotland, ed. Sir J. Sinclair, 1791–99. 21 vols (Edinburgh, repr by county in 20 vols, ed. D. J. Withrington & I. R. Grant, Wakefield, 1976–83).

Ostrom, E., 1990. *Governing the Commons: the evolution of institutions for collective action* (Cambridge).

Owen, T. M., 1969. 'Historical aspects of peat-cutting in Wales', in *Studies in Folk Life. Essays in honour of Iorwerth C. Peate*, ed. G. Jenkins (London), pp. 123-55.

Padel, O., 1985. *Cornish Place-Name Elements*, Engl Place-Name Soc Vols 56-7 (Nottingham).

Palmer, M., & Neaverson, D., 1998. *Industrial Archaeology: principles and practice* (London).

Parry, B. R., 1970. 'The Vaynol estate: end of 400 years of history', *Royal Welsh Agric Soc J*, 16, pp. 15-18.

Parry, M. L., 1975. 'Secular climatic change and marginal land', *Trans Inst Br Geogr*, 64, pp. 1-13.

Parry, M. L., 1978. *Climate Change, Agriculture and Settlement* (Folkestone).

Parry, M. L., 1981. 'Climate change and the agricultural frontier: a research strategy', in *Climate and History*, ed. T. M. L. Wigley, M. J. Ingram & G. Farmer (Cambridge), pp. 319-36.

Parry, M. L., 1985. *Mid-Wales Upland Study* (Cheltenham).

Parry, M. L. & Carter, T. R., 1985. 'The effect of climatic variations on agricultural risk', *Climatic Change*, 7, pp. 95-110.

Parry, M. L., & Slater, T., 1980. *The Making of the Scottish Landscape* (London).

Pearsall, W. H., 1950. *Mountains and Moorlands* (London).

Pearsall, W. H., & Pennington W., 1973. *The Lake District* (London).

Pearse Chope, R., 1918. *Early Tours in Devon and Cornwall* (repr New York, 1968).

Peate, I. C., 1944. *The Welsh House* (Liverpool).

Peate, I. C., 1972. *Tradition and Folk Life: a Welsh view* (London).

Penfold, N., Francis, I. S., Hughes, E. J., & Aitchison, J. W., 1990. *Biological Survey of Common Land. No. 10: Radnor district, Powys* (Peterborough).

Pepper, D., 1996. *Modern Environmentalism: an introduction* (London).

Perkins, D. F., 1978. 'Snowdonia grassland: introduction, vegetation and climate', in *Production Ecology of British Moors and Mountain Grasslands III: Snowdonia Grasslands*, ed. O. W. Heal & D. F. Perkins (New York), pp. 289-96.

Peter, D., 1984. *In and Around Silverdale: the story of a North Lancashire village* (Carnforth).

Pimlott, J. A. R., 1947. *The Englishman's Holiday: a social history* (London).

Plomer, W. (ed.), 1977. *Kilvert's Diary, 1870–1879* (London).

Pollard, A., 2000. 'In them thar hills: the archaeology of the Kildonan gold rush', in *Townships and Farmsteads: rural settlement studies in Scotland, England and Wales*, ed. J. A. Atkinson, I. Banks & G. MacGregor, Br Archaeol Rep, Br ser 293 (Oxford), pp.188-96.

Pollard, S., 1997. *Marginal Europe: the contribution of marginal lands since the middle ages* (Oxford).

Pontefract, E., & Hartley, M., 1934. *Swaledale* (London).

Porteous, C., 1950. *Derbyshire* (London).

Porteous, J. M., 1876. *God's Treasure House in Scotland* (Glasgow).

Potts, R. (ed.), 1974. *A Calendar of Cornish Glebe Terriers 1673–1735*, Devon & Cornwall Rec Soc No. 19 (Torquay).

Pounds, N. J. G., 1978. 'William Carnsew of Bokelly and his Diary, 1576–7', *J R Inst Cornwall*, 8.1, pp. 14-60.

Pounds, N. J. G. (ed.), 1982. *The Parliamentary Survey of the Duchy of Cornwall 1649–50*, Devon & Cornwall Rec Soc No. 25 (Torquay).

Preece, R. A., 1981. *Patterns of development control in the Cotswolds AONB*, School of Geography, Univ Oxford, Res Pap 27 (Oxford).

Preston-Jones, A., & Rose, P., 1986. 'Medieval Cornwall', *Cornish Archaeol*, 25, pp. 135-85.

Pringle, D., 1994. *The Forestry Commission: the first 75 years* (Edinburgh).

QW Placita de Quo Warranto, Rec Comm, 1818 (London).

Rackham, O., 1980. *Ancient Woodland: its history, vegetation and uses in England* (London).

Rackham, O., 1986. *The History of the Countryside* (London).

Ragg, F. W., 1910. 'De Lancaster', *Trans Cumberland & Westmorland Antiq & Archaeol Soc*, new ser, 10, pp. 395-494.

Raistrick, A., & Jennings, B., 1965. *A History of Lead Mining in the Pennines* (London).

Ratcliffe, D. A., 1977. *A Nature Conservation Review* (Cambridge).

Ravenhill, W. L. D., 1979 (1st edn 1967). 'Cornwall', in *The Domesday Geography of South-West England*, ed. H. C. Darby & R. Welldon Finn (Cambridge), pp. 296-347.

RCAHMS, 1956. Royal Commission on the Ancient and Historical Monuments of Scotland, *The County of Roxburgh* (Edinburgh).

RCAHMS, 1957. Royal Commission on the Ancient and Historical Monuments of Scotland, *The County of Selkirk* (Edinburgh).

RCAHMS, 1967. Royal Commission on the Ancient and Historical Monuments of Scotland, *Peebles-shire* (Edinburgh).

RCAHMS, 1980. Royal Commission on the Ancient and Historical Monuments of Scotland, *Argyll. Vol III* (Edinburgh).

RCAHMS, 1991. Royal Commission on the Ancient and Historical Monuments of Scotland, *'Well Sheltered & Watered'. Menstrie Glen, a Farming Landscape Near Stirling*, (Edinburgh).

RCAHMS, 1994. *South-East Perthshire: an archaeological landscape* (Edinburgh).

RCAHMW, 1956–7. Royal Commission on Ancient and Historic Monuments of Wales, *An Inventory of the Ancient Monuments in Caernarvonshire Vols I–III* (London).

RCAHMW, 2002. Royal Commission on the Ancient and Historical Monuments of Wales, *Houses and History in the Welsh Marches: the late-medieval and Tudor houses of Radnorshire and their transformations*, (Aberystwyth).

Redfern, R. A., 1965. *Rambles in Peakland* (London).

Rees, W., 1924. *South Wales and the March, 1284–1415: a social and agrarian study*. (Oxford)

Rees, W., 1932. *Map of South Wales and the Border in the fourteenth century* (Southampton).

Rees, W., 1966. *The Great Forest of Brecknock* (Brecon).

Richards, A. R., 1961. 'Facing up to the sixties: Vaynol, part I — the problems', *J Chart Land Agents Soc*, 60, pp. 126-32.

Riley, H., & Wilson-North, R., 2001. *The Field Archaeology of Exmoor* (Swindon).

Roberts, B. K., Turner, J., & Ward, P. F., 1973. 'Recent forest history and land use in Weardale, northern England', in *Quaternary Plant Ecology*, ed. H. J. B. Birks & R. G. West (Oxford), pp. 207-22.

Roberts, R. A., 1949. 'The historical development of hill farming in Wales', *Agric Prog*, 24, pp. 25-9.

Roberts, R. O., 1959. 'Ecology of human occupation and land use in Snowdonia', *J Ecol*, 47, pp. 317-23.

Roberts, R. O., 1973. *Farming in Caernarvonshire around 1800* (Denbigh).

Robinson, G. M., 1994a. *Conflict and Change in the Countryside: rural economy, society and planning in the developed world* (revised edn, Chichester & New York).

Robinson, G. M., 1994b. 'The greening of agricultural policy: Scotland's Environ-mentally Sensitive Areas (ESAs)', *J Environ Plann & Manage*, 37, pp. 215-25.

Robinson, G. M., 1999. 'Countryside recreation management', in *Applied Geography: principles and practice*, ed. M. Pacione (London), pp. 257-73.

Rodgers, C. P., 1999. 'Environmental management of common land: towards a new legal framework?', *J Environ Law*, 11 (2), pp. 231-55.

Rose, G., 1993. *Feminism and Geography: the limits of geographical knowledge* (Cambridge).

Rotherham, I. D., 1995. 'Urban heathlands: their conservation, restoration and creation', *Land Contamination and Restoration*, 3 (2), pp. 99-100.

Rotherham, I. D., 1996. 'Habitat fragmentation and isolation in relict urban heathlands — the ecological consequences and future potential' (abstract paper), *Proc 28th Intern Geogr Congr: Land, Sea and Human Effort, 4–10 August 1996* (The Hague, The Netherlands), p. 396.

Rotherham, I. D. (ed.), 1999a. 'Peatland ecology and archaeology: management of a cultural landscape', *Landscape Archaeol & Ecol*, 4, pp. 1-100.

Rotherham, I. D., 1999b. 'Peat cutters and their Landscapes: fundamental change in a fragile environment', in Rotherham 1999a, 'Peatland ecology', pp. 28-51.

Rotherham, I. D., Ardron, P. A., & Gilbert, O. L., 1998. 'Peat-cutting and upland landscapes: case-studies from the South Pennines', *Landscape Archaeol & Ecol*, 3, pp. 65-69.

Rowlandson, T., 1846. 'Agriculture of North Wales', *J R Agric Soc*, 7, pp. 553-89.

Rowley, R. T., 1970. 'The Clee forest: a study in common rights', *Trans Shropshire Archaeol Soc*, 58 (for 1965–8), pp. 48-67.

Rowley, T., 1972. *The Shropshire Landscape* (London).

Rowse, A. L., 1941. *Tudor Cornwall: portrait of a society* (London).

Royal Commission on Land in Wales and Monmouthshire, 1895. *Minutes of evidence, Vol. III* (London).

RSPB, 2001. Royal Society for the Protection of Birds, *Futurescapes: large-scale habitat restoration for wildlife and people* (Sandy, Bedfordshire).

Rumsby, B. T., & Macklin, M. G., 1996. 'River response to the last neoglacial (the "Little Ice Age") in northern, western and central Europe', in *Global Continental Changes: the context of palaeohydrology*, ed. J. Branson, A. G. Brown & K. J. Gregory (London), pp. 217-34.

Russel, A. J. F., 1983. 'Meeting the feed requirements of the hill ewe', in *Sheep Production*, ed. Haresign, 1983, pp. 210-38.

Ryder, M. L., 1983. *Sheep & Man* (London).

Salt, T., 1887. 'Ancient documents relating to the honor, forest and burgh of Clun', *Trans Shropshire Archaeol & Nat Hist Soc*, 11, pp. 244-71.

Samuel, R., 1998. *Island Stories: unravelling Britain. Theatres of Memory, Vol. II* (London).

Sansom, A. L., 1999. 'Upland vegetation management: the impacts of overstocking', *Water Sci & Technol*, 12, pp. 85-92.

Sayce, R. U., 1942. 'Popular enclosures and the one-night house', *Montgomeryshire Collect*, 47.2, pp. 1-12.

Schama, S., 1996. *Landscape and Memory* (London).

Schweitzer, A., 1997. 'Mid/late Holocene landscape development in the Cheviot Hills: a palynological investigation', unpubl Diploma diss, Johann Wolfgang Goethe Institut, Frankfurt.

SCR Sheffield Clarion Ramblers.

Sculthorpe, H., 1993. *Freedom to Roam* (London).

Searle, C. E., 1993. 'Customary tenants and the enclosure of the Cumbrian commons', *Northern Hist*, 29, pp. 126-53.

Searle, C. E., 1995. 'Cumbria's Parliamentary enclosure movement: a comparative case study in rural quiescence', *Trans Cumberland & Westmorland Antiq & Archaeol Soc*, new ser, 95, pp. 247-71.

Seddon, B., 1957. 'Late glacial cwm glaciers in Wales', *J Glaciol*, 3, pp. 94-9.

Seddon, B., 1962. 'Late glacial deposits at Llyn Dwythwch and Nant Ffrancon, Caernarvonshire', *Phil Trans R Soc London*, B, 244, pp. 459-81.

Sellgren, J. M. A., 1986. 'Areas of Outstanding Natural Beauty: a case for positive management', *Ecos*, 7, pp. 29-33.

Sellgren, J. M. A., 1988. 'Planning policies in Areas of Outstanding Natural Beauty: the role of county and district councils', in *The Role of Institutions in Countryside Management*, ed. P. Hart, & M. Atherden (Rural Geogr Stud Group, Inst Br Geogr, Coll Ripon & York St John, Harrogate), pp. 17-23.

Selman, P. (ed.), 1988. *Countryside Planning in Practice: the Scottish experience* (Stirling).

Shaw, R. C., 1956. *The Royal Forest of Lancaster* (Preston).

Shaw-Lefevre, G., 1894. *English Commons and Forests: the story of the battle during the last thirty years for public rights over the commons and forests of England and Wales* (London).

Sheail, J., 1971. *Rabbits and their History* (Newton Abbot).

Sheail, J., 1981. *Rural Conservation in Inter-War Britain* (Oxford).

Sheail, J., 1995a. 'War and the development of nature conservation in Britain', *J Environ Manage*, 44, pp. 267-83.

Sheail, J., 1995b. 'John Dower, national parks, and town and country planning in Britain', *Plann Perspect*, 10, pp. 1-16.

Sheail, J., 1998. *Nature Conservation in Britain: the formative years* (London).

Sheail, J., 2000. 'The Countryside (Scotland) Act of 1967 revisited', *Scott Geogr J*, 116, pp. 25-40.

Shepherd, N., 1977. *The Living Mountain: a celebration of the Cairngorm mountains of Scotland* (Aberdeen).

Shields, R., 1991. *Places on the Margin: alternative geographies of modernity* (London).

Shoard, M., 1982. 'The lure of the moors', in *Valued Environments*, ed. J. R. Gold & J. Burgess (London), pp. 55-73.

Shoard, M., 1987. *This Land is Our Land: the struggle for Britain's countryside* (London).

Shorter, A. H., Ravenhill, W. L. D., & Gregory, K. J., 1969. *South West England* (London).

Silvester, R. J., forthcoming. 'Deserted rural settlements in mid and north-east Wales', in *Deserted Rural Settlements in Wales* (forthcoming Counc Br Archaeol Res Rep).

Simmons, I. G., & Innes, J. B., 1996. 'An episode of prehistoric canopy manipulation at North Gill, North Yorkshire, England', *J Archaeol Sci*, 23, pp. 337-41.

Simpson, S., & Robinson, G. M., 2001. 'Agri-environment policies, post-productivism and sustainability: England's Countryside Stewardship Scheme', in *Proc Second Anglo-Spanish Symp on Rural Geography, University of Valladolid, July 2000*, ed. F. Molinero, E. Baraja, & M. Alario (Univ Valladolid, Spain), sect 3-3, pp. 1-16.

Singleton, S., 2000. 'Co-operation or capture? The paradox of co-management and community participation in natural resource management and environmental policy-making', *Environ Polit*, 9 (2), pp. 1-21.

Sissons, D., 1992. 'A Sheffield Clarion Rambler: some aspects of the life and work of G. H. Ward (1876–1957)', unpubl Univ Sheffield Local Hist M.A. diss.

Skene, W. F., (ed.), 1890. *Celtic Scotland* (Edinburgh).
Slack, W. J., 1951. *The Lordship of Oswestry 1393–1607* (Shrewsbury).
Slater, F., 1988. *The Nature of Central Wales* (Buckingham).
Smil, V., 1990. 'Nitrogen and Phosphorus', in *The Earth as Transformed by Human Action*, ed. B. L. Turner, W. C. Clark, R. W. Gates, J. F. Richards, J. T. Mathews & W. B. Meyer (Cambridge), pp. 423-36.
Smirke, E., 1843. *The Case of Vice against Thomas, determined on appeal before the Lord Warden of the Stannaries of Cornwall; with an appendix of records and documents illustrating the early history of the tin mines in Cornwall* (London).
Smith, A. H., 1961. *The Place-Names of the West Riding of Yorkshire, Part 6*, Engl Place-Name Soc Vol. 35 (Cambridge).
Smith, A. H. H., 1997. 'A history of two Border woodlands', in *Scottish Woodland History*, ed. Smout, pp. 147-61.
Smith, D. (ed.), 1951. *The Third Statistical Account of Scotland. XXIX. The County of Kincardine* (Edinburgh).
Smith, G. C., 1896. *Book of Islay* (Glasgow).
Smith, J. B. (ed.), 1972. *Medieval Welsh society: selected essays by T. Jones Pierce* (Cardiff).
Smith, L. O. W., 1971. 'The Lordships of Chirk and Oswestry 1282–1415', unpubl Univ London Ph.D. thesis.
Smith, M. S., 1987. 'Deserted farm and shielings in the Braemar area of Deeside', *Proc Soc Antiq Scotland*, 116, pp. 447-53.
Smith, R. B., 1961. *Blackburnshire: a study in early Lancashire history* (Leicester).
Smout, T. C., 1972. *A History of the Scottish People 1560–1830* (London).
Smout, T. C. (ed.), 1997a. *Scottish Woodland History* (Edinburgh).
Smout, T. C., 1997b. 'Bogs and people since 1600', in *Conserving Peatlands*, ed. L. Parkyn, R. E. Stoneman & H. A. P. Ingram (Oxford), pp. 162-7.
Smout, T. C., 2000. *Nature Contested: environmental history in Scotland and northern England since 1600* (Edinburgh).
SNPA, 2001. Snowdonia National Park Authority Press Releases, 26 Feb., 2 March, 20 April, 7 May 2001.
Spence, R. T., 1991. 'Mining and smelting by the Cliffords, earls of Cumberland, in the early seventeenth century', *Trans Cumberland & Westmorland Antiq & Archaeol Soc*, new ser, 91, pp. 101-17.
Spooner, B. C., 1942. 'The boundaries of Twelve Men's Moor in the parish of North Hill', *Devon & Cornwall Notes & Queries*, 22.2, pp. 49-55.
Spratt, D. A., & Harris, A., 1991. 'The rabbit warrens of the Tabular Hills, North Yorkshire', *Yorkshire Archaeol J*, 63, pp. 177-206.
Spratt, D. A., & Harrison, B. J. D. (eds), 1989. *The North York Moors: Landscape Heritage* (Newton Abbot).
Stamp, L. D., 1962. *The Land of Britain: its use and misuse* (3rd edn, London).
Stamp, L. D., & Hoskins, W. G., 1963. *The Common Lands of England & Wales* (London).
Statham, D. C., 1993. 'Managing the wilder countryside', in *Leisure and the Environment: essays in honour of Professor J. A. Patmore*, ed. S. Glyptis (London), pp. 236-52.
Statistical Account of Scotland, ed. Sir J. Sinclair, 1791–99. 21 vols (Edinburgh).
Stevenson, A. C., & Birks, J. J. B., 1995. 'Heaths and Moorland: long-term ecological changes, and interactions with climate and people', in *Heaths and Moorland*, ed. Thompson, Hester & Usher, pp. 224-39.
Stevenson, A. C., & Thompson, D. B. A., 1993. 'Long-term changes in heather moorland in upland Britain and Ireland: palaeoecological evidence for the importance of grazing', *The Holocene*, 3, pp. 70-6.
Stewart O. H., & Stewart, M. B., 1988. 'A Highland longhouse — Lianach, Balquhidder, Perthshire', *Proc Soc Antiq Scot*, 118, pp. 301-17.
Strong, R. (ed.), 2000. *Lockton Remembered: memories of a moorland village in the early 1900s* (place of publ).
Stuart, D. R. M., 1961. 'Facing up to the sixties: Vaynol, part II — the solution', *J Chart Land Agents Soc*, 60, pp. 154-62.
Stuiver, M., & Reimer, P. J., 1993. 'Extended ^{14}C base and revised CALIB 3.03 ^{14}C age calibration program', *Radiocarbon*, 35, pp. 215-30.
Suffling, E. R., 1885. *The Land of the Broads* (London).
Sugita, S., Gaillard, M-J., & Brostrom, A., 1999. 'Landscape openness and pollen records: a simulation approach', *The Holocene*, 9, pp. 409-21.
Sylvester, D., 1969. *The Rural Landscape of the Welsh Borderland* (London).
Tansley, A. G., 1939. *The British Isles and their Vegetation* (Cambridge).
Tate & Turner 1978: Tate, W. E., 1978. *A Domesday of English Enclosure Acts and Awards*, ed. M. E. Turner (Reading).
Taylor, J., 1994. *A Dream of England: landscape, photography and the tourist's imagination* (Manchester).
TeBrake, W. H., 1985. *Medieval Frontier: culture and ecology in Rinjland* (College Station, Texas).
Thirsk, J. (ed.), 2000. *The English Rural Landscape* (Oxford).
Thomas, A. C., 1964. 'Settlement history in early Cornwall: 1, the Hundreds', *Cornish Archaeol*, 3, pp. 70-9.
Thomas, A. H., 1924. 'Some Hallamshire rolls of the fifteenth century', *Trans Hunter Archaeol Soc*, 2, pp. 65-79.
Thomas, C., 1967. 'Enclosure and the rural landscape of Merioneth in the sixteenth century', *Trans Inst Br Geogr*, 42, pp. 153-62.
Thomas, C., 1968. 'Thirteenth century farm economies in North Wales', *Agric Hist Rev*, 16, pp. 1-14.
Thomas, C., 1978. 'The rural landscape of North Wales in the later Middle Ages', *Geographia Polonica*, 38, pp. 271-7.
Thomas, C., 1989. 'Rural settlements in the modern period', in *Settlement and Society in Wales*, ed. D. Huw Owen (Cardiff), pp. 249-67.
Thomas, C., 1992. 'A cultural-ecological model of agrarian colonisation in upland Wales', *Landscape Hist*, 14, pp. 37-50.
Thomas, D., 1963. *Agriculture in Wales during the Napoleonic Wars* (Cardiff).
Thomas, K., 1983. *Man and the Natural World: changing attitudes in England 1500–1800* (London).
Thompson, D. B., Hester, A. J., & Usher, M.B. (eds), 1995. *Heaths and Moorland: cultural landscapes* (Edinburgh).
Thompson, E. P., 1993. *Customs in Common: studies in traditional popular culture* (New York).
Thorn, C., & Thorn, F., 1979. *Domesday Book: 10 Cornwall*, from a translation by O. Padel (Chichester).
Tipping, R., 1992. 'The determination of cause in the generation of major prehistoric valley fills in the Cheviot Hills, Anglo-Scottish Border', in *Alluvial Archaeology in Britain*, ed. S. Needham & M. G. Macklin (Oxford), pp. 111-21.
Tipping, R., 1994. 'Fluvial chronology and valley floor evolution of the upper Bowmont Valley, Borders Region, Scotland', *Earth Surface Processes & Landforms*, 19, pp. 641-57.
Tipping, R., 1995a. 'Holocene evolution of a lowland Scottish landscape: Kirkpatrick Fleming. I. Peat- and pollen-stratigraphic evidence for raised moss development and climatic change', *The Holocene*, 5, pp. 69-81.
Tipping, R., 1995b. 'Holocene landscape change at Carn Dubh, near Pitlochry, Perthshire', *J Quaternary Sci*, 10, pp. 59-75.
Tipping, R., 1996. 'The neolithic landscapes of the Cheviot Hills and hinterland -palaeoenvironmental evidence', in *The Neolithic of Northern England*, ed. P. Frodsham (Newcastle), pp. 17-35.
Tipping, R., 1997. 'Pollen analysis, late Iron Age and Roman agriculture around Hadrian's Wall', in *Reconstructing Iron Age Societies*, ed. A. Gwilt & C. Haselgrove (Oxford), pp. 239-47.

Tipping, R., 1998a. 'The chronology of Late Quaternary fluvial activity in part of the Milfield Basin, northeast England', *Earth Surface Processes & Landforms*, 23, pp. 845-56.

Tipping, R., 1998b. 'Cereal cultivation on the Anglo-Scottish Border during the "Little Ice Age"', in *Life on the Edge: human settlement & marginality*, ed. C. M. Mills & G. Coles (Oxford), pp. 1-12.

Tipping, R., 1999. 'Towards an environmental history of the Bowmont Valley and the northern Cheviot Hills', *Landscape Hist*, 20, pp. 41-50.

Tipping, R., 2000. 'Palaeoecological approaches to historic problems: a comparison of sheep-grazing intensities in the Cheviot Hills in the medieval and later periods', in *Townships to Farmsteads: rural settlement studies in Scotland, England and Wales*, ed. J. Atkinson, I. Banks & G. MacGregor, (Oxford), pp. 30-43.

Tipping, R., Carter, S. P., Davidson, D. A., Long, D. J., & Tyler, A. N., 1997. 'Soil pollen analysis: a new approach to understanding the stratigraphic integrity of data', in *Archaeological Sciences*, ed. R. Tipping, D. A. Gowlett & E. A. Slater (Oxford), pp. 221-32.

Tipping, R., & Watson, F., 1999. 'Environmental history in Scotland — the past as the key to the future', *Scott Assoc Geogr Teachers J*, 28, pp. 23-30.

Todd, J. M. (ed.), 1997. *The Lanercost Cartulary*, Surtees Soc 203 (Gateshead).

Tough, D. L. W., 1928. *The Last Years of a Frontier* (Oxford).

Trinder, B., 1982. *The Making of the Industrial Landscape* (London).

Tsouvalis, J., 2000. *A Critical Geography of Britain's State Forests* (Oxford).

Tubbs, C. R., 1986. *The New Forest* (London).

Tuck, A., 1979. *Border Warfare: a history of conflict on the Anglo-Scottish border* (London).

Tuke, J., 1800. *A General View of the Agriculture of the North Riding of Yorkshire* (London).

Tupling, G. H., 1927. *The Economic History of Rossendale*, Chetham Soc, new ser 86 (Manchester).

Turner, J., & Peglar, S. M., 1988. 'Temporally-precise studies of vegetation history', in *Vegetation History*, ed. B. Huntley & T. Webb III (Dordrecht), pp. 753-77.

Turner, M., 1980. *English Parliamentary Enclosure: its historical geography and economic history* (Folkestone).

Turner, V., 1998. *Ancient Shetland* (London).

Turton, R. B. (ed.), 1894–97. *The Honor and Forest of Pickering*, 4 vols, North Riding Rec Soc, new ser, 1-4, (London).

Tyson, B., 1984. 'The Troutbeck Park slate quarries, their management and markets 1753–1760', *Trans Cumberland & Westmorland Antiq & Archaeol Soc*, new ser, 84, pp. 167-90.

Unwin, D. J., 1973. 'The distribution and orientation of corries in northern Snowdonia', *Trans Inst Br Geogr*, 58, pp. 85-97.

Unwin, D. J., 1975. 'The nature and origin of the corrie moraines of Snowdonia', *Cambria*, 2, pp. 20-33.

VCH The Victoria Histories of the Counties of England (in progress).

The Victoria History of the County of Chester II, 1979, ed. B. E. Harris (London).

The Victoria History of the County of Derby I, 1905, ed. W. Page (London).

The Victoria History of the County of Shropshire IV, Agriculture, 1989, ed. G. C. Baugh (Oxford).

The Victoria History of the County of Shropshire VIII, 1968, ed. A. T. Gaydon (Oxford).

The Victoria History of the County of Shropshire X, Wenlock, Upper Corve Dale, and the Stretton Hills, 1998, ed. G. C. Baugh (Oxford).

The Victoria History of the County of Stafford VII, Leek and the moorland, 1996, ed. M. W. Greenslade (Oxford).

The Victoria History of the County of Yorkshire North Riding I, 1914, ed. W. Page (London).

The Victoria History of the County of Yorkshire North Riding II, 1923, ed. W. Page (London).

Walker, D., Head, M. J., Hancock, G. J., & Murray, A. S., 2000. 'Establishing a chronology for the last 1000 years of laminated sediment accumulation at Lake Barrine, a tropical upland maar lake, northeastern Australia', *The Holocene*, 10, pp. 415-28.

Walker, S. S. (ed.), 1983. *Court Rolls of Manor of Wakefield from October 1331 to September 1333*, Yorkshire Archaeol Soc Wakefield Court Rolls Ser 3 (Leeds).

Walker, M. J. C., 1989. 'Environmental evidence', in Austin *et al.*, 'Tin and agriculture', pp. 179-223.

Ward, A., 1997. 'Transhumance and settlement on the Welsh uplands: a view from the Black Mountain', in *Landscape and Settlement in Medieval Wales*, ed. N. Edwards (Oxford), pp. 97-111.

Watt, H., 2000. *Welsh Manors and their Records* (Aberystwyth).

Webb, N., 1986. *Heathlands* (London).

Welch, D., 1975. 'Three Elizabethan documents concerning Milburn Fell', *Trans Cumberland & Westmorland Antiq & Archaeol Soc*, new ser, 75, pp. 136-49.

White, R., 1997. *Yorkshire Dales* (London).

Whittington, G., & Edwards, K. J., 1990. 'The cultivation and utilization of hemp in Scotland', *Scott Geogr Mag*, 106, pp. 167-73.

Whittington, G., & Gordon, A. D., 1987. 'The differentiation of the pollen of *Cannabis sativa* L. from that of *Humulus lupulus* L.', *Pollen et Spores*, 29, pp. 111-20.

Whittington, G., & Whyte, I. D. (eds), 1983. *An Historical Geography of Scotland* (London).

Whittow, J., & Ball, D.F., 1970. 'North West Wales', in *Glaciation of Wales* ed. C. A. Lewis (London).

Whyte, I. D., 1979. *Agriculture and Society in Seventeenth Century Scotland* (Edinburgh).

Whyte, I. D., 2000a. 'Patterns of parliamentary enclosure of waste in Cumbria: a case study from North Westmorland', *Landscape Hist*, 22, pp. 77-89.

Whyte, I., 2000b. 'William Wordsworth's *Guide to the Lakes* and the geographical tradition', *Area*, 32, pp. 101-6.

Whyte, I., & Whyte, K., 1987. *Exploring Scotland's Historic Landscape* (Edinburgh).

Whyte, I., & Whyte, K., 1991. *The Changing Scottish Landscape 1500–1800* (London).

Wickham-Jones, C. R., 2001. *The Landscape of Scotland: a hidden history* (Stroud).

Wiley, M., 1998. *Romantic Geography: Wordsworth and Anglo-European spaces* (London).

Wiliam, E., 1988. *Home-made Homes: dwellings of the rural poor in Wales* (Cardiff).

Williams, D. H., 2001. *The Welsh Cistercians* (Leominster).

Williams, D., 1927. 'The geology of Snowdon', *Quarterly J Geol Soc London*, 83, pp. 346-431.

Williams, D., 1930. 'The geology of the country between Nant Peris and Nant Ffrancon', *Quarterly J Geol Soc London*, 86, pp. 191-233.

Williams, D., 1941. 'An eye-witness account of agrarian conditions in Caernavonshire during the Napoleonic era', *Trans Caernavonshire Hist Soc*, 3, pp. 72-84.

Williams, G. H., 1981. 'Farming in Stuart Caernarvonshire', *Trans Caernavonshire Hist Soc*, 42, pp. 49-80.

Williams, M., 1970. 'The enclosure and reclamation of waste land in England and Wales in the eighteenth and nineteenth centuries', *Trans Inst Brit Geogr*, 51, pp. 55-69

Williams, W. H., 1965. *The Commons Open Spaces and Footpaths Preservation Society 1865–1965* (London).

Williamson, T., & Loveday, R., 1988. 'Rabbits or ritual? Artificial warrens and the Neolithic long mound tradition', *Archaeol J*, 145, pp. 290-313.

Wilson, G. A., 1996. 'Farmer environmental attitudes and ESA participation', *Geoforum*, 27, pp. 115-31.

Wilson, J. (ed.), 1915. *The Register of the Priory of St Bees*, Surtees Soc 126 (Durham).

Winchester, A. J. L., 1987. *Landscape & Society in Medieval Cumbria* (Edinburgh).

Winchester, A. J. L., 2000a. *The Harvest of the Hills: rural life in northern England and the Scottish Borders, 1400–1700* (Edinburgh).

Winchester, A. J. L., 2000b. 'Hill farming landscapes of medieval northern England', in *Landscape: the richest historical record*, ed. D. Hooke (Birmingham), pp. 75-84.

Withers, C. J., 1996. 'Conceptions of cultural landscape change in upland Wales: a case study of Llanbedr-y-Cennin and Caerhun parishes, *c.* 1560–*c.* 1891', *Landscape Hist*, 17, pp. 35-47.

Withington, L. (ed.), 1899. *Elizabethan England* (London).

Woodland, W. A., Charman, D. J., & Sims, P. C., 1998. 'Quantitative estimates of water tables and soil moisture in Holocene peatlands from testate amoebae', *The Holocene*, 8, pp. 261-74.

Woodward, D., 1998. 'Straw, bracken and the Wicklow Whale: the exploitation of natural resources in England since 1500', *Past & Present*, 159, pp. 43-76.

Wordsworth, J., Abrams, M. H., & Gill, S (eds), 1979. *The Prelude* by William Wordsworth (New York & London).

Wordsworth, J., Jaye, M. C., & Woof, R., 1987. *William Wordsworth and the age of English Romanticism* (New Brunswick & London).

Wordsworth, W., 1810. 'Introduction: description of the scenery of the lakes', in Wilkinson, J., *Select Views in Cumberland, Westmorland and Lancashire* (London).

Wright, L., 1964. *Home Fires Burning: the history of domestic heating and cooking* (London).

Wynne, B., 1991. 'After Chernobyl: science made too simple', *New Sci*, January 1991, pp. 44-6.

Wynne, B., 1996. 'May the sheep safely graze? A reflexive view of the expert-lay knowledge divide', in *Risk, Environment and Modernity*, ed. S. Lash, B. Szerszynski, & B. Wynne (London), pp. 28-43.

Young, C. R., 1979. *The Royal Forests of Medieval England* (Leicester).

Youngson, A. J., 1973. *After the Forty-Five* (Edinburgh).

Index